AS HER WHIMSEY TOOK HER

As Her Whimsey
Took Her

CRITICAL ESSAYS ON THE WORK
OF DOROTHY L. SAYERS

edited by Margaret P. Hannay

THE KENT STATE UNIVERSITY PRESS

Copyright© 1979 by The Kent State University Press, Kent, Ohio 44242
All rights reserved
Library of Congress Catalog Card Number 79-10933
ISBN: 87338-227-7
Printed in the United States of America
Second Printing, 1980

Library of Congress Cataloging in Publication Data
Main entry under title:

As her whimsey took her.
    "Dorothy L. Sayers's manuscripts and letters in public collections in the United States, by Joe R. Christopher, E. R. Gregory, and Margaret P. Hannay": p.
    Includes index.
    1. Sayers, Dorothy Leigh, 1893-1957—Criticism and interpretation—Addresses, essays, lectures. I. Hannay, Margaret P.
PR6037.A95Z6   823'.9'12   79-10933
ISBN 0-87338-227-7

Contents

Editions of Frequently Used Texts

Because of the enormous and continuing popularity of the Lord Peter Wimsey novels, their publication history is complex, involving reprints by as many as nine different publishers. Since the original English editions (Benn, Unwin, and Gollancz) are difficult to obtain in the United States, and since the original American edition (Harcourt) has rarely crossed the Atlantic, it was impossible to find one edition which would be useful in both the United States and England. Therefore, all references to the Wimsey novels are given by chapter, not by page, and can be used with any edition.

For Sayers's other works, the first American edition has been cited whenever possible; this is frequently identical to the first English edition.

ESSAYS

Are Women Human? (Grand Rapids, Michigan: William B. Eerdmans, 1969)

Christian Letters to a Post Christian World (Grand Rapids, Michigan: William B. Eerdmans, 1969)

Creed or Chaos (New York: Harcourt, 1949)

Further Papers on Dante (New York: Harper, 1957)

Introductory Papers on Dante (New York: Harper, 1954)

A Matter of Eternity (Grand Rapids, Michigan: William Eerdmans, 1973)

The Poetry of Search and the Poetry of Statement (London: Gollancz,
    1963)
Unpopular Opinions (New York: Harcourt, 1947)
The Mind of the Maker (New York: Harcourt, 1941; rpt. Westport,
    Conn: Greenwood Press, 1970)

DRAMA

The Emperor Constantine (New York: Harper, 1951)
Four Sacred Plays (London: Gollancz, 1948)
The Man Born to Be King (New York: Harper, 1943; rpt. Eerdmans,
    1971)

POETRY

Catholic Tales and Christian Songs (Oxford: Basil E. Blackwell,
    1918)
Op. I (Oxford: Basil E. Blackwell, 1916)

TRANSLATIONS

The Comedy of Dante Alighieri (Harmondsworth: Penguin, 1949)
The Song of Roland (Harmondsworth: Penguin, 1957)
Tristan in Brittany (London: Ernest Benn, 1929)

Preface

THE WORKS of Dorothy L. Sayers are just beginning to receive serious attention from literary scholars; prior to 1970, Sayers was famous as the creator of Lord Peter Wimsey, but was nearly unknown as a philosopher of aesthetics, a dramatist, or a translator. The growing interest in her work is reflected in the publication of new collections of her stories and essays, in the reprinting of her dramas and her study of aesthetics, in the seminars devoted to her work held at the Modern Language Association since 1974, in the founding of the Dorothy L. Sayers Society in Witham, England (1976), and in the publication of *The Sayers Review* (1976).

Because Sayers studies are in their infancy, the few secondary sources now available aim to establish the canon of her works or to reveal the details of her life. The essays in this collection, however, are literary criticism, approaching Sayers as artist. Our attention is focused on "the writer alive in her works": biography is mentioned rarely and only as it is directly relevant to the critical discussion of her art. The final section of this volume, a bibliography of unpublished materials available to the scholar in the United States, is included for those who seek to continue this study of her art. Our goal is not to present, at this early date, the definitive study of Sayers, but rather to serve as a first critical study, a catalyst to further work on this remarkable creative mind.

Most of these articles are revised from scholarly papers read at the Dorothy L. Sayers Seminars at the Modern Language Association conventions: Robert Dunn (1974); R. B. Reaves, Terrie Curran, Barbara Dunlap (1975); Alzina Dale, Margaret Hannay, Robert Stock (1976);

Nancy Tischler (1977); Richard Harp, William Reynolds (1978). Five of those seminar papers have appeared in *The Sayers Review:* Terrie Curran (Sept. 1976), Alzina Dale (Jan. 1977), Margaret Hannay (June 1978), Richard Harp (Sept. 1978), William Reynolds (Sept. 1978).

The papers by Lewis Thorpe and Richard Webster were originally read as part of a week-end residential course on "The life and work of Dorothy L. Sayers" at Moor Park College, Farnham, Surrey (22–24 April 1977). Barbara Reynolds's paper was first presented at Wheaton College (5 May 1975).

We are grateful to the Marion E. Wade Collection at Wheaton College, the Houghton Library at Harvard University, the Humanities Research Center at the University of Texas (Austin), and the University of Michigan (Ann Arbor) for opening their collections of unpublished Sayers materials to us, and permitting us to publish an annotated listing of those collections. We also thank the Marion E. Wade Collection for permission to quote from manuscripts in their possession.

Through David Higham Ltd. permission to quote from the following works of Dorothy L. Sayers has been granted by Mr. A. Fleming and the Sayers estate: *Le Roman de Tristan* (London: Ernest Benn Publishers, 1929); *Op. 1* (Oxford: Basil Blackwell and Company, 1916); *The Song of Roland* (Harmondsworth: Penguin Books, 1957). I am also grateful to Holt, Rinehart, and Winston for permission to reprint "Two Tramps in Mud Time" by Robert Frost, and to Doubleday and Company for permission to reprint "To William Camden" and "On My First Sonne" by Ben Jonson.

I should personally like to thank Professor William Reynolds for supplying the papers of the early MLA seminars on Sayers, and for offering his advice and encouragement. Professor Peter Schakel contributed to this collection in a variety of quiet, helpful gestures. Professor Kilby, Barbara Griffin, and Marjorie Mead at the Wade Collection were unfailingly cheerful in the face of many requests for information; Col. Ralph Clarke, founder of the Dorothy L. Sayers Society in Witham, opened his home and his manuscripts to me. Finally, my greatest debt is to my husband, David, who provides "that still centre."

M. P. H.

Margaret P. Hannay

Introduction

I know it is no accident that *Gaudy Night,* coming towards the end of a long development in detective fiction, should be a manifestation of precisely the same theme as the play *The Zeal of Thy House*, which followed it and was the first of a series of creatures embodying a Christian theology. They are variations upon a hymn to the Master Maker: and now, after nearly twenty years, I can hear in *Whose Body?* the notes of that tune sounding unmistakably under the tripping melody of a very different descant: and further back still. I hear it again, in a youthful set of stanzas in *Catholic Tales*. . . . The end is clearly there in the beginning.

[*The Mind of the Maker,* p. 207]

THE sacramental value of work is the theme which unifies Dorothy L. Sayers's writings in many genres. Whether she is plotting detective stories, staging drama, or translating medieval poetry she is concerned with craftsmanship; her most explicit statements on work are presented in *The Mind of the Maker,* her original and provocative approach to aesthetics.

In *The Mind of the Maker* Sayers counters the Puritan ethic of duty by declaring that there is more nobility in doing things "out of sheer love of the job" than out of a sense of duty; the merit lies *in* the enjoyment. For the creator should not seek to escape his work or "to bully it," but "to serve it." Yet "To serve it he must love it. If he does so he will realize that its service is perfect freedom."

In all her essays on work, Sayers stresses that it must not be considered merely in economic, political, or social terms, but "as being in itself a sacrament and manifestation of man's creative energy." Like Robert Frost in "Two Tramps in Mud-Time" she would declare that work should not be chosen for economic gain alone, that "Only where love and need are one,/ And the work is play for mortal stakes,/ Is the deed ever really done/ For Heaven and the future's sakes."

This idea of serving the work, rather than merely working for pay, is present from the beginning in her detective stories. Lord Peter Wimsey, rich and leisured, must cope with the moral dilemma of his avocation. Is it just to hunt down criminals as a hobby? Or is the hunt legitimate only if it is one's paid work, as it is for Inspector Charles Parker? The question recurs, both in the novels and in the reviews of the novels, erupting finally in Miss Barton's condemnation of "this dilettante gentleman" whose hobbies are "detecting crimes and collecting books, and, I be- lieve, playing cricket in his off-time." Harriet, speaking no doubt for Sayers, fumes "Why should he do anything else? Catching murderers isn't a soft job, or an easy job. It takes a lot of time and energy, and you may very easily get injured or killed. I dare say he does it for fun, but at any rate, he does do it. Scores of people must have . . . reason to thank him" [*Gaudy Night,* ch. 2]. The fact that Lord Peter enjoys his work is not to be held against him so long as it is worth doing and he does it well.

The theme of work well done occurs in a variety of other ways in this detective series. For example, Philip Boyes's friend Vaughan complains that Harriet failed him by getting "the bug all these damned women have got—fancy they can do things. They hate a man and his work. You'd think it would have been enough for her to help and look after a genius like Phil, wouldn't you?" [*Strong Poison,* ch. 8]. This gives Sayers the opportunity to establish a woman's need for her *own* work, a theme treated in more detail in the essay "Are Women Human?"

Strong Poison also presents this theme of loving one's work in the humorous guise of Bill Rumm, the reformed safecracker. He still takes pleasure in a job well done, complaining "there ain't many of 'em now-a- days . . . that can do a real artistic job. It fair goes to my 'eart to see a elegant bit o' stuff like that blowed all to bits with gelignite." Mrs. Rumm makes the obvious reply "Ef anybody's goin' ter do sech a wicked thing as breakin' safes, wot do it matter whether it's done artistic or inartistic" [ch. 13], but we are left with the conviction that somehow it *does* matter.

In *Gaudy Night* the theme of integrity in one's work is central both to the mystery and to the love story; it provides the mainspring of the plot and also the opportunity for Harriet and Peter to become engaged. Arthur Robinson has cheated on his thesis, suppressing evidence which would mean beginning anew on his research; the cost of such dishonest craftsmanship is appalling, leading eventually to his own suicide, the mutilation of Miss Lydgate's proofs, the attempted murder of Harriet Vane, and his own wife's criminal insanity. This dishonest work counterpoints Harriet's discovery of her own worth through the integrity of her work; Harriet becomes an independent person, able to meet Lord Peter on an equal plane. Early in the novel she decides that "to be true to one's calling, whatever follies one might commit in one's emotional life, that was the way to spiritual peace" [ch. 2]. That decision is never questioned; the emphasis of the novel falls on doing one's *proper* job, despite the interference of parents, friends, or circumstances. She can finally accept Lord Peter's proposal only because he respects her work.

The craft of the detective novel itself is admirably defended in this novel, as we follow Harriet's creation of *Death 'twixt Wind and Water*. Peter confronts her with the shallowness of the story; it is merely a verbal puzzle. She is challenged to make Wilfrid *real,* to write a novel, not a conundrum. When she realizes that "It might go too near the bone. . . . It would hurt like hell," Peter shocks her by replying "What would that matter, if it made a good book?" [ch. 15]. We know that Sayers did not spare herself in attempting to create a detective novel that was more like a novel and less like a puzzle. Now that her notebooks are available in the Wade Collection we can see the care with which she structured her work so that the secondary world would be totally consistent and believable. When she wrote she did an enormous amount of research; if change-ringing was to be part of *The Nine Tailors,* it was obvious to her that she must spend two years learning that art. What did the cost matter if it made a good book?

Sayers managed to take her profession seriously without losing her sense of fun. She gave many lectures on the history and form of detective fiction, arguing quite plausibly that Aristotle's rules for tragedy are admirably suited to the detective story. She was a Baker Street Irregular, approaching the Holmes canon with that perfect solemnity of scholarship which is a crucial part of the game. She provided a significant commentary on detection in her introductions to the three volumes entitled *Great Short Stories of Detection, Mystery, and Horror* (published in the United States as *The Omnibus of Crime*), which she edited for Gollancz. And, with such other notable detective writers as G. K. Chesterton, E. C. Bentley, and Marjorie Allingham, she founded the Detective Club. Each member was required to respond to a catechism in the form of a baptismal questioning before admission to the club, taking an oath with one hand on a skull named Eric; it was all grand fun, but Sayers was quite serious when she had writers swear that their plots would abide by the rules of probability. The work should be done *well*.

When Sayers turned from detective fiction to theological drama and translation, she continued to stress the importance of work well done. It is no surprise that *The Zeal of Thy House,* written close to *Gaudy Night,* should also treat the theme of integrity in the work. As Robert Dunn points out, in this drama we see William of Sens, a lustful, lying, cheating, but faithful worker, learn the harder lesson, that *his* work is not only serious, but also insignificant; it is God's work that matters, and that can be carried on by other hands.

In her study of aesthetics, Sayers declares that the "desire and ability to make things is the characteristic God and man have in common." She finds in this theory of art as *creation* "the one important contribution that Christianity has made to aesthetics." The doctrine of the Trinity has "set free all the images, by showing that the true Image subsisted within the Godhead Itself—it was neither copy, nor imitation, nor representation, nor inferior, nor subsequent, but the brightness of the glory, and the express image of the Person. . . ." The creative act of the Trinity is expressed through the Creative Idea (the Father, analogous to the artist), the Creative Energy (the Son, analogous to the artifact itself), and the Creative Power (the workings of the Holy Ghost, analogous to the effect of the work on the audience). The significance and application of this original approach to aesthetics are discussed in the final section of this collection. Nancy Tischler stresses the theme of vocation, of the love of the craft, and explains Sayers's aesthetic theory in some detail. Richard Webster puts that theory into philosophic context, comparing it to phenomenology; Richard Harp studies the origins of her artistic trinity and applies it to the analysis of poems by Ben Jonson and Robert Frost.

When Uncle Paul Delagardie "wrote" his biography of Lord Peter in 1935, he remembers being worried about Peter after his breakdown: "I could not but think it dangerous that a man of his ability should have no job to occupy his mind, and I told him so." This, retroactively presented, is the start of Peter's detective career. Since the series is founded in Peter's need for meaningful work, it is inevitable that this theme recurs in our discussion of his cases. Robert D. and Barbara Stock find that the villains typically pervert their own work: Urquhart betrays his work as solicitor, Whittaker uses her vocation of nursing to murder her aunt, Tallboy plants information for a drug ring in his own advertising copy.

R. B. Reaves adds to this theme the conflict between Lord Peter, who seeks Truth, and Sir Impey Biggs, who wants to win the case by any means available; it is significant that Peter later hires Biggs to defend

Crutchley, who he knows is guilty. Lionel Basney stresses the centrality of the change-ringing, "the solemn intoxication that comes of intricate ritual faultlessly performed" which is ironically the instrument of death, involving all the ringers in the guilt. E. R. Gregory, pointing to the accuracy of detail and craftsmanship of Sayers's biography of Wilkie Collins, notes her belief that work well done becomes sacramental.

In their analysis of *The Man Born to Be King,* Terrie Curran and Alzina Stone Dale differ on her craftsmanship, and on the success of Judas as a character in the play cycle. Curran also points to Proclus, the Roman centurion, as a man concerned with doing his job well. He refuses to slaughter the innocents despite Herod's command: "Sir, I am a soldier, not a butcher." Yet his compassion for Christ on the cross is tempered by the same ethic: "if there was anything I could do —consistent with my duty, that is. . . ."

William Reynolds notes the centrality of the sacrament of work in *The Zeal of Thy House,* as well as Lisa's work for the master's soul in *The Devil to Pay*; in both cases work is seen as a form of prayer. *The Just Vengeance* is presented as the story of God's work of redemption.

The essays on Sayers's translations constantly stress her concern for accuracy in translation as she sought to preserve not only the word but also the metrics and the tone of the original. Lewis Thorpe emphasizes "the scrupulous care with which she had preserved the masculine and feminine assonances, the tonic beat and the break at the caesura, and the extreme rigidity of the end-stopped line" in her Roland. But she does more —she avoids the pedantic style of many translators, capturing the original picture of "gay and unconquerable youth." Barbara Reynolds discusses Sayers's delight in Dante's craftsmanship, his audacity in choosing for his expansive story "the most rigid form conceivable," his success in making us "believe in the Inferno as we believe in Robinson Crusoe's island —because we have trudged on our own two feet from end to end of it." She demonstrates also Sayers's own concern for detail, particularly as evidenced in her long letter about the progress of Dante's shadow. And throughout the essay Reynolds stresses Sayers's superb preparation for the study of Dante.

Barbara Dunlap analyzes the critical reception of Sayers's Dante, again stressing her concern with the accuracy of work and tone. It is the *tone* of her translation which has caused the most furor; Sayers presented Dante as humorous and charming, finding in the *Commedia* more comedy than some scholars will accept. Yet few would criticize her research, or the care with which she approached even the smallest details. "Honoring Dante as she did," Dunlap observes, "she became possessed by the need not to dishonor him by unworthy work."

The final essay, by Robert Dunn, integrates her many genres, stressing that "the way of the artist, who lovingly accepts the limitations of the medium as an opportunity for creation, is the way of the Christian religion, and of human and social reintegration." This is not to imply that Sayers wrote in order to serve society: she reminds us that "to aim directly at serving the community is to falsify the work; the only way to serve the community is to forget the community and serve the work. . . . If your heart is not wholly in the work, the work will not be good—and work that is not good serves neither God nor the community; it only serves Mammon."

In her many roles—detective novelist, dramatist, translator, and philosopher of aesthetics—Dorothy L. Sayers faithfully served the work.

I: DETECTION

R. B. Reaves

Crime and Punishment in the Detective Fiction of Dorothy L. Sayers

DETECTIVE fiction does not invariably deal with punishment of crime; perhaps the only invariable element is the detection of crime, or, as in the Montague Egg stories of Dorothy L. Sayers, the uncovering of a crucial clue. But in Sayers's detective novels the question of crime and punishment is raised repeatedly, and a chronological examination of her works reveals both a recurring treatment and an evolving attitude toward the subject. It is unlikely that Sayers began her career as a detective novelist with the preconceived design of an exhaustive and elaborate exploration of the subject. But the fact that the problem is raised in novel after novel clearly suggests that the issue interested her; as she matured as an artist her treatment of it becomes more varied and subtle.

Few readers fail to notice the recurrence of suicide in the first four of her novels, and most readers probably realize that suicide, and accidental death as well, are in fact used as extralegal means of effecting punishment for culprits who are perhaps otherwise able to evade conviction or appropriate punishment. That Sayers so frequently employed these extralegal means to achieve justice in her fiction raises a number of issues with moral and aesthetic implications. Perhaps the central moral issue concerns the question of the varying degrees of responsibility of those who cause the death or the serious injury of others. And though it seems that crime, when detected, ought to be punished through the workings of the legal system, often in Sayers's novels situations conspire to prevent the system from achieving justice—exonerating the innocent

1

and convicting the guilty. In a few instances Sayers shows the legal system erroneously prosecuting the innocent and protecting the guilty. Usually her courtroom scenes are treated farcically.

All of this leads to the conclusion that the rational process of crime detection is not necessarily followed by a similarly rational process of trial and conviction. But whether by the legal system or by some extralegal means, almost every villain in her novels is punished, or is at least apprehended with such evidence that leaves no doubt of eventual conviction. Finally, Sayers seems concerned that crime and punishment be viewed beyond the narrow scope of simple retributive justice. Especially in the later novels there is the clear suggestion that the victimizer as well as the victim may become a subject for pity as well as for punishment.

Sayers introduced the element of suicide in her first novel, *Whose Body?* (1923). Sir Julian Freke, after confessing his guilt in a letter to Lord Peter, adds a postscript announcing his intention to kill himself, presumably by the same method he had used on his victim and had attempted to use on Wimsey. Both the confession and the attempted suicide are seen as acts perfectly natural to a man of such strong will as Sir Julian. As Peter observes, "All that coolness, all those brains—and then he couldn't resist writing a confession to show how clever he was, even to keep his head out of the noose" [ch. 13]. The unrepentant and sinister Sir Julian is the first of basically two types in Sayers's gallery of rogues—villains who are totally unscrupulous and apparently incapable of remorse and who deserve severe and swift punishment.

In *Clouds of Witness* (1926), the crux of the plot is the fact that Cathcart was not killed by Gerald, Peter's brother, but that he had died by his own hand. And again the use of the confession, or here more properly a farewell or suicide note, provides the evidence sufficient to resolve the case. Cathcart, in the second category of villains, is hardly a sinister figure. Cathcart's misdeeds are merely a matter of his moral bankruptcy. He is a sad character who is unable to live without deceit: but he is not held up for either much censure or sympathy. He is finally seen as a rather disappointing cad who happily recognized that the world might be better off without him.

But in Mary Whittaker, the murderer in Sayers's third novel, *Unnatural Death* (1927), we are confronted with a villain who surpasses Sir Julian in cold-bloodedness and ingenuity. In this case the evidence against this most cunning and unnatural of all Sayers's criminals is somewhat circumstantial, speculative, and certainly inconclusive on several counts. Here we have a fiend who almost succeeds in committing a series of perfect crimes. Peter remarks that "the Dawson murder was beautiful in its ease and simplicity." And Parker further laments the lack of evidence for the first of her crimes: "If she had stuck to that and left well alone, we could never have proved anything. We can't prove it now, which is why I left it off the charge-sheet. I don't think I've ever met a more greedy and heartless murderer. She probably really thought that anyone who inconvenienced her had no right to exist" [ch. 23].

Although Mary Whittaker could be tried and convicted only for the murder of Bertha Gotobed and Vera Findlater, and for the attempted murder of Miss Climpson, there is a fortunate side-effect to the otherwise disappointing fact that the Dawson murder cannot be proved. The Dawson estate belonged to Mary Whittaker. As Parker explains, "We know it [the estate] was gained by crime, but we haven't charged her with the crime, so that legally no such crime was committed" [ch. 23]. If the crime were proved, the estate would be forfeit, but as matters stand, Cousin Hallelujah and Mary Whittaker's first cousin, Allcock, "a very decent fellow," will receive their part of the inheritance. This turn of events is an example of benefit arising out of the failure to prove a crime. The case is finally closed when word comes that Mary Whittaker "strangled herself with a sheet" [ch. 23]. The suicide happily preempts the discovery of the Dawson murder.

The suicide of the villain at the end of *Unnatural Death* and of the next novel, *The Unpleasantness at the Bellona Club* (1928), effects not only extralegal punishment, but also rewards for certain innocent victims of crime. In the fourth novel it is almost as if Peter has come to recognize the usefulness of suicide as a means of resolving the crime and punishment question. Peter, realizing that the evidence against Penberthy is rather slim, gets him to sign a confession—this is a means to clear Ann Dorland, who is under suspicion of murder. ' "Write a clear account of what actually happened,' said Wimsey. 'Make a clean job of it for those other people. Make it clear that Miss Dorland had nothing to do with it.' " Penberthy then asks Peter what his next step should be, and Peter responds, "Then do as you like. In your place I know what I should do" [ch. 22]. A few minutes later Colonel Marchbanks reiterates the hint, suggesting to Penberthy that he "take another way out of the situation," and then leaves his pistol conveniently nearby [ch. 22].

It is not until 1933 in her ninth novel that Sayers returns to the subject of suicide. Near the end of *Murder Must Advertise* Lord Peter confronts Tallboy, who had killed Victor Dean. Tallboy, a frustrated and somewhat pathetic figure who had got over his head in involvement with an elaborate narcotics ring, is disturbed that his arrest and conviction would mean that his wife and child would be "pointed at all their lives," and bear part of the shame for his guilt. Peter hints to Tallboy, as he had to Penberthy in *The Unpleasantness at the Bellona Club,* that there is an alternative. Tallboy acknowledges the hint of suicide, "the public school way out of it," as he phrases it. The overly self-conscious Tallboy, unnecessarily ashamed of his nonprestige schooling, sees suicide as a way to at last "achieve the Eton touch." But Peter no doubt recalls the newspaper account of Milligan's "execution":

> At 3 o'clock this afternoon a heavy lorry skidded and mounted the pavement in Piccadilly, fatally injuring Major 'Tod' Milligan, the well-known clubman, who was standing at the kerb. [ch. 17]

Wimsey thus instructs Tallboy to leave "on foot, and not too fast. And don't look behind you" [ch. 20].

Peter's expectation is realized, and as he watches from his window, seeing Tallboy walk away followed by a shadowy figure, he speaks the judge's sentence: " —and from thence to the place of execution . . . and may the Lord have mercy upon your soul" [ch. 20]. Even though Tallboy does not die by his own hand, he in effect commits suicide by putting himself in harm's way: the death of Tallboy is the last example of suicide as an extralegal means of punishment for capital crime in Sayers's novels. [1]

Closely akin to the use of suicide as a means of extralegal punishment is the use of accidental death and murder as methods of punishment for villains who are out of the reach of the law. Grimethorpe, in *Clouds of Witness,* is guilty of brutalizing his wife, and, of course, he does attempt to murder the man he believes to be his wife's lover. Grimethorpe is dispatched when he is accidentally struck and killed by an automobile. His death frees his distressed wife in a way his imprisonment could not. She has his estate in recompense for all his injuries to her. Another example of accidental death, or perhaps it is manslaughter, is the killing of the fiendish Loder in the short story, "The Abominable History of the Man with Copper Fingers." More to the point are the circumstances of the death of Tod Milligan, the drug trafficker, who is seen as a more dangerous criminal than Tallboy the murderer in *Murder Must Advertise.* Peter and Parker raise the question of appropriate punishment for crime. Parker observes that "Dope-runners are murderers, fifty times over. They slay hundreds of people, soul and body, besides indirectly causing all sorts of crimes among the victims. Compared with that, slugging one inconsiderable pip-squeak over the head is almost meritorious." Peter, obviously pleased with such an "enlightened" response from a "religious" man like Parker, further remarks on the injustice: "Hang the one [the murderer] and give the other [the dope-runner] a few weeks in jail —or, if of good social position, bind him over or put him on remand for six months under promise of good behaviour" [ch. 15]. Milligan's execution by his fellow gangsters, and similarly the murder of Mr. Mountjoy, another small-fry in the syndicate, are just punishments for these "murderers, fifty times over."

The questions of accidental death and that of the varying degrees of responsibility for harm done are raised in *Five Red Herrings* (1931). Just as the plot of *Clouds of Witness* revolves around a suicide which is perceived as a murder, so in *Five Red Herrings* the plot concerns manslaughter, really an accidental death, which is perceived as well-plotted, cold-blooded murder. In some ways this novel seems to turn the tables on the crime and punishment problem by creating an unsympathetic victim, the hot-headed and vindictive Campbell, who had made so many enemies that the case is confused with suspects, all of whom had motive enough. Clearly Campbell deserved what he got. "Murder is murder, you know," observes the Chief Constable, remarking on the Campbell case, to which Wimsey replies curtly, "Not always" [ch. 29]. Ferguson, it seems, accidentally killed Campbell in a fight, but since he had previously publicly threatened Campbell, he feared he would be charged with murder, and thus he contrived to make the death look like an accident. His elaborate scheme ironically takes on the appearance of a contrived murder.

Geoffrey Deacon in *The Nine Tailors* (1934) is killed by accident: tied in the bell chamber by Will Thoday, Deacon faced a death which Peter describes as "stroke, apoplexy, shock," caused by the ringing of the bells for nine long hours. The Rector of Fenchurch concludes that Deacon was punished by God: "Perhaps God speaks through those mouths of inarticulate metal. He is a righteous judge, strong and patient, and is provoked every day."[2] The victim in this case is in fact the villain in a plot, a theft, which takes place years before the action of this novel, and which sets in motion a chain of events with cumulative effects much more enormous than the original misdeed. And it is ironic that Deacon's return to Fenchurch has the effect of reopening a long-forgotten case with the result that the lost jewels are discovered and restored to the heirs of the family that had suffered from their loss. Upon his return to the scene of the crime, Deacon is at last punished for his wrongdoing.

Because he was responsible for imprisoning Deacon in the bell chamber, Will Thoday is partly responsible, as is James Thoday for mutilating and burying the corpse to protect his brother who he believes has killed Deacon. Before Peter discovers the cause of Deacon's death the authorities are uncertain of what action to take against Will and Jim: "If either were charged separately, there would always be sufficient doubt about the other to secure an acquittal, while, if they were charged together, their joint story might well have the same effect upon the jury that it had already had upon the police. They would be acquitted and left under suspicion in the minds of their neighbours, and that would be unsatisfactory too. Or they might, of course, both be hanged."[3] The police take no action. Jim, leaving the community, is spared the constant reminder of his part, and Will, later trying to save a drowning boy from the flood, dies in the attempt. "Poor Will . . . died finely and his sins died with him,"[4] is his obituary. His accidental death and his valiant act serve as punishment and expiation.

In several novels both suicide and accidental death bring not only punishing justice but also rewarding justice: Penberthy's suicide and confession protect Ann Dorland; Grimethorpe's death frees his wife; Mary Whittaker's death benefits Cousin Hallelujah; and Tallboy's death spares his family. Such satisfactory resolutions are not necessarily the rule in Sayers's fiction: in two of her novels the plots are resolved with the complete detection of the crime but without the assurance that the culprits will be punished. But even in these two works the issue is raised, if not resolved.

At the end of *Documents in the Case* (1930), Paul Harrison, the compiler of this file, observes that the "unsatisfactory part of the case is . . . that which concerns the woman, Margaret Harrison. . . . That she instigated and inspired it [the murder] is, to my mind, certain; but Lathom will strenuously deny this, and I have failed to secure any reliable evidence against her. I trust that you [the prosecutor] will use every possible endeavour to prevent this abominable woman from getting off scot-free" [#53]. There is apparently no resolution to this problem since all the reader learns subsequently, from the appended newspaper clipping, is that Lathom was tried, convicted, and hanged.

The conclusion to *Have His Carcase* (1932) is perhaps even more "unsatisfactory" in this regard. In this novel the victim, Paul Alexis, a Russian-born gigolo tricked into believing that he is the last of the

Romanovs, is brutally murdered in an elaborate and highly calculated plot contrived by Mr. and Mrs. Morecambe and Henry Weldon. Although the crime is solved and the murderers and their methods are exposed, there is the difficulty in making a good case. As Parker observes, "It's so complicated . . . that I don't believe we'll ever get any jury to believe it. . . . See here, my lord, if we do prosecute, d'you really think we've a hope in Hades?" Harriet Vane responds by observing that the release of the culprits would possibly result in further bloodshed. Peter has the last word. He seems to assume that the murderers will be convicted and his comments are worth noting: "Well . . . isn't that a damned awful, bitter, bloody farce? The old fool who wanted a lover and the young fool who wanted an empire. One throat cut and three people hanged, and £130,000 going begging for the next man who likes to sell his body and soul for it. God! What a jape! King Death has asses' ears with a vengeance" [ch. 34]. Even in these two novels which have no clear punishment, legal or extralegal, promised for the villains, the idea that crime deserves punishment is still asserted, even though it cannot always be realized. That crimes go unpunished and that innocents are sometimes unjustly convicted are facts of life that are fully asserted in Sayers's fiction. Both Parker and Peter realize that even crimes which may be detected cannot always be proved. In *Murder Must Advertise,* for example, they realize further that with a crime such as trafficking in narcotics, the mere conviction of the culprit does not begin to eradicate the evil done. The syndicate itself is seen as a kind of hydra-headed monster constantly repairing itself. "It's no good worrying about it," says Parker. "My job is to catch the heads of the gangs if I can, and, after that, as many as possible of the little people. I can't overthrow cities and burn the population." Peter's rejoinder is perhaps prophetic: "'Tis the Last Judgment's fire must cure this place . . . calcine its clods and set its prisoners free" [ch. 15].

At one point in her commentary on the *Divine Comedy* Sayers asserts that there are certain acts with natural consequences which are punishments for those acts. In discussing the punishments of Dante's Hell she notes that the poet "speaks indifferently of the torments, the pains, the penalties, or the punishments of Hell; and this language often prompts people to suppose that the torments are punishments arbitrarily inflicted, as a man might beat a boy for stealing sweets." But, as she continues, "the intimate analogy between the sin and the penalty shows that the suffering of Hell is punishment only in the sense that a stomach-ache, and not a beating, is 'punishment' for greed."[5]

Sayers recognized the artistic danger in the insistence that the good be rewarded and that the evil be punished. In *Mind of the Maker,* she unequivocally asserts that the arbitrary imposition of rewards and punishments in a work of fiction, what we usually term "poetic justice," is a serious artistic flaw. The creative writer, she explains, certainly can "intervene at any moment in the development of his own story; he is absolute master, able to perform any miracle he likes." The writer "can twist either character or plot from the course of its nature by an exertion of arbitrary power. He can slay inconvenient characters, effect abrupt conversions, or bring about accidents or convulsions of nature to rescue the characters from the consequences of their own conduct."[6] Sayers complains that Dickens gave in to this weakness in *David Copperfield* when he allows something at last to turn up for Micawber. Micawber, she explains, "is a 'good' character . . . and it is desired to reward him with a 'happy ending'. He is therefore packed off to Australia, where, in defiance of his own nature and in defiance of the nature of Australian civic life in the last century, he becomes a prosperous magistrate."[7] Sayers insists that the artist has to restrain these impulses to reward and punish in a manner that is inconsistent with either the nature of the character or of the world as we recognize it. " 'Poetic justice' (the name often given to artistic miracle-mongering) may be comforting, but we regretfully recognize that it is very bad art. 'Poetic justice' is indeed the wrong name to give it, since it is neither poetry nor justice; there is a true poetic justice, which we know better by the name of 'tragic irony', which is of the nature of judgment and is the most tremendous power in literature as in life—but in it there is no element of miracle."[8]

In Sayers's fiction the accidents that either resolve or help resolve the plots by punishing and rewarding characters are, if we look closely, generally well prepared for and are, in short, far from *deus ex machina* resolutions. The flood at Fenchurch at the close of *The Nine Tailors* comes as no surprise, nor does the discovery that Milligan, in *Murder Must Advertise,* is murdered by his cohorts in the narcotics syndicate. It is not necessary to demonstrate that each instance of extralegal punishment in these novels is artistically flawless, but most of these are clearly the natural consequences of acts, just as a stomachache is the consequence of eating stolen sweets. The suicides of Sir Julian Freke and Mary Whittaker, for example, are not arbitrary endings, but inevitable though not always expected acts of arrogant overreachers who scorn the rule of law. Their suicides are in character, just as the accidental death-suicide of Tallboy is appropriate for a man who was merely a pawn in an enterprise not of his own making.

Another aspect of the crime and punishment theme evident in the novels is that the legal system, the law, the courts, the lawyers, the judges, are frequently imperfect instruments for achieving justice. Such a notion is by no means extraordinary. The legal system has long been a target for the satirist, and it would indeed be surprising to find in detective fiction of the sort Sayers wrote a blind faith in the legal system. Nevertheless, in her fiction we are repeatedly reminded not only that the legal system is often unable to provide justice, but also that often the system is an active agent of injustice. Of course, such a view is consistent with Sayers's theology. In "Creed or Chaos?" Sayers asserts that "Law like every other product of human activity, shares the integral human imperfection: it is in the old Calvinistic phrase: 'of the nature of sin.' That is to say: all legality, if erected into an absolute value, contains within itself the seeds of judgment and catastrophe. The law," she maintains, "is necessary, but only, as it were, as a protective fence against the forces of evil, behind which the divine activity of grace may do its redeeming work. We can, for example, never make a positive peace or a positive righteousness by enactments against offenders; law is always prohibitive, negative, and corrupted by the interior contradictions of man's divided nature; it belongs to the category of judgment."[9]

Parker and Peter, as we have already seen, recognize throughout the novels that their brilliant detection may be frustrated, or come to naught because of failings in the legal system. In particular their resentment is directed to the citizens on the jury who make the final determination, to the judges who preside, and to the lawyers who perform in these cases.

At the close of *The Unpleasantness at the Bellona Club,* Peter remarks that it was a "damned unsatisfactory case, Charles. Not the kind I like. No real proof." Parker responds in a similar vein: "Nothing in it for us, of course. Just as well it never came to trial, though. With juries you never know."[10] And, of course, in *Five Red Herrings* one of the principal reasons Ferguson concocts his elaborate scheme is his fear that no jury would ever believe what really happened. Gerald's trial before a jury of his peers, the House of Lords, in *Clouds of Witness,* is treated as an elaborate farce, something out of Gilbert and Sullivan. " 'Of all the farces!' grumbled Lord Attenbury," presumably commenting on the outrage of Denver's trial, though the comment clearly describes the scene of "three hundred or so British peers . . . sheepishly struggling into their robes" preparing for the processional [ch. 14].

The judge in *Strong Poison* is pure caricature. In this novel Peter must discover the murderer of Philip Boyes to vindicate Harriet Vane, whose guilt is assumed by this judge and almost all of the jurymen in the case. "The judge," we are told, "was an old man; so old he seemed to have outlived time and change and death. His parrot-face and parrot-voice were dry, like his old, heavily-veined hands" [ch. 1]. This "hostile judge," as Salcombe Hardy describes him, and the jury bring to mind Pope's couplet:

> The hungry Judges soon the Sentence sign,
> And Wretches hang that Jury-men may Dine.

It is only through the good instincts of Miss Climpson, a member of this jury, that Harriet is saved from conviction.

Sayers reserves her severest comments for the lawyers. In *Clouds of Witness* the comic-opera atmosphere of Gerald's trial is enhanced by the antics of the lawyers, Sir Impey Biggs and Sir Wigmore Wrinching. Peter, when he finally takes the stand to clear his brother and to reveal the truth, cannot help taunting the lawyers:

> "Biggy and Wiggy
> Were two pretty men
> They went into court
> When the clock — — —."
> [ch. 17]

Sir Impey Biggs who defends Gerald, and later Harriet in *Strong Poison,* and who is hired by Peter to defend Frank Crutchley, the murderer in *Busman's Honeymoon* (1938), is characterized as a brilliant, eloquent, and devious lawyer. In this last novel we see Sir Impey cleverly throwing dust in the jury's eyes in his defense of the guilty Crutchley, but the case is not successful. Biggs had not been able to sway the judge and jury in *Strong Poison,* and, of course, it is Peter and not Sir Impey who at last clears Gerald. But it is not the number of cases Sir Impey wins or loses that should concern us. Sayers focuses on Sir Impey's attitude toward his profession, his view of the law. During a discussion of the case against Gerald in *Clouds of Witness* Peter remarks to Sir Impey Biggs: "Damn it all, we want to get at the truth!" Sir Impey's reply expresses disapproval of Lord Peter's meddling, but his comment clearly reveals his limited moral outlook:

"Do you?" said Sir Impey drily. "I don't. I don't care twopence about the truth. I want a case. It doesn't matter to me who killed Cathcart, provided I can prove it wasn't Denver. Here's a client comes to me with a story of a quarrel, a suspicious revolver, a refusal to produce evidence of his statements, and a totally inadequate and idiotic alibi. I arrange to obfuscate the jury with mysterious footprints, a discrepancy as to time, a young woman with a secret, and a general vague suggestion of something between a burglary and a *crime passionel*. And here you come explaining the footprints, exculpating the unknown man, abolishing the discrepancies, clearing up the motives of the young woman, and most carefully throwing back suspicion to where it rested in the first place. What *do* you expect?"

Peter's retort is curt: "I've always said," growled Peter "that the professional advocate was the most immoral fellow on the face of the earth, and now I know for certain" [ch. 10].

The criticism of Sir Impey, that he is only playing a grand game and that he has no concern for the truth, may also be applicable to Inspector Parker and Lord Peter. Parker, a decent and religious man, though certainly no fool like the incompetent and overzealous Inspector Sugg, is seen as a fallible human being. And Lord Peter's views on the truth, on justice, on crime and punishment are perhaps draconian at times, and they are certainly partial. The limits of Peter's vision are examined in the final novels of the Wimsey series. In *Gaudy Night* (1935) and in *Busman's Honeymoon,* Sayers expands her discussion to consider the implications of human judgment and human justice. These last two novels suggest that the detection and punishment of crime are not the only requirements for a satisfactory resolution to a case.

Gaudy Night, more of an academic novel than a novel of detection, does not deal directly with capital crime, but rather with a series of pranks, some with serious implications, which are revealed at last to be the work of a misguided, perhaps unbalanced, woman who is seeking vengeance for what she believes the wrong done to her suicide husband. Arthur Robinson had been deprived of his M.A. when it was discovered that he had withheld evidence that "absolutely contradicted" the argument of his thesis. The Dean of the College, commenting on a wife's likely reaction to the discovery of her husband's academic dishonesty, asks, "How many women care two hoots about anybody's intellectual integrity? Only over-educated women like us. So long as the man didn't forge a cheque or rob the till or do something socially degrading most women would think he was perfectly justified. Ask Mrs. Bones the Butcher's Wife or Miss Tape the Tailor's Daughter how much they would worry about suppressing a fact in a mouldy old historical thesis" [ch. 17]. Peter, when he at last confronts Annie Robinson, acknowledges that she may have a "justifiable grievance" against the scholars who she believes caused her husband's disgrace, dishonor, and suicide [ch. 22]. Annie's hatred for Miss de Vine, and, by extension, all women academics, is not abated and she lashes out at everyone in her sight. Miss de Vine feels she is to blame, not, she explains, for the "original action, which was unavoidable," but for the consequences of her action [ch. 22]. This realization does not blur the distinction between right and wrong, nor does it invalidate the scholar's code or the rule of law. It does affirm that the suffering which results from a rule of law demands human compassion in response.

In the last Wimsey novel, Lord Peter himself comes to feel what Miss de Vine had at the conclusion of *Gaudy Night*. In *Busman's Honeymoon,* Peter discovers the murderer of William Noakes, Frank Crutchley, an unfortunate young man who felt himself cheated by Noakes. Although Frank was guilty of cold-blooded premeditated murder, rather fiendishly contrived in fact, and although he angrily turns on Peter "panting and snarling" [ch. 20], Crutchley has Peter's sympathy. Peter does not withhold evidence, nor does he seem reluctant to expose Crutchley, yet he engages Sir Impey Biggs for the defense. Peter is, in a way, of two minds about the case. Peter feels that it was a strange twist of fate that on his own honeymoon he finds himself responsible for the arrest, conviction, and execution of a "poor devil who hasn't got a bean in the world and hasn't done *us* any harm."[11]

Sir Impey Biggs attempts a clever defense, but Crutchley is convicted, acknowledges his deed, and remains unrepentant. In the hours before Crutchley's execution Peter and Harriet ruminate upon the crime and its punishment. Peter in a rambling manner makes a number of observations: "It's a merciful death compared with most natural ones. . . . It's only the waiting and knowing beforehand. . . . And the ugliness. . . . Old Johnson was right; the procession to Tyburn was kinder. . . . 'The hangman with his gardener's gloves comes through the padded door.' . . . I got permission to see a hanging once. . . . I thought I'd better know . . . but it hasn't cured me of meddling."[12] Harriet reminds him that his meddling had saved her from the gallows, and, of course, his meddling had saved his brother. But the Wimsey we see in his final scene is not the Lord Peter who could so coolly recommend to Penberthy or Tallboy the "public school way out." Peter's last words in this last novel, "Oh damn!" his first words in the first novel, are followed by his sobs as the moment of execution arrives.

This compassion of Wimsey's is ineffectual, and perhaps that is part of the truth that Sayers is asserting. The rule of law requires obedience to the proposition that actions have their consequences. Crime must be punished, and in an imperfect world the legal process may become a farcical game that winks at the truth. Victims may, in fact, be scoundrels who, in a sense, deserve what they get; villains, even calculating ones, may be poor devils who have rashly acted out of desperation. But before the law, Sayers asserts, there is no difference between a Frank Crutchley, a Tallboy, or a Sir Julian Freke—all are guilty of premeditated murder. Sayers finally suggests that the rule of law requires of Christians, and perhaps ideally of everyone, that human sympathy, human compassion, be extended to the guilty as well as to the innocent victims of crime.

It may be argued that what Sayers is about is not an exploration of themes of justice, crime, and punishment, but rather the creation of elegantly written, though perhaps morally simplistic, romantic fiction, catering to popular taste with the conventions of success and happiness for the virtuous and punishment for the villainous. Indeed, if we had only her first novel, or perhaps only the first few, we might conclude just that. But what emerges from an examination of these issues as they appear throughout her fiction from first to last leads us to conclude that we are dealing with more than mere formulas of popular literature. This examination of crime and punishment in Sayers's detective fiction, it is hoped, should indicate not only the nature of some of the moral concerns which underlie the plots, but also some measure of her artistic accomplishment in integrating these moral concerns into the fabric of her work.

R. D. Stock and Barbara Stock

The Agents of Evil and Justice in the Novels of Dorothy L. Sayers

By dealing with the unsleeping sentinels who guard the outposts of society.[detective fiction] tends to remind us that we live in an armed camp, making war with a chaotic world, and that the criminals, the children of chaos, are nothing but the traitors within our gates . . . . it is the agent of social justice who is the original and poetic figure, while the burglars and footpads are merely placid old cosmic conservatives, happy in the immemorial respectability of apes and wolves. —G. K. CHESTERTON

LIKE Chesterton and others who have written "escapist" fiction, Dorothy L. Sayers was a moralist. She censures Goethe, whose *Faust*, she believes, depreciates the power of sin and the notion that "any act or choice could be final or irrevocable." Christopher Marlowe, she continues, did much better with the theme, but Dante best grasped the nature of evil, its "idiot and slobbering horror."[1] It is hardly remarkable, then, that she should have been attracted to detective fiction as an apt arena for exhibiting the conflict of good and evil. "Of all forms of modern fiction, the detective story alone makes virtue *ex hypothesi* more interesting than vice, the detective more beloved than the criminal."[2] That Sayers had an ethical aim in her novels is clear enough. That her morality was traditional is suggested by her disdain for the ambiguities in Goethe's play and her preference for the damnation unequivocally described in Marlowe's. But like any good craftsman, Sayers understood the difference between pious propaganda and true art, and studied how the dualism of good and evil might be shown with most effect.[3]

14

We should like to urge that the concern for justice is as strong in Sayers's early novels, sometimes demeaned as melodrama, as in her later, allegedly more substantial works. But we shall argue that she alters her method of delineating moral dualism, and that this change can best be observed by examining specifically her representatives of good and evil. She begins with egregious villains, true "traitors within our gates," and with an agent of social justice who is perhaps an "original," and certainly a "poetic figure." By the middle of the series the criminals have become more mundane, and Lord Peter's insouciance is no longer impenetrable. Sayers's belief in the horror and irrevocability of evil remains firm, but characterization becomes less melodramatic and the portrayal of good and evil, in general, more like Dante's. We shall dwell on one later novel, *Murder Must Advertise*, as the most successful example of the new pattern, and glance briefly, by way of conclusion, at her own version of the Faust story, *The Devil To Pay*.

In later years Sayers regretted the conventionality of her first novel, *Whose Body?* (1923), but the concoction of Lord Peter out of Bertie Wooster and Sherlock Holmes is ingenious. Of the former character there is, of course, the apparent flippancy and prattle. Like Holmes, Lord Peter has a plenitude of side-interests: he is a bibliophile and no mean amateur pianist, to say nothing of his cricket-playing and facility with a motor car; he is also a neat dresser. But he contrasts with Holmes in his philandering, of which we are told much but shown little, and in his opulent and tidy flat. Sayers, indeed, rather overdoes the Woosterism, and later deplored such levity as altogether incompatible with homicide. But even here Lord Peter is discomposed when he uncovers the murderer's identity [ch. 8]. This villain, aptly named Sir Julian Freke, is powerful, famous, socially significant; he possesses and indeed exercises the capacity to benefit mankind. Clues to his character are provided by his biological determinism [chs. 6, 8], which denies the validity of the individual conscience, and by his unfeeling contempt for antivivisectionists. Whether this determinism is the cause or effect of his character is not decided, though a connection is clearly established between his philosophy and his conduct. Freke is truly a traitor within the gates, the murderer of the nameless vagrant as well as of Levy, glacially remorseless even in his confession and suicide attempt, doubly dangerous because of his artfulness, his respectability, and—what he shares with Lord Peter—his whimsical humor concerning crime. He is an amoral intellectual, a professional, an egoist, whose talents are as romantically magnified as Lord Peter's; but he is fatally flawed by pride [ch. 10].

Though we are never invited to admire him, his character introduces into the novel some old tragic themes: the perversion and waste of potential, and the inexorability of justice.

In *Clouds of Witness* (1926), turning as it does on suicide, Cathcart is merely a cad, not a villain, more an agent of disorder than of evil. But in *Unnatural Death* (1927) the murderer, Miss Whittaker, is truly congener to Dr. Freke: a professional (she is nurse as well as relative to the victim) who grossly abuses her trust. Like Freke she is relentless and remorseless; unlike him she is successful in the ultimate crime of suicide. But whether she is congenitally evil, or like a Macbeth is debauched through repeated and progressively desperate acts of atrocity, Sayers fails to indicate. As an agent of justice, Peter is delighted at the prospect of a new case, but he is several times forced to confront the moral responsibilities of his amateur sleuthing. Believing at first that the murder is merely the hastening to her last reward of a terminally ill and senile old woman, he wonders whether he should interfere. In an unusual fit of self-questioning he asks the humble vicar of St. Onesimus whether the killing of such a person, though assuredly criminal, is really so bad. The damage done by such a murder, Mr. Tredgold replies, is less to the victim than to society and indeed, to the malefactor. Moreover, after one murder another may supervene. We must therefore do what we think right and leave the consequences to God. This advice is both trite and true enough, but the novel does not probe much further into ethical questions.

The Unpleasantness at the Bellona Club (1928) is nicely decorated with satire on modern biology and postwar nihilism, but thematically it breaks no new ground. The culprit, Dr. Penberthy, is a somewhat humanized Freke: intelligent, though by no means so brilliant and lionized, he too propounds scientific theories inimical to such antiquated doctrines as original sin and human responsibility; he too is contemptuous of such "sentimental old women" as the antivivisectionists; he too, if less notably, is something of an idealist and benefactor of mankind. Like Whittaker he violates a capital trust in killing his patient, General Fentiman, and he is willing to compound the murder by letting George Fentiman take the rap. Like both Freke and Whittaker, he is quite unrepentant as regards the deed itself, though he confesses manfully enough his shabby treatment of Ann Dorland. As in *Unnatural Death*, the victim is old, and Peter again wonders whether it is so very bad to shuffle such a person off the stage. He decides, of course, that it is.

Peter's Woosterism is less extravagant in this novel, and he takes little delight in the case as a whole. His relationship with Parker is deepened, his relentless devotion to the truth is more robustly assailed than ever before by the John Bullish Robert Fentiman, and he handles the maladroit Ann Dorland with a tact and solicitude hitherto unexhibited. Peter's powers of life and death are exercised most conspicuously in his encouraging Penberthy to commit suicide [ch. 22]. That this solution, humane as it is in several ways, has more in common with Stoicism than Christianity, is evident; but we must remember that Lord Peter has nowhere professed to be more than a nominal Christian, and that Sayers deliberately refused, despite much hounding on this point, to convert him. [4] Of course we ought to recollect, too, that on leaving Penberthy for the last time, Peter puts his hand on his shoulder for a moment. Of conscience and compassion, this is all we are given.

In her introduction to *The Omnibus of Crime* (1929) Sayers predicted the exhaustion and ultimate desuetude of the traditional detective novel. The next year saw two books in which she attempted to reinvigorate the form. In *Strong Poison* she introduces what she and other theorists of detective fiction had earlier reproved—a love interest. And in *The Documents of the Case* she very adroitly revives Wilkie Collins's trick of conducting a mystery through the viewpoints of diverse and contrasting characters. In *Documents*, the novelist Munting, though by his own admission blown about by every wind of false doctrine, modern, and cynical, is nevertheless a moral traditionalist, fond of the prickly and conservative victim Mr. Harrison, resentful of behaviorism and educational relativism, a slightly ironic and embarrassed admirer of suburban respectability. As the agent of justice, he has neither Peter's levity nor his self-confidence. Because the murderer, Lathom, is an old school acquaintance and present friend, he endures squalls of doubt and perturbations of conscience far beyond anything we have seen in Peter.

Lathom is Munting's friend, but spiritually his opposite number: the avant-garde artist, gifted indeed, but egotistic, contemptuous of the little watercolors of Harrison, whom, however, he hypocritically flatters; disdainful of bourgeois values, on which, however, he is willing to trade. He is a Bohemian version of Freke; and Munting, like Peter in that first novel, must poise the claims of genius against those of justice: "he was a great painter—something would be lost to the world if they hanged Lathom." Harrison, fatally imperceptive of character, prefers Lathom to Munting. And so it is no wonder that Mrs. Harrison, a modern and even more repellent Madame Bovary, drawing from fantasy her personalities as well as her ideals, should be captivated by his glamor, as he is captivated by her histrionic and protean charm. Lathom, then, like Sayers's previous murderers, is an ingenious and amoral intellectual, while Mrs. Harrison represents the untrammelled indulgence of the emotions and the imaginative life. Mrs. Harrison, it is to be noted, is never exposed or punished; but Lathom, the obvious suspect, is snared by not so obvious means. Startling scientific methods elucidate the factitious nature of the poison he employed, thus discrediting the notion that Harrison, in his culinary adventures, had accidentally poisoned himself. Lathom, tripped up as he is by "a miserable asymmetric molecule," is an interesting variation on the type of murderer characteristic of the early novels, but the book explores ethical problems and modern, philosophical views far more strenuously than any previous work; and Munting, like the later Lord Peter, is a less relentless and more squeamish agent of justice.

Strong Poison strikes out in something of a new direction. Never has Peter been more passionately involved in a case, and never has his intuition—his certain if illogical knowledge that Harriet could not have committed the murder—operated more forcibly. The murderer, Urquhart, though not exactly a genius, *is* a professional who, like Freke, Whittaker, and Penberthy, icily betrays his responsibilities as a solicitor. His means of covering himself, though not unprecedented, are ingenious, and require resourcefulness and expertise. As for Lord Peter, his sleuthing has become no longer a mere hobby, but a means to happiness; and he has ceased to be, as Marjorie Phelps puts it, "the comfortable sort of person that nothing could touch." The old Peter does re-emerge in the false-poisoning scene at the end, however, and as an agent of justice he has never proceeded more relentlessly than in that last interview with Urquhart.

But if Urquhart is in the same general category as Freke, Lathom, or Whittaker, he is decidedly not of the first class. There is nothing romantic and little spectacular in his crime. And so with *Strong Poison*, half-way through the series, this species of murderer vanishes forever. *Five Red Herrings* (1931), for all its banausic elaborations of plot, has but a commonplace villain. *Have His Carcase* (1932) is a shrewd study in the "dangerous prevalence of the imagination"; but the murderers are a tedious pair of fortune-hunters operating from the usual mundane motives of greed. Of *The Nine Tailors* (1934) one remembers its atmosphere and symbolism, its range of campanological lore; but the initial crime, jewel theft, is one of the most jejune, at least in detective fiction, and the criminals are no Napoleons of crime. The agent of evil in *Gaudy Night* (1935) is merely demented and pathetic. In the final book, *Busman's Honeymoon* (1937), Crutchley is at once one of Sayers's most repulsive and undistinguished murderers. Yet over this person Lord Peter, at the term of the novel, experiences such pangs of conscience as would have been impossible to his younger self. Compared with the *sang-froid* with which Peter had treated the more sympathetic Penberthy, this emotionalism is remarkable, and shows his enlarged capacity for reflection and vicarious suffering.

To sum up, the agents of evil, beginning with *Five Red Herrings*, have become commonplace (but not necessarily more sympathetic), while Lord Peter, beginning with *Strong Poison*, grows less flamboyant and overwrought. But though the changes in Peter commence with *Strong Poison*, they are not much developed in the intervening novels, and emerge convincingly only in *Busman's Honeymoon*. Of all these later books, *Murder Must Advertise* most superbly exemplifies this newer pattern.

In *Murder Must Advertise* (1933) Sayers evokes two modern worlds, that of the workaday advertising agency and that of the leisured *beau monde*. Both are shown to be shallow, frivolous, morally vapid, with the difference, of course, that the world of the Bright Young People is infected with malignity and malaise, whereas at the ad agency, Pym's, there is camaraderie and institutional loyalty. Then too, Pym's is inhabited by characters of real intelligence and wit, such as Ingleby and Miss Meteyard. It is to be noted that the notorious "de Momerie crowd" are but one part of the aristocratic class, and no synecdoche; when they crash Helen's party, they are immediately discerned and ejected. They are, in fine, dopers, clever in some things but obtuse in others, vicious but humdrum, profane but superstitious; and like the baser sort of criminals there is no unity but perfidy in them; their house cannot stand. In the conventional manner, Sayers represents their spiritual degeneration by their physical decay: she dilates on the blemished complexions of both Major Milligan and Dian de Momerie, setting them against Lord Peter's nearly super-human prowess—his acrobatics as harlequin (especially that strenuous dive from the fountain), and his agility at cricket.

We sympathize with none of these characters, nor indeed with the victim, Victor Dean. Dean was a blackmailer, and in detective fiction blackmailers, because they are the one type of criminal usually immune from the law, are invariably odious. Consequently, Tallboy is Sayers's most appealing murderer: hardly more than a dabster at crime, weak but essentially decent, driven to desperation by the fatality of his first naive acquiescence, his pressing domestic situation, his paltry philandering, and finally his harassment by the verminous Dean. "As the villain is allowed more good streaks in his composition," Sayers had written five years before, "so the detective must achieve a tenderer human feeling beneath his frivolity or machine-like efficiency."[5] She endows Peter with that trait here. Yet to spare Tallboy's family the public humiliation, Peter gives Tallboy an unpleasant choice: the hangman, or violent death from the doping gang still at large. Tallboy chooses the second, and as he leaves Peter's flat, that gentleman admonishes him not to look back. Resembling somewhat Penberthy's choice at the end of the *Bellona Club*, this is yet more perplexing morally. Tallboy is merely wretched, not villainous, and Peter explicitly sympathizes with Tallboy's lack of remorse [ch. 20]. Much of the guilt has been transferred to the dopers, and Peter's self-disgust at the end is strong. Nowhere does Sayers's morality seem more uncompromising and Hebraic: however extenuated, the act is everything and must be atoned for. As the title of the book facetiously suggests, murder will out.

This is not only Sayers's most forcible novel morally, it is also her first sustained attempt to depict a coherent world view, that of a cynical and amoral modernism, deluding and self-deluding. Pym's world may be more agreeable than that of the dopers, but it shares in the decadence, for it is an enterprise based on deceit and manipulation. Both worlds, in respect of their inanition and unmeaning activity, put one in mind of Dante's Hell, though Pym's, doubtless, occupies a higher circle. It is the fundamental irony of the book that the dope traffic should be directed from an agency that in its daily operations must be ever on guard to avoid offending the public morals. Pym's employees may not smoke and must watch their language when the Brotherhood representatives are present, and women must cover their shoulders. The great Nutrax row, which gave Lord Peter a valuable clue, is caused by a salacious innuendo in a newspaper ad. When Peter reveals the connection between Dean's death and the dope-running from his agency, Pym gasps, "Dope? From this office? What on earth will our clients say? How shall I face the Board? The publicity . . ." [ch. 16]. The last thing Pym desires is publicity about what *really* is going on in his agency. The professional deceivers have been deceived.

Disguise is employed to point up the theme of deception. Lord Peter, agent of retribution, appears as Mr. Death Bredon, the new copywriter who reminds everyone of Bertie Wooster and who at length is discovered to be Peter's unsavory, unscrupulous—and nonexistent—cousin. Peter also disguises himself as the romantic and sinister harlequin, high-diver and automobile racer *par excellence*, who like Pan piping hidden in the woods, springs from tree to tree to infatuate and terrorize the urban but superstitious Dian.

The representation of good and bad, then, is quite different in this novel. To call Tallboy an agent of evil is to mislabel and mislead, for the real evil emanates from a degenerate and soulless class. As an agent of justice, Lord Peter is not the poetic figure of the earlier books, and though he has preserved abilities touching on the superhuman, these have assumed a different purpose. For example, his Woosterism is mightily revived, but it is part of a deliberate deception, as are his escapades as Harlequin. In other words, these "poetic" aspects are *recognized* as guises. The levity and high-jinks are acceptable, for we know throughout the novel, and most conspicuously at the end, that Peter's humanity is fully engaged in the personal tragedy which he has exposed and to which he has perforce contributed. In fine, the idiocy of evil is embodied, not in some vulpine egoist, but in a deracinated and aimless class; while the romance and poetry of detecting are centered, not in the middle-aged Lord Peter, but in his sometime protégé, the eager and adolescent officeboy, Ginger Joe.

Through the first half of the series, Sayers typically pitted a grandiose or exceptional criminal against a superhuman and relentless sleuth. This dualism, figuratively speaking, is a species of the Manichean heresy, and while it well represents the high blasphemy of evil, it may at the same time distract us from its idiocy and horror. In the later novels, the agents of evil become less melodramatic, and, more gradually, the agent of justice acquires a keener conscience. Of the later works, *Murder Must Advertise*, we believe, most vividly evokes the horror, while *Busman's Honeymoon* considerably accelerates the moral development of Lord Peter.

As the 1930s elapse, the Wimsey books leave behind them the *genre tranché* of detective fiction and assume the familiar form of the novel of manners.[6] Even the scattered vestiges of the old form are clearly a clog and a vexation to her in the final two books, and at length she gives it up altogether and turns to plays and essays on Christian themes. Between her dramatic version of the Faust story, *The Devil To Pay* (1939), and her early *Whose Body?* yawns a chasm of 15 years; but the aesthetic gap is still greater. If Freke is the swollen egoist sinning grandly, Sayers's Faustus is a supersensitive humanitarian who sins through love, whose increasingly desperate and frustrated acts of idealism serve only to produce more and more tangible evil, till, losing a sense of good and bad, he sinks to brutishness. The play, which allows the possibility of Faustus's final salvation, is a more subtle study of evil than *Whose Body?*. This greater sophistication is owing partly to Sayers's greater knowledge of life, but also, we suspect, to her developing interest in Dante. And yet the play shares with the novel two themes: the irrevocability of the evil deed, and the interplay of thought and action. Freke's conscience is counteracted by his biological determinism, and Faustus's moral sense is stifled by his secular humanism and primitivistic nostalgia. In all her imaginative works Sayers enforces the notion that we inhabit a moral world where evil, once embraced, scores itself ineradicably on the soul. To this belief she adheres, however much she may grow in her understanding of the deviousness and mundane subtlety of that evil. At the last, she turned to translating Dante, who had described it all so well so long ago.

Lionel Basney

The Nine Tailors and the Complexity of Innocence

THE NINE TAILORS (1934) was the tenth of Dorothy L. Sayers's 12 mystery novels. It came at a crucial point in her career; according to her own testimony, *Murder Must Advertise* (1933) was the first novel in which she approached serious fiction—a "criticism of life" along with the murder, the detection, and Peter Wimsey's charming flippancy. In this she was only partially successful. The novel's analysis of modern commercial motives is clear enough, and congruent with what she would say later in her wartime social commentary. But the thought is not completely integrated with the mystery. The story's excitement, and Lord Peter's charm, seem to float above the heavy business of the theme.

In contrast, the book following *The Nine Tailors, Gaudy Night* (1935), is not a murder mystery at all. Harriet Vane and Oxford dominate the story; Lord Peter proposes, and Harriet accepts, as we knew she would. Plot and theme are thoroughly integrated here; but the whole project is clearly an outright novel, and ought to be judged as such.[1]

Between these books—the murder mystery with theme attached, and the serious novel with mystery attached—came *The Nine Tailors*, the most successful of Sayers's stories at integrating detective interest and a seriously intended "criticism of life." This makes it a definite achievement, one of the very few mystery stories that may be considered an interesting novel as well. A detective story is not often expected to carry intellectual or ethical implication. It is, wrote W. H. Wright, "a complicated and extended puzzle cast in fictional form" in which style and thought are out of place.[2] On the contrary, Sayers's fiction had always had style. In *The Nine Tailors*, moreover, it is the murder mystery's essential ingredient—the murder and its detection—which initiates a coherent and moving statement about the nature of human experience.

Despite this, the book's reputation has always been shallow. Among casual mystery readers it is rumored a masterpiece. Among purists it tends to be dismissed as "that book about campanology." The lore of English change-ringing is, in fact, central to the story, and accounts in part for its instantaneous popularity. But the book is "about" campanology in roughly the same way as *King Lear* is "about" the weather. The storms that whip through the tragedy are impressive stage business; but insofar as they have metaphoric value they are, by definition, about something else. Similarly, bells and bell-ringing are part of the materials of *The Nine Tailors*, which is clearly about something else altogether.

The book's real impact arises not from its materials but from skillful invention and construction; Sayers succeeded in making both narrative momentum and conceptual substance flow naturally from the same set of circumstances. The novel's deepest concerns are functions of its perfection as a murder mystery. To approach them, therefore, we must consider the mystery plot in some detail.

The plot satisfies beautifully the two main requirements of a mystery "gimmick": it is virtually unguessable, and utterly convincing. In the best tradition of detective writing, it turns on a bit of evidence which has been unmistakably present throughout the story, and has been ignored for very familiarity. The murder is committed by no one, or rather by several people, as innocently and indifferently as if it were a natural castastrophe. The murderers are nine bell ringers, who get their man by ringing an eight-hour peal in the church of Fenchurch St. Paul. Their victim, tied in the bell chamber itself, can neither escape nor make his presence known. He is killed by the anatomical effects of long-continued noise in the closed space of the belfry. The people responsible for his death are ignorant of his presence; the people responsible for his presence have no part in the peal that kills him; the direct agents of death are the bells, which do nothing that is not mechanically dictated to them by the skilled but unknowing hands below.

Sayers's identification of the two acts—murder and bell peal, one carrying guilt, the other an expression of innocent devotion and pleasure—makes for a fine harvest of ironies. Will Thoday, who put the victim in the bell chamber, is a bell ringer himself. But, stricken with unexpected illness, he can neither participate in the peal nor rescue his acquaintance. In fact, his illness would have stopped the peal (read murder) altogether, but for the chance appearance of Lord Peter Wimsey, who, it turns out, has rung changes himself in his youth. Theodore Venables, rector of Fenchurch St. Paul, reads Wimsey's arrival as the decree of Providence—as God's sanction on the peal (read murder): " 'Positively, I cannot get over the amazing coincidence of your arrival. It shows the wonderful way in which Heaven provides for our pleasures, if they be innocent.' "[3]

It is, to say the least, an unusual crime. But in judging it we must distinguish between the rules of detective writing and its normal conventions. Sayers has carefully obeyed the rules; the solution to the mystery is always at hand. The murder is no more technical than homicide by an unknown aboriginal poison, and a good deal more credible than homicide by a slingshot icicle (this is not an invented example). The book contains a number of suspects, and no "Australian cousins" turning up at the last moment to solve an otherwise insoluble crime. If Wimsey's solution of the mystery is finally somewhat by chance, he does solve a number of subsidiary mysteries by the normal route of clues and logic; too, the final discovery of things by a concurrence of events beyond Wimsey's foresight is fully in line with a story that began with coincidence, and contributes importantly to the meaning of the whole tale.

On the other hand, Sayers rode hard but confidently over a number of mystery writing's conventions. First, Wimsey is as much involved in the death as the other bell ringers. Here we see Sayers arranging ahead of time for Wimsey's customary loss of detachment. Unless, like Chesterton's Father Brown, he has a special moral vocation, the classical detective tends to remain "objective," personally detached from the crimes to be investigated. Holmes himself is a "consulting detective" whose professionalism guarantees his neutrality; he is there to solve puzzles. But Wimsey is in this affair from beginning to end, robbed involuntarily of his detective's distance and objectivity. His responsibility for the death in the belfry is immediate; it is not a matter of empathy, or of delicate social situations, as when he must investigate friends or family, or even of personal sympathy with the murderer. It is a matter of complicity; his hands are as red as anyone's.

Second, and perhaps even more important, there is no single murderer on whom all the guilt of murder may be laid. The scapegoat theory of murder mysteries will not work here: no individual can expiate society's corruption by being executed. Further, none of the people involved with the murder has a murderer's conscious guilt to hide. They are all, in various ways, innocent and responsible at the same time. Again Sayers violates a convention. As Chesterton wrote: "The chief difficulty [with the mystery novel] is that the detective story is, after all, a drama of masks and not of faces. It depends on men's false characters rather than their real characters." Sayers made the same observation more than once in her criticism of the form.[4] But in *The Nine Tailors* this is not true, or it is true only in limited fashion. The true murderers have nothing to hide, being unconscious of their deed. They therefore wear no masks. We live and move among ordinary men who have killed one of their kind, and we see their real faces. Wimsey sees them too, and becomes their friend—is, in the essential sense, one of them.

The death's third consequence is not in violation of a convention, but requires the special use of one. Some varieties of the detective story— particularly those featuring a scientist or policeman—depend upon esoteric knowledge for solutions. The murder by unknown poison cannot be explained by a layman. Sometimes the detective's display of knowledge seems miraculous, solving an utterly opaque mystery in a way no reader could have done; in these cases it is a defect in the story's construction. *The Nine Tailors* appeals to unusual knowledge, the lore of change-ringing. But the information is not sprung on us, nor is it Wimsey's long-secret specialty come suddenly to light. Wimsey learns about the bells from a pamphlet quoted in the text, and so may we. Finally, moreover, the technicalities of change-ringing are not necessary to the central mystery, though Sayers uses them to solve subordinate ones (here she is scrupulously fair) and to remind us of the bells' presence and importance.

The murder actually occurs by force of cumulative coincidence. But no one knows this, and as a result Sayers is free to heighten the mystery by any means available. For this purpose the bells provide an almost inexhaustible source of eerie suggestion. Her specific technique is a discreet touch of pathetic fallacy. Have the bells some dim preternatural consciousness? Several characters testify to their strangeness; they seem almost alive. What Sayers is doing is equivocating about the agents and meaning of the murder.

Of course we know the bells have no life; this is no Gothic horror story. But Sayers will not leave the hint alone. The bells have subtle, coercive effects on people; and forthright assertions of their consciousness appear only among characters whose naivete or hysteria Sayers can trust to disarm our natural suspicions. *She* does not tell us they are alive, or ask insinuatingly if they are. In fact, however, the close association of the bells with certain characters tends to heighten rather than lessen their suggestiveness. Hezekiah Lavender has rung Tailor Paul, the passing bell, for decades, and feels a comradely acceptance of the bell's significance:

> Mr. Lavender pushed his chair back and quavered to his ancient feet.
>
> "In the midst of life," he said solemnly, "we are in death. Terrible true that is, to be sure. If so be as you'll kindly excuse me, ma'am, I'll be leaving you now, and thank you kindly. Good mornin' to you all. That were a fine peal as we rung, none the more for that, and now I'll be gettin' to work on old Tailor Paul again."
>
> He shuffled sturdily out, and within five minutes they heard the deep and melancholy voice of the bell. . . .[5]

Sayers's hand is light enough to allow us humor at the old man's expense, his sententious attitude toward death sounding both naive and oddly adequate. (There is, too, the Biblical undertone to his saying, "In the midst of life, we are in death"—see St. Paul—and "the body of this death." The actual phrase appears in the Order for the Burial of the Dead, the Book of Common Prayer.) Tailor Paul, moreover, the enormous tenor of the ring, is an important item in Lavender's moral security, and of his security in his community, for which the bells ring at every christening, marriage, and death, marking time for the minutiae of village life.

Further, the bells are associated explicitly with moral retribution. The church caretaker will let no one "visit" Batty Thomas, because "she's a bell that has her fancies"; he explains with two stories of fatal accidents, neither, to his mind, mere chance. Our comfortable distance from his superstition does not erase its suggestion. Lavender is more forthright: " 'They bells du know well who's a-haulin' of 'un. . . . They can't abide a wicked man. They lays in wait to overthrow 'un.' "[6] To which Wimsey, in the way of his courteous secularity, responds with an "Oh, quite" that is meant to be embarrassed and inadequate. We are impatient with Wimsey for having no stronger response. We do not believe Lavender, of course; but it is his simple faith that carries conviction. Besides, Wimsey himself has thought in Scriptural terms—"If their tongues could speak they could tell him what they had seen, but they had neither speech nor language."[7] We are in no position, at this point, to free our knowledge of this small world from the implications building around the bells.

In addition, some passages in the novel are plainly metaphoric:

> To the ordinary man . . . the pealing of bells is a monotonous jangle and a nuisance, tolerable only when mitigated by remote distance and sentimental association. . . .

But the change-ringer's passion—and it is a passion—finds its satisfaction in mathematical completeness and mechanical perfection, and as his bell weaves her way rhythmically up from lead to hinder place, and down again, he is filled with the solemn intoxication that comes of intricate ritual faultlessly performed. [8]

Here Sayers is speaking directly to us; she makes of the ring an explicit image, figuring order in apparent disorder, harmony in chaos, skill and intention manifested superficially as monotonous confusion—the promise of justice within the flux of phenomena. Indeed, the bells act as factors of order in village life, marking years and lives, warning, celebrating, and, because they are passed on from generation to generation and do not die, forming a palpable continuity with the far past. Their carefully prepared but veiled menace is balanced by practical benevolence, just as the peal's apparent randomness is balanced by its actual discipline. And the suggestion that they possess some active initiative, freedom, or moral awareness is balanced by their actual mechanical passivity.

Sayers keeps these hints and values alive throughout the story, largely by involving us in the systole and diastole of opinion among the characters closely associated with the mystery. What they think, the terms they use, affect what we think. Like them, we are around the bells so much that we come to think of them as more than mere objects. Cosmopolitan that he is, Wimsey finds himself talking to the bells, studying their history, playing with the riddles of their mottoes and change patterns, drawn by a sense of hidden significance. Sayers uses his curiosity to place the bells in a richer context than village opinion, the nest of campanological terms and practices. These in turn add to the image the tones of great age, of vast size and latent power, beauty, and the awe of religious tradition.

My discussion of the bells as image has bypassed the novel's busy surface, where the daily routine of clues and witnesses gradually assembles the pieces of the mystery's answer. But in the routine Wimsey comes up against something closely associated with the bells, the unpretentious but solid life of the village itself. The parish of Fenchurch St. Paul is not large (340 souls), but in its unity and its devotion to the foci of village life, particularly the church, it seems remarkable. Their distinction between "us" and "them" is the clearest thing the villagers know. But they do not apply it uncharitably. When the belfry's victim turns up, they give him a proper funeral, as if he were "one of ourselves." He is rung out by Tailor Paul, like any other Christian soul. (Sayers underlines the religious quality of their charity with a reference to Luke 12:6—"Are not five sparrows sold for two farthings, and not one of them is forgotten before God?"—referring to the victim's anonymity; the reference appears on Wimsey's funeral wreath.)

A more vivid revelation of the communal life comes at the inquest into the victim's decease. The whole village turns out; all present take each question to heart, as if addressed to them all; they think together, discuss their common judgments, jog the witness's memory, answer on his behalf, supply him with extra information; they simply ignore the coroner's feeble effort to separate the individual knowledge of a witness from the corporate knowledge of the town. The momentum of the village life hardly notices the law's quibbling decorum.

Apart from such broadly comic scenes, the book is, like many mysteries, a rather private one. Wimsey must be about his trade of detecting; he inquires, indulges in various schemes to obtain evidence, makes a brief visit to France. The absence of violent incident is filled by subplots resting on the main investigation. Wimsey must identify the corpse, and explain how it came to Fenchurch St. Paul; he finds a necklace whose disappearance has caused grave misfortune to the local gentry. None of these really clarifies the opacity of the murder itself. Indeed, the discovery of the necklace serves as a minor, ironic peripety—for it solves an old police case, and at the same moment reveals to Wimsey that he is hopelessly mistaken about the central mystery.

In the business of detection, like most of Sayers's books, *The Nine Tailors* is most satisfactory. But its special interest, as I have said, arises when this business impinges on deeper thematic concerns. How are the two levels to be united? One tactic for this is Sayer's use of a consciously literary, allusive style. In *The Mind of the Maker,* for instance, Sayers assembled 10 quotations which "were obviously hovering in my memory when I wrote a phrase in *The Nine Tailors.* "[9] The passage describes the church roof as Wimsey stands beneath:

> Incredibly aloof, flinging back the light in a dusky shimmer of bright hair and gilded outspread wings, soared the ranked angels, cherubim and seraphim, choir over choir, from corbel and hammerbeam, floating face to face uplifted.[10]

It is a Paradisal vision; it quiets even the invincibly secular Wimsey. Behind it Sayers ranges quotations from the Bible, Milton's *Nativity Ode* ("The cherubick host in thousand quires"), Keats, Browning, T. S. Eliot, and Donne ("a bracelet of bright hair"). Though she modestly points out the disparity between sources and use, the allusions have something concrete to do with the passage's excitement. The allusive richness images an aesthetic excellence which is itself the image of a deeper exultation.

Another example, unconfessed, is more interesting because it is not part of a descriptive set piece:

> The air was so heavy with water, that not till they had passed Frog's Bridge did they hear the sweet, dull jangle of sound that told them that the ringers were practising their Christmas peal; it drifted through the streaming rain with an aching and intolerable melancholy, like the noise of the bells of a drowned city pulsing up through the overwhelming sea.[11]

Along with the Atlantis image and (perhaps) a glance toward Claude Debussy's *La Cathedrale engloutie,* the passage is enriched by its deliberate echoing of *Hamlet* III.i.162 ("Like sweet bells jangled, out of tune and harsh"), itself parodied in its own century by Thomas Shadwell (*The Virtuoso,* 1676). The passage seems to mingle archetypes: bell, temple, flood, sea. Where Sayers uses Biblical quotation or style, this archetypal depth also appears. We have quoted Wimsey's thought—the bells "had neither speech nor language"—deriving from Psalm 19:3 ("There is no speech nor language, where their voice is not heard"). The same allusive effect joins with the flood archetype to produce: "And over all, the bells tumbled and wrangled, shouting their alarm across the country. . . . awake! make haste! save yourselves! The deep waters have gone over us!"[12]

That the novel's style can open out to this sort of connotation does not detract from its more usual clear, witty narrative tone. The allusions undergird the style, at crucial points giving us to know that the story goes deeper than its surface bustle. But this stylistic development of certain of the story's features is also essential to the significance of the murder mystery itself. Sayers's use of a semipastoral village setting connects the murder with a representative human community; suggestions about religious mystery, as in the image of the bells and the Biblical allusions, help to work out the murder's ethical complication. For the murder was, in a sense, a corporate action of the community in its human agents both conscious and unconscious of the circumstances, and in the bells, which are an image for the village's common life. To this, religious allusion adds a delicate if undefinable sense of purpose. The bells seem to be implying something else, an impersonal justice beyond the capacities of any of the humans to grasp.

For though the bell ringers are ignorant of it, the act of murder is a kind of execution. The book's only thorough villain is the dead man, Jeff Deacon, a thief, liar, deserter, bigamist, and murderer in his own right. Making the victim a villain is not an original turn. It can be done in order to preserve our sympathy for the murderer and increase our respect for a detective who, for sympathy, conceals the solution. Sayers had done it in *Five Red Herrings,* and would again in *Busman's Honeymoon,* in the first to multiply suspects, in the second to increase the psychological pressure on Wimsey.

Only in *The Nine Tailors,* however, does the idea have greater import. It makes the murder just, so to speak, in spite of itself: " 'whoever killed him,' " says Wimsey in a moment of frustration, " 'was a public benefactor.' "[13] But the bell ringers had formed no vigilante committee: they did not know what they were doing. The justice of their action was neither intended nor anticipated. Ordered by a judge and effected by proper means, the death would have been legal as well as just: Deacon is guilty of an unsolved murder. But the death was not sanctioned or planned. It was done apparently by chance, in a moment of pious celebration.

It is therefore morally and legally ambiguous. It lacks clear legal sanction. Strictly speaking, it was unpremeditated: though Deacon's presence in the belfry was not by chance, the man who put him there did not intend to kill him. He does, however, feel responsible. Morally, the murder seems justified, if we grant the community's right to free itself from its own degenerate elements; but as an act of the community, it might be said to have a legal dimension—does not formal justice act in the community's name and on its behalf? But, of course, the death was not legal, because it was effected not through law, which controls the latent violence of human communities, but through chance. We seem to be forced into the conclusion that what guilt Deacon's death generates must be borne by "innocent" men—and, further, that these innocent men were obeying, unknown to themselves, a form of overruling justice.

It is in the community, then, that the murder's ambiguities come to rest. The community is responsible. Here also we come to Sayers's basic theme and her most striking alteration of detective story convention. As W. H. Auden wrote in his fine essay, "The Guilty Vicarage" (1946), the discovery of a murderer usually leads society from a state of apparent innocence to one of true innocence.[14] Evil is identified and rooted out, because responsibility for it is placed on a single agent, who is then disposed of. But this moral simplification is the very thing Sayers is working to destroy. She achieves a more difficult and realistic vision than this. Her representative society, the village, moves from apparent innocence toward the realization of true guilt.

The genre's limits are nevertheless present. The villagers as a group do not grasp the murder's implications. The book is, in fact, about Wimsey's own perceptions, and secondarily about Fenchurch St. Paul. He understands; he is the village's surrogate, and his insight is ours also. Deacon's death has been "doubly determined." It was caused by the chance that ties him in the bell chamber and prevents his being freed; also, by the mute but actual justice of the event, which Sayers will neither state nor ignore. Will Thoday grasps his degree of responsibility; his reaction, extreme but not absurd, is suicide. Wimsey's reaction is less drastic, though it cancels his habitual flippancy. He is never exhilarated by his successful solution of the murder; there is no wine of victory. Rather he is shocked and daunted by the case's unexpected ironies, and by his own place in its tangle of human motives, accident, and physical necessity.

We should pause here to emphasize that these implications arise directly from the form of Sayers's murder "gimmick." They constitute a moral explication of the event of the murder, and a metaphoric development of the main object involved, the bells. That Wimsey comes to understand these implications is also inherent in the mystery form. He is the detective. It is for him to uncover facts and place responsibility. As he does so, however, he comes to see how difficult the placing of responsibility must be.

This difficulty is further reinforced by the novel's last major incident, the fen flood. This is only slightly foreshadowed in the story. Sayers places it between the discovery of Deacon's identity, which solves half the mystery, and Wimsey's own discovery of the cause of death. It comes at a moment when the detective plot is stalled; the rhythm of the novel is virtually at a stop, and with some daring Sayers brings in a piece of stage business with no obvious connection with anything. The flood intrudes on the novel's symmetry. It seems to violate the unity of action by starting a second plot. It does not, in fact, because it testifies to the novel's theme clearly and on several levels. What the mystery has hitherto left distant and potential, the flood makes immediate: the deep orderliness of village life, punctuated by mishap and tragedy, morally ambivalent as all human life is ambivalent, but stable, continuing, self-enriching.

It would almost be true to say that at this point the novel changes heroes, from Wimsey to the village. It would be more accurate, however, to say that Wimsey moves closer to his final discovery by moving closer to the village. Trapped with it by the flood waters, he is no longer observing its operations from the outside. He is absorbed, and becomes a working member. The village preoccupies our attention for the moment; but it is also working as an agent of Wimsey's discovery.

Here Sayers's carefully nurtured symbols come to full fruition. The church, as the only high ground on the surrounding fen, becomes the logical sanctuary for the village, people, livestock, belongings. It no longer symbolizes the community; it is the community. The bells, too, are brought from the detachment of size and legend to intimate involvement in the village's moment of trouble. They spread the flood alarm; they ring to bed and rising; they mark a christening. The suggestiveness which has cloaked church and bells attaches to the village, and to the neglected quest for the truth about Deacon's death.

For there are definite similarities between the murder and the flood. The self-confident preparations of engineers parallel the innocent enthusiasm of the bell ringers. The flood reduces the preparations to nothing; the coincidence of Deacon's death marks the peal. In both cases the best-laid plans *gang agley,* and in both cases "nature"—or the mechanical necessity of the bells—has its way despite human interference.

The community, therefore, exists between the threats of nature and the accidents of its own humanity. It survives by coping with both as best it can: Venables, the curate, has a detailed, effective plan ready for the flood emergency; and the village has a sententious, humane, but protected response for Deacon's death. Wimsey is perfectly willing to work within Venables's emergency plans. But Deacon troubles him; the case stands open, its rationale incomplete. Sayers leaves the motives of Wimsey's final discovery obscure. They may amount to no more than his surrendering, finally, to the bells' tacit appeal. There is, too, the same half-intended chance that left Deacon in the belfry—an accident the outcome of which is too rational to be accidental. In any case, Wimsey climbs into the bell chamber during a peal, and the climb becomes an inverted Purgatorial journey, up toward heaven, toward death:

> Through the brazen clash and clatter there went one high note, shrill and sustained, that was like a sword in the brain. All the blood of his body seemed to rush to his head, swelling it to the bursting-point. He released his hold of the ladder and tried to shut out the uproar with his fingers. . . .[15]

To this point, Sayers has played a wary, reticent game with the image of the bells, inviting and rebuking pathetic fallacy to deepen the mystery. Here no such game is necessary; the simple physical pressure of the sound is quite sufficient to make her point. The bells' indifference to Wimsey's presence and suffering clinches the ambiguity of Deacon's death at the same moment that it explains its mechanism. That Deacon, this man "deserving" death, should have come to be there at this moment—though easily explained in terms of circumstances—becomes the greater mystery.

Wimsey's experience in the bell chamber revokes his earlier disgust for Deacon and receives the murdered man again into the community of mutual responsibility. Any one of the villagers could have been in the bell chamber, and the bell ringers would have murdered that person instead of Deacon, with the indifferent complicity of the bells. As the detective, Wimsey properly uncovers this fact. Perhaps ironically, however, he feels it most deeply, though he is only a transient member of the village, and though he, unlike the villagers, bears Deacon no lasting ill will. Wimsey not only comprehends the sense of the event. He summarizes it within his own experience. He is one of the murderers and, through their shared experience of the bell chamber, the murdered as well. He thus represents in its clearest form the novel's theme—the juxtaposition of innocence and guilt, of responsibility and the inability to make an adequate response to tragedy. He feels what Auden, very perceptively, calls the "sense of sin": "to feel guilt at there being an ethical choice to make, a guilt which, however 'good' I may become, remains unchanged."[16] It remains unchanged, of course, because responsibility remains unchanged. There is no shrugging it off onto someone else's shoulders. On behalf of the villagers, Wimsey carries the burden of moral knowledge.

As with other aspects of *The Nine Tailors,* therefore, its resolution falls partially within and partially outside the normal boundaries of mystery fiction. Sayers makes a deeper use of the genre's conventions, drawing her thematic concerns out of the mystery's typical preoccupation with event and circumstance. But most detectives manage to retain scientific (or aesthetic) detachment from their cases; they have a neat, *a priori* and, in their terms, adequate response to tragedy. They "solve" mysteries, resolving tension and reinstating the primacy of induction. Wimsey, on the other hand, loses his detachment. His solution reinstates not reason but charity, the necessary sharing of pain and guilt. One cannot explain death without to some degree explaining it away. For this reason, Wimsey's identification with both parties to the murder makes the most suitable closing to the novel's ambiguous case. Other viewpoints are offered. The district constable simply closes the investigation. Venables raises the old superstitions about the bells. But Wimsey's profound discomfort remains the most realistic and humane response. It completes, without releasing us from, the moral tension of the murder itself.

Margaret P. Hannay

Harriet's Influence on the Characterization of Lord Peter Wimsey

IN HER early essay "A Sport of Noble Minds" Dorothy L. Sayers establishes the principle that the detective story "does not, and by hypothesis never can, attain the loftiest level of literary achievement . . . . it rarely touches the heights and depths of human passion."[1] In this same essay, she declares that even the love interest, which had become *de rigueur*, is inappropriate to the detective genre. Lord Peter Wimsey rather cheerfully complies with these requirements until introduced to Harriet Vane in *Strong Poison*; from that point on, he gradually develops a human face behind his monocle. So far does Sayers stray from her earlier dictum that she subtitles *Busman's Honeymoon* "A Love Story with Detective Interruptions," prompting critics, such as Elizabeth Hurling, to bewail her abandonment of the detective story.

Lord Peter had begun life as a detective persona who combined the characteristics of E. C. Bentley's Philip Trent[2] and P. G. Wodehouse's Bertie Wooster. The Wooster pose was intended to conceal Wimsey's brilliant mind from the criminal; similar "disguises" were used by Chesterton when he made his detective a priest and by Agatha Christie when she used an elderly spinster to solve the crime. Lord Peter's pose was essential to the mystery plot, but it left him particularly vulnerable to critical indignation. When John Strachey called Wimsey "a preposterous young aristocrat"[3] he was seeing the persona only, not the person whom Sayers had gradually created behind the pose.

Sayers had two obstacles to overcome in giving Lord Peter a personality behind the persona: his "silly-ass-about-town" pose itself, and his superhuman abilities. Sayers introduces Harriet to counteract his Woosterism, but she defends his abilities as necessitated by the mystery plot.

In an unpublished address on "The Craft of Detective Fiction," apparently written after *Busman's Honeymoon,* Sayers defends Wimsey's prowess. Because she believes that those who ridicule the "marvelous assortment of qualities" possessed by the amateur detective do not understand the artistic problems involved, she lists the basic practical necessities for the detective hero:

1. The detective must be in a position to be brought into crimes and enabled to work with the police. (Lord Peter develops a close friendship with Inspector Parker.)
2. He must be able to drop everything at a moment and go off somewhere to investigate the crime. (Lord Peter has no professional obligations which would keep him in an office from nine to five, for example.)
3. He must be able "to tackle anything from a subtle poisoning to an elaborate alibi produced by mechanical means" if he is to be the hero of a series of books. One cannot always have the solution to the mystery depend upon poisoning if there is to be any suspense. Nor can the detective waste valuable space running around seeking expert opinions on every detail. (Lord Peter is notoriously versatile.)
4. He must have the physical equipment to be able to cope with violent criminals. (Since guns are considered rather vulgar for English detectives, Lord Peter must have physical strength. As his creator has made him rather short, he is agile, surprisingly strong for his size, and knows karate or its equivalent.)
5. He "must be *leisured* and *rich*" (italics hers). (Lord Peter cannot be deterred by such minor considerations as the cost of chartering a plane to cross the Atlantic, or the months he must disappear as Lord Peter if he is to maintain the character of Death Bredon.)
6. If he is to figure in a series of books, he should not be too old to start with, he should have some loose ends hanging out to be developed later, and his character should evolve gradually.[4]

Sayers, operating on the assumption that "to cramp your detective's possibilities cramps the action of the story," has been careful to endow Lord Peter with all these necessary attributes. The wealth and leisure permit him to follow interesting cases to appropriate settings; the title permits him access to the upper reaches of British society including, in *Clouds of Witness*, the king.

But the question remains, has Sayers overdone it? Q. D. Leavis charges:

> Miss Sayers has overstepped the limits of what even a best-seller's public can be expected to swallow without suspicion. Lord Peter is not only of ducal stock and all that a Ouida hero was plus modern sophistication and modern accomplishments — such as being adored by his men during the Great War and able to talk like a P. G. Wodehouse moron — he is also a distinguished scholar in history, a celebrated cricketeer, an authority on antiques, a musician, a brilliant wit, a diplomat on whom the F.O. leans during international crises, a wide and deep reader and no doubt some other things I've overlooked.[5]

Leavis has overlooked the physical prowess, the book he wrote on methods of murder, and the expertise on incunabula, among other things. But her list is suggestive of the things which caused W. H. Auden to call Lord Peter a "priggish superman . . . having no motive for being a detective except caprice."[6]

It is the purpose of this paper to demonstrate that Sayers was thoroughly aware of Lord Peter's overabundant abilities and underdeveloped character, that she deliberately set about to change her creature from a cardboard detective into a human being, and that she used the character of Harriet Vane to provide both the necessity and the means for this difficult metamorphosis.

The essay "Gaudy Night" makes her intentions quite clear. She recounts that when she first started to write a Lord Peter book, "It was with the avowed intention of producing something 'less like a conventional detective story and more like a novel.' Re-reading *Whose Body?* at this distance of time I observe, with regret, that it is conventional to the last degree, and no more like a novel than I to Hercules."[7] She had, as she admits, been preaching that to survive, the detective story "must get back to where it began in the hands of Collins and Le Fanu, and become once more a novel of manners instead of a pure crossword puzzle" [p. 76]. She traces the evolution of her plots to indicate that "each successive book of mine worked gradually nearer to the sort of thing I had in view." The progress from pure detection to something "more like a novel" was not, however, nearly so smooth as that comment implies.

Even in *Whose Body?* we note that Lord Peter, whose "long, amiable face looked as if it had generated spontaneously from his top hat"[8] did have some elements of life, some "loose ends" which could be woven together later. His sensitive hands, for example, at their best playing Bach or a Scarlatti sonata, figure prominently in *Gaudy Night* and *Busman's Honeymoon* as the hands of the lover and the hangman; the passion for collecting rare volumes leads naturally into a profound knowledge of Elizabethan literature in the later books; the "bad knock after the war" turns out to have been Barbara, the "moonlight princess"; his habit of quotation, begun quietly, leads to the rollicking tossing of quotations "not for edification" in *Busman's Honeymoon*; the gift for talking piffle later makes him invaluable to the foreign office.

In the second Wimsey book, *Clouds of Witness,* Peter is provided with a complete background, dropped into the story like a lump in a pudding:

> But to Lord Peter the world presented itself as an entertaining labyrinth of side-issues. He was a respectable scholar in five or six languages, a musician of some skill and more understanding, something of an expert in toxicology, a collector of rare editions, an entertaining man-about-town, and a common sensationalist. He had been seen at half-past twelve on a Sunday morning walking in Hyde Park in a top-hat and frock-coat, reading the *News of the World.* His passion for the unexplored led him to hunt up obscure pamphlets in the British Museum, to unravel the emotional history of income tax collectors, and to find out where his own drains led to.[9]

The next two novels add a few details to Lord Peter's personality. In *Unnatural Death* we find that he is writing *The Murderer's Vade-Mecum,* that he leaves all the mundane dreary work to Parker or Miss Climpson, that he is surprisingly familiar with the works of St. Augustine, and that he frequents the British Museum to collate a twelfth-century manuscript of Tristan. *The Unpleasantness at the Bellona Club* shows us the same person. His facade as rich man-about-town still convinces people "I'm too well-off to have any brains."[10] The superdetective is rather overplayed, as when he notes the corpse's loose swinging knee: "The change in him was almost startling—it was as if a steel blade had whipped suddenly out of its velvet scabbard" [ch. 4]. The most interesting character in the book is Ann Dorland, a precursor of Harriet Vane. Like Harriet, she has had a previous affair in which she was treated brutally; she has been falsely accused of murder and rescued by Lord Peter; she knows too much about poison and detective stories; she is intelligent, but not beautiful. Peter advises her that what she needs is "not an artist, not a bohemian, and not a professional man—a man of the world." He compares her to a Romanée Conti, too rough now, a bit unfinished but "it'll be a grand wine in ten years' time." Of course "It takes a fairly experienced palate to appreciate it" [ch. 21]. (Peter, we realize, is naturally far more the man of the world than is the Major Fentiman who presumably ends up appreciating Ann Dorland, and his choice of a woman is also inexplicable to those who prefer conventional beauty.)

Peter has come as far into humanity as he could on his own. If he is to progress into fuller life, he needs help. Sayers provides that help in the person of Harriet Vane, who is the catalyst of Peter's humanity in several important ways: she provides the necessity for developing his character; she serves as an indirect narrator in love with the hero, thus relieving the author of that charge; she functions as a *ficelle* within the story, allowing Peter to reveal both his crushing sense of responsibility for getting people hanged and his many personal weaknesses.

Harriet forced Peter toward humanity almost against the will of her creator. Sayers claims that she "rather timidly introduced the 'love element' into the Peter Wimsey story" with the intention "of marrying him off and getting rid of him."[11] She was thwarted by Peter's growing popularity and by Harriet's character. Harriet, a full person from the start, had been put in such a position that she could not accept Peter without "loss of self-respect." According to the traditional plot, "the heroine, after treating the hero for interminable chapters as though he were something the cat had brought in, is rescued by him under peculiarly humiliating circumstances and immediately falls into his arms in a passion of gratitude and affection."[12] Harriet and Peter would not comply. "When I looked at the situation I saw that it was in every respect false and degrading; and the puppets had somehow got just so much flesh and blood in them that I could not force them to accept it without shocking myself."[13]

Sayers decided to take Lord Peter away and perform a major operation on him, to make him a suitable lover for Harriet. He had to be made "a complete human being, with a past and a future . . . with a complicated psychology and even the rudiments of a religious outlook" [p. 80]. She remembers that "I laid him out firmly on the operating-table and chipped away at his internal mechanism through three longish books. At the end of the process he was five years older than he was in *Strong Poison,* and twelve years older than he was when he started" [p. 80]. But the process cannot have been that simple. *The Five Red Herrings* (1931) was, as she admits, a throwback to the puzzle form of the detective story. Presumably that book does not count. *Have His Carcase* (1932) is generally considered the weakest of the Wimsey stories, needing much more of the chisel on its padded frame. The most important developments are that details are often given from Harriet's point of view and that it is made increasingly clear that Harriet is attracted to Peter, though held back by her crushing sense of inferiority. We can see that the two puppets are developing a friendship, a camaraderie from working together on the murder problem, which bodes well for their future in *Gaudy Night.* The next two volumes, *Murder Must Advertise* and *The Nine Tailors,* are superb detection stories, presenting complex problems of guilt and responsibility.

By 1935 Peter has enough reality to be reunited with Harriet if "some device [is]found for putting Harriet back on a footing of equality with her lover."[14] The "device" is to bring her to Oxford and to give her the scholar's mind. "On the intellectual platform, alone of all others, Harriet could stand free and equal with Peter, since in that sphere she had never been false to her own standards" [p. 82]. But there must be a corollary movement which knocks Peter off his pedestal, which presents him as more of a man and less of a superman. This is accomplished by giving him a conscience and by revealing his weaknesses. The presence of Harriet Vane in Wimsey's world is essential if Peter is to develop fully these elements of humanity.

In *Whose Body?* Lord Peter begins with a rather casual attitude toward murder; he turns the corpse over and "inspect[s] it with his head on one side, bringing his monocle into play with the air of the late Joseph Chamberlain approving a rare orchid" [ch. 1]. Such flippancy is abhorred by Sayers some 10 years later. In "The Craft of Detective Fiction" she observes that often the detective "seems to take the whole thing as a mere piece of intellectual fun," noting that this is "especially unpleasant in [the] amateur detective." Peter's delight that a corpse has been found *is* thoroughly unpleasant. But even in this first book Sayers introduces some element of remorse. Peter confesses to Parker that finding the murderer is just a game "to begin with, and I go on cheerfully, and then I suddenly see that somebody is going to be hurt, and I want out of it."[15] Inspector Parker acts as his conscience, scolding him for wanting to treat life like a football match: "You can't be a sportsman. You're a responsible person." One important element in the Wimsey series is the increasing internalization of the conscience here represented by the Evangelical Parker; Peter himself comes to believe that it is essential to find the truth and that he must be willing to accept the consequences of his inquiry. This scholarly emphasis on *facts* becomes one of the central themes in *Gaudy Night,* but even in *Clouds of Witnesses* Peter admits that "the best thing we can do . . . is to look the evidence in the face, however ugly" [ch. 6]. After all, "whoever did it, it's better the right person should suffer than the wrong" [ch. 5].

The best early attempt to give Peter a conscience occurs when he wanders into church in *Unnatural Death* and asks Mr. Tredgold about the moral propriety of his interference with the murderer—interference which had led to other murders. Peter is told that "sin is in the intention, not the deed." This applies to the murderer, but also to himself. The rector concludes that he should not feel too responsible if he is not serving a private vengeance. "Probably the murderer's own guilty fears would have led him into fresh crimes even without your interference." But the presentation of guilt and absolution is not totally successful here. Tredgold can view Peter only from the outside, and his conclusion is almost comical:

> "Dear, dear," he said, "how nice they are. So kindly and scrupulous and so vague outside their public-school code. And much more nervous and sensitive than people think. A very difficult class to reach. I must make a special intention for him at Mass tomorrow."[16]

He knots his handkerchief to help him remember to say the prayer.

Strong Poison, involving Harriet in the role of victim, forces Lord Peter to reconsider his involvement in detection. He catches himself saying, "When I blow my brains out—" quickly adding "I hope I shaln't want to . . . . I hope I shaln't need to want to . . . . but I'm beginning to dislike this job of getting people hanged."[17] He also begins to resent the fact that his own flippancy convinces even Parker that he is not to be taken seriously. When he cries that Biggy ought to "fry in hell and be served up with cayenne pepper on a red-hot dish" for not believing in Harriet's innocence, Parker is unimpressed. "Anybody would think you'd gone goopey over the girl." Parker is shocked to find that Peter is indeed serious, as he retorts "bitterly": "I'm not expected to be serious. A buffoon, that's what I am" [ch. 5]. His new seriousness about Harriet makes the reader believe in his new seriousness about his detection. His work is no longer presented as merely the hobby it had been in *Whose Body?*. Though Peter understandably displays little remorse over Urquhart's hanging, his new attitude is underscored in *Murder Must Advertise* and *The Nine Tailors* so that the reader is prepared for Harriet's passionate defense of his vocation in *Gaudy Night*. When Miss Barton is indignant because "this dilettante gentleman" devotes all his time to his hobbies—collecting books, playing cricket, and detecting crimes, Harriet explodes:

> 'Does it matter? Why should he do anything else? Catching murderers isn't a soft job, or a sheltered job. It takes a lot of time and energy, and you may very easily get injured or killed. I dare say he does it for fun, but at any rate, he does do it. Scores of people must have as much reason to thank him as I have. You can't call that nothing.'[18]

Here Harriet nearly absolves the author of the charge of being in love with her creation; although she will not yet admit it to herself, Harriet defends Peter's work with the passionate understanding of a woman in love. In *Gaudy Night* a new conscience is projected *back* into earlier books as he tells Harriet about his cases.

The case in *Murder Must Advertise* is mentioned in *Gaudy Night;* from Harriet's perspective, early in the novel, we see that Peter "had found office life entertaining; but the thing had come to a strange and painful conclusion." Peter showed up for a dinner appointment so ill with a headache and fever that Harriet had to convey him home to Bunter, who reassured her that it was just reaction "of frequent occurrence at the end of a trying case, but soon over." Indeed, Peter rang up shortly thereafter and displayed "a quite remarkable effervescence of spirits" [ch. 4]. Because Harriet is keeping her distance from Peter, she cannot yet function as a *ficelle* in the Jamesian sense.

After the river episode, when they both realize she loves him, Peter can be more open in her presence, projecting his doubts back into early cases. For example, *Unnatural Death* has displayed just enough hint of conscience so that the reader can believe Peter when he tells Harriet and the dons that the execution of the guilty is not nearly such a burden as the execution of the innocent: "I happened to find out that a young woman had murdered an old one for her money. It didn't matter much: the old woman was dying in any case, and the girl (though she didn't know that) would have inherited the money in any case. As soon as I started to meddle, the girl set to work again, killed two innocent people to cover her tracks and murderously attacked three others. Finally she killed herself. If I'd left her alone, there might have been only one death instead of four" [ch. 17]. The dons absolve him of responsibility, agreeing that one must "establish the facts, no matter what comes of it;" Peter then steers the discussion toward the conflict between private loyalties and

public responsibilities, a discussion which provides the crucial clue of
the mystery. But what is important to us here is that Sayers, using
Harriet's perspective, has established the utter seriousness of Peter's
detection; he does not investigate merely out of inquisitiveness, as he
seems to in *Whose Body?*, but out of a deep sense of public responsibility.

What we have seen only through Harriet's eyes—Peter's crushing
sense of responsibility for the results of his detection—is underscored in
the postscript to *Gaudy Night*, "written" by Paul Delagardie: "The only
trouble about Peter's new hobby was that it had to be more than a hobby.
. . . You cannot get murderers hanged for your private enjoyment.
Peter's intellect pulled him one way and his nerves another, till I began
to be afraid they would pull him to pieces. At the end of every case he had
the old nightmares and shellshock again." With the words of "Uncle
Pandarus" to verify Harriet's new realization of Peter's conscience, we
are prepared for *Busman's Honeymoon.*

Sayers observes that the premise of the play is that "To occupy one's
honeymoon in getting a fellow-creature hanged (however rightly and
deservedly) is no very agreeable thing for any gentleman; and is liable to
lead to a certain amount of emotional conflict."[19] She discovered that
people are "so used to taking detection callously" that the "managements
could not understand why Peter could not merrily get on with the job, or
why we chose to encumber the play with his distastes and scruples and
emotional reactions."

If Sayers is to dramatize these "distastes and scruples and emotional
reactions," Harriet must serve as the *ficelle*. An author who respects the
integrity of her characters as much as Sayers does would hardly have
Lord Peter sobbing in Bunter's arms or covering his ears to avoid the
striking clock in the presence of Inspector Parker. Nor could he have
revealed his suffering with Harriet still opposing him. It is a reasonable
premise that a man may show his inner torments to his wife but not to his
colleagues. Sayers uses this premise, together with emphasis on the
flippant persona which protects Peter's sensibilities, to imply that he has
had this delicate conscience all along but has never been able to reveal it.

As Crutchley is dragged off by the police, Peter asks Harriet, "Come
and hold my hand. . . . This part of the business always gets me
down."[20] The closing section of the book, entitled "Epithalamion,"
presents Lord Peter stripped of his protective disguise, the Peter known
only to his wife. Harriet contrasts the outcome of her own detective
novels, wherein Mr. Robert Templeton always ends on a "top note . . .

leaving somebody else to cope with the trivial details of putting the case together," with "real life," wherein Lord Peter and his household spend most of the day at the police station "making an interminable statement." Peter is officially requested to hold himself ready to be a witness and not to leave town. But he also has a private conscience, which requires hiring the famous Sir Impey Biggs for the defense, making arrangements for the care of Crutchley's pregnant girlfriend, begging the forgiveness of the criminal, and building a wall of protective fortification around his sensitivities. From Harriet's perspective we see that his "determined courtesy and cheerfulness" are "punctuated by fits of exigent and exhausting passion," alarming both because they are so intense and because they are "apparently automatic and almost impersonal."[21] The Dowager Duchess had explained that it is Peter's nervous breakdown after the war which leaves him in this vulnerable state; he always becomes ill after a case. "He doesn't like responsibility you know . . . and the War . . . was bad for people that way."[22] After much lonely suffering, Peter finally does come upstairs, to share his torment with his wife. He tells Harriet, "I got permission to see a hanging once. . . . I thought I'd better know . . . but it hasn't cured me of meddling" [ch. III]. She is able to reassure him more effectively than could Mr. Tredgold: "If you hadn't meddled six years ago, it would almost certainly have been me." Peter, thankful for her presence, compares himself to Coriolanus relying on his wife, an analogy impossible to the flippant Peter of *Whose Body?*. He begs her, "Harriet, for God's sake, hold onto me . . . get me out of this . . . break down the door. . . . " Then suddenly he says "Oh damn!" and begins to cry—"in an awkward, unpractised way at first, and then more easily." Certainly this man who cries in his wife's arms because he has caused a hanging can no longer be accused of being "priggish." But Peter also needs to be given some human foibles to make him less of a superman.

Another of Harriet's major functions in the Wimsey novels is to reveal Peter's personal frailties, making him more human and less cardboard. Sayers gives the "priggish superman" these human frailties in the same way that she gives him a tender conscience. Using the narrative technique of limited omniscience, she presents Peter as seen through Harriet's eyes; using references to past episodes, she builds in the troubled childhood of a sensitive and idealistic lad; using his love for Harriet, she presents a man troubled by his own mortality and fallibility; using Harriet as a *ficelle*, she presents Peter's pessimism about the European situation and the approaching war.

This process is carefully begun in *Strong Poison*. For the first time we see our great detective at a loss. He sits in his luxurious apartment, surrounded by his rare volumes:

> All that wisdom and all that beauty, and they could not show him how to save the woman he imperiously wanted from a sordid death by hanging. And he had thought himself rather clever at that kind of thing. The enormous and complicated imbecility of things was all around him like a trap. [ch. 15]

Catching sight of his "fair, foolish face" in the mirror, he wants to smash the glass to destroy the image of his own helplessness. This passage is significant on three counts. First, Lord Peter is stymied and in great personal distress over his inability to solve a problem. Second, he is ready to remove the Wooster mask which has made even Parker unable to believe he is serious about Harriet. Third, he wants Harriet "imperiously," here seeming to care as much about his own inability to achieve his ends as about Harriet herself; as yet he has none of the sympathetic understanding he achieves in *Gaudy Night*. *Strong Poison* also shows Peter, for the first time, affected by musings on mutability:

> Like the poisoned Athulf in *Fool's Tragedy*, he could have cried, "Oh, I am changing, changing, fearfully changing."
> Whether his present enterprise failed or succeeded, things would never be the same again. It was not that his heart would be broken by disastrous love—he had outlived the luxurious agonies of youthful blood, and in this very freedom from illusion he recognized the loss of something. From now on, every hour of light-heartedness would be, not a prerogative but an achievement—one more axe or case-bottle or fowling-piece, rescued, Crusoe-fashion, from a sinking ship. [ch. 8]

Also, for the first time, his personal feelings are strong enough to cloud his mind: "He was fumbling—grasping uncertainly here and there at fugitive and mocking possibilities . . . and the shortness of the time, which would once have stimulated, now frightened and confused him" [ch. 8]. Harriet has the power to bring the superman into doubt; perhaps that is the most crucial step in making him human.

Have His Carcase contributes little to the development of either Harriet or Peter; they seem to emerge new-born in *Gaudy Night* some three years after they had fled Wilvercombe. When Peter calls Harriet, his voice betrays "a curious huskiness and uncertainty" [ch. 4], returning to his attitude in *Strong Poison*; even when she is not in danger, she undermines his breezy self-confidence.

Harriet provides the author with an indirect way to undercut the Bertie Wooster pose. When Miss Armstrong mentions that she had met Peter once at a dog show, "giving the perfect imitation of the silly-ass-about-town," Harriet can explain, "Then he was either frightfully bored or detecting something. . . . I know that frivolous mood, and it's mostly camouflage—but one doesn't always know for what" [ch. 2]. The superman image is also undercut when Peter takes her to dinner. She finds that the great detective is not utterly indestructible, after all—he is troubled by a few broken ribs and irritating sticking plaster. Harriet, seeing him vulnerable, vehemently declares: "I'm *damned* if I'll have you wiped out by plug-uglies or anonymous letter-writers!" Then she lends "a strong arm to extricate him, swearing loudly, from the difficult depths of the couch" [ch. 4].

The meeting with the young Viscount St. George (who apparently serves as Peter's alter ego, his egotistical and impudent younger self) serves once again to alter their relative positions. The letter she reads to the battered young nephew "displayed . . . almost everything that she resented most in Peter; the condescending superiority, the arrogance of caste and the generosity that was like a blow in the face." This is a turning point:

> For the first time in their acquaintance, she had the upper hand of Peter Wimsey, and could rub his aristocratic nose in the dirt if she wanted to. Since she had been looking for such an opportunity for five years, it would be odd if she did not hasten to take advantage of it. [ch. 9]

But, of course, she does not take advantage of it; she puts a full two hours into composing her brief letter, concerned that however she puts the situation "all this is going to hurt his pride damnably. . . . Poor old Peter!" The narrator observes: "The remark probably deserves to be included in an anthology of Great First Occasions."

When Peter finally does arrive at Oxford, he says, " 'Hello-ullo!' " with a faint echo of the old, flippant manner" [ch. 14]. The flippancy objectionable to Harriet and critics alike is fading rapidly. Harriet notices that he looks terribly tired; her sympathy encourages him to tell her his utter weariness with the European negotiations and his fear that he is changing: "Don't say I'm getting to look my age. . . . An eternal childishness is my one diplomatic asset."[23] At the same interview she confesses that she recognized Jerry as a Wimsey by his hands. He is flattered: "It amused and touched her to discover this childish streak of vanity in him." Then they talk about the Denver estate, with Peter sighing: "Our kind of show

is dead and done for. What the hell good does it do anybody these days?"
Peter is shown to be tired, vain, getting old, and with his age, pessimistic
about the future of the aristocracy and the freedom of Europe:

> Harriet could find nothing to say to him. She had fought him for five years, and found
> out nothing but his strength; now, within half an hour he had exposed all his
> weaknesses, one after another. And she could not in honesty say: "Why didn't you tell
> me before?" because she knew perfectly well what the answer ought to be. [ch. 14]

By her skillful use of Harriet's perspective Sayers lulls the readers into
thinking there is good reason for *them* not to have seen this side of Peter
before. The truth is, of course, that these weaknesses did not exist before
this novel, but they have been skillfully projected back into the past.

But Harriet has not yet seen all his weaknesses. The next step comes
in the sentimental interlude on the river, when he commits the absurdity
of falling asleep in public: "From a height of conscious superiority we
look down on the sleeper, thus exposing himself in all his frailty" [ch.
15]. As Peter sleeps, Harriet finds a copy of *Religio Medici* in his blazer
pocket. Reading Browne's observation that "The first day of our jubilee
is death," she realizes that she does not want Peter to make any personal
application of the passage: "She would rather have him secure and happy
in order that she might resent his happy security."

For the bulk of the novel, of course, Peter shows his strengths: his
brilliant mind, his knowledge of Aristotle in the original Greek, his
familiarity with the European political situation and with history, his
ability to gain access to rare manuscript collections, his penetrating
insight into Harriet and into the motivations of the dons, his self-control,
his witty self-assurance at formal dinners. But Sayers includes examples
of Peter's jealousy of undergraduates to make him seem realistically
middle-aged. The first such incident occurs when Jerry kisses Harriet
under the SCR window; Peter is jealous of "the careless young egotism"
which makes such uncomplicated relations possible.

He is also envious of Reggie Pomfret. This other, and most engaging,
evidence of Peter's jealous weakness has led Edith Hamilton to accuse
him of still being a superman. Because of the attempt to make the book
more of a novel, she explains, she is "bothered by . . . Lord Peter's
ability to quell the rage of a husky undergraduate, bent upon knocking
him out, by seizing 'one' of his wrists 'in an iron grip.' "[24] Of course the
iron grip shows strength, but it is not really so unbelievable that a man of
forty-five who knows karate could pin the arm of a flailing, drunken
undergraduate. The emphasis in the novel is clearly on his sensitivity to

his age and to his height. He writes a pompous note to Pomfret, considers challenging him, and brags about the three duels he has been involved in. Harriet understands the symptoms: "Peter . . . I believe you're showing off." He replies: "I believe I am. . . . I hate being loomed over by gigantic undergraduates and made to feel my age."[25]

Busman's Honeymoon does not contribute nearly so much to the character development of Lord Peter as does *Gaudy Night*. The novel operates on Bunter's principle of judging people "by their behavior, not in great crises, but, in the minor adjustments of daily life" [ch. 1]. Both bride and bridegroom manage to keep their tempers admirably in the material discomforts of Talboys and the presence of the corpse; however, it is only fair to add that their work mostly consists of supervising Mrs. Ruddle and sympathizing with Bunter. Peter is humanized by his puttering way of dressing in the morning, his singing of French songs, and his concern that Mrs. Murdle (the car) be properly cared for. When the corpse is discovered and the police are called, Peter goes up to change:

> "Of course," thought Harriet, secretly entertained. "Someone has died in our house, so we put on a collar and tie. Nothing could be more obvious. How absurd men are! And how clever in devising protective armour for themselves!" [ch. 7]

Such charming absurdity comes better from Harriet than directly from the author. We have already noted that we see Peter's concern for Crutchley through Harriet's eyes. But it is Mrs. Goodacre, the vicar's wife, who puts the problem most succinctly:

> "But that's men all over. They want the thing done and then, of course, they don't like the consequences. Poor dears, they can't help it. They haven't got logical minds." ["Epithalamion," ch. III]

In one sense, of course, Lord Peter has one of the most logical minds in detective fiction, but Mrs. Goodacre is noting the way his heart wars with his head. This is the conflict Sayers intended to portray: "The essential Peter is seen to be the familiar figure of the interpretative artist, the romantic soul at war with the realistic brain."[26] Mrs. Goodacre's comment functions on the level of comedy as well, reducing Lord Peter to mortal stature. It is very difficult to picture the flippant Lord Peter of *Whose Body?* suffering mental tortures sufficient to produce the pity of a village vicar's wife, nor is it likely that he would have been called a "poor dear." Priggish supermen are not, after all, poor dears.

Dorothy L. Sayers did not mean for the Wimseys' career to end with the tears over Crutchley's execution. In the essay "Gaudy Night" she admits:

> I can see no end to Peter this side of the grave. . . . Formerly a periodic visitation, he has become a permanent resident in the house of my mind. . . . He darkens the future, so that I cannot now contrive an episode in his career without considering how it will affect him and his in ten years' time. . . . He sprawls over the past like an octopus. [pp. 93–94]

Thrones, Dominations, her unfinished novel, continues the progression of Lord Peter from pasteboard paragon toward a full humanity. As we continue to see through Harriet's eyes, his personal vanity becomes increasingly clear—his interminable dawdling in the bathroom, his agonized fears over pimples, his terror that he will come to need false teeth. We find that his accomplishments as a pianist and collector of rare books necessitate taking the temperature of the music room and library with irritating frequency. We note his pride of ancestry and tradition; he capitulates to the ancient ritual which requires husband and wife to sit 10 feet apart at a solitary meal. We also see him involved in more "real" problems, as opposed to detective problems; we are given considerable detail about how Peter runs his blocks of flats, for example. We hear of the death of the king and the consequent necessity to buy mourning clothes; Harriet's search for the proper black frock weaves the Wimseys into the fabric of English history.

At a dinner scene (which is extant in at least two versions) a Lady Croppingford "delivered a merciless assault on [Peter's] sensibilities." He retreats into the old "silly-ass-about-town" pose familiar to us from the early books: clowning, assuming a "fixed vacuity of countenance," and "dropping all his g's."[27] From the beginning, Sayers had shown us that a brilliant mind was working behind the monocle. By introducing Harriet Vane and showing us Peter through her eyes, Sayers has been able to establish that a sensitive conscience, a passionate heart, and some very human frailties have been hidden by that persona. So far has Lord Peter progressed from his early days as a cardboard detective that this last, unfinished chronicle contains no murder, and no problem for detection at all—not even stolen peaches. He is left managing his estate, feeling vaguely discontent. Perhaps he was to come across another corpse shortly; there are characters in the manuscript who almost beg to be murdered. But to our great loss, Lord Peter Wimsey had become so nearly real that he wandered out of the detective novel altogether.[28]

E. R. Gregory

Wilkie Collins and Dorothy L. Sayers

SELDOM in literary history can the case for one author's influence upon another be made with such authority as the case for Wilkie Collins's influence on Dorothy L. Sayers.[1] The external evidence for it is compelling by virtue of the massive quantities of documentation available. Even without the documentation, however, her writings give ample evidence of the influence. The section on Collins in the *Cambridge Bibliography of English Literature*, the introduction to the Everyman Library edition of *The Moonstone*, the uncompleted biography, the discussions of him in her essays, the allusions in her novels—all attest to her interest in Collins. A study of him, then, should help in understanding her, and it does. To be sure, however, it leaves much unexplained. The most Collinsean of her novels, *The Documents in the Case*, is unmistakably Sayers, not Collins. Still, a knowledge of Collins helps to restore perspective that an overly biographical reading of Sayers has destroyed, and suggests qualities of thought like great sensitivity to accuracy of detail that underlie all her work, fiction, and criticism alike.

The documentation for her interest in him is enormous. Most of it is at the Humanities Research Center, Austin, Texas (hereafter referred to as HRC). Over the years, Sayers collected a number of Collins's manuscripts, editions of his books, and books about him. After her death, these and her own materials—the fragment of her biography, her note-cards, notebooks (with two exceptions), and correspondence on Collins—were offered for sale. Since the HRC does not open its files to scholars, the following must be taken as its official statement of how it acquired these materials:

The Dorothy Sayers collection was first brought to our attention during the summer of 1960 by Mr. Lew David Feldman (House of El Dieff, New York). The collection of manuscripts, books, and related materials was at that time the property of Mr. Anthony Fleming, son of the late Dr. Sayers. Acting as Fleming's agent was Mr. Robert Barry, Jr. (C. A. Stonehill, Inc., New Haven). A twenty-page list of the materials was made available for our consideration. It was mentioned that the collection being offered at the time did not represent the complete manuscript and book holdings of the Estate.

On 28 October 1960, we ordered the Sayers collection through Mr. Feldman. In July, 1961, we received word that Mr. Barry had received the materials, had carefully checked them against the list provided, and was shipping them directly to Texas. Barry mentioned that the list was not completely accurate—a few items were not included in the collection, although there were some materials present which had not been listed. The materials arrived here on 3 August 1961.[2]

That the list was not completely accurate creates problems because the HRC did not keep the collection together. Thus we cannot know for certain whether Sayers continued to purchase books about Collins during her last years. Among the books that the sale catalog lists are Robert P. Ashley's *Wilkie Collins* (1952) and Nuel Pharr Davis's *Life of Wilkie Collins* (1956). The HRC's copies of these books, however, contain no evidence—bookplate, signature, marginalia—that they belonged to Sayers. Other evidence, which we shall examine, suggests that her interest in Collins continued through her last years, so she probably did buy books on Collins as they appeared. Proof positive that this is so, however, is lacking.

Still, the story that the collection tells is clear enough: Sayers was deeply interested in Collins. The first letter referring to him is from the bookseller, Myles Radford, 15 June 1921: "When," he asks, "are you going to get your 'Life' published? I really think you ought to have it out shortly, and I feel sure you have as much information about Wilkie as is likely to come to light, and a great deal more than most 'Memoirs' contain." The last letter is from Sayers to T. I. F. Armstrong, July 1957. In it, she writes of "regrets that pressure of other business has prevented her from proceeding with the Biography of Wilkie Collins, although she still hopes to finish it, if and when old age brings leisure."[3]

We have, then, a documentable interest span of 36 years. Since Sayers was contemplating a biography in 1921, she had probably read the entire canon by that time. Be that as it may, her interest in Collins continued to grow for the next several years and reached its height in the late 1920s and early 1930s, as an abundance of material proves. I indicated above that the HRC got all of Sayers's Collins materials, with two exceptions. One is a notebook now in the Wade Collection at Wheaton College; the other, a notebook still in the possession of Mr. Anthony Fleming. They were separated from the other materials because they also contained some Lord Peter material. The notebook in the Wade Collection is of the same manufacture as one of the notebooks in the HRC, so that Sayers probably purchased and worked on them both at about the same time. Fortunately, the materials in the Wade Collection's notebook help in establishing when that time was. They include a Lord Peter story, "The Fantastic Horror of the Cat in the Bag," and a list of books and articles about Collins. The Lord Peter story had been written by November 1927, when Sayers discussed its publication with Gollancz;[4] the first entry in the list is the Oxford University Press's edition of *The Moonstone*, published in 1928. She therefore worked on this notebook around 1927-28.

The notebook in Mr. Fleming's possession she probably worked on a bit earlier, for it contains notes for, and Chapter I of, a detective novel entitled *The Three Spinsters*, subsequently published as *Unnatural Death* in 1927. The Collins material is either an address or the extensive preparation for an address made to a group described in the text as the "Newcastle Lit. Phil." It is entitled "Wilkie Collins, 1824-1889," covers all of Collins's life, and runs to about 20,000 words. Although I have not seen the manuscript itself, the extracts that I have read are very close in wording to the biographical fragment in the HRC, albeit shorter and less polished.[5]

Further evidence of Sayers's interest in Collins during these years has been provided by John Lehmann. In a letter to me, 2 October 1976, he wrote: "I have a clear memory of Dorothy Sayers working on the Wilkie Collins project in the library of our home by the Thames—but it must be at least 45 years ago!" When I pressed him to recall more precisely when this might have been, he replied (3 November 1976): "I think the occasion of Dorothy Sayers' visit to our family home by the Thames ("Fieldhead," Bourne End) *must* have been after my father's death in January 1929, and *must* have been before my departure to live in Vienna (not all the year) in the autumn of 1932." The manuscript of Sayers's biography confirms the first part of Lehmann's recollection, for it refers in Chapter I to the portrait of Collins by his father as "now in the possession of Mrs. R. Lehmann." Since the Collins connection was through Mr. Lehmann, Sayers's designation of ownership indicates that she worked at Fieldhead after his death.

The biography itself she cannot have begun much before 1931. It begins with Collins's antecedents and proceeds, chapter by chapter, to November 1855. No reason exists to suppose that any sizable portion is missing, and it is therefore reasonable to assume that she composed the chapters in sequential order. The rough draft of Chapter I refers to Stewart M. Ellis's *Wilkie Collins, Le Fanu, and Others*, published in 1931; thus, the *terminus a quo*.

The *terminus ad quem* is more difficult to establish. Interestingly enough, the biography refers to no book published later than Ellis's. In 1933, she was still sufficiently interested in the project to hire A. May Osler as a research assistant, and 21 letters from Osler to Sayers survive, dating from 18 February 1933 to 2 October 1933/34. The letter of 2 October does not give the year in its date. Although it could have been written in 1933, I date it 1934 because it implies that a period has elapsed in which she and Sayers have not communicated.

Sayers's correspondence thereafter suggests that she has laid the biography aside. On 20 February 1936, she writes to a bookseller, Raphael King, who had sent her the typescript of two Collins letters: "I have been terribly busy lately and unable to do any work on Collins, but some day I hope to be able to get to work on him again." Eight years later, she uses almost the same words in a letter to the American scholar, James Sandoe: "I am very glad to have these [copies of Collins letters], since I am always hoping some day to be able to get on with my life of him . . ." (6 January 1944). Finally, in 1948, she wrote to Robert P. Ashley, who had asked her a number of questions about her research: "Dear Sir, If I were to put in about six weeks' intensive work on the material I laid aside fifteen years ago, I might be able to answer some of your questions fully; but I fear that under present conditions I cannot find the time."[6] Sayers may, of course, have been using "fifteen years" in a general and imprecise way; but the neatness with which 1933 fits into the pattern of evidence suggests that she was writing with characteristic precision and, in fact, did little on the biography thereafter.

Indeed, she probably did little work on Collins at all after the mid-1930s. The subsequent publication dates of work on Collins do not prove much. Although the section on him that she did for the *Cambridge Bibliography of English Literature* was not published until 1941, the form letter from F. W. Bateson enclosing the galley proofs is dated 5 August 1935. Similarly, the brief though brilliant introduction to the Everyman Library edition of *The Moonstone* appeared in June 1944; but it had been commissioned by February 1941 and draws heavily on notes that she had jotted down years earlier.[7]

Consider, for example, the following passage about "Wilkie's Women" in one of the notebooks at the HRC:

> Their idea of unconventionality & idependance [*sic*] does not mean, as usually with writers of that time, liberty to *love* where they like, but to *act*.
>
> Meredith, for instance, like Tennyson wants women freed & educated so as to be better companions for men. Wilkie is hardly interested in woman as a complement to man. He sees her as a creature of independent personality & intelligence. This is rare & in advance of his time.

The following passage in the introduction is an expanded and polished version of the same thoughts:

> In his whole treatment of women he stands leagues apart from his period—infinitely more "modern" than Meredith and (strange as it may seem) in certain ways more penetrating. He was not interested in feminist movements—in fact, he disliked what he knew of them; yet he is the most genuinely feminist of all the nineteenth-century novelists, because he is the only one capable of seeing women without sexual bias and of respecting them as human individuals in their own right, and not as "the ladies, God bless them!"
>
> The women of Collins are strong, resolute, and intellectual; they move actively towards a purpose, which is not always, nor indeed usually, conditioned by their attitude to a husband or a lover. They are not unfeminine; yet they are capable, like men, of desiring knowledge or action for its own sake, rather than for its personal implications. Marion Halcombe in *The Woman in White*, Magdalen Vanstone in *No Name*, Madame Pratolungo in *Poor Miss Finch*, cannot be classed as "female characters"; they are simply characters, for whom other things than passion guide the plot. [8]

The notebook from which I quote lists, among other things, the contents of an artist's satchel—material used in writing *Five Red Herrings* (1931). It also refers to a novel about Basque life and lists Basque names—material used in writing "The Incredible Elopement of Lord Peter Wimsey," published in *Hangman's Holiday* (1933). [9] Once again, then, the facts point to the early 1930s; and so the introduction to *The Moonstone*, though written later, is essentially a production of the same period as the other notebooks, the bibliography, and the biography.

Of the work she produced on Collins during this period, the biography, even in its unfinished state, is the most impressive achievement. It consists of approximately 141 pages of handwritten rough draft, divided into five chapters. With it are two tentative tables of contents. One projects 22 chapters for the complete work; the other, 19. These do not unfortunately establish exactly the amount of the work envisaged by Sayers that we have, because in neither table do the chapter headings fit the chapters completed. I would estimate that she completed about one-fourth of the work she planned. Incomplete, unrevised, and, in some respects, outmoded though it is, it is nevertheless in some ways the most perceptive, and certainly the most elaborate, critique of Collins yet done. Had she completed it on the scale she began, it would far exceed in amplitude of treatment any biography of Collins that has yet been published.

As one would expect, a bit of judicious pruning would improve some passages; and yet, the overall impression that the work leaves is not one of prolixity. On the contrary, seldom has so much information been so condensed and so elegantly phrased. Thus she sums up the case against *Antonina*, Collins's early excursion into historical fiction à la George Bulwer-Lytton, in the following well-crafted sentence: "The historical facts are there, but not the historical sense; Goths and Romans alike hail from Wardour Street; the fifth-century Christians are nineteenth-century Protestants; the stock villain, virgin, and fanatic utter the stock sentiments appropriate to villainy, virginity, and fanaticism." To be sure, this is amusing; but, more important, it is accurate. Seldom indeed does Sayers engage in wit at the expense of accuracy. Throughout, the biography reveals a thorough familiarity with its subject and an admirable ability to separate the wheat from the chaff where a lesser individual would have been overwhelmed by the sheer quantities of chaff. Having held up the chaff in *Antonina* to well-deserved ridicule, she goes on to point out ways in which it reveals characteristically Collinsean traits— dramatic instinct, passion for documentation, tendency to tuck in the threads of the plot very neatly.

In addition to the section on Collins in the *Cambridge Bibliography of English Literature*, the introduction to *The Moonstone*, and the biography, her works contain numerous references to him. Often, in her essays, she uses his work to illustrate various points about the detective story. In "Aristotle on Detective Fiction," for instance, she notes that Collins's description of the Shivering Sands in *The Moonstone* does what any purple passage in a detective story should do—contain "some vital clue to the solution, which cannot be omitted or transposed to any other part of the story."[10] Later in the same essay, she cites *No Name* as an example of a story in which the knowledge of the villain's identity is made agreeable "by showing the moves and counter-moves made successively by villain and detective . . ." [p. 184].

The novels, too, allude to Collins; and as one would expect of a conscious artist like Sayers, the allusions are often highly functional.

Through alluding to Collins, John Munting confirms the humorous self-deprecation that he has shown elsewhere in *The Documents in the Case*. In section 52, he says: "At present I feel rather like the good lady in *The Moonstone*, who wanted to know when the explosion would take place." The good lady in question, Mrs. Merridew, is also a rather silly lady who can by no means be persuaded that experiments can take place without explosions following. [11]

More sophisticated still is Lord Peter's remark in *Five Red Herrings:* "Bunter . . . this case resembles the plot of a Wilkie Collins novel, in which everything happens just too late to prevent the story from coming to a premature happy ending" [ch. XV]. Thus she wittily reminds the reader that he has before him a consciously crafted piece of art and not the raw data of life. The autonomy of art was an issue that Sayers always felt strongly about. Although she may not have articulated her ideas as completely as she later did, no reason exists to suppose that she felt differently in 1931 from the way she did when she wrote "Toward a Christian Aesthetic." [12] On the contrary, the analyses that she had already written, her very choice of the detective story as a genre—these suggest that never at any time did she feel the artist should merely tell it like it is.

In other instances, the allusions are more hidden and difficult to assess. No student of Collins can doubt that Sayers derived the name of Martha Ruddle in *Busman's Honeymoon* from his mistress, Martha Rudd. The names are too close to be accidental, but the little we know about Collins's mistress suggests that the two share little other than their names. On the one hand, Martha Rudd bore Collins three children out of wedlock and ended up meekly tending the grave where he and his other mistress were buried; on the other hand, Martha Ruddle greets Peter and Harriet with the comment, " 'film-actors, by the look of yer. And—' (with a withering glance at Harriet's furs) 'no better than you should be, I'll be bound' " [ch. I]. Some connection may have existed in Sayers's mind between these two seemingly dissimilar persons; but since she disliked private symbolism in general, it cannot have been very important. [13]

In yet other instances, allusions to Collins blend with other material. The Dowager Duchess of Denver characteristically rattles on in *Strong Poison* about detective writers as solvers of crime in real life:

I don't suppose detective writers detect much in real life, do they, except Edgar Wallace of course, who always seems to be everywhere and dear Conan Doyle and the black man what was his name and of course the Slater person, such a scandal, though now I come to think of it that was in Scotland where they have such very odd laws about everything particularly getting married. [ch. III]

Doubtless, an important element in Sayers's understanding of Scottish law was Collins's *Man and Wife*, where the "very odd laws about everything particularly getting married" are explored in detail. Here, as elsewhere, Sayers knew that one could count on Collins to get his facts right; and indeed she praised this novel as "an outstanding example" of this tendency of his in her introduction to *The Moonstone* [p. vi]. Still, though *Man and Wife* may have been in the back of Sayers's mind when she crafted the Dowager Duchess's comments, she knew about Scottish law from sources other than Collins; and so this can count at most as only a partial allusion to him.

The Dowager Duchess's comments exemplify in miniature the problem that the source hunter never fully solves. Having established through external documentation and her own work that Collins very likely influenced Sayers, how do we trace his influence in her work? We might, for example, assume with good reason that he influenced her greatly in the area of plot construction. This is an area where both writers have received high praise and where Sayers certainly respected Collins. Citing various of his strong points, she singled out "the architecture of his plots" as especially praiseworthy:

Taking everything into consideration, *The Moonstone* is probably the very finest detective story ever written. By comparison with its wide scope, its dovetailed completeness and the marvellous variety and soundness of its characterisation, modern fiction looks thin and mechanical. Nothing human is perfect, but *The Moonstone* comes about as near perfection as anything of its kind can be.[14]

Still, examination of Sayers's most Collinsean novel, *The Documents in the Case*, suggests that his influence on her in plotting is not unmediated. In his greatest novels, Collins's most impressive achievement as a plotter lies in his distribution of incident from section to section. Since a different character relates each section, the reader finds that his knowledge of the plot advances simultaneously with his perception of the characters. In this regard, Sayers's novel hardly competes. Our understanding of the characters in Sayers advances almost independently of our knowledge of how the murder was committed. *The Documents in the Case* being a murder mystery, this cannot be completely true; but even the technical point on which the murder's solution depends, though it has been thematically prepared for, is not mentioned until late in the novel.

On the other hand, Sayers's novel suggests the complexity of reality in a way that Collins's do not. William H. Marshall has argued ingeniously that "the structure of the total narrative [in *The Moonstone*] resembles an arrangement of mirrors reflecting mirrors, no one of which directly reflects full reality" and that it "anticipated the greater fragmentation of the sensibility of modern man, as perhaps no other major Victorian novel was to do."[15] One may legitimately wonder, however, how many readers, Victorian or modern, have been disturbed by the metaphysical implications of *The Moonstone*, or indeed even noticed them. The metaphysical implications of *The Documents in the Case*, on the other hand, are obvious. Marshall's comments, in fact, accord with it far better than they do with *The Moonstone*. Significantly, John Munting resorts to the image of the prism again and again to describe Margaret Harrison. Into George Harrison's "outer manner, her radiance sank and was quenched." Munting's own "diffusion left her dead glass. But in Lathom's concentration she shone." At the art exhibit where Lathom's portrait of her is first shown, Harrison writes that "for the first time I saw her in full prismatic loveliness, soaked and vibrating with colour and light." Finally, he wonders whether Lathom "has realised that the only real part of her was vulgar and bad, and the rest merely the brilliant refraction of himself."

On the societal level that demands an eye for an eye, Harrison's judgment is not only accurate, but, in Sayers's view, irremediably final. Her affinities of thought are with the Victorians like Collins and Browning rather than her contemporaries like Luigi Pirandello and James Joyce. She is interested, that is, in demonstrating the complexity of reality rather than in questioning its nature. Still, because she lived when the older epistemological bases had already been shaken, she was far better able than Collins to convey a sense of the radical unfairness and peculiarity of life. Browning, of course, surpasses her; but we must in all honesty observe that the monumental art of *The Ring and the Book* is achieved finally through an equally monumental indifference to readability. As a popular novelist, Sayers has gone as far as she can in underscoring the questions of how bad lives provide the raw material for good art, of how a mediocre life is to be weighed against a great artist's achievement.

In short, knowledge of Collins only partially illuminates *The Documents in the Case*. The partial illumination that he affords, however, is not without value. Though other factors were involved, *The Moonstone* and *The Woman in White* adequately explain why, in 1930, Sayers relied entirely on the no longer fashionable method of narration through documents—letters, memoranda, newspaper clippings. [16] Collins's passion for factual accuracy explains why she called in a collaborator, Robert Eustace, to validate the abstruse chemical point on which her *dénouement* depends. [17] Collins's characters teach us to view skeptically such simple-minded biographical identifications as Janet Hitchman proffers. Agatha Milsom, Hitchman tells us, is a "cruel but accurate portrait of a Miss Drennan, who had been an extremely inefficient copytypist at Benson's."[18] Perhaps so, but the reader of Collins inevitably recalls that equally embittered and unpleasant old maid, Drusilla Clack.

This last point, obviously, has ramifications extending far beyond *The Documents in the Case*. It raises the basic question of whether one should read Sayers's or any author's work as public document or private revelation. All literature partakes, of course, of both; but readers should have firmly fixed in their own minds where their interests lie; for upon their preferences depends whether they regard source study or biography as more illuminating. In all fairness, Hitchman makes no secret of her preference. With regard to Sayers's most famous feminine character, Harriet Vane, she writes: "There is no doubt that Harriet is Dorothy, as she saw herself," and she lists a number of characteristics that they share:

> Harriet resembles Dorothy in looks, being tall and dark haired, not by any means beautiful. She had "a nice throat" with "a kind of arum lily quality." She wrote detective stories, and always signed her name Harriet *D*. Vane, an echo of Dorothy's insistence on her L. Like Dorothy, she had a beautiful speaking voice. [p. 98]

If this kind of thing appeals to one, the list can be extended. Both were brought up on strictly religious principles; both smoke; both are working on biographies of early detective-story writers, etc. Some of the details do not fit. Mary Ellen Chase has commented on how Sayers "seemingly had no neck at all. Her head appeared to be closely joined to the regions directly between her shoulder blades in back and her collar bone in front."[19] Under the circumstances, one would think it rather difficult to have a nice throat with a kind of arum lily quality, but one can't have everything.

What Sayers would have thought of this is clear enough, for she believed that "art draws its chief sustenance from the art of the past, and not (as people often like to imagine) directly from life."[20] She explicitly stated her own interpretation of Harriet and Peter in her essay on *Gaudy Night*:

> Peter is . . . the familiar figure of the interpretative artist, the romantic soul at war with the realistic brain. Harriet, with her lively and inquisitive mind and her soul grounded upon reality, is his complement—the creative artist; her make-up is more stable than his, and far more capable of self-dependence.[21]

Having cut our teeth on Wimsatt and Beardsley, we know that this may not do; but the point is one that Sayers would readily have conceded, for she was committed to the public reading of literature, including her own.

The question, as I have suggested, is a matter of one's interests. If one is interested in literature as psychobiography, then Hitchman is probably right; if one is interested in literature as art, then study of Agatha Milsom and Harriet Vane in terms of their Collinsean antecedents pays more handsome dividends. Setting Agatha Milsom beside Drusilla Clack, we note that their manias express themselves in superficially dissimilar ways: Agatha Milsom's in Freudian psychology; Drusilla Clack's in Evangelical Christianity. That, underneath, they are so similar reflects the satirical view that human nature does not change, though the expressions of its folly vary from age to age; reflects the comic view that any system of thought, uncritically accepted, renders its accepter less human, more mechanical, and more justly an object of ridicule.

Harriet, like the Collins heroines Sayers praised, is "strong, resolute, and intellectual." Like Marion Halcombe, she is "not by any means beautiful"; like Anne Sylvester in *Man and Wife*, she has been deeply compromised by a love relationship with a man whom she no longer respects. In no instance are the details exactly the same, any more than the details of Hitchman's identification of Harriet and Sayers are exactly the same. The ideas that emerge from such comparisons, however, strike me as more significant than those emanating from a view of Harriet as wish-fulfillment: the woman for whom something other than love spins the plot usually has rather a hard time of it, whether in the Victorian period or our own time; the heroine who is "not by any means beautiful" often makes for a more interesting story than the one who is.

As with plot, so with character: Collins only partially illuminates. He had no patent on the plain yet interesting heroine. From the same general mold have come good characters like Jane Eyre and bad ones like Rose Armiger in Henry James's *The Other House*. Finally, of course, Harriet has qualities that are quite her own, is probably in a sense "wish-fulfilment," though not in the straightforward way that Hitchman has it.

Turning our attention from Sayers's fiction to the entire canon of her writings, we can observe that perceptions she gained in studying Collins made her a better critic when she turned to study, translation, and explication of Dante. To some extent, her whole career as a writer of detective stories is involved; but Collins was the writer she studied the most closely; and some of her perceptions of Dante formed themselves round earlier perceptions of Collins. Consider the following quotations:

> in order to gain the reader's attention in the first place, and in order to secure his belief in far more astonishing parts of the narrative, the writer, if he knows his business, will strive for the utmost and most exact realism in the details of everything that happens "within the reader's own experience."

> If you want the reader not only to follow but to accept and believe a tale of marvels, you can do it best by the accumulation of precise and even prosaic detail.

The first statement refers to Collins; the second, to Dante.[22] Without context, no one could distinguish them.

A lifetime spent in academic circles might in some ways have been a better preparation for Sayers's work on Dante than her study of Collins and work as a novelist, but it could not have prepared her any better to appreciate "the accumulation of precise and even prosaic detail" as a strategy in Dantean art. In her biography of Collins, she notes again and again his passion for factual accuracy:

> The passion for documentation, the confident appeal to historical fact, with which the sensation novelists of the century defended themselves against the charge of improbability are already present in the preface to *Antonina*. There are the accents of the same voice which in *Basil* protests: "I have founded the main event out of which this story springs, on a fact within my own knowledge"; which called in "professional men" to witness the accuracy of the law, medicine and chemistry of *Armadale*; which in *Heart and Science* adduces the evidence of *The Times* and *Chambers's Encyclopaedia* in support of Mrs. Gallillee's researches into "the idea of atoms" and the "Diathermancy of Ebonite"; which cites the Report of the Royal Commission with reference to the marriage laws discussed in *Man and Wife*; which explains in the preface to *Jezebel's Daughter* "that the accessories of the scenes in the Deadhouse of Frankfort have been studied on the spot"; and which, in *Blind Love*, tells the story of the von Scheurer Insurance Fraud with hardly a detail changed. [Ch. III]

The effect of this on her own fiction we have already noted in the effort she made to get the chemistry of *The Documents in the Case* right. An even more impressive example is her effort to get the details of change-ringing right in *The Nine Tailors*. The notebooks at Wheaton College, which contain page after page of mathematical formulae, testify to the exhaustive nature of this effort. That the novel needed such effort becomes apparent only when its plot is laid out sequentially, as John G. Cawelti has done. Then, one notes the "incredible tissue of improbability, coincidence, and turgid sensationalism" upon which the novel is built.[23] As he immediately goes on to say, this is not the impression the novel leaves; and although there are other reasons it does not, high on any list must be "the accumulation of precise and even prosaic detail" by which Sayers has captured her reader's confidence.

Small wonder, then, that she exhorts the reader of the *Purgatory*

> to remember that he is at the Antipodes, and not to get his compass-points muddled up. Dante, though he had never in his life crossed the Line, has no moments of forgetfulness or confusion, which is more than can be said for most of us who live beneath the Wain. Readers in Australia, New Zealand, and South Africa will find that (for once, in a European literary classic) the Sun is in the right part of the sky. [*Purgatory*, p. 71]

In short, study of Sayers's relation to Collins confirms the growing impression among her admirers that underlying her work, despite its variety of expression, is the unity of a solid and enduring personality. A good storyteller herself, she prized both Collins and Dante as storytellers: the possessors, she believed, of a gift that is innate and not acquired. Of this gift, she wrote that "it is mightiest in the mighty: by itself, it can produce the minor immortality of a *Sherlock Holmes* or a *Three Musketeers*; in the hands of a great poet it produces the major immortality of an *Odyssey*, a *Paradise Lost*, or a *Divine Comedy*."[24]

Collins's immortality she doubtless considered of the "minor" variety. The qualities of intellectual and moral grandeur that attracted her to Dante he did not have. Yet he was more in her view than just a good storyteller. Though she did little work on him after the mid-1930s, she could never bring herself completely to abandon him. When Kenneth Robinson, who was writing a biography of Collins, asked her about the state of her work in 1948, she wrote (9 March): "I will not say that I have altogether given up the idea of some time writing something about Wilkie Collins, but I have had to put off the scheme indefinitely, in favour of more urgent work, and there is nothing at all to prevent you from writing the biography you have in mind."

In light of this letter, Robinson was surprised to read in Hesketh Pearson's *Dickens* that "Miss Dorothy Sayers informed the present writer that it was 'the extreme obscurity which surrounds the whole of Collins's private life which discouraged me from getting on with the biography that I had contemplated.' "[25] Assuming that Pearson was correct, Robinson wrote Sayers again, asking if he might see her Collins materials. She replied (4 November 1949):

> I don't think I told Mr. Pearson quite that. I never "definitely abandon" anything. No doubt I shall one day have definitely to abandon life—but even then I shall probably [do] so with the greatest reluctance, protesting that there were still a great many things I had intended to do with it. All my Wilkie Collins stuff is at present stored away—but I mean to do something with it sometime if I can manage it, though it may not be exactly a biography (the fellow really had no "life" to speak of, had he?) but something more in the nature of a critical study.
>
> But if Atropos uses the shears before I get to that point, I will leave all the material to the nation, and then it will be available to everybody.[26]

The facts, then, meager though they are, suggest that Sayers's interest in and respect for Collins continued to the end of her life: she probably continued to buy books on him as they appeared; she certainly stated a number of times that she hoped to finish her work on him; she specifically told her friend, Barbara Reynolds, that she planned someday to finish her biography.[27] That this is so suggests that he was more to her than just a good storyteller. Her admiring comments about his feminine characters indicate that she found in him at least some of the qualities that transform mere competence into artistic greatness. Certainly, study of her feminine characters in conjunction with his illuminates the traditional and artistic—as opposed to the biographical—dimension of her art.

Were "mere competence" all that Sayers derived from Collins, her debt might yet be greater than the phrase indicates; for it was a deeply held tenet of her religious faith that any work, truly well done, becomes sacramental. Collins, one of the most carefully conscientious craftsmen who ever wrote, gave to Sayers a heightened awareness of the tools of her trade that made her a better novelist and a better critic. Because of this, I suspect, she continued to the very end not only to respect his work, but to love it as well.

II: DRAMA

Terrie Curran

The Word Made Flesh: The Christian Aesthetic in Dorothy L. Sayers's *The Man Born to Be King*

IT IS neither fashionable nor prudent to view Dorothy L. Sayers as renegade writer, fleeing the trifles of detective fiction for the eternal concerns of Christianity. Aesthetic theory was always a primary factor governing her fiction, drama, and translations, and as she came to recognize the limits and artificiality of the detective fiction mode,[1] she (along with T. S. Eliot, Charles Williams, and C. S. Lewis), began to examine Christianity for its philosophic and aesthetic potential.

Certainly Sayers moved in this direction from both Christian and artistic motivation; the spiritual aridity of England in the 1930s disturbed her sufficiently to declare that "The brutal fact is that in this Christian country not one person in a hundred has the faintest notion what the Church teaches about God or man or society or the person of Jesus Christ."[2] But the artist in her recognized the danger to integrity should aesthetic concerns be overriden by evangelism.[3]

Sayers was involved in working out this line of thought both in theoretical terms and in her dramatic works in the 1930s. In her essay "Toward a Christian Aesthetic," she traces the uneasy relationship historically existing between art and Christianity, and concludes that since art is creation, an analogy can be drawn between the creative artist and the Holy Trinity.[4] The analogy is most succinctly stated in her play, *The Zeal of Thy House:*

> First, [not in time, but merely in order of enumeration] there is the Creative Idea, passionless, timeless, beholding the whole work complete at once, the end in the beginning: and this is the image of the Father.

67

Second, there is the Creative Energy [or Activity] begotten of that idea, working in time from the beginning to the end, with sweat and passion, being incarnate in the bonds of matter: and this is the image of the Word.

Third, there is the Creative Power, the meaning of the work and its response in the lively soul; and this is the image of the indwelling Spirit.[5]

In contrast to the Greek theory based on a mimetic view of art—that art imitates and perfects reality—Sayers held that the Christian aesthetic is based on art as actualization, or, using the Christian analogy, that art is the word made flesh.

In practice, therefore, she insisted that the dramatist "must set out, not to instruct but to show forth; not to point a moral but to tell a story; not to produce a Divinity Lesson with illustrations in dialogue, but to write a good piece of theatre."[6] And if indeed the result is "a good piece of theatre," the fusion of dogma and drama, of word and flesh, would be realized.

The difficulty of maintaining that delicate fusion is illustrated in two of Sayers's early dramas: her verse play, *The Zeal of Thy House* (1937), and her redaction of the Faust legend, *The Devil to Pay* (1939). While both achieved a considerable degree of commercial success on the London stage, the protagonist in each has occasional lapses into cardboard allegory. The problem of dogma overwhelming the drama was far less evident when Sayers chose specifically biblical material and thus made dogma into drama. Her radio play, *He That Should Come* (broadcast on 25 December 1938), was so well received that the BBC commissioned her to write a cycle drama on the life of Christ. Sayers agreed on three conditions, then considered severe, but which demonstrated her demand to maintain artistic integrity: that she could use the character of Christ, provide contemporary realism, and employ modern speech. Although both she and the BBC were plagued with censorship problems (the impersonation of the Godhead was considered blasphemous)[7] and violently divided public opinion (some believed "that Singapore fell because these plays were broadcast, and appealed for them to be taken off before a like fate came to Australia! They were answered by the supporter who thanked [BBC] for the plays which . . . 'made possible the November victories in Libya and Russia'!"),[8] the plays reveal Sayers's most ambitious manifestation of the Christian aesthetic.

Though Sayers believed that "it is scarcely the business of Christian writers to introduce novelties into the fundamental Christian doctrines,"[9] she also was aware of the necessity of stripping away from those doctrines the tedium accrued over years of rote recitation of archaic

English. The historical Jesus, a rather wearisome bore to churchgoers and randomly understood through "a string of parables, a bunch of miracles, a discourse, a set of 'sayings,' a flash of apocalyptic thunder—here a little and there a little,"[10] could hardly have been such to his contemporaries. The whole point of the Incarnation is precisely that God lived among men not unlike ourselves. The inherent irony that "God was executed by people painfully like us"[11] is a fact that no fictive drama could ever match.[12]

The modern world, viewing the events from a postresurrection perspective, is oblivious of its possible analogous complicity, since even if we are capable of feeling any genuine horror over the execution, the nasty deed can easily be sloughed off on those two archvillains, Judas and Pontius Pilate. To be sure, the point of placing Jesus back into his historical context—with all the complexities of social and political existence alongside casual unawareness of the events—is not to induce the twentieth-century Christian into self-flagellation, but rather, Sayers believed, by making the event shockingly real, by making the word flesh for our era, to elicit a genuine response to the question *"What think ye of Christ?"*[13]

If one chooses to call this an evangelical motive, so be it; but from the point of view of the aesthetic, Sayers's use of realism is the means for reconciling the sublime and humble, the temporal events and the eternal plan of God, which, to be obvious, are the very reconciliations manifested in the Incarnation. That "the dogma *is* the drama" is not glib alliteration;[14] though nearly two millennia of ecclesiasts and writers (with some—largely medieval—exceptions) have succeeded in obliterating the irony and thereby the drama of the event.

Sayers's 12-play cycle, *The Man Born to Be King,* was a qualitative and quantitative extension of the motives and methods she had successfully employed in her single Nativity play, *He That Should Come.*[15] But the task of writing 12 plays (broadcast at monthly intervals) which retain individual autonomy and yet contribute to the unfolding of a single plot raises a host of technical problems. No doubt Sayers's First in Medieval Literature at Oxford provided help, since at least some of the solutions could be found in the medieval mystery cycles. But the medieval pageants had sufficiently different scope, focus, and purpose to render the reduplication of their means for achieving artistic integrity unfeasible.

Whereas the mystery cycles employed typological correspondence of figure and fulfillment as the cohesive basis for the Idea of dramatizing all history, Sayers's restricted Idea (the life of Christ) could cohere, with judicious improvisation, on the basis of character continuity. One kind of improvisation consisted in combining historical fact with—where history was lacking—an educated imagination to yield what she called 'tie-rods,' or characters and situations which, by their reappearance, thread the plays together. But a mere string of core characters involved in a plot, no matter how intriguing, is not dramatically innovative, nor does such a linear approach make the fullest use of a Christian aesthetic; it even violates the idea of *cycle* that was typologically evident in the medieval plays. So Sayers had to reshape the linear plot to give it theologically valid form. In this instance, a medieval solution could be adopted.

The artistically tidy medieval mind was fascinated by the symbolic worth and actual realization of circularity, that all things come from God and return to Him. Taking this as a basic structure of creation, medieval writers were inclined to frame their works accordingly, hence the conspicuousness of artistic circularity, of ends echoing beginnings (e.g., *Beowulf, Sir Gawain and the Green Knight, Pearl, The Canterbury Tales*, etc.). Sayers employs this structure by "planting" characters, ideas and gestures at the Bethlehem scene which, with necessary alteration, are made to reappear at Calvary Hill. For example, the youngest of the Magi, Balthazar, brings the gift of myrrh (symbol of death and love) to the Christ child, and again reading the stars aright, he reappears, sufficiently aged, at the Crucifixion. At the foot of the Cross he meets the Roman centurion, Proclus, whom he last saw some 30 years previously at Bethlehem. While their mutual recognition may strain plausibility, their individual presence at Calvary has had dramatic preparation. There is no question about Balthazar, for he is one of the blessed who believed before he saw, and by his faith in the star's revelation, he is led to witness the fulfillment of his Nativity gift.

Proclus, on the other hand, requires greater dramatic justification. He is a composite figure of the Roman soldier in the best sense, a means for "tightening up the dramatic construction and avoiding the unnecessary multiplication of characters."[16] But he is an important example of Sayers's success with the artistic trinity of Idea, Energy, and Power. Being essentially fictive,[17] Proclus could be endowed with any qualities Sayers chose; she maximized the opportunity by substantiating his presence on both political and spiritual grounds. In Bethlehem, the young Proclus helps to establish the political context of the Incarnation; he also reveals an instinctual sense of what is right, good and just. When

Herod outlines his plans for the slaughter of the innocents, Proclus responds: "Sir, I am a soldier, not a butcher."[18] In the fourth play, 30 years later, he reappears exhibiting similar political and spiritual characteristics. The expository scene, designed to keep us aware of sample —if not typical—Roman views, has Proclus and an old friend chat about the "carpenter's son from Nazareth." Proclus remarks, "I've only seen him once, but I liked the look of him. A good man, I thought, with something godlike in his face."[19] Shortly thereafter, when his servant falls ill, Proclus goes to Jesus with the conviction that Jesus can restore the servant's health. Proclus does not see Jesus as the Messiah in either the political or spiritual sense, but his army experience and good instincts lead him to his conviction. He tells Jesus:

> Sir, I have only to look at you. I know authority when I see it. I've been a soldier all my life. I've had to obey my colonel, and my men have had to obey me. I say to the corporal, 'Come here,' and he comes, and to another man, 'Go there,' and he goes; or I tell my batman 'Do this,' and he does it. And I know very well that when you command, you are obeyed. [scene iii]

If we can call this faith, however, it is a faith in the goodness and not the god-ness of Jesus.

We meet Proclus twice more, once in the eighth play, as Sayers admits, "to get his presence in Jerusalem 'planted' for the Crucifixion"[20] so that here he merely bustles about with Passover preparations. His last appearance, in the Crucifixion play, is one of necessary understatement, since he is on the periphery of the event and its significance. Ordered to stand guard at the Cross, his Roman sense of duty overcomes his reluctance, but his good instincts lead him to offer what comfort he can: "If there was anything I could do—consistent with my duty, that is—,"[21] whereupon he makes himself useful by administering the vinegar sop. When Jesus dies and Balthazar reaches the Cross, Proclus points out to him "Jesus of Nazareth, whom they called King of the Jews" [iii, seq. 8]. He is conspicuously noncommittal about what *he* believes Jesus' status to be, but Balthazar's mention of the Nativity star strikes a chord of recognition in Proclus: "Is that he? . . . Herod told me to slay him and I refused. But you see they have killed him at last—and here I stand. . . . Son of God he called himself—and so I believe he was" [*ibid*]. His words are carefully chosen to illustrate his ambiguous state of mind: pride, self-exemption, complicity, belief in the Son of God who no longer lives.

Though Proclus does not proportionately warrant lengthy discussion, he is an important illustration of Sayers's full employment of Idea, Energy, Power. Sayers's Idea, seeing "the end in the beginning," is evidently manifested in Proclus, since his presence at Bethlehem and Calvary Hill helps reinforce the Christian premise that the Crucifixion was inherent in the Nativity, and so the end of the play-cycle recalls the beginning in persons, gestures and beliefs. Energy is provided by his tie-rod role, which helps not only to lend coherence of character to the whole cycle, but his presence fuses the political and religious atmosphere and supports Sayers's intentions for contemporary realism to develop the irony of events. His character also manifests Power, "the meaning of the work and its response in the lively soul," since he serves as a typological figure of the incipient believer. His part in Powering the Energized Idea was adapted from medieval typology which, in addition to serving as a means of cohesion between widely separated persons or events, implicitly compared the persons or events to make a theological point.

Medieval typology maximizes the similarities between the figure and fulfillment to exhibit the cohesion of God's Plan. But typological comparisons were also drawn to demonstrate the differences between events. The Sacrifice of Isaac by Abraham foreshadows that of Christ by God, but equally important is that Isaac's death was averted, typologically suggesting the Resurrection as well. In such a manner is the tie-rod role of Proclus two-pronged. His role functions not only to draw together the Nativity and Crucifixion with like characters, etc., to demonstrate the Divine Plan, but his slightly altered perspective—from seeing "something godlike" in Jesus to ambiguous recognition of His divinity— suggests another theological point: the greater possibility for real faith to be born after the Resurrection, as has been the case for all subsequent Christians.

That the single character of Proclus dramatically fuses contemporary political realism (as a Roman soldier) with doctrinal significance (his spiritual perplexity), and both are exhibited structurally (in his tie-rod capacity), illustrates Sayers's fusion of character, content and form. The word has been made flesh.

Because Proclus is essentially fictive, Sayers could choose his character, circumstances and role to suit the needs of the drama. But this was not the case with those characters who have historical reality. In such cases the artist's Idea is external fact that must be preserved. Sayers had to retain the Idea that Herod was ambitious to keep Caesar off his back; that Pilate wasn't terribly enthusiastic about the liquidation and tried to wash his hands of the whole affair; that Caiaphas, a conservative Jewish leader, was no less politically motivated in convicting Christ than Marshal Pétain in donating France to the Nazis. Obviously, Sayers could and did shape the facts, cull and excise medieval dramatic precedents, and embroider the Idea to form credible characters who demonstrate the machinations of the contemporary world. By providing political and psychological complexity to nullify the clichéd stereotypes promulgated by tradition, Sayers was able to further her premise that "God was executed by people painfully like us." When it came to the character of Judas, however, not only was the Idea of Him rigidly fixed, but Sayers's Energy was necessarily confined by theological considerations: both unavoidable restrictions diffused (and perhaps confused) the Power of Judas's role.

The character of Judas suffers from being interpreted from the viewpoint of two millennia of hindsight; his deed is so infamous that little else is known about him. He appears in the Gospels with minimal background, and even when not in the throes of the betrayal, he is consistently identified with epithets of "Judas, who betrayed Jesus," or "Judas, the traitor."[22] While in essential agreement about the procedure of the betrayal, the Gospel writers ascribe variant, though complementary, motivations to Judas. In all four Gospels Judas is the instigator, though according to Matthew, Mark and John, the betrayal results from Judas's resentment over Jesus' wastefulness of precious perfume,[23] while Luke (and John additionally) believes Satan to have entered Judas.[24] John singularly suggests greed as yet another motivation: Judas, as group treasurer, could not resist dipping his fingers into the apostolic till.[25] Matthew singularly bothers to narrate Judas's post facto remorse and suicide.[26]

Given this skeletal Idea, several possibilities for interpretation of Judas's character exist. One could simply leave well enough alone and present Judas as a resentful traitor impelled by nebulous motives—i.e., an enigma. Such a solution—if it can be called such—would be, however, a dramatic failure, and for Sayers would result in an automatic lapse of Power. Or one could cull the medieval dramatic tradition and note that there Judas is not enigmatic, but is viewed as a Satanic tool in the Divine Plan. This is most conspicuously illustrated in the Wakefield Cycle, in which a separate play is accorded to substantiating Judas's thorough villainy. "The Hanging of Judas" is a fragment monolog in which Judas pulls out all his dirty laundry with masochistic glee. Apparently his career as "accursed caitiff" only concluded with the betrayal of

Christ, for he had previously slain his father and slept with his mother, to mention but a few of his colorful accomplishments. Whereas the Middle Ages caricatured Judas by his sins (particularly covetousness and wanhope), from Sayers's perspective, perpetuating this caricature would not only negate the irony she intended to manifest, but, given modern skepticism, would force the conclusion that either Jesus wasn't terribly perceptive about human nature to have chosen Judas as a disciple, or that He deliberately set out to be crucified.

To make Judas both theologically valid and humanistically credible would be Sayers's major problem. Even by excising caricature and probing more seriously into Judas's attributed sins, Sayers would have a rather thin dramatic character. But just as she maximized her opportunities with the minor figure of Proclus, so too she would attempt a similar substantiation for Judas: she would conjoin Judas's spiritual role as disciple with a political role.

Because there is no evidence for Judas's political machinations, Sayers had to invent both the motivation and circumstance. These, however, could not be consciously devious, for she also had to endow Judas with good qualities or else implicitly label Jesus a fool. Hence she conceived of him as "infinitely the most intelligent of all the disciples," and because of his intelligence, he would have "the greatest possibilities of them all for good, and therefore for evil."[27]

While Christianity is replete with paradoxes, they tend to fare better in matters of faith than they do in dramatic characterization. That Sayers was aware of the problem of paradox slipping into contradiction is evident from the lengthy notes she supplies for Judas at each of his appearances; and not unlike Eliot's notes on *The Waste Land*, the clarification tends to contribute to the problem. For instance, Sayers notes that Judas

is passionately sincere. He means to be faithful—and he will be faithful—to the light which he sees so brilliantly. What he sees is the true light—only he does not see it directly, but only its reflection in the mirror of his own brain; and in the end that mirror will twist and distort the reflection and send it dancing away over the bog like a will o' the wisp.[28]

Perhaps here Sayers is getting too far into the complexity she is trying to convey: who does not see except by the mirror of the brain? What happens in the drama (which is what counts) is that Judas will be led to believe that Jesus has turned ambitious and seeks a political kingdom. That Judas has unconscious and abstract motivations scarcely makes him unique, but that he, with all his experience of Jesus and his own superior intelligence, should fall into obvious traps, strains credibility and impedes the Power of the drama.

Clearly the Roman leaders fear that Christ's Kingdom, no matter what He says to the contrary, will impinge on their political power (or, as Herod says in the first play, "Religion has been the pretext for political ambition"),[29] so they have obvious motivation to destroy Jesus. The Zealot Baruch, representing the Jewish hope for political liberty from Rome, fears Jesus may bungle the possibility for a coup d'état, and so attempts to enlist Judas's aid in organizing Jesus' revolutionary affairs. Though Baruch evidently does not understand the nature of Jesus ("He is a man. Every man has his pride. . . ."),[30] he does claim to know Judas better than Judas himself, and can plant seeds of doubt in Judas's mind about Jesus' motivations. That one glib politician can so completely subvert Judas's extraordinary intelligence is the core of the problem. If we are to believe that Judas does sincerely understand the person and kingdom of Jesus, why does he fail to counter Baruch's statement—that Jesus is only a man? It is on this claim that the whole of Baruch's argument rests. On numerous occasions, both before and after his discussion with Baruch, Judas had made evident his own understanding of Jesus and the Kingdom: "He is the Christ. But he is the Messiah, not of an earthly but of a spiritual Kingdom."[31] With the possible exception of John, Judas is the only disciple to understand the real nature of the kingdom; the rest reveal their anxiety even at the Last Supper where they joke about their future posts in the new government.[32]

That Sayers was aware of the need to clarify Judas's character for dramatic plausibility is clear from her introduction of Baruch, the only totally fictional character in the cycle. Baruch establishes his credibility in character assessment with his glimmering (and then ultimate) recognition that Jesus is incorruptible. But his real importance is to substantiate Judas's character. He says that he understands Judas:

> He has a subtle mind and would see through any crude efforts to corrupt him. But, he may be led into deceiving himself with specious arguments. That is the weakness of all clever people. Intellectual dishonesty springing from intellectual pride—the sin by which Adam fell.[33]

What Baruch is saying only reiterates the paradox of Judas: that a truly intelligent (and not merely clever) person can be swayed by speciousness may be plausible, but that an intelligent person would be conned into choosing speciousness over his firmly established convictions is less plausible. What we really have with Baruch is a convenient character whose 'substantiation' of Judas's character allows Sayers to mask the problem: by encouraging us to believe that *someone* understands Judas, we are then forced to assume that his character is understandable; if we do not understand, the problem is ours.

While Judas, because of Baruch's "specious arguments," loses faith in the person of Jesus, he does not lose faith in the Kingdom, since it is to preserve that cause that he betrays Jesus. The Kingdom of God means, as he says, "that all must be endured, and the cup of humiliation drunk to the very dregs."[34] And yet in the end when he realizes the fact of his betrayal of Jesus, Judas's eloquent analysis of the situation reverses his beliefs—from mistrust of Jesus and belief in the cause, to belief in Jesus and mistrust in the cause:

> It was written that he must suffer—Yes! And why?—Because there are too many men in the world like me. . . . I was in love with suffering, because I wanted to see him suffer. I wanted to believe him guilty, because I could not endure his innocence: He was greater than I, and I hated him. And now I hate myself. . . . If I crawled to the gallows' foot and asked his pardon, he would forgive me—and my soul would writhe for ever under the torment of that forgiveness.[35]

Jesus is restored, in Judas's eyes, as the manifestation of the Godhead, yet the love and forgiveness which He represents, and the Kingdom which He rules are forfeited by Judas. Judas cannot accept the totality of Jesus' cause. Not to accept these greatest of gifts is to deny the import of the sacrifice: that even the greatest of sinners can be reborn.

What we have then in Judas is a confused variation on the Satanic archetype. Perhaps that is as he was, but from the point of view of dramatizing the irony that "God was executed by people painfully like us," he fails. His character is no more nor less rationally comprehensible than is his medieval counterpart illustrating the sins of covetousness and wanhope. But whereas the Middle Ages necessarily eschewed mundane logic and realism, Sayers does not. She is hampered by the Idea of Judas: that he could believe *and* betray Jesus, believe *and* deny the result of Jesus' sacrifice is a theological paradox. In the context of dramatic realism, however, paradox succumbs to contradiction. Sayers attempts to support Judas's character with the logical character of Baruch, and therefore we are implicitly asked to judge him on logical grounds. Paradox, by definition, is logically inexplicable and results in dramatic equivocation.

In trying to avoid the simplistic approach adopted by the Middle Ages, and to make Judas's actions credible to a modern audience, Sayers included a fair number of red herrings, but when we sort them out, we are left with an ultimate personification of Pride illustrating an obvious moral. But whereas for the Middle Ages aesthetic considerations ("chaff") were subservient to moral instruction ("wheat"), Sayers sought "not to point a moral but to tell a story; not to produce a Divinity Lesson with illustrations in dialogue, but to write a good piece of theatre." And where her material was pliable, where she could realize the trinity of Idea, Energy, and Power, she created good theater. She never lost her gift for drawing realistic characters when she could allow them freedom of development. In addition to the character of Proclus, *The Man Born to Be King* is replete with delightful characters reminiscent of her detective fiction: children asking 'dreadful' questions, Jewish mothers bustling about with births and deaths, holiday crowds rushing to see "some chaps" being crucified, Madison Avenue entrepreneurs trying to convince Lazarus to "tour the country" as a living advertisement. But when it came to her having restrictions placed on her material, when the Idea was fixed by historical fact and the Energy confined by theology, the resulting aesthetic impact could not be of Sayers's free devising. In this case, the historical and theological restrictions ran counter to the Power, which is dependent for its full effect upon the use of logic and realism.

The character of Judas represents one illustration of the predicament, and not altogether a fair one since his villainous deed has overshadowed his person, and yet his further development is bound by theological as well as psychological considerations. He represents the problem, at its most extreme, of the Christian aesthetic, and if he is not an evident success as a dramatic character, neither was he in reality. The word is made flesh?

The Man Born to Be King:
Dorothy L. Sayers's Best Mystery Plot

THERE IS still a great tendency on the part of her critics to divide Dorothy L. Sayers, like all Gaul, into three parts. Some seem to feel that she could not be a successful writer of mysteries, an effective playwright, and a masterly translator of Dante, while others assume that she grew, or was converted, from one category into the next. What these people all miss when they try to pigeonhole Miss Sayers is that her sly, whimsical sense of humor, her remarkable ability to translate ideas from one generation to another, and her Christian convictions appear in everything she wrote. What she learned in one aspect of the craft of writing she applied to any other job she undertook, for part of her peculiar genius was to see connections and similarities between situations and concepts that to ordinary people might appear widely different. This trait is nowhere better illustrated than in her creation of the plot of *The Man Born to Be King.*

It is only fair to say that part of her commentators' confusion has come from Miss Sayers's own fondness for bland, sweeping disclaimers that have been taken too seriously, while she was also a highly educated, self-examining writer who liked to take apart what she had made to show what she had done. The important thing to keep in mind in considering her plays on the life of Christ is that she accepted the Christian understanding of human nature and history throughout her entire life. She was not converted to Christianity as an adult, nor did she embark suddenly upon the work of an apologist. Her gradual emergence as an apologist for Christianity grew out of her own experience and her trade as writer, while the gift for translating ideas from traditional language to contemporary speech was hers from the start of her career.

Her theory of Christian aesthetics, written up after she had become known as a Christian apologist through her speeches and articles and Canterbury plays, was never meant to be used as a vehicle of conversion. She did not postulate a theory and then write a book or play to dramatize it. Instead, in *The Mind of the Maker* and articles like "Towards A Christian Aesthetic," she took her own work apart to show her reader how it was constructed, and by doing so demonstrated that her understanding of Christian aesthetics reflected the very act of creation that she had experienced as a writer.

The key word is "experience," because it was her conviction that Christianity itself is only understood through personal experience, which shows one the truth of its credal statements. The Christianity she believed in was not her personal invention but the faith of the historical Christian church. Discovering that so many of her contemporaries were unfamiliar with the source of their own religious and ethical convictions, she began to put more of her time into translating these statements into modern idioms, in as many ways and in as many places as she could. As a result she became one of the great popularizers of Christianity.

In trying to define Dorothy Sayers's peculiar talent as a translator, I am greatly indebted to Dr. Barbara Reynolds. In her series of lectures on Dorothy Sayers given the summer of 1976 at Wheaton College, Dr. Reynolds brought out in great detail the sense in which she considers Miss Sayers to have been a translator above all else, not only in her dealing with Dante and Roland, but in her other work as well.[1]

Miss Sayers herself realized this fact quite clearly, but typically made light of it when she said,

> (Translating) is a kind of congenital disease. . . . I began to suffer from it as soon as I was able to think in any language but my own. At school I wasted my prep time producing metrical translations. . . .When I took my scholarship exam at Somerville, the French Unseen paper presented me with a sonnet . . . which I succeeded in rendering . . . in strict Petrarchian form. . . .[2]

·But Dr. Reynolds uses the term "translating" to mean far more than a kind of linguistic facility. She sees Dorothy Sayers at work translating ideas, terms, and concepts which, stated originally in old-fashioned or traditional language, have not only lost their power to shock but their actual meaning for modern man. Her translations were a deliberate effort to make the content of these ideas available to her contemporaries.

The more her translations worked, the more we take them for granted. This is particularly true of *The Man Born to Be King,* in which Miss Sayers created the plot structure, and in so doing, translated the Gospels into modern terms. In her sly way she tells us what she did, but we only half believe her. The only way to see what she created is to follow in her footsteps as she writes these plays and take them apart to see how they were made, following the clues she provided.

Although like many of her university generation Dorothy Sayers had first been published as a poet, she was really a playwright whose major tools were plot and dialog. She tended to view literature architecturally, seeing the *Divine Comedy,* for example, as if it were a magnificent Gothic cathedral. The skeleton of her writing was always clearly articulated no matter what she was writing, from mystery novels to forceful essays presenting her particular point of view.

The plays that make up *The Man Born to Be King* were an outstanding popular success, but it is easy to take her success for granted and not look too closely at the methods she used to achieve her purpose. Hunting for clues among her copious notes makes one startling thing clear: both her plot and its protagonists, Jesus Bar Joseph and Judas Iscariot, were not really present in her source material, for which, true to her Oxford education, she had gone back to the Greek New Testament as the primary source. She passed lightly over the enormous body of secondary commentary and refused to be limited by its current conventional wisdom. The world she created within these plays grew from her own capacious brain, and its dramatic structure was the result of her own engineering, but its purpose, always, was to tell the Gospel story compellingly. The chief reason this series of plays is not always recognized as having her most successful plot is that the Gospel story is considered a "given," but she did do what she said she did: flesh out an existing tale.

In writing these plays she had been assigned a job for which there were "no modern precedents to offer a guide as to treatment or to prepare the minds of the critics and audience for what they were to hear." She had to write 12 plays to be heard a month apart by a general audience, originally children, who might listen to one or two, or get sufficiently interested to keep tuning in. She had material "that began with the birth in Bethlehem and ended with Passion Week in Jerusalem," with the rest of Christ's so-called "life" nothing but a "string of parables, a bunch of miracles, a discourse, a set of sayings, a flash of apocalyptic thunder—here a little, and there a little."[3]

As models she found the medieval mystery plays "too remote in period and atmosphere." They not only contained much legendary material drawn from dubious sources, but also characters who did not change. A typical mystery cycle had a cast of thousands, each of whom stood symbolically for a single trait or event. This kind of drama did not provide her with an action plot, nor with any useful clues for the psychological makeup of her chief characters.

The first clue to her own creation lies in the fact that she called these plays a "play-cycle," but it is necessary to consider and dismiss several meanings for "cycle" before her point is clear. Two dictionary definitions of "cycle" do not fit *The Man Born to Be King.* They are a "recurring succession of events" and "a group of plays treating the same theme." The third definition from *Webster's Collegiate Dictionary,* however, is "a series of narratives dealing typically with the exploits of a legendary hero."

The Man Born to Be King fits this third definition perfectly. Miss Sayers had been familiar since her college days with the famous medieval cycles dealing with legendary figures like Roland, the nephew of Charlemagne. But it is the Matter of Britain, or the story of Arthur and its accrued legends like the Holy Grail, which is the closest match.

Like the life of Christ, the Arthurian legend has a highly dramatic birth story complete with royal parents, indicating that this baby is "born to be king," as well as an account of the hero's obscure upbringing by Merlin and Sir Ector. Then Arthur as a young man is recognized as king in the dramatic episode of the sword in the stone. At the end of Arthur's life, parallel to the Passion of Christ, there is the story of the Morte d'Arthur, which begins with his betrayal by Guinevere and Lancelot, includes Mordred's treason and the last great battle of Camlann, and ends with Arthur's disappearance to the Isle of Avalon, where he awaits Britain's call. Each story gains depth and universality from these mythic elements, but also makes both heroes sound like legendary demigods, an effect Miss Sayers was far from wishing to create with her own plays.

For her, anyhow, the significant parallel in terms of plot construction was the fact that "between the Nativity and the Passion, there is no real story at all." In the Arthurian legend, the middle becomes separate tales of his knights' adventures, while in the Gospels, the middle of the Ministry, especially in the synoptic Gospels, is arranged more according to topic than chronology.

Fortunately, the job of making up a "middle" was one for which Miss Sayers was well qualified. She knew the difference between getting a bright opening idea, such as a body in a bath, and working out the story to dramatize that curious event. She also not only liked mental puzzles, but was a master of the "divided mind," in which the author knows what is really happening but the reader does not.

As one can tell from her notes to the producers and actors, she attacked the project with her usual combination of humor, thoroughness, and irreverence, and she was so successful that her creation has been taken for granted, or passed over lightly in the patronizing tone of Roderick Jellema when he calls her, "the audacious author of a radio dramatization of the life of Christ . . . in which . . . his ragtag disciples speak cockney."[4] She did not just dress the disciples in modern costume, but told a new version of an old story in which the drama is created by the interaction of her two protagonists, Jesus Bar Joseph and Judas Iscariot, who is one of the representatives of contemporary humanity.

To demonstrate her at work, it has been very helpful to consult the early, undated drafts of these plays, which are in the Marion Wade Collection at Wheaton College. Among these papers are bits and pieces of the plays, including some whole scenes, scratched-out lines of dialog, notes, and instructions she later edited for the published version. These papers all have one thing in common: she continually redrew her scenes in an effort not to preach at the audience but to allow her characters to demonstrate her ideas in action.

For example, in an early version of the baptism scene in the second play, "The King's Herald," she has Judas actually making blunt statements about his interest in power for its own sake. But in the final version of this scene, Judas is only shown as recognizing the source of power first in John the Baptist, then in Jesus Bar Joseph. His co-conspirator, Baruch the Zealot, was not even given a name until she had rewritten the first three plays and found out how Baruch could help her create her Judas.

One of her building-blocks was the theme-structure concerning the nature of heavenly and earthly kingdoms from which the whole series took its name. It reflected not only philosophical concerns about power common to both the first and twentieth centuries, but also, by using the British Empire as a modern parallel to Rome, she made the plays real. It was a method very like Dante's when he used real people known to his readers as symbols of the stages of sin. Instead of describing simony and calling it "Pope," Dante described Boniface VIII, knowing that the Italians would instantly grasp the particular nature of the sin Boniface represented. The British public had grown up among the diverse elements of the British Empire with its many people and laws and could accept a more distant Roman Empire when it was presented to them in a similar light.

But just as vital for the plot was the way in which she tackled the problem of building a middle for the plays. In an early list at Wheaton College she had the first three plays, consisting of the Nativity, Baptism, and Cana, neatly ticked off, corresponding roughly to the final version of these plays. Then she had blanks numbered 4, 5, 6, while 7 is already the entry into Jerusalem, and 8, 9, 10, 11 and 12 are the Passion story. Plays 4 through 8, then, needed a chronology and a focus to make the whole cycle dramatic, but each must also stand on its own feet with a structural unity and beginning, middle and end, or there would be no plays at all, only "lengths cut arbitrarily from an interminable Scripture lesson."

She found her greatest single help in the Gospel of John, who always showed a logical connection between events, and often their chronological order as well. She used John's chronology wherever she could, but she was determined not to be an innovator so much as a synthesizer of Gospel events, so she harmonized accounts of the Ministry by making a list of the events which must be included in the most logical order of their happening. As an example of the work she did, there is a list in parallel columns, one for actions, one for dialog, for each of the four Gospel accounts of the feeding of the 4,000, escape across the lake, and walking on water. Ultimately, this list was dramatized in the fifth play, "The Bread of Heaven," where she fitted all the accounts together in believable sequence and provided the logic for the actions themselves.

Once she had her outline of events, she developed her system of using minor characters as "tie-rods"; that is, having them appear early and later on, which allowed them growth and logic as characters instead of mystery play walk-on parts. By this device she also reduced the confusion of the "number of persons who flit" through the Gospels, and she snatched every change to tighten her dramatic construction by "combining" people.

That her invented character, Proclus the centurion, is present at Herod's court in the nativity play, has a sick servant for Jesus to heal in the fourth play, is on duty in Jerusalem during Passion Week, and is finally stationed at the Cross, seems so natural that we take it for granted. In some cases she borrowed traditional identifications, such as Mary Magdalen and Mary of Bethany, the sister of Lazarus, which had been approved by St. Augustine. Others like Shadrach, the colleague of

Nicodemus and Joseph of Arimathea, were given names and personalities as she went along.

All authors use this economy of characterization; but these plays represent a master craftsman's performance, for Miss Sayers took each and every chance for such doubles, from Claudia's Tyro-Phoenician handmaiden Eunice, who is also the foreign woman with the sick child, to her remarkable decision to identify *all* of Christ's major disciples with those who had first followed John the Baptist. In addition, she doubled up like parables on the logical grounds that their similarity shows that Jesus, like any good teacher, used His own materials over and over.

These "tie-rods" also served her ultimate purpose of making Jesus Bar Joseph realistic by showing Him in convincingly dramatic situations. They let her demonstrate that His goodness was not static, that "there was that clash between His environment and Himself which is the mainspring of drama." But her basic plot sprang also from her conviction that Jesus did not deliberately stage His fulfillment of prophecies about the Messiah, both because that made a story that could not be acted and a character who was a fraud who "produced" his own life.

So like any detective story writer, she did precisely what her character Harriet Vane said was the proper way to write such plots: begin at the end. For dramatic purposes, Miss Sayers took the beginning of Passion Week, or Palm Sunday, as the beginning of the end. By that point in the Gospel, the die is clearly cast. Jesus is not popular with the rulers of this world, whether they are Jewry, as represented by Caiaphas, Pharisees, Sadducees or Scribes, or Rome. His refusal to provide free bread and circuses has made Him less of a charismatic, populist leader, too, but to the Zealots, still hoping for a sudden, successful armed rebellion, He is still a possible hope. Then, at that precise moment, Judas is suddenly center stage in the Gospel story, egotistically convinced that either Jesus is betraying him or that only he, Judas, can weld the sources of power and support together to bring in the Kingdom.

Miss Sayers reasoned that because the original records did not show that the disciples knew where the ass came from for the procession into Jerusalem, that need not mean there was no logical explanation for its appearance. So she had the ass there because Baruch the Zealot was hoping to get a clearcut sign from Jesus that He was willing to be the leader of an uprising. Baruch had been in touch with Judas behind Jesus' back, trying to learn what sort of person Jesus was. While the other disciples were surprised but accepted an ass ready to ride, she made Judas see it as damning proof of his worst suspicions that Jesus was a traitor. In that moment, filled with irony for us looking on, Judas is given the motivation to betray Jesus.

Next Miss Sayers followed her own rule and worked backward to establish the circumstances in which her Judas would think her Jesus might sell out. Her characterization of Judas was in fact her real creation, for the Gospel account is lacking any explanation of his motives, apart from the magical idea that it was "written" that one of His own would betray Him and the suggestion that Judas was a thief whose personality Jesus understood. She needed her Judas three-dimensional so that he could help her characterize her Jesus Bar Joseph.

She realized that Judas's connection with the Zealots was not just another "tie-rod," but the mainspring of her plot. She also saw that she was free to make anything she liked out of Judas, so long as he fitted into her Palm Sunday ending and contributed to the characterization of her other protagonist. Judas's validity, therefore, was determined by her success in "translating" Jesus out of the Gospel account into a real, believable person, for the two characters depend upon one another. In Judas, as she developed him, she had her "unreliable narrator" who was highly intelligent but morally deficient, who like Othello could only see clearly what he had destroyed after he killed it.

As she explains in the notes to the actor, he must play Judas "real," not go off into a stock Richard III stance of "I am determined to prove a villain." If Judas was bad because he was born that way with no reasons given, then his choice as a disciple makes Jesus look like a fool, and that in turn will destroy her chances of making Him real and compelling. But so far as her Gospel sources are concerned, Judas is an enigma, who appears abruptly, near the close of the story, "all set for villainy." As she said, "we are not told how he came to be a disciple, nor what motives drove him to betray his Master [but] when he had done his worst and saw what he had done, he brought back the reward of iniquity and went out and hanged himself. He seems a strange mixture of the sensitive and the insensitive."[5] She therefore took her cue from the modern world and made Judas not only an intellectual with strong opinions on how to do good, but also an organization man, intrigued by power and determined to wield it.

Her first brilliant stroke in Judas's characterization was to bring him into the story early in a place where he fits quite naturally, but never appeared in any Gospel versions. In her second play, "The King's Herald," Judas, like Peter, Andrew, James and John, appears as a disciple of John the Baptist. Like them, he was involved in the Ministry from its beginning and he is first shown to us as a capable organization man, herding converts down to the Jordan.

In an early version of this play Judas talked directly to Jesus who is standing quietly in line to be baptized, saying to Him,

> Sir! I see you have been greatly moved by John's preaching. You, too, I think are a worker for the Kingdom . . . or—is it possible that you are the greater teacher of whom John speaks?

Jesus replies by saying, "And if I were, what then? Would you follow me?" and Judas tells him, "I would follow any man that could bring in the Kingdom with power. And there is power in your face and voice."[6] This exchange is terribly didactic, not letting us see Jesus clearly enough to understand why He compelled this sudden attention. In rewriting, Sayers cut it out completely. Judas never notices Jesus at all, but is subtly sounded out by Baruch the Zealot about his political interests, while it is John the Baptist himself that recognizes Who Jesus is. In the next scene in this play John the Baptist is talking with his disciples, Judas, Andrew, Peter, James, and John, whose presence here gives dramatic continuity to the idea of John as the forerunner of Jesus. Most of the conversation is between John the Baptist and Judas, underlining the fact that Judas understands John better than the rest. When John the Baptist is arrested and the other disciples scatter, Judas chooses to stay with John, foreshadowing his passion for power that will overwhelm his better judgment as he says, "I'm not afraid. Herod's only bluffing. . . . There will be great opportunities in Tiberias . . . I've established certain contacts."[7] Clever Judas is thinking of the coup it would be if they baptized Herod Antipater. He is not dealing in eternal verities, but in campaigns to win votes.

Dorothy Sayers said that she deliberately chose to make Judas not only a modern, but "one of us," that is, a part of the intellectual elite. Since Jesus spoke of him sternly, far more so than He did of Peter and his impetuous sins, she deduced that Judas was guilty of the deadly corruption of the proud virtues, or, as we would say, of tremendous gifts of intelligence and leadership. As he appeared in her plays Judas is a very realistic portrait of a political animal we have seen often in the twentieth century. He is not only determined to save Israel from itself at all costs, but also well aware of his superior status as the star pupil, first of John the Baptist, and then of Jesus Himself. Several times in her original notes Miss Sayers crossed out the single word "intellectual" to describe him; it is what she meant, but saying it was too much of a shortcut dramatically.

Instead, she put him in the forefront of the action in the second through tenth plays and gave her audience plenty of opportunity to see him as the kind of bright young man who has haunted our recent political campaigns, smarter than his charismatic puppet candidate, self-righteously angry at the squandering of campaign money on perfume when it might have been used for buying votes. His kind have ended up in court on SDS charges, or as defendants at Watergate, quite surprised at the turn events have taken. But they are as deluded as Judas, who was ". . . faithful . . . to the light which he sees so brilliantly . . . only he does not see it directly, but only its reflection in the mirror of his own brain. . . ."[8]

But while she was busily creating her Judas, Miss Sayers also had to fight the fact that "at the name of Jesus every voice goes plummy, every gesture becomes pontifical, and a fearful, creeping paralysis slows down the pace of the dialogue," while she must also make it plain that, "of course the minute you take Christ as somebody real, you've landed in theology—[but] you've got to translate the thing into terms of life and action. . . ."[9] Her first step was to give Him a real name like the other characters, calling him Jesus Bar Joseph, not Jesus Christ, and letting Him appear onstage without any supernatural effects such as heightened language like poetry, or lead-ins, until the last play, in which His Resurrection appearances are deliberately heralded by angels or occur with a magical quickness that scares His own followers.

In examining her characterization of Jesus Bar Joseph, we must also remember that it was only after her *Man Born to Be King* that the vogue for modernizing Him really began, with popular translations of the Bible, secular and contemporary liturgies, rock musicals with hippy disciples, or plays and novels in which Judas is the real hero. In her day He was never shown on stage, and no audience had had a chance to experience directly His wit and intelligence, His argumentative ability, or the truth of what He said about the human condition.

In seeking to dramatize for us that "clash between His environment and Himself which is the mainspring of drama," she hit upon the magnificent device of making Judas the kind of person who can give Jesus dramatic opportunities to demonstrate this clash. Not only does Judas fill the need of any great leader for someone who is capable of understanding what he is doing, but potentially, he is the one best suited to carry out the Gospel afterwards. In *The Man Born to Be King*, Judas emerges as someone who might easily have become a Saint Paul. In dramatic terms, moreover, a dialog or an argument between these two, carried on in front of the other disciples who act as a kind of chorus, is a very natural way of seeing what is happening. Each stage of the Ministry is shown in this way with Judas's assumptions and reservations illuminating Jesus Bar Joseph's mission.

It is also vital to remember that Miss Sayers made full use of the fact that her audience is watching both Jesus and Judas from a Post-Nicene point of view, aware that Judas is more and more arrogantly mistrusting Jesus, thinking only he can bring in the Kingdom. We know, too, in an ironic, hideous way, that his betrayal will do precisely that. This knowledge of ours provides the dramatic irony as the shape and search of the Ministry shifts from the popularist movement of a miracle worker to a deep comprehension of the human condition, seen by a few but misunderstood and feared by many.

A good example of the use she makes of Judas in her dramatization of Jesus Bar Joseph occurs in the fourth play, "The Heirs of the Kingdom," which is the key play in their relationship since they are thrust together in it for good or ill. In this play Jesus Bar Joseph's friends and foes, both open and secret, are forming into two camps, when "into [His] camp comes Judas; the man of brilliant gifts and intellect, bringing just those qualities the other disciples lack."[10]

Along with Andrew, Peter, James and John, Judas becomes John the Baptist's legacy to Jesus, and he is the one most fitted to be the cornerstone of the new creation. In an earlier version of the first scene of the fourth play, Jesus is with His disciples when Judas comes seeking Him with the news that John is dead. Aware of his own importance, Judas greets Jesus formally, "God prosper you, honored Rabbi." He then recites a speech, which remained in the final version, concerning John the Baptist's gift of him to Jesus, but when Philip naively tries to hand him their money for safekeeping, Judas again speaks directly to Jesus, saying, "If Jesus is willing, I am willing."

This remark is too full of overtones of Calvary, and Miss Sayers cut it out, instead having Jesus question Judas subtly about his motives. Judas quickly understands Him, characteristically explaining, "If I set my hand to the plough, I will never look back. . . ." to which Jesus replies in the elliptical fashion these two use with one another, ". . . take care lest it turn out truer than you think. But if you are resolved, then come and follow me."[11]

The link here between Jesus and Judas, as it is again on Palm Sunday, is a prophecy of betrayal made real and believable by the circumstances. Following the Gospel of John, who said that He knew what Judas was, she then has Jesus withdraw to meditate not only upon the fate of His cousin, but also upon this new disciple, until He returns for their evening Scripture reading. She modified this particular Scripture reading three times, seeking the best way to dramatize that Jesus wanted to show Judas not only what the Kingdom is, but also to warn him that he is not guaranteed the place at Jesus' right hand.

First, she chose the *Book of Deuteronomy,* in which Moses preached upon his mission and made clear the role of Joshua, to whom her Judas had already compared Jesus. Then she switched to *Isaiah* and the Suffering Servant, but finally she had Jesus tell the parable of the Draw-Net, in which good and bad fish are both caught and sorted out later. In this way she has Jesus warning Judas that not everyone who is called will be chosen.[12]

The remainder of the fourth play has two scenes, one in which Baruch and Caiaphas join in unholy alliance, planning to use Judas as their tool by playing upon his intellectual egotism, and the last scene in which the other heirs to the kingdom, like Proclus the centurion and Eunice the slavegirl, come from the far corners of the earth to sit at the wedding feast in place of Israel. The total effect of the play is to make us, the audience, extremely tense, aware that Judas is a threat, but also aware that his choice as a disciple by Jesus was not perverse, but natural and inevitable, given his gifts and his position as the favorite disciple of John the Baptist. None of this characterization came from her sources; it all came from her.

During the fifth, sixth and seventh plays before the Passion begins, we grow accustomed to having Judas understand what Jesus is saying, to having him understand everything except Whom he is dealing with, an understanding that, ironically, comes to the other major disciples quite naturally at the Transfiguration. When Jesus' message becomes harder and they lose followers, He can say to Judas, teasing him, "At any rate, Judas, it does not look like being a popular doctrine. The crowd is drifting away. Comfort yourself with the reflection that they are not likely to crown me king today."[13] As we have come to expect, Judas understands Him, even though he is also misled by the fact that Jesus recognizes his anxieties into false suspicions. Judas becomes more watchful and more distrustful as he and Jesus talk to one another over the heads of the other disciples. Judas expects Jesus also to take nothing on faith and question all motives, just as he is also developing a good case for a martyr who will help the cause, an ironic but understandable inversion of the real meaning of the Cross.

In the earlier version of the sixth play, "The Feast of Tabernacles," when the other disciples are dismayed at the popular desertions and worry, too, over Jesus' physical safety, one says, "It's all going wrong," and Judas replies, "No, it's all going right." Then Thomas asks him, "Do you understand it, Judas?" and Judas smugly replies, "Yes, I'm the only one who really understands." But Miss Sayers cut that out and instead used Judas's secret reports to Caiaphas and Baruch to show us his blindness.[14]

She makes the Zealots responsible for that ass of prophecy, but she also uses that situation to convince Judas that Jesus has betrayed their cause, so that his own betrayal inevitably follows. At the same time, once Judas sees what he has done, he is not repentant, but illuminated, bursting into prophecy himself, shrieking aloud to the appalled Sanhedrin in Scene II of the play "The Princes of This World," "Do you know what hell-fire is? It is the light of God's unbearable innocence that sears and shrivels you like flame."[15] To speak in tongues was given to the other disciples only after Pentecost, but her Judas had it all along. It is her creation of him as a character with that kind of sweep and depth, matching the personality of her Jesus Bar Joseph (watched by an audience who know Who He is and how the story must end), that makes these plays work dramatically. We have all seen other men of great gifts worship themselves to their own and others' destruction.

These plays represent a triumph of dramatic development made from static materials of such symbolic nature that the modern world did not take them seriously. Without her character of Judas to involve Jesus closely with someone whom He can neither convince nor control, she could not have succeeded in making her Jesus Bar Joseph real. By creating her "workmanlike" plot, hidden from the participants until the end, while gradually revealed to us, colored by the irony of the story's familiarity, she did far more than she admitted when she said, "To make an *adequate* dramatic presentation of the Life of God . . . would require superhuman genius. . . . Nevertheless, when a story is great enough, any honest craftsman may succeed in producing something not altogether unworthy. . . ."[16] But in fact we have here a very superior craftsman, and when she is onstage in her favorite persona of the "writer Dorothy L. Sayers," then, as she pointed out in her analysis of Dante the author and Dante the character, we must be careful not to confuse the two and refuse to give credit to the author for his own creation.

William Reynolds

Dorothy Sayers and the Drama of Orthodoxy

SINCE the publication of *Christian Letters to a Post-Christian World* and of a new edition of *The Man Born to Be King,* Dorothy Sayers's noncyclical plays (*The Zeal of Thy House* [1937], *He That Should Come* [1938], *The Devil to Pay* [1939], *The Just Vengeance* [1946], and *The Emperor Constantine* [1951]) have become the least accessible of her works.[1] This situation is particularly unfortunate, for while the essays collected in *Christian Letters to a Post-Christian World* adequately summarize the range of Sayers's thought, *The Man Born to Be King* does not and cannot represent plays which differ as radically as do these five.

In fact, so marked are these differences that any thematic analysis of these plays seems doomed from the start. The subtle political intrigue and still more subtle theology that characterize *The Emperor Constantine* are absent from *He That Should Come,* a straightforward account of the birth of Christ. *The Zeal of Thy House* discusses the relationship of artists to their art in order to supply a supernatural interpretation of a piece of human history, while *The Devil to Pay,* Sayers's interpretation of the Faust story, furnishes a human interpretation of a supernatural legend.[2] *The Just Vengeance* mixes the human (Samuel Johnson and George Fox), the supernatural (Gabriel and the Recording Angel of Lichfield), the historical (Cain's murder of Abel and Judas's betrayal of Jesus), and the imaginary (Adam's invention of the ax and God's healing of Samuel Johnson's dimmed vision) into an examination of atonement and redemption.

But beneath this very real diversity of content and method is a single intention. Commenting on the status of British Christianity, Sayers writes: "The brutal fact is that in this Christian country not one person in a hundred has the faintest notion what the Church teaches about God or man or society or the person of Jesus Christ."[3] But Sayers manages to find some grounds for optimism: "Theologically, this country is at present in a state of utter chaos. . . . We are not happy in this condition and there are signs of a very great eagerness, especially among the younger people, to find a creed to which they can give wholehearted adherence."[4] The purpose of the plays, then, is simply to present the truths of Christianity in such a way as to "drag out the Divine Drama from under the dreadful accumulation of slipshod thinking and trashy sentiment heaped upon it, and set it on an open stage to startle the world into some sort of vigorous reaction."[5] The truths she emphasizes and the devices she uses to "startle" the theatergoer differ from play to play, but the plays are united by their author's desire to show the effects of the Timeless irrupting into time.[6]

HE THAT SHOULD COME

The least complex of the plays is *He That Should Come,* first performed on the London National Transmission of the BBC on 25 December 1938, and subsequently adapted for the stage by Sayers herself. The play opens with a prolog in which Melchior, Caspar, and Balthazar detail their reasons for following the Star: Melchoir the Just, a Greek ruler, is not interested in dogma but in a religion that insures good government; Caspar the Wise, an astrologer, hopes that the god about to be born will speak "the ultimate wisdom,/ the unalterable truth behind and above the appearance";[7] Balthazar the Servant, King of Ethiopia, searches for a god to stand beside him, "bearing the weight of His own creation" [p. 227]. The prolog closes with the three gazing into Balthazar's crystal and observing the events taking place in Bethlehem.

Most of the play takes place at an inn in Bethlehem. Mixed with traditional episodes, like the innkeeper's housing Joseph and Mary in a stable, are events which reveal the social and historical background of the period. A merchant complains to his friends about the Roman taxes, then asks a centurion to find someone to travel with him to Beth-Horon; a zealous Pharisee berates a young Jewish gentleman who has adopted Roman habits; a Greek gentleman tries to comprehend what the Jews expect from their Messiah. The play ends with Caspar, Melchior, and

Balthazar hastening in pursuit of the Star, each having found in Jesus what he sought:

> CASPAR: I looked for wisdom—and behold! the wisdom of the innocent.
> MELCHIOR: I looked for power—and behold! the power of the helpless.
> BALTHA⁄AR: I looked for the manhood in God—and behold! A God made man.
>
> [p. 273]

Sayers's account of her intent is succinct: "The whole idea in writing . . . [this play] was to show the miracle that was to change the whole course of human life enacted in a world casual, inattentive, contemptuous, absorbed in its own affairs and completely unaware of what was happening; to illustrate, in fact, the tremendous irony of history" [p. 218]. In a world where Christianity had become for many "unreal, shadowy, 'a tale to be told'" [p. 219], Sayers realized that before people could be startled by the Incarnation they must realize "that the thing actually happened—that it is, and was from the beginning, closely in contact with real life" [p. 219].

The success of *He That Should Come* is difficult to assess. Most of the characters are individualized and believable; careful attention to detail brings the period to life, and Sayers relates that after the play's first broadcast she received letters remarking how well it brought home the real humanity of Jesus. But she likewise admits that because it was originally a radio play, *He That Should Come* poses certain problems, like maneuvering some 24 characters on, off, and around the stage. A more serious problem is that the audience may grow bored with the long speeches the three kings direct to one another, and with the even longer discussion of the Messiah's character conducted by the people staying at the inn. In addition, the kings' lines smack of the "ecclesiastical intonation" and "religious unction" Sayers warns about in her introduction; and while the debate about the Messiah counterpoints the change in the three kings' expectations, the exchanges often seem wooden and pedantic, as if every variant were systematically being cataloged by an industrious Ph.D. candidate. *He That Should Come* has its successes, but it is the least of Sayers's plays.

THE ZEAL OF THY HOUSE

The Zeal of Thy House, first presented at the Canterbury Festival (1937), is more successful in bringing dramatic life to Sayers's ideas.

perhaps because the historical matter it treats is more susceptible to artistic interpretation than is the Nativity story. After a brief prolog, the play opens with the Cathedral Chapter meeting to choose an architect to rebuild the Choir of Canterbury Cathedral after the great fire of 1174. After reviewing the plans submitted by John of Kent, William of Sens, and Henry of York, the Chapter (with help from the Archangel Gabriel) selects William of Sens. His competitors question William's methods and motives, but William replies that "one has to damn one's soul for the sake of the work."[8]

William's statement seems to be the bold defiance of a hero rebelling against the restrictions placed on him by a backward-looking Church, and the middle section of the play adds to this impression. William juggles the books, using an illegal commission to purchase a better grade of lime than he had been authorized to purchase, and carries on a blatant affair with the Lady Ursula de Warbois.

But the reality of William's situation is far different. The Archangel Michael directs Cassiel, the Recording Angel, to write of William:

> A schedule here,
> Long as my sword, crammed full of deadly sins;
> Jugglings with truth, and gross lusts of the body,
> Drink, drabbing, swearing; slothfulness in prayer;
> That challenges disaster.
>
> [p. 37]

Yet when Gabriel lists William's credits, he echoes William's view:

> Six columns, and their aisles, with covering vaults
> From wall to arcading, and from thence again
> To the centre, with the keystones locking them,
> All well and truly laid without a fault.
>
> [p. 37]

Raphael does likewise:

> Behold, he prayeth; not with the lips alone,
> But with the hand and with the cunning brain. . . .
> So, when the mouth is dumb, the works shall speak
> And save the workman.
>
> [p. 38]

And the great tragedy of the play, William's fall from a scaffold, comes about because Fr. Theodatus is so intent upon William's private sins that he ignores his own work and permits a flawed rope to lift the scaffold to the top of the great arch. The prior's words to Fr. Theodatus make this part of the play's dogma explicit:

> This is thy sin: thou hast betrayed the work;
> Thou hast betrayed the Church; thou hast betrayed
> Christ, in the person of His fellow-man.

[p. 75]

The fourth act adds much to the play's message. Six months after his devastating accident, William still refuses to resign his appointment even though his efforts to supervise the work are obviously killing him and the work itself is not going well. William confesses his sins, but Michael accuses him of regarding himself as indispensable when even God Himself, risen from the dead, left His work for others to carry on. All at once, William realizes why his conscience is still troubled:

> I have sinned. The eldest sin of all,
> Pride, that struck down the morning star from Heaven
> Hath struck down me.

[p. 98]

William then prays that God will spare his work, but Michael reassures him:

> Thou shalt not surely die
> Save as He died; nor suffer, save with Him;
> Nor lie in hell, for He hath conquered hell
> And flung the gates wide open.

[p. 100]

Following his vision, William admits that others can do his work as well as he, announces his resolution to return to France, and promises to make amends to all—except to God to whom he owes no debt since "He from the treasure of His great heart hath paid/ The whole sum due, and cancelled out the bond" [p. 102]. Michael closes the play by proclaiming the doctrine that every work of creation is three-fold: the Creative Idea, the Creative Energy, and the Creative Power.

As Charles Moorman points out, the major theme of the play is William's recognition that in his excess pride he has failed to understand "the proper relationship of man to God and of man the creator to his creation."[9] William has not seen that unless "the Lord build the house,

their labour is but/ lost that build it" [p. 70]. In addition to this key
theme, one which also animates *Gaudy Night*, Sayers presents at least
two other ideas worthy of some attention.

The first is that William's original idea about the importance of work
has merit. Gabriel and Raphael agree that in William's case, "to labour is
to pray" [p. 38]; and the prior tells Theodatus:

> He [God] that bestowed the skill and the desire
> To do great work is surely glad to see
> That skill used in His service.
>
> [p. 60]

Raphael voices one justification for William's view when he answers
Cassiel's "By man came sin" with "O felix culpa, quae/ Talis et tanti
meruit Redemptoris!" [p. 62]; Michael develops the same doctrine by
echoing the parable of the Prodigal Son in his description of William's
conversion:

> when he is come,
> The angelic trumpets split their golden throats
> Triumphant, to the stars singing together
> And all the sons of God shouting for joy.
>
> [p. 100]

The prior presents an alternative when he tells Theodatus:

> He [God] can,
> Being the alchemist's stone, the stone of Solomon,
> Turn stone to gold, and purge the gold itself
> From dross, till all is gold.
>
> [p. 60]

The Zeal of Thy House also develops the folly of the Cross theme
suggested in the final scene of *He That Should Come*. When William
imagines that God will punish him for refusing to relinquish his work,
Michael demonstrates that Jesus Himself has already suffered everything
that William fears:

> He [Jesus] made no reservation of Himself
> Nor of the godlike stamp that franked His gold,
> But in good time let time supplant Him too. . . .
> He, unshaken, with exultant voice

Cried "It is finished!" and gave up the ghost.
"Finished"—when men had thought it scarce begun.

[p. 97]

THE DEVIL TO PAY

In her next play, *The Devil to Pay*, originally produced at the Canterbury Cathedral Festival, 10-17 June 1939, Sayers turned from investing historical events with larger significance to suggesting the contemporary significance of the already well-established Faust myth. The best commentaries on Sayers's intentions are her introduction to the play and her essay "The Faust Legend and the Idea of the Devil." She observes that because her generation did not need to be warned against the pursuit of knowledge for its own sake, she presented Faustus as the "impulsive reformer, oversensitive to suffering, impatient of the facts, eager to set the world right by a sudden overthrow, in his own strength and regardless of the ineluctable nature of things."[10] In the first phase of the play, "the idea that evil is a means to good reaches its almost inevitable conclusion: i.e. it is *consciously* accepted and exploited. Faustus, sickened by the human suffering about him, tries to take the short cut to a remedy, and to cast out bodily evil by invoking the aid of spiritual evil."[11]

The Mephistopheles who answers Faustus's summons presents himself to Faustus as a fellow humanitarian, telling Faustus exactly what he is predisposed to hear; when, for example, Faustus asks how evil came into the world, Mephistopheles places the blame on an inefficient God whose efforts to set things right resulted only in His own death and a set of ambiguous statements which men have spent nearly 2,000 years trying to puzzle out. The minor characters are also different. Sayers adds a female servant named Lisa and transmutes Wagner (to whom she gives the symbolic name Christopher) from a clown into a loyal helper whose actions show by contrast what Faustus's should be.

In the second scene of the play, Faustus's resolution weakens when he sees the failure of his attempts to use the devil's power to do God's work. Lisa and Wagner try to persuade him to abjure magic and return with them to Wittenberg. But Mephistopheles counters by producing Helen of Troy who tells Faustus:

None may touch my lips
While on his own hangs still the fatal taste
Of Eve's sharp apple.

[p. 162]

Enflamed with desire for Helen, Faustus denies the reality of evil and of personal responsibility for evil, and the second phase of the play begins. He agrees to give up his soul in exchange for a 24 year period of eternal youth and the primal innocence enjoyed before the Fall. Lisa sounds the only optimistic note, one reminiscent of *The Zeal of Thy House*:

> And we will try to do his work—help the poor and heal the sick with the remedies he taught us. And when God sees what we are doing, He will say: That is the real Faustus; that's what he really meant to do. . . . So you see, our work will plead for our master's soul.

[p. 168]

The third scene reveals Faustus's corruption: the saintly Lisa has died, but Faustus can think only of himself; he who had professed to love all men sends the legions of Hell to support the Emperor's attack on Rome. Finally, Faustus is struck down; but when Mephistopheles claims his soul from Azrael, angel of the souls of the dead, nothing is to be found except a black dog. The scene ends with Azrael and Mephistopheles threatening court action.

The fourth scene is set in the court of heaven. God explains that by taking away Faustus's knowledge of good and evil, Mephistopheles has reduced him to the level of an animal. God then restores the soul of Faustus as he was before he signed the devil's contract and calls him before the bar of justice. Here, where no lying is possible, Mephistopheles reveals to Faustus that God did indeed create evil but in the same way as the light creates the shadow:

> God is only light,
> And in the heart of the light, no shadow standeth,
> Nor can I dwell within the light of Heaven
> Where God is all.

[p. 206]

God offers Faustus two choices: to resume his animal soul, become "Incapable alike of hell or heaven,/ [and] Wander for evermore between the worlds" [p. 204] or go to Hell. Finally seeing things as they are, Faustus chooses the latter, echoing the Scriptures in his resolve:

> If I go down to hell
> He is there also; or if He stand without,

My hands shall batter against hell's brazen gates
Till the strong bars burst asunder and let Him in.

[p. 209]

But the result of Faustus's decision is, surprisingly, not Hell but Purgatory. In choosing to be deprived of God over being ignorant of Him, Faustus has gained the kingdom of heaven. Thus, God warns Mephistopheles not to destroy Faustus but to purge the dross so he will be ready for God when they meet at the gates of Hell.

The play, then, concentrates on an examination of the nature of evil and the nature and necessity of human freedom. God (light) is presented as primary; evil (darkness) as secondary and derivative. Evil is depicted as " 'the price that all things (i. e. all created things . . .) pay for being' — that is, for existing in created and material form. There is, for them, along with the reality of God, the possibility of not-God . . . to the self-conscious creature the not-God is known as change, as pain, and *also* as intellectual error and moral evil; and it is at this point that it becomes evil in the profoundest sense of the word, because it can be embraced and made active by the will."[12] Further, the play demonstrates that "damnation, or hell, is the permanent choice of the not-God. God does not (in the monstrous old-fashioned phrase) 'send' anybody to hell; hell is that state of the soul in which its choice becomes obdurate and fixed; the punishment (so to call it) of that soul is to remain eternally in that state which it has chosen."[13]

THE JUST VENGEANCE

In *The Just Vengeance,* originally performed in Lichfield Cathedral, 15-26 June 1946, Sayers again attempted something new. Instead of relying as she had before on already established story lines, she mixed actual history with extrapolated history and with pure invention to treat the doctrines of the Atonement and the Coinherence of Christ in the Church, His mystical body.

"In form, the drama is a miracle-play of Man's insufficiency and God's redemptive act, set against the background of contemporary crisis. The whole action takes place in the moment of the death of an Airman shot down during [World War II]. In that moment, his spirit finds itself drawn into the fellowship of his native city of Lichfield; there, being shown in an image the meaning of the Atonement, he accepts the Cross, and passes, in that act of choice, from the image to the reality."[14]

Lichfield takes on, as Charles Moorman points out, the character of Charles Williams's City—the City of God on Earth.[15] The Airman is met by the Quaker George Fox, who gradually leads him to the realization that he has died. The Airman grows angry because he has been a violent man while Fox allowed the Lord to exact judgment; he asks to meet the souls of others who have also shed blood. But Fox informs him that "there is no fraternity/ And no exchange, except in the blood of Christ" [p. 289], and before him appear the victims of the City's violence.

After his exposure to this side of the City, the Airman is asked by the recording angel of Lichfield why he claims citizenship in the City. When the Airman attempts to enunciate his creed, he is drowned out by the voice of the City reciting the Apostles' Creed. Still, the Airman does not understand and tells the angel:

I believe in man, and in the hope of the future,
The steady growth of knowledge and power over things,
The equality of all labouring for the community,
And a just world where everyone will be happy.

[p. 297]

But the Airman has forgotten that he is now a part of the past, not the future; and the City must show him that he cannot divorce himself from it, that all are "victims together/ Or guilty together" [p. 299]. The Airman remains troubled; he tells the angel:

I want to know why we have no choice;
I want to know why there is no justice . . .
I want to know what it is all about,
And whether the thing makes sense. I have lived; I have died;
I have a right to know.

[p. 299]

The City then presents a play to teach the Airman the true nature of things. When he tells Eve "It is our [man's] privilege to know good and evil/ And choose the good" [p. 302], Eve tells him that she and Adam had believed the serpent when he had said the same things, but

had forgotten we were creatures.
We could not know as God knows, by pure knowledge
Only as men know, by experience.
What we desired in knowing good and evil

Was simply the experience of evil:
We chose it and we had it.

[p. 302]

Next, the City enacts Cain's murder of Abel to teach the Airman that

Though you slay innocence and outlaw guilt
You cannot undo the brotherhood of the blood.
Every man and every woman . . .
Is the whole seed of Adam, not divided
But fearfully joined in the darkness of the double self.

[p. 313]

When the chorus calls for justice to be done to Cain, Eve, who sees clearly that men desire justice only for the other and not for themselves, prays instead for "A kind of mercy that is not unjust,/ A not unmerciful justice" [pp. 315–16]. In answer, the *Persona Dei* descends from heaven, becomes Incarnate, and heals the victims of the City. Jesus' teaching on retribution is simple:

there is no justice in the Gospel,
There's only love, which does not seek its own,
But finds its whole delight in giving joy
Unasked.

[p. 327]

Hearing this, the Airman asks Jesus:

Was it worth while—forgive my bluntness, sir—
That God should be made man, only to say
To man, "Be perfect," when it can't be done?

[p. 329]

Jesus replies that human beings cannot keep His law unless He comes to be within each human being. He gives His body to be broken that it may be distributed to all people so they too may break and give themselves for all the world. Thereupon, Jesus is taken prisoner. When Pilate offers the crowd the choice of Barabbas (portrayed as Cain) or Jesus, the Chorus shouts:

Barabbas! we're accustomed to Barabbas—
Let us have back our old familiar sin!
Give us Barabbas! we will have Barabbas!

[p. 335]

They demand that Jesus be crucified because

> His kingship makes too great demands on us—
> He would be king of body and soul and all,
> There would be nothing left of us.
>
> [p. 336]

Next, true to the Gospel account, the Chorus accepts responsibility for the death of Jesus: "His blood be upon us and upon our children" [p. 336].

At this climactic moment Adam exclaims, "O sons and daughters . . . you have pulled the judgment of Cain upon you;/ You are all the children of one father" [p. 337]; and Eve continues, "you have pulled the death of Abel upon you. . . . Now you are all involved in the same disaster,/ In the intimate bond of blood" [p. 337]. The truth of their statements comes home to the Airman when all the other voices grow still, and he alone is left shouting "Crucify! Crucify!" His situation, like that of all humanity, seems hopeless. As Judas says:

> This guilt is yours and mine—altogether yours,
> Altogether mine.
>
> [p. 338]

But while the situation is hopeless for human beings alone, it is not so for God. Jesus tells the people:

> Because our brotherhood is not in the sin
> But in the blood—the fatherhood of God
> And the motherhood of the first and the second Eve
> The yours and the mine can belong to both and either
> By division or exchange, if you choose to make it so.
> Say that the guilt is Mine; give it to Me
> And I will take it away to be crucified.
>
> [pp. 338–39]

Jesus' words seem meaningless to some; but the Chorus and the Airman accept Jesus' offer, secure in His promise: "The moment when you meet Me is never too late,/ Though the moment of death and moment of choice were one" [p. 345].

Jesus is crucified and dies. The Atonement has been accomplished. But Sayers does not end the play here; instead, she reveals the risen Jesus standing before the Cross of glory. He assures everyone that no matter what it is they do,

> it is I that stand and suffer with you,
> Adding My innocence to redeem your guilt,
> And yours with Mine, to ransom all mankind.

[p. 350]

Jesus then rises into Heaven; the people follow and are received into the joy which their Lord had promised.

THE EMPEROR CONSTANTINE

Like *The Just Vengeance,* Sayers's last play, *The Emperor Constantine: A Chronicle* (1951), deals with guilt, punishment, and forgiveness; but it poses a different set of problems for playwright and audience. As Sayers puts it, much is known about Constantine, yet "all that is known remains in a manner ambiguous. . . . The playwright, groping among the lights and shadows of history, must interpret the facts as best he may, so as to distill from them a reasonable and consistent story."[16] Sayers attempts a double task: to trace Constantine's developing consciousness of Christ and to render intelligible the theological debate which led to the decrees of the Council of Nicaea.

As the play opens in 303 A.D., Constantine Chlorus and Helena meet for the first time in 10 years, and Helena is reunited with their son Constantine whom she has not seen since he was 11 years old. Constantine is pleased to learn that the Christian Church regards him not only as Constantine Chlorus's legitimate son, but as his only legitimate child; for this he decides he owes Christ something. This is the first stage of Constantine's relationship with Christ: knowing Christ as one god among many.

Constantine Chlorus dies, and during a troubled time when the title of Augustus of the West is claimed by five men, Constantine is also acclaimed Augustus. Thus begins Constantine's rise to Emperor, as had been prophesied by the visionary King Coel when he hailed his grandson as "Son of the old Rome, father of the New" [p. 26]. Constantine's next step is to formulate an alliance with Maxentius and Maximian, who recognizes him as Augustus on equal terms with full jurisdiction in Gaul and Britain. A few years later at the Battle of the Milvian Bridge, Constantine, recognizing Christ, who has appeared to him in a dream as a warrior god fighting on his side, defeats Maxentius and becomes sole Augustus of the West; he immediately frees the Christian Church from taxes and begins to endow it. But Constantine has not finished. In 324

A.D. Constantine defeats Licinius, the Augustus of the East, and becomes sole Augustus of both Empires. Constantine unwisely spares Licinius, and the latter plots against him, taking advantage of Constantine's second wife's jealousy of her stepson Crispus.

In the midst of these plots, Constantine must also confront a doctrinal controversy which threatens to tear the Christian Church apart. Arius of Alexandria maintains that "before the Son was generated. . . . He was not, since He is not unbegotten" [pp. 79-80]. As a result, he and his followers have been excommunicated. At first, Constantine does not grasp the importance of the issue; but when he does, he resolves, as Christ's viceroy on Earth, to summon a council of all the churches and to enforce whatever decision this council arrives at. Thus Constantine comes to know yet another Christ: the Christ of the theologians.

Though the theologians want a creed, Constantine desires only peace in the Church. But Constantine also realizes that peace is possible only if as chairman he is able "to guide the meeting toward some iron-clad expression of meaning which by no conceivable ingenuity can be twisted into meaning anything that Arius and his friends could possibly dream of accepting" [p. 116]. Eventually, Constantine himself supplies the formula ("consubstantial," in Greek "Homoousios") which the council adopts as the Church's official teaching, anathematizing Arius and his followers.

The play's final section is devoted to Constantine the man. He brings tragedy upon himself when he executes his son Crispus because of his wife's claim that he had attempted to rape her. Too late, Constantine learns that his wife had joined a conspiracy whose next step would have been Constantine's death. Constantine answers in blood; he orders the death of all involved, exclaiming as he does so: "How fortunate that I was never baptised! I can damn myself with a clear conscience" [p. 179].

It is only after he has shed so much blood that Constantine comes to know Christ in yet another way: as Redeemer. He asks his mother if God ever spares man and learns from her the doctrine of *The Zeal of Thy House* and *The Just Vengeance:* "He did not spare Himself. The price is always paid . . . By the blood of the innocent. . . . Every man's innocence belongs to Christ, and Christ's to him. And innocence alone can pardon without injustice, because it has paid the price . . . there is no redemption except in the cross of Christ" [pp. 182–83]. But Constantine's actual baptism is saved for an epilog set 11 years in the future (337 A.D.). Constantine's final repentance and baptism are presented realistically, but their effect is made more powerful by the symbolic reappearance of the long dead King Coel, who reviews Constantine's life and achievements and shows that all before has led to this climactic moment—Constantine's salvation. The play ends with the recitation of the Apostles' Creed.

Sayers is more successful in her account of Constantine's journey to faith than in dealing with the conflict between Arianism and Catholicism or with the Council of Nicaea. The basic material of Constantine's life is exciting to begin with; characters like Constantine, Helena, and Togi (Constantine's servant) come alive; and Sayers's skill in constructing detective plots helps her work out reasonable connections between events. But while Sayers generally provides sufficient motivation for Constantine's movement from one stage of his relationship with Christ to the next, her juxtaposition of the scene in which Constantine sees his need for salvation with the scene depicting his baptism and death conceals rather than explains Constantine's 11-year deferral of his public acceptance of Christianity, and leads one to question the sincerity Constantine displays in the former scene.

The sections dealing with the theological controversy are more interesting to a general audience than might be expected; Sayers stresses the plots of two sides attempting to outsmart each other and sufficiently individualizes the characters that one can appreciate the clashes between Arius and Athanasius without understanding the differences between them or seeing what significance their differences can have. But ultimately the exact nature of the relationship of one Divine Person to another is so mysterious that it is hard for the audience to take more than an academic interest in what is taking place. Further, the characters are more reminiscent of attorneys arguing a point of law than of Faustus, William of Sens, the Airman, or Constantine, whose interactions with the Divine involve more than their intellects and reveal more fully the nature of the God Who is Love than do the formulae of philsophers and theologians.

Sayers's plays are more than Christmas pageants or Sunday school teaching aids. They are the work of a woman skilled in both dramaturgy and theology. Much remains to be written about such topics as the relationship between the methods Sayers utilizes in her novels and those she employs in her plays, and about her ability to write plays to be performed on the radio and in great cathedrals as well as on traditional stages. Nor has this essay said all that could be said about her theology. But what is most central to her plays from a religious perspective is that all five are Christocentric. The same Jesus whose birth is treated in *He*

That Should Come and whose divinity is one of the foci of *The Emperor Constantine* redeems Faustus, William of Sens, the Airman, and Constantine. Further, Redemption occurs in the same, orthodox way in every play: the protagonists recognize that they are not a law unto themselves, admit that they have violated God's law, and ask for forgiveness; God grants forgiveness, an action made possible because perfect Innocence—Christ—has destroyed humanity's guilt in His own death; the protagonist is united with God forever.

III: TRANSLATION

Dorothy L. Sayers as a Translator of *Le Roman de Tristan* and *La Chanson de Roland*

IN 1912, when she was 19, Dorothy L. Sayers went to Somerville as a scholar. She read French Language and Literature and, after working for three years, received first class Honours. While she was an undergraduate, certain aspects of medieval French literature aroused her interest and enthusiasm, particularly works written in or connected with Anglo-Norman.

The Final Honour School of Mediaeval and Modern Languages had been established at Oxford only in 1903. In Dorothy Sayers's time there was no tuition in French or any other modern language by specifically University teachers. There were the Taylorian Professor of Romance Languages, paid partly by private endowment, with a small financial contribution from the University, and two Taylorian Lecturers in French; and there were the tutors appointed by the colleges. Of the Taylorian Lecturers, the only one who could possibly have given her encouragement in her studies in medieval French was E. G. R. Waters of Keble, a young graduate not much older than herself, who had been appointed on a part-time basis in December 1911. She nowhere mentions him, and it is probable that her only teacher in this branch of her studies was Mildred K. Pope, her tutor at Somerville.

To generations of undergraduates Mildred Pope has been well known as the author of an intricate and fascinating volume called *From Latin to Modern French, with especial consideration of Anglo-Norman phonology and morphology*. She had been a tutor at Somerville since 1894. Thirty-four years later, in 1928, she was appointed University

Reader in French Philology. In 1934, after 40 years of service at Oxford, she was made first Visiting Professor and then Professor of French Language and Romance Philology at Manchester, which post she held until her second retirement in 1939. She died in September 1956 at the age of 84.

I remember her well in her last years, when we both used to attend the meetings of the Anglo-Norman Dictionary committee. She was a tall and dignified person, severe in feature, always dressed in black. She would enter the room ceremoniously on the arm of Professor Eugène Vinaver and be led to an armchair, into which she would settle herself with some care and no small relief. I myself had attended occasional lectures by Joseph Bédier, then a very old man, at the Collège de France and at University College, London, but I was filled with awe by this elderly scholar who had studied in the 1890s under Fritz Neumann in Heidelberg, and with Gaston Paris and Paul Meyer in Paris. By then her hearing was impaired, and this obviously hampered her. When addressed directly, or when she chose to make a comment, her face would light up with enthusiasm, and she was clearly a most sympathetic and lovable person. Dorothy Sayers obviously found her so, and gained great inspiration from her teaching. She is Miss Lydgate in *Gaudy Night*, Harriet Vane's former tutor, who is described with great affection.[1] *Gaudy Night* came out in November 1935, just after Mildred Pope's move from Oxford to Manchester. *From Latin to Modern French* had appeared the previous year. The typescript must have been extremely complicated, and in the preface the author thanks her printers, "who have borne with my inconsistencies and vagaries with exemplary patience." Dorothy Sayers was frequently in Oxford at this time, and was a guest speaker at the Somerville gaudy in 1934. While there, she must have watched Mildred Pope struggling with her galleys.[2] By then, she had herself produced 16 books, although none even approaching *From Latin to Modern French* in complexity, and she was familiar with all the problems of authorship. In *Gaudy Night*, Miss Lydgate is tutor in English, not French, and the subject of her book is lightly disguised, but otherwise the portrait is taken from life.

I have begun this talk with Mildred Pope because it was the work Dorothy Sayers did with her tutor at Somerville that inspired her to write parts of *Op. I*, and because, down the years, it was the memory of that work which led her to make her verse translations of the two Old French poems, *Tristan in Brittany* and *The Song of Roland*. These three works span her whole creative life. *Op. I*, published by Blackwell in 1916, was obviously her first book. *Tristan in Brittany* was brought out by Benn in 1929. *The Song of Roland*, in the Penguin Classics series, was her last work, for it was published in 1957, shortly before her death.

The copy of *Op. I* which I am using is inscribed to my wife Barbara Reynolds in Dorothy Sayers's handwriting: *Gemina Geminae d.d.d. Id. Jun. MCMLVII*, i.e., "To her twin-spirit her sister presented this as a gift and dedicated it on 13 June 1957," six months before Dorothy's sudden death on 17 December of that same year. The little book of 79 pages was published by Basil Blackwell in 1916, when she was in her first year as Modern Languages Mistress at the High School for Girls, Hull. It was No. 9 in the "Adventurers All: a series of young poets unknown to fame," price 2s. On the back page is printed: "The object of this Series is to remove from the work of young poets the reproach of insolvency. The Series will be confined to such work as would seem to deserve publicity. It is hoped that these Adventurers may justly claim the attention of those intellects which, in resisting the enervating influence of the novel, look for something of permanent value in the more arduous pursuit of poetry." It seems unlikely that Dorothy Sayers's share of the two shillings for which each copy was sold can have removed her work from "the reproach of insolvency"; but this her failure to resist "the enervating influence of the novel" was soon to do.

Op. I contains 37 lyrics, 12 of them grouped under the title *Lay* (to Oxford), 11, together with an introductory passage, in *The Last Castle*, and three in *The Elder Knight*. The rondeau which ends the collection, *Last morning in Oxford*, is dated "June 23rd, 1915." Three of the poems, *Lay* (to Oxford), Songs IV and V, and *The Elder Knight*, Poem III, contain references to Arthurian incidents and to Arthurian characters, Perceval, the Lady of the Lake, Merlin, Lancelot. One, called *Matter of Brittany*, which had already been published in *The Fritillary*, the magazine of the Oxford Women's Colleges, is an Arthurian pastiche in lyric verse, containing the lines:

> And first of all I'll tell the tale to you,
>   And you shall tell the next to me: . . .
> While your dim shadow moving on the wall
> Might be Sir Tristram's, as he harped in hall
> Before Iseult of Ireland, always true,
>   Or white Iseult of Brittany.[3]

Two of the other poems are taken wholly from the story of Tristan and Iseult, and they prove how warmly and directly Dorothy Sayers was inspired by her reading of the Tristan legends during her three years at Somerville. They are lyrics of intense feeling and great beauty, and I quote them in full. The first, Poem X in the *Lay* (to Oxford), gives the wounded Tristan's lament, as he lay dying in Brittany and waiting for the boat which might bring Queen Iseult back to him:

"Iseult, Iseult! day follows day
With weary feet; the bitter spray
Flies fitfully over the waterway.
        The gull's harsh crying
Is cruel as death. O far away
Are the years when we made holiday;
My hair and beard show very grey
In the bed where I am lying.

"All the wonderful songs of May
Roundel, madrigal, virelay,
I cannot remember them now to play,
        For yesternight I was trying
To bring them back, but the harp-strings fray,
And I only know that the songs were gay."
Thus and thus did Sir Tristram say
        In the hour that he was dying.[4]

The second, Song I in *The Last Castle*, entitled *War-time*, describes Iseult's answering anguish, as, far away in Cornwall, she looked out across the sea to where her lover lay:

The splendour of the year, no less
Is on thy loveliness,
The light in no less glory falls
On thy unchanging walls
Now, than in other days;
No sorrow can displace
The ordered beauty of thy face;
Yet thou dost watch the water-ways
For thy lost lovers, with a grave and panoplied distress;

Like Iseult looking over-sea
With wan face wearily
Under the coils of braided gold
Resplendent fold on fold,
And girded queenliwise
With jewels of rich price,
With vair, and scarlet of fine dyes,
But still with shadow-haunted eyes,
Straining to Tristram hard bested in far-off Brittany.[5]

For Dorothy Sayers *Tristan in Brittany* means the 10 fragments which, by a series of happy chances, we still possess of a long narrative poem in octosyllabic couplets called *Le roman de Tristan* and composed in the twelfth century by a poet who names himself twice as Thomas. I say which we still possess, but in effect all but two of these fragments have disappeared or been destroyed during the last 100 years. By good fortune we have reliable modern transcripts of the eight lost fragments. The two which still exist are in the Cambridge University Library and in the Bodleian Library in Oxford. When set in proper sequence, these 10 fragments, some of which overlap, make up to a poem of 3,144 lines, with many gaps. Of the author Thomas we know virtually nothing. From certain of his comments[6] and from the fact that of the 10 fragments all but one show strong traces of Anglo-Norman spelling and pronunciation, it is deduced that he lived in England and was an Anglo-Norman speaker. The date of his poem is difficult to establish. Thomas was certainly writing after 1155, for it can be proved that he used passages from *Le roman de Brut* by Robert Wace, which appeared in that year. He was certainly writing before Chrétien de Troyes composed his Arthurian romance *Cligés*, for in *Cligés* Chrétien shows debts to Thomas. The most recent suggestion of a date for *Cligés* is 1185-1187.[7] These extreme dates of 1155 and 1187 make it probable that Thomas wrote his poem before the *Tristan* of Béroul[8] and maybe before the lost Tristan of Chrétien de Troyes.[9]

In 1902-1905 Joseph Bédier brought out his edition of *Le roman de Tristan par Thomas, poème du XIIe siècle*, in two volumes in the *Société des Anciens Textes Français* series. It is the Bédier edition, both volumes, and those alone, which Dorothy Sayers used when she was writing *Tristan in Brittany*. There is no doubt about this. The most casual reading of *Tristan in Brittany* makes it clear. In her "Translator's Note" she writes:

> My most grateful thanks are due to M. Joseph Bédier, for the chivalrous kindness with which he has permitted me to make use of his edition of the poem, as well as for his noble work of reconstruction and interpretation.[10]

And again:

> From his great work (published in two volumes by the Société des Anciens Textes Français) I have, with his generous permission, prepared the brief prose sketch which links up the various fragments of the poem, so that English-speaking readers may get some sort of idea of the shape and proportions of Thomas's work as he originally wrote it.[11]

They were obviously in communication. In the first of his two volumes, Bédier printed the 3,144 extant lines of Thomas's poem, completed and woven together by his own prose passages, which are adapted from the five derivatives we possess, in Old Norse, German, English, Anglo-Norman, and Italian. He estimated that the original poem probably contained between 17,000 and 20,000 lines.[12] Bédier's second volume contains his vast critical apparatus. There seems little doubt that Dorothy Sayers worked over part at least of the 3,144 lines of Thomas's *Le roman de Tristan* in the Bédier edition with her tutor during her three years at Somerville, and that it was these supervisions by Mildred Pope which inspired her, while still an undergraduate, to write parts of *Op. I*, notably the two poems about Tristan and Iseult that I have quoted in full. She began *Tristan in Brittany* some time later,[13] after graduating at Oxford; but it seems probable that much of this work overlapped, at least, the two novels published in 1928.[14]

Tristan in Brittany, published in July 1929, was No. 15 in the series called Benn's Essex Library. It is a slim volume of 220 pages. It is dedicated to M.K.P., and in her "Translator's Note" Dorothy Sayers expresses her thanks "to Miss M. K. Pope of Somerville College, Oxford, who has carefully gone over the text to expunge mistranslations and obscurities."[15] To it is prefixed an enthusiastic but discursive and self-regarding introduction by George Saintsbury, one-time Professor of Rhetoric and English Literature in the University of Edinburgh, but by then in his eighty-fifth year. My wife remembers Dorothy Sayers saying that she was "very lucky to get him."

Le roman de Tristan is one of the great love stories of the world. What remains of Thomas's poem aroused the greatest possible admiration and enthusiasm in the mind of Dorothy Sayers, and this for a series of reasons that are not difficult to understand. In the 14 years between her leaving Oxford and the publication of *Tristan in Brittany* she had proved herself to be a fluent teller of tales, and Thomas's story, "the old, brutal incidents of the original Tristan tradition,"[16] was an immensely powerful piece of storytelling. As an example of the strength of the narrative line, I quote the incident of the ship with the black and white sails, the passage in which Tristan, married to Iseult of the White Hands, has in fulfillment of his promise to the woman he loves, refused to consummate the marriage. Now, dying of a wound far away in Brittany, he sends his brother-in-law Kaherdin to summon Queen Iseult to his bedside:

"I know not what her love is worth
If she desert me in my dearth,
And little her love profiteth
Save she me succour against death,
And love hath brought me little wealth
If she will help me not to health.
Kaherdin, I know not to say
How strongly for this boon I pray:
Do all thou canst and strive amain,
Greet for me many times Brangwain,
Show her how sore my anguish is:
Save God me help, I'll die of this,
I cannot live for very long
To feel such pain, such torment strong.
Think, friend, to do this happily
And swiftly to return to me,
For save thou come in little space,
Know, thou shalt no more see my face.
I give thee till the fortieth day;
And if thou do the thing I say,
So that Iseult comes home with you,
Take heed none knows it save we two.
Let not thy sister learn thereof,
Or have suspicion of our love:
Give out it is a cunning wife
Come from afar to save my life.
And thou shalt take my vessel fair,
And place a double sail in her:
One shall be black, the other white;
And if thou bring Iseult aright,
And if she come to heal my pain,
Sail with the white sail home again,
But if of Iseult thou shouldst lack
Sail hither with the sail of black.
Further to say I do not know;
May God our Saviour with thee go,
And bring thee safe and sound once more."[17]

The weeks pass. Kaherdin returns across the sea. Queen Iseult comes with him and, as his ship crosses the horizon, he hoists the white sail. Iseult of the White Hands has overheard Tristan's instructions to her brother. She tells her husband that the sail is black.

Amid this anguish and great strife
Before him comes Iseult his wife,

A cunning plot her mind within,
And saith: "Friend, here comes Kaherdin;
I've seen his ship come sailing free,
Scarce yet in sight, across the sea,
Yet well enough I saw, to know
It is his ship comes sailing so;
God grant such news he may bring in
That you at heart may comfort win!"
Then at that word Tristan upstart,
And cried to Iseult: "Fair, sweet heart,
Is that his ship, his, without fail?
Tell me, what colour is the sail?"
Then said Iseult: "In sooth, alack!
Know that the sail is all of black,
And hoist aloft, and high outspread
Because the wind is slack and dead."
Such bitter dole had Tristan then
As ne'er hath been, nor shall again,
So to the wall he turned his head:
"God save Iseult and me," he said,
"For if thou wilt not come to me,
Then I must die for love of thee;
I can no more, my life must end,
For thee I die, Iseult, sweet friend;
Thou hast no pity for my pain,
Yet by my death thy tears I'll gain;
Love, this makes me a little glad,
That thou for my death will be sad.
True love Iseult," three times he said,
And at the fourth time he was dead.[18]

The uncontrolled violence and the unremitting strength of the passion of Tristan and Iseult appealed to something strong and primitive that lay beneath Dorothy Sayers's scholarly intellect. "The fatal love of Tristan and Iseult," she writes, "is an obsorbing passion, before which every other consideration must give way, ..."[19] "There is a kind of desperate beauty in this mutual passion, faithful through years of sin and unfaith on both sides, and careless of lies and shifts and incredible dishonour."[20] Thomas's description of how, in King Mark's own bedroom, with the King gone out to hear matins, Tristan contrives to come to Iseult in the night, has been lost, but I quote Dorothy Sayers's word-for-word translation of Joseph Bédier's prose reconstruction:

One day, it chanced that King Mark had sent for the surgeon to bleed him, and both Iseult and Tristan were let blood also. And at night there were in the king's chamber only Iseult, Tristan, Brangwain and the evil dwarf, who had contrived a fresh plot to entrap the lovers.

Then Mark, counselled by the dwarf, bade Tristan put out all the lights. And when it was dark, the dwarf rose secretly and strewed flour upon the floor between Tristan's bed and the queen's. But the watchful Brangwain saw him, and warned Tristan.

In the middle of the night, the king rose, and called the dwarf to follow him, saying that he was going to hear matins. Then Tristan wondered how he might come to Iseult without leaving footmarks in the flour; and standing upon the edge of his bed he leapt with both feet together into the queen's bed. But with the exertion, the vein that had been bled opened again, and drenched the bed with blood. And when he had taken his pleasure with Iseult, Tristan leaped back into his own bed again.

When morning was come, the king returned. He looked at the floor, and saw no footmarks in the flour. But he saw the bed of Iseult stained with blood. He asked her how this was, and Iseult answered that her arm had bled where she had been let blood.

Then the king looked at Tristan's bed, and saw that it also was bloody, and his heart was filled with grief, for he knew that Iseult had lied to him.[21]

Thomas's *Tristan* had strong claims upon Dorothy Sayers other than its gripping narrative and its compelling portrayal of physical desire and remorseless passion. "Thomas," she writes, "is a thoughtful and competent psychologist."[22] She greatly admired the many passages in which the poet analyzes in depth the feelings of Tristan and Iseult for each other. "Unlike many poets of his day, he is not really interested in fights with giants, magical marvels and adventures by sea and land; he scrambles hurriedly over these incidents, to spread himself with loving care over long dialogues and monologues containing elaborate analysis of feelings, motives and problems of morality."[23] As an example I quote part of the long passage in which, in desperation, the exiled Tristan, who is about to marry Iseult of the White Hands, mediates upon his feelings for the Queen.

"How can man's will be ever moved
To have in hate what he has loved,
Or ever carry hate and ire
Thither, where he has set desire?
What he hath loved he cannot hate.
Natheless, he may withdraw him straight,
And turn away and far remove,
When he sees no good cause to love.
Both hate and love he ought to shun
If he should find good cause for none.
He that doth deeds of good report
Mingled with deeds of baser sort,
His nobler acts we ought to weigh
And never ill for ill repay.

The one the other so alloys,
The two things hang in counterpoise;
Not too much love, because of ill,
Nor, for good's sake, too much ill-will,
Since love is due to what is good,
But evil ought to be withstood.
For the good's sake, I will not hate,
Nor, for the evil, on her wait.
Because Iseult once loved me so,
And semblance of such joy did show,
I must not hate her now at all,
For anything that may befall.
But since she casts her love behind
I ought to put her from my mind,
Must neither love her any more,
Nor bear her any hate therefore;
But I will draw my heart away,
As she has done, if so I may,
And work and deed I will employ
To see if I can win me joy,
By that same deed in love's despite
Wherein with Mark she finds delight.

Dorothy Sayers loved what she saw, partly no doubt in her imagination, as Thomas's Englishness. "The care he takes to stress the power and importance of King Mark, making him king, not of Cornwall only, but of all England; and the glowing passage in which he sings the praise of London —'mult riche cité, meliur n'ad en cristienté'—make it probable that he was either an Englishman or at least attached to England by some very close link." Above all she loved the clear ring of his octosyllabic couplets. "Whoever he may have been, Thomas was a poet of very great gifts. His verse at its best has that rare singing quality which the romance-writers of the langue d'oïl seldom attained. It is on an altogether different plane from the pedestrian couplets of that prolific society novelist, Chrestien de Troyes, and sometimes achieves a really lyric level of stark and moving simplicity." This "stark and moving simplicity" we shall find again as we turn to her translation of *La chanson de Roland*.

In 1953 I prepared the index raisonné for Dorothy Sayers's *Introductory papers on Dante*, which Methuen published in 1954.[28] On 2 December of that year we began exchanging letters about her translation of *La chanson de Roland*, which was already moving on fast, for she was then at laisse 50, about one-sixth of the way through. The correspondence went on apace, sometimes in typescript, but more often in longhand, which means that for much of it I have her letters to me but no copies of my answers. At intervals she sent me long sections of her translation, with arrangements for us to meet and discuss outstanding problems.[29] On 23 August 1956 came the typescript of the whole poem, and soon afterwards that of the Introduction. On 21 June 1957 she sent me the page proofs of the entire volume. The book came out in September of that year. It has since sold over 50,000 copies.

As we have seen, *The Song of Roland* was Dorothy Sayers's last work, apart from those published after her death. Soon after leaving Somerville in 1915 she had begun a rhymed translation of the epic. In her lecture "The Translation of Verse," which she gave at Oxford in March 1957, she said: "Shortly after going down, I embarked on a translation of the *Song of Roland*, in the original metre, but in rhyme instead of assonance. I still have it. It is very bad. I completed the task much later—in assonance this time, and I hope with better results. It was nice to get something finished that had been lying about for forty years or so."[30] In her acknowledgments for *The Song of Roland* Dorothy Sayers wrote: "My first debt of gratitude is, of course, to my old tutor Mildred K. Pope, with whom I read the Roland at Oxford, and to whom I owe such Old French scholarship as I possess."[31] Once again, as for *Tristan in Brittany*, at the center of the enterprise sat the figure of Mildred Pope; and once again the edition which Dorothy Sayers was using was that of Joseph Bédier.[32] There is nothing extraordinary in this; indeed, it would be odd if it were not true; but it is interesting to note the neat repetition of events.

Dorothy Sayers had translated *Le roman de Tristan* into octosyllabic couplets, the verse-form of the original. In Ms. Digby 23 in the Bodleian Library, *La chanson de Roland* consists of 4,002 decasyllables divided into 291 laisses of irregular length, the lines of each laisse being linked by assonance. Dorothy Sayers again reproduced the verse-form of the original. She explained to the reader the scrupulous care with which she had preserved the masculine and feminine assonances, the tonic beat and the break at the caesura, and "the extreme rigidity of the end-stopped line."[33] To help herself she made free use of the variable tonic accent in the subject and object case of some proper names and place names. In her English she used a few deliberate archaisms. To the translation is prefixed, not a "Translator's Note" as for *Tristan in Brittany*, but a spirited Introduction of 43 pages, much of it devoted to an explanation of the military and social conventions of the eleventh century in Normandy. The first of the nine sections of this Introduction deals with "The Poem," and here Dorothy Sayers has many valuable points to make: the mysterious transformation of the unimportant historical event of 778 into "a vast epic of heroic proportions and strong ideological significance";[34] the transmission of the legend; the epic style; the characterization; the Christian message; the Baligant episode, and the alleged breaking of the unity of subject. Her enthusiasm for the French Middle Ages is fresh and compelling. "But the picture that remains most vividly with us is that of gay and unconquerable youth. No other epic hero strikes this note so ringingly," she writes of Roland:

> Through Gate of Spain Roland goes riding past,
> On Veillantif, his swiftly-running barb;
> Well it becomes him to go equipped in arms,
> Bravely he goes and tosses up his lance,
> High in the sky he lifts the lancehead far,
> A milk-white pennon is fixed upon the shaft,
> Whose falling fringes whip his hand on the haft.
> Nobly he bears him, with open face he laughs;
> And his companion behind him follows hard.
> The Frenchmen all acclaim him their strong guard.
> On Saracens he throws a haughty glance,
> But meek and mild upon the men of France,
> To whom he speaks out of a courteous heart—[35]

So he rides out, into that new-washed world of clear sun and glittering colour which we call the Middle Age (as though it were middle-aged), but which has perhaps a better right than the blown summer of the Renaissance to be called the Age of Re-birth. It is a world full of blood and death and naked brutality, but also of frank emotions, innocent simplicities, and abounding self-confidence—a world with which we have so utterly lost touch that we have fallen into using the words 'feudal' and 'mediaeval' as mere epithets for outer darkness. Anyone who sees gleams of brightness in that world is accused of romantic nostalgia for a Golden Age which never existed. But the figure of Roland stands there to give us the lie: he is the Young Age as that age saw itself.[36]

In the ninth section of the Introduction, she sets out some of the difficulties she had to face: the case forms, the marginal A.O.I. instructions, the threefold repetition, the mystery of the authorship, the flood of outlandish names.

There are, of course, many translations of *La chanson de Roland*, into French, into English, into other languages. In none of her difficulties can Dorothy Sayers have lacked help, or, failing that, fellow-feeling. Again, as with *Le roman de Tristan*, the narrative line of the story is magnificent. This is a tale of virile action, of battle scenes described with immense relish, of the triumph of good over evil, of Christian ethics "as näive and uncomplicated as might be found at any time in the simplest village church,"[37] of welling blood and gushing entrails. "Le style est simple, ferme, efficace," wrote Gaston Paris in 1887; "il ne manque par endroits ni de grandeur ni d'émotion; mais il est sans éclat, sans nuances, sans véritable poésie et sans aucune recherche d'effet; il n'est ni plat ni prolixe, comme celui de beaucoup de poèmes postérieurs, mais on peut dire qu'il est terne, monotone, quelque peu triste."[38] Lytton Strachey re-echoed Gaston Paris: "This great work — bleak, bare, gaunt, majestic —stands out, to the readers of today, like some huge mass of ancient granite on the far horizon of the literature of France."[39] "Of all the great poems in the world," wrote Dorothy Sayers in her turn, "the *Roland* is perhaps the starkest, not only in theme but in treatment. The style is wholly unadorned: direct statement, direct speech; there are scarcely any general reflections."[40] Stark; bleak, bare, gaunt, majestic; terne, monotone, quelque peu triste; sans éclat, sans nuances, sans véritable poésie. As a counterpart to Roland riding bravely past in the midst of the battle, I quote part of the description of his death, to see in what measure these adjectives apply:

Now Roland feels that he is at death's door;
Out of his ears the brain is running forth.
Now for his peers he prays God call them all,
And for himself St. Gabriel's aid implores;
Then in each hand he takes, lest shame befal,
His Olifant and Durendal his sword.
Far as a quarrel flies from a cross-bow drawn,
Toward land of Spain he goes, to a wide lawn,
And climbs a mound where grows a fair tree tall,
And marble stones beneath it stand by four.
Face downward there on the green grass he falls,
And swoons away for he is at death's door.[41]

Now Roland feels his time is at an end;
On the steep hill-side, toward Spain he's turned his head,
And with one hand he beats upon his breast;
Saith: "Mea culpa; Thy mercy, Lord, I beg
For all the sins, both the great and the less,
That e'er I did since first I drew my breath
Unto this day, when I'm struck down by death."
His right-hand glove he unto God extends;
Angels from Heaven now to his side descend.

The County Roland lay down beneath a pine;
To land of Spain he's turned him as he lies,

And many things begins to call to mind:
All the broad lands he conquered in his time,
And fairest France, and the men of his line,
And Charles his lord, who bred him from a child;
He cannot help but weep for them and sigh.
Yet of himself he is mindful betimes;
He beats his breast and on God's mercy cries:
"Father most true, in whom there is no lie,
Who didst from death St Lazarus make to rise,
And bring out Daniel safe from the lions' might,
Save Thou my soul from danger and despite
Of all the sins I did in all my life."
His right-hand glove he's tendered unto Christ,
And from his hand Gabriel accepts the sign.
Straightway his head upon his arm declines;
With folded hands he makes an end and dies.
God sent to him His Angel Cherubine,
And great St Michael of Peril-by-the-Tide;
St Gabriel too was with them at his side;
The County's soul they bear to Paradise.[42]

The story does not quite end there. At some time in 1956 I asked Dorothy Sayers to write for the periodical *Nottingham Mediaeval Studies*,[43] which I was then in the process of founding, an article "On translating *La chanson de Roland*" which was to be a companion-piece to her lecture "On translating the *Divina Commedia*." On 18 February 1957 she wrote: "I haven't forgotten about that article you want. I will try and do something about it when I have polished off a lecture which I have foolishly undertaken to deliver at Oxford on 'The Translation of Verse.' "[44] Shortly before her death on 17 December 1957, she sent me a longhand draft of the first 17 pages of this article. I have never had the heart to print them.

Barbara Reynolds

Dorothy L. Sayers, Interpreter of Dante

VIVUS PER ORA VIRUM, alive on men's lips, poets alive in their writings: this phrase perhaps best sums up what Dorothy L. Sayers set out to reveal in her interpretation of Dante.

The sense of exhilaration Dorothy Sayers obtained from Dante's narrative took her by surprise. Though she was well read in European literature and though she had specialized in medieval French at Oxford and had published a translation of the Old French romance of *Tristan* by Thomas, she had left unread the greatest medieval poet of all. It is true that Lord Peter Wimsey buys an early edition of Dante in her first detective novel, *Whose Body?*, and that the scene of exhumation in that same novel contains a comparison that suggests a knowledge of *Inferno*. But these two references have their origin in general knowledge such as any cultured person might have been expected to possess, particularly in the years soon after 1921, the sixth centenary of Dante's death.

Dorothy Sayers herself says that she first decided to read the *Commedia* only after reading Charles Williams's book, *The Figure of Beatrice:*

> While I still knew Dante chiefly by his repute, *The Figure of Beatrice* was published, and I read it—not because it was about Dante, but because it was by Charles Williams. It became immediately evident that here was an Image and here an Image-maker, with whom one had to reckon, and that the world had been right to call Dante a Great Poet—perhaps the greatest. But it was still some time before I made up my mind to tackle Dante in person. . . . It was only a sense of shame and a series of accidents that made me at last blow the dust from the three volumes of the Temple *Divine Comedy* which had originally belonged, I think, to my grandmother, and sit

123

down to *Inferno, Canto* I, resolute, but inwardly convinced that I should read perhaps ten cantos with conscientious and self-conscious interest and attention, and then—in the way these things happen—one day forget to go on.[1]

And she continues:

It did not happen that way. Coming to him as I did, for the first time, rather late in life, the impact of Dante *upon my unprepared mind* was not in the least what I had expected.[2]

The phrase "unprepared mind" requires qualification; that qualification is the subject of this article.

The Figure of Beatrice by Charles Williams was published in 1943. This, Dorothy Sayers tells us, was the initial spur, and Williams's insights were to become increasingly important to her as she progressed. She was nevertheless too independent-minded to be a mere sounding-board and the extent of Williams's influence has yet to be determined. It is clear, then, from her own words, *why* she began to read Dante: because *The Figure of Beatrice* impressed her. As to *when*, the answer is some time after 1943. The *circumstances* in which she began to read Dante are also known: they are mentioned in passing in the article from which the above quotation is taken and they are confirmed in a letter to me in which she says she has written to Professor Cesare Foligno:

I am offering him a pathetic picture of me clutching Dante to my heart in the air-raid shelter while the bombers roared overhead—and that is also quite, quite true.[3]

The mention of "doodle-bugs" in the article[4] clinches the matter: this was the nickname for Hitler's V-1's. The time was the summer of 1944.

There is probably an optimum moment for reading every great work. Sometimes we have the good fortune that our impulse to read coincides with it. In the case of Dorothy Sayers and Dante, the initial spur (Charles Williams) and the moment (1944, at the age of 51, in the midst of a bombardment in World War II) were of paramount significance.

The shock of surprise and delight which Dante's *Commedia* made upon her "unprepared mind" supplied the dynamism for all her future work:

Neither the world, nor the theologians, nor even Charles Williams had told me the one great, obvious, glaring fact about Dante Alighieri of Florence—that he was simply the most incomparable story-teller who ever set pen to paper. . . . When I say that Dante is a miraculous story-teller, I mean that he enthralled me with his story-telling.[5]

It is her professional assessment of Dante's skill as a storyteller, as a *writer* in that sense of the word, which constitutes one of her most original contributions to Dante criticism. In her Introduction to her translation of *Inferno* she stresses "the vigour of the story-telling and the swift movement of the verse."[6] Many of her subsequent lectures are a commentary upon these two features of Dante's art.

There are six aspects of Dante's technique to which her admiration is addressed. First, the immediacy of the beginning; this particularly delighted her:

> The poem does not start off like an epic, but with the disarming simplicity of a ballad or a romance or a fairy-tale. . . . Dante has acknowledged his debt to his classical masters; but there must be, I think, also an unacknowledged debt to the romance-writers of the northern tradition, whom, after all, he had read. They are apt to begin with this kind of abruptness. . . . [but whereas] they are rambling and diffuse, he is pregnant, articulated, and architectural.[7]

This second aspect of Dante's technique, the architectural structure, she found "in every way astonishing":

> Assuming that a story-teller is going to attempt this remarkable mixture of . . . satire, romance, autobiography, and adventure, what kind of form would one expect him, nowadays, to give it? The obvious answer is, the most elastic form possible, capable of the utmost variety . . . a broad treatment, without too much finicking detail and, above all, freedom from any suggestion of sameness or monotony.
>
> What Dante in fact does is to take the whole thing and cramp it, as though into a steel corset, into three sets of concentric and similar rings. . . . He need not have done it like that; the ten circular Heavens may have been imposed on him by Ptolemaic astronomy; the twenty-four circles of Hell and the ten ascents of Purgatory he went out of his way to invent. He liked it like that; he deliberately chose for his material the most rigid form conceivable, because he was a superb story-teller and knew, first, that you can hold disparate material much better together if you box it in so that it can't fall out; secondly, that you can hold people's attention more closely to the matter in hand if you focus it resolutely on some undeviating purpose (which is one reason why detective stories are popular . . .); finally, that if you want the reader not only to follow but to accept and believe a tale of marvels, you can do it best by the accumulation of precise and even prosaic detail.[8]

Expert herself in creating an illusory world in which her readers delightedly believe, she recognized such a power in Dante and could estimate its just technical value:

> We believe in the Inferno as we believe in Robinson Crusoe's island—because we have trudged on our own two feet from end to end of it.[9]

She recognized too

> that quality without which a tale may indeed take captive the imagination but can never root itself in the affections—the power to create a whole universe of breathing characters. It is often a fatal weakness in allegory to be populated by droves of frigid abstractions and perambulating labels; it is on his ability to endow these figures with the breath of life that the allegorist depends for his enduring persuasiveness. In this art Bunyan is, I suppose, acknowledged master, and it would be a bold man who should maintain that even Dante equalled or surpassed him. What one can say is that Dante, by an inspired tact in choosing his subject, side-stepped this besetting difficulty of allegory. His fable is such that he can fill his poem with real people who do not cease to be their earthly selves because they also typify everybody's sins and virtues.[10]

Among the characters whom Dante creates is the protagonist "Dante" himself. This brings us to the fifth aspect of his technique, concerning which Dorothy Sayers makes an original and characteristic observation:

> The danger [of the autobiographical method] is that the adventuring ego will become either a self-glorifying bore or else a characterless mirror for the reception of fleeting impressions. Dante avoids both these pitfalls by a brilliant technical expedient for which he has never (I think) been given sufficient credit. Except for those clearly indicated passages in which he allows his prophetic function, and not himself, to speak by his mouth, he has conceived his own character from start to finish in a consistent spirit of comedy. Seldom has an autobiographer presented the world with a less heroic picture of himself, or presented his own absurdities so lovably.[11]

For saying this, Dorothy Sayers was rebuked by several Dante scholars and she has been much misrepresented on this point. She does not seriously mean that Dante saw himself as funny; it is more subtle than that. With a self-awareness which links him endearingly to the reader, he sees himself as frail, doubting, bewildered and frightened:

> I do not think this is just a craftsman's device—I think it is, on the contrary, a sincere and touching humility. The fact remains that no other treatment of himself could have served his artistic ends so well.[12]

This is a penetrating observation and it took a professional writer to make it. "I reaffirm," she continues, "my (possibly revolutionary) opinion that Dante Alighieri is a very great comic artist indeed, with a range extending from Swift on the one hand to Jane Austen on the other; and that his comic spirit is an enormous asset to his story-telling."[13] Here again is the professional writer, aware from her own experience over many years, of the difficulties which confront the writer of fiction. As a craftsman she is fascinated to watch Dante handle certain situations. She applauds that trick of narration which "consists largely in the avoidance of unnecessary difficulties and imprudently-placed explanations."[14] In other words, good management; and this is the sixth aspect of Dante's technique which aroused her admiration. In letters to me she expressed delight at Dante's skill in this respect:

I am at present translating the Ante-Purgatory. It's quite true, as you say, that the "feel" of the time of day does most beautifully and subtly accompany the progress up the mountain. I hadn't noticed about the blinded Envious and the noonday sun, but very likely it was in the back of Milton's mind. He borrows more from Dante than most people realise. The thing that has been striking me is the incredible cleverness with which Dante uses his "time of day" to vary and make plausible all the stuff about his shadow; and how the two things help to establish one another. For instance, when he meets the Excommunicate, and they see the shadow "run from him to the rock": you see that *long* shadow and are reminded that it is still quite early. Then, he and Virgil climb up to the second Terrace and sit down looking back eastward, and he notices the sun "driving on his left hand, between them and Aquilo." They hear Belacqua speak, look round, and see a rock and go and investigate. The shades are *behind* the rock, resting *in the shadow*, and are so lazy that they don't look up till Dante is standing quite close to them, *in* the shadow, so that *his* shadow is invisible. Then he goes, and they (a little more awake by this time) look after him, and see his shadow on his left. Look how that places his direction again—he sits looking back east, and the *sun* is on his left; he walks on up the mountain, and the *shadow* is on his left: nothing's left vague—you *see* the change of direction.

But the masterpiece is the enormous ingenuity which delays Dante's recognition by Sordello and the people in the Valley of the Rulers. For the moment, he has rung almost every possible change on shadows and recognitions, and he's just had the scene of the *gioco della zara* and here comes another whole crowd of people and he doesn't want to repeat his effects. So what?

First, a chat with Virgil about the length of the journey, in the course of which Virgil observes with what seems to us rather clumsy circumlocution: "You will not get to the top before you have seen him return who is now so low behind the mountain *that you cast no shadow*." They meet Sordello; he greets his fellow Mantuan; long digression about Italy. Sordello says: "Who are you?" (in the plural). If Dante is explained *now*, there will be trouble when we get to the valley, because Sordello will come rushing along with the news, and the whole thing will blow up too soon and without dramatic effect. So Virgil says: "I am Virgil"—and that distracts Sordello from Dante altogether. The huge, great, obvious thing about Dante—the shadow—has been taken away quietly at the beginning of the previous canto; so it's quite natural that Sordello should devote himself entirely to Virgil and ignore his silent companion. So we go on, undisturbed, to the valley and hear all the gossip about the Rulers. Then we go down into the valley, where it's almost too dark to see at all, and Nino's recognition of Dante takes place quite quietly. Then Dante does reveal that he's alive, and Nino has only just time to call out to Conrad before in comes the serpent and down swoop the angels. After which we proceed quietly, Conrad does his stuff, Dante falls asleep, and we may imagine that Virgil gave all the necessary explanations about both of them to the assembled company. But it's so accomplished just as a bit of narrative technique, the way it's all broken up and held in suspense, and keyed to that almost unnoticeable little bit of periphrasis about

> colui che già si copre della costa,
> sì che i suoi raggi tu romper non fai.

It's absurd of me to go on telling you what you know perfectly well already. But when one sees a thing so exquisitely and neatly done, it's difficult not to say, "Hi! look at that!"[15]

Dorothy Sayers understood perfectly well that Dante's intention was not merely to entertain. He sought to impress on his readers certain truths. Those truths were more important than the story, but without the story they could not be adequately conveyed. Dorothy Sayers puts this in an unforgettable and moving way in her lecture "The Eighth Bolgia":

> . . . whether we like it or not, we have to acknowledge that the whole vast structure of Dante-study and Dante-criticism—theological, philosophical, historical, philological, poetical and what-not—beneath which the bookshelves of Christendom sag, is carried upon the sturdy bones of a narrative, as the reality of all the universe once endured to be carried upon a donkey.[16]

In this one telling image, she makes manifest the nature and function of Dante's allegory.

I think I have now discovered how Dorothy Sayers arrived at her exceptionally clear understanding of Dante's allegory and in particular at her unique awareness of the canto of Ulysses, the subject of "The Eighth Bolgia." It was not only that she understood the techniques of narrative fiction and the means by which a plot can be made to carry a theme. There is another, more profound explanation. Not long before she began to read Dante, she had explored in an original way the mysterious indivisibility of the three components of art: Idea, Energy, and Power. I refer to *The Mind of the Maker*, published in 1941, five years before she delivered the lecture in question,[17] and three years before she read Dante. In this book she examines an analogy between artistic creation and the Trinity: the Idea of a work may be seen as an image of the Father; the Energy, resulting in the Form, as an image of the Son Incarnate; the Power of a work to evoke response, as an image of the Holy Ghost. In the chapter entitled "Scalene Trinities," she discusses works which manifest various degrees of imbalance or irregularity in respect of their authors' trinity. Writers tend, she says, to be "father-ridden," "son-ridden," or "ghost-ridden."

Dorothy Sayers spoke of coming to Dante with an "unprepared mind." But the mind that had been exploring concepts such as these was, on the contrary, well prepared to respond to Dante's poem. In the *Commedia*, above all in Canto XXVI of *Inferno*, she must have recognized with delight a writer whose trinity was anything but scalene.

To the *selva oscura* of the interpretation of Dante's allegory she brought not an "unprepared mind," but an energy and clarity of mind and a talent for exposition possessed by few.[18] But she not only revealed the meaning, she asked if that meaning was true. She has described how she came to see the importance of this question:

> It was, I remember, while trying to write a helpful note upon the Giants who stand round the Well which forms the division between Malebolge and the frozen Lake of Cocytus at the bottom of the Pit, that I found myself asking the question: "Why in the world did Dante put the Giants just here?" And while looking for the answer, I quite suddenly saw a vision of the whole depth of the Abyss—perhaps as Dante saw it, but quite certainly as we can see it here and now: a single logical, coherent, and inevitable progress of corruption. . . . I saw the whole lay-out of Hell as something actual and contemporary; something that one can see by looking into one's self, or into the pages of tomorrow's newspaper, unaffected by its literary or dogmatic origins; and I recognized at the same moment that the judgment was true.[19]

She expresses surprise that it should so seldom occur to anybody to ask: "However Dante arrived at this infernal arrangement, is it sound, is it relevant, does it correspond to anything at all within the living experience of you and me *now*?"[20]

It is not in the nature of academic scholars to ask these questions; or at least, they seldom regard it as their academic function to comment on a text in the light of any answers they may have arrived at. Dorothy Sayers had the training of a scholar. She understood and used the tools of learning. She could marshal evidence, submit it to critical analysis, and state a conclusion in the approved manner. But she did more: she examined that conclusion in relation to her experience and view of life.

In her interpretation of the first of the nonliteral meanings of Dante's allegory (what is sometimes called the political meaning and what she has termed the Way of the City), Dorothy Sayers departed, and was well aware that she departed, from the main current of Dante commentary:

> Now, if we hold fast to the principle that, just as the *literal* meaning of the *Commedia* deals exclusively with the life of man after death, so the *allegorical* meanings deal exclusively with the life of man in *this* world, we shall be led at once to a very simple conclusion. We shall conclude that, where the political meaning is

concerned, the *Inferno* will show us the picture of a corrupt society—*Città Dolente*, the City of Destruction; the *Purgatorio* will show society engaged in purging off that corruption and returning to the ideal constitution which was God's intention for it when He created man as a "social animal"; the *Paradiso* will show the ideal constitution in working order—the *Civitas Dei*. And that, I believe, is precisely what they do show us. . . . But I am aware that in saying this I am setting up my opinion against that of many modern scholars who are far more learned and authoritative and better equipped than I am. These other writers all show a strong disinclination to carry the perfected social life on into the *Paradiso*. They are inclined to take it as far as the Earthly Paradise and abandon it there; and some of them suggest that Dante, despairing of, or changing his mind about the feasibility of, a perfected social life on earth, ended by preaching that man should withdraw from the world and find perfection either in a purely contemplative religious life, or only in Heaven after death.[21]

The central point of disagreement concerns the interpretation of the Earthly Paradise on the summit of Mount Purgatory. Many Dante scholars have taken it to be the symbol of the perfection of the Active Life, a point of arrival rather than a point of new departure. Dorothy Sayers finds the perfection of the Active Life not in the Earthly Paradise but in the Celestial:

. . . if anyone asks, "Where, in the *Commedia*, has Dante found room for that perfection of the Active Life, and the Perfect Universal State of which his earlier writings are so full?" the answer is: Here; not in the Earthly Paradise, but in the Heavenly, where all perfection is. Here, with its law-makers and lovers and poets, its scholars and warriors; here, with its civic decencies and family affections; here, with its order and empire and justice. This is the picture of the world as it might be; as, if the Kingdom come, please God it will be; as, in so far as the Kingdom is already here and at work, it already is; Here, not hereafter; though it shall be hereafter; and in the Heaven which knows neither before nor after, it eternally exists.[22]

The pattern of reiteration, here . . . here . . . here . . ., is a chime echoing an earlier work. As her exploration of the analogy of the Trinity and creative art in *The Mind of the Maker* had rendered Dorothy Sayers uniquely alert to the integration in the *Commedia* of Idea, Energy, and Power, so, to account for her perception of the relevance of the allegory of the *Commedia* to the enduring patterns of world affairs, I now refer to a work published in January 1940, but written during the first two or three months of World War II. The work is entitled *Begin Here*.

Of all the many books put out in wartime, this is surely one of the most remarkable and the most original. Since those days are long past, it might be thought to be out of date, but it is not; and for the purposes of understanding Dorothy Sayers as an interpreter of Dante it is strikingly relevant. Examining attempts to achieve world order in the past, she describes "the first structure of Western-Mediterranean-Christian civilisation," which she identifies as "theological." This lasted, "as the theoretical basis of European society, from the Christianization of Europe to the Reformation. . . . It referred all problems to one absolute Authority beyond history and beyond humanity; and as a scheme for the satisfactory fulfilment of the individual and the world-community it was and remains complete and unassailable."

Why then, she asks, did it break down?

> It did not fail because the theory itself collapsed when brought into contact with real life; but because the human instruments who had to carry it out failed to realise the implications of their own theory. The shards and fragments of this shattered structure—the most grandiose, the most universal and the most exact ever planned since the beginning of history—are with us to this day, and are built into every edifice of society erected upon its ruins.
>
> In this tremendous conception of human life, nothing was omitted or neglected; nothing was too great or small for inclusion. It embraced the world eternal as well as the world of time; it provided minutely for the most trifling acts of daily life as well as for the rule of empires, and it regulated all human activities alike by the same universal law. . . .
>
> Freedom was understood . . . in a . . . philosophical sense: the freedom to be true to man's real nature . . . As a stone, left free to follow its own natural law, falls to the ground, so the spirit of man, made free to follow its own natural law, flies to God.

If we had not her own word for it to the contrary, we might be forgiven for deducing that she had Dante's *Purgatorio* Canto VI in mind, or at least his strictures upon Boniface VIII, when she wrote:

> The Christian world-state invoked a Divine authority, but how was that authority to be exerted? . . . The rulers of the Church put themselves in a strong financial position, and they availed themselves of the power of the temporal arm. Possibly they would have done better to abide by their spiritual weapons and trust that God would work His purpose out in His own way . . . the temporal arm dragged the dignitaries of the Church into the tangle of political intrigue and subjected the Divine authority to worldly expediency, so that the Pope frequently appeared, less as a supreme head, under God, of a world-state than as one prince struggling, among a crowd of his equals, for the possession of political advantage.

No mind could have been better prepared for the coming encounter with Dante. She had no intention then of reading him. The sequence of events is as follows: war is declared on 3 September 1939; she at once puts her thoughts—the fruit of reading and thinking about the past in the light of Christianity—at the disposal of her fellow-countrymen; in 1941 she publishes her work on the Trinity of creation, *The Mind of the Maker;* in 1943, Charles Williams's book, *The Figure of Beatrice*, is published and she reads it; this makes her resolve to read Dante but some months go by before she does so. We now, from our point of perspective, can see into her future. We move on, along the line of time, to the summer of 1944; we place her in our minds in the air-raid shelter, physically in the very midst of destructive forces, and bring her face to face with Dante. It was a moment of intersection in her life: her intellect, her reading, had reached a peak of maturity; she had been thinking thoughts and contemplating concepts which belonged to the same universe as Dante's; it was a moment of crisis for her country, for the Western world, and for Christendom.

Barbara J. Dunlap

Through a Dark Wood of Criticism:
The Rationale and Reception of Dorothy L. Sayers's
Translation of Dante

IN 1941 Dorothy L. Sayers published *The Mind of the Maker,* in which she drew striking analogies between the creative process and the concept of the Trinity. Her work on Dante—both the translation and the several essays which resulted from it—reveal her as a craftsman intent on manifesting the mind and art of the maker of the *Commedia.* How well did she suceed? Sayers's version of the *Inferno* and *Purgatorio* has been criticized for insisting that Dante's mind had a humorous cast. While the question of his humorous intent probably cannot be resolved on this side of the grave, a look at the history of Dante in English translation will suggest why such a view commended itself to her own basically humorous cast of mind. A second major criticism of her version has been that in choosing to use Dante's own terza rima (a not uncommon choice among previous translators) she locked herself into a verse form incompatible with poetic success in the English language. An examination of her theory of verse translation will explain why terza rima had to be her inevitable choice. Quotation from letters she wrote while engaged on this project will reveal that Dorothy L. Sayers was a truly critical translator. She both questioned the possible meanings and implications of Dante's own choice of words, and scrutinized the choices of past translators and commentators. Finally, a look at the informed critical reception of her *Hell* and *Purgatory* (as she titled them) should help dispel any notion that her version was scoffingly received because of her past career as a detective novelist. Sayers's translation received both great acclaim and acid criticism, as have other translations whether in verse or prose.

The history of Dante in English goes back to Chaucer, who wrote two passages in close imitation of lines in the *Inferno* and *Paradiso,* and although the *Commedia* continued to have some English readers, it was *not* among the works of Italian literature that inspired Tudor translators. A few scattered passages were translated but not published in the seventeenth and eighteenth centuries, including one of the Count Ugolino episode by Thomas Gray, and a complete translation in heroic couplets, now lost, was left by William Huggins at his death in 1761.[1] The first published version of Dante in English did not appear until 1782, when Charles Rogers published his blank-verse version of the *Inferno.*[2] The Reverend Henry Francis Cary published his translation between 1805 and 1814. Coleridge's discussion of Dante in his lectures on Gothic literature and art in 1818 helped advance interest in Dante and in Cary's translation.[3] From the time of Rogers's work to 1962, when the Sayers/Reynolds version of the *Paradiso* appeared, 82 translations into English of one or more books of the *Commedia* had appeared. Of these, 31 were in terza rima or some modification thereof. Other modes of translation have included prose, blank verse, rhymed six-line stanzas, rhymed quatrains, irregular and heroic couplets, blank tercets, rhymed nine-line stanzas, Marvellian stanzas (using the four-line meter of the poet's "An Horatian Ode Upon Cromwell's Return from Ireland"—hendesyllabic blank tercets), unrhymed amphibractic tetrameter tercets, rhymed decasyllabic verse and unrhymed hendesyllabic verse.

Behind this welter of forms lie various theories of the aim and method of the translation process. Rogers and Henry Boyd, influenced by the neoclassical canons of taste, sought to renovate the "Gothick" of Dante into something more seemly;[4] they not only changed his vivid, often concrete verse into ponderous abstractions, but interpolated explanations and allusions of their own. In *INFERNO,* for example, Dante is humanly curious to hear the stories of the damned and sometimes has to be reprimanded by Vergil for vulgarity. The pity he feels for Paolo and Francesca causes him to swoon, but in Boyd's version Dante sententiously offers an excuse for wishing to hear the stories of Francesca and others:

> Could aught the captive souls persuade
> To tell the trains for their seductions laid,

Millions might shun their fate, by
Heav'n inspired.

And so on. At the same time that Rogers and Boyd were attempting to
turn Dante into a neoclassical poet, the purveyors of the Gothic taste,
both writers and artists, seized eagerly on the story of Count Ugolino,
far outdistancing Dante. Their descriptions of "clotted blood" and
"mangled hair" made explicit what Dante had merely suggested; and
his suggestiveness causes the greater *frisson*.[5] The succeeding generation of Romantic translators rejected this attempt to remodel Dante.
Their aim was to subdue their age and individual personalities to the
original and "mirror the aesthetic qualities of their model."[6] The
barrier to bringing off the "mirror trick" in translation was the fact that
terza rima was not a poetic form which had found acceptance in English
poetry, ostensibly because of the shortage of rhyme words in English as
compared to Italian. Various modifications were experimented with.
Byron objected to Cary's use of blank verse, and his own version of the
story of Paola and Francesca in terza rima is far more a direct translation than Cary's; but then Byron did not sustain his efforts.[7] Cary's
work, in Sayers's words, "for the first time offered to the English reader
a translation which was at once complete, readable, accurate, and
supplied with a sufficiency of helpful notes." She remarks against his
detractors that he "deserves all honour as the man who made the whole
English people aware not merely of Dante's existence, but of his poetic
power and importance."[8]

The Romantic translators tended to dwell on the religious and lyric
strains in Dante, and viewed their role as re-creative. Victorian translators, on the whole, concentrated on substance rather than form and
produced prose paraphrases and versions in several of the meters previously mentioned. Their translations stressed accuracy over beauty.
These literalists included John A. Carlyle (younger brother of Thomas),
William Michael Rossetti, Henry Wadsworth Longfellow and Charles
Eliot Norton. Norton was acutely aware that not even the most faithful
literal rendering could convey the connotative associations words had in
the original. He contended also that when there is an obscurity in Dante,
it is frequently in the rhyme word; even Dante's mastery of the resources
of the Italian language forced him to "exact from words such service as
they did not naturally render."[9] Moreover, unlike most Victorian translators, he refused to accept the "form/content" dichotomy of poetry.[10]
The great achievement of the literalist Victorian translators was to pass

on a heritage of respect for the text and for the goal of accuracy to the translators of this century.

Although he made no translation himself, T. S. Eliot's writings on Dante had wide influence. His admiration for Dante's precise but evocative language and its application in "clear visual images" was not new, but Eliot was original in his stress on the formal qualities of Dante's art over his content.[11] While twentieth-century translators—Binyon, Bickersteth, Hows, Bergin, Ciardi—are eclectic in their approaches, they all tend to stress accuracy, the unadorned style and vividness in their statements of aims. The translators realize the impossibility of reproducing Dante, or any other poet of the past, in the "spirit of his age," and are wary of claiming to have captured the spirit of the present age in their work. They aim to reproduce the effect the poem had on *them*. In this aim, Dorothy Sayers concurs. She considered impossible Arnold's suggestion that the translator of a "classic" or "period" poet should try to produce "upon the best scholars the same effect which the original produces in them," as *no* translation can ever be satisfactory to such scholars, and translations are intended for persons who cannot read the original with ease.[12] She wrote, "I believe that the only thing a translator can hope to produce, or should aim at reproducing, is the effect of the original upon *himself.*" Competency in the language and a knowledge of the period are indispensable requirements if this "impression" is to have any validity. Each generation feels a poet's greatness differently and praises him for qualities other generations will neglect or scorn: "Just as no translator can escape from his own personality neither can he escape from the habit of mind of his own contemporaries."[13]

Whatever else Sayers's translation may or may not succeed in doing, it *does* reproduce the "effect of the original" upon her. She wrote of her first encounter, "I can remember nothing like it since I read *The Three Musketeers* at the age of thirteen." She was enthralled by Dante the storyteller and by her discovery that he was "a very great comic writer."[14] She was delighted when, as World War II was ending, the opportunity was offered by Dr. E. V. Rieu to "indulge" herself in translating the *Commedia* for the ambitious Penguin Classics series. She was determined that her version should convey Dante's speed and skill as a narrator as well as his humor. Accuracy would be assured by using his own verse form, a point to which I will return. In her view, previous translators had failed to communicate Dante's frequent raciness and the "punch" of his verse. Even more serious was their collective fault of having "hopelessly obscured" his humor, and his "charming self-mockery [which] has no parallel that I know of outside the pages of Jane Austen."[15] In a letter written while working on the *Inferno,* Sayers declared, "He is so lively and they [other commentators and translators] make him so stiff and portentous. . . . I like his personality—he *isn't* all grim and sour; he's humourous and charming—though I admit he didn't suffer fools gladly. But, after all, twenty years of being a refugee and evacuee are apt to try the temper—as we all ought to know by this time."[16] The wish to communicate this vision of Dante, and to append to the translation commentaries which would make the theological and historical backgrounds clear and relevant for the uninstructed reader were the rationales behind the Penguin version.

Sayers's commentaries and essays are frequently concerned to disabuse her readers of the notion that the *Commedia* is "permeated" by "unmitigated Grimth." This view arises from the twentieth-century prejudice that religion should be merely soothing. Moreover, modern readers' minds have been so contaminated by journalism that they are almost incapable of reading a long poem as a connected whole, and Dante's humor is evident not so much in lines and episodes as in a "comic attitude, a diffused spirit of high comedy permeating the whole tone." This attitude springs from the "characterization (particularly where Dante's own self-portrait is concerned) and the satiric intention."[17] As the poem affects her so strongly in this way, her writings on Dante are full of examples in which she is at great pains to point out how the humor—designed to evoke "a soft chuckle of inward delight"— springs out of the context. One example occurs in *Inferno* III, 72–75, where Dante and Vergil are approaching the River Acheron:

> "Maestro, or mi concedi
> Ch'io sappia quali sono e qual costume
> le fa di trapassar parer si pronte,
> com'io discerno per lo fioco lume."

> "Sir," said I, "pray tell
> Who these are, what their custom, why they seem
> So eager to pass over and be gone—
> If I may trust my sight in this pale gleam."

Dante's "cramming of two or three questions within as many lines, and . . . final confession that the talker can't really see the people he is talking about, stands for a whole spate of excited chatter that would do credit to Miss Bates. . . ."[18]

Sayers acknowledged that Dante is often grim, but also frequently found him to be "bubbling over with ecstasy."[19] She did some bubbling of her own. In the midst of working out a problem presented by the text she could write, "Dear Dante! What a lot of fun he gives us to be sure!"[20] This joyfulness, yoked to a sensitive ear for metrics, a refusal to accept mechanically the received translations of difficult phrases, and her gift for lucid and lively commentary inform her translation.

In putting Dante into English, Dorothy L. Sayers was constantly concerned to render image and tone accurately. She believed Dante's own terza rima to be the only proper vehicle for a translation, and disavowed the cliche that a prose translation is necessarily more faithful than one in verse. Rhyme, she counters, can be an aid to accuracy as it forces the translator to penetrate deeply into the meaning of a passage rather than merely to transcribe words "without regard to their original sense."[21] Blank verse shares this disability and is fatally "easy to write badly."[22] Sayers cast aside objections that English does not offer sufficient rhymes to make terza rima practicable by proclaiming it a less exacting form in that respect than the Spenserian stanza. The choice of any other stanza form "involves the placing of stanza-breaks at places where he [Dante] did not choose to place them," and thus demolishes his tightly woven verbal and intellectual structure."[23]

An even stronger argument to her own mind for verse translation is her belief that "for the verse translator with the bug in his veins, prose translation lacks all the fun of the game." Certain rules must be observed if the game is to be well played. If the translator's language possesses a meter exactly or nearly equivalent to that of the original, that meter *must* be used. The original stanza form must be used, and although tonic stresses and rhymes may not fall upon the same words as in the original, they "should perform their task of distributing the emphasis in a manner corresponding to the original." Meter, rhyme, and stanza-form serve to "paragraph" a long poem, and its shape is distorted or lost by a translator who has chosen badly in these matters.[24]

For Sayers every good translation involves the making of choices and, in some cases, the sacrifice of one quality of the original in order to retain another more important *in a particular passage*. Of the features which cannot be sacrificed, the first is accuracy.[25] The most damaging kind of inaccuracy is not mere mistranslation but "the failure to render precisely the point of a simile or image." Such errors too often go unnoticed by critics. Readability is the second important factor, as a too crabbed translation will repel the reader. Dorothy Sayers believed that disagreements about tone and style were at the core of disagreements over translations. While writers such as Milton and Ariosto have an unmistakable tone and style, generations have disagreed about the tone and style of Dante and Homer. Moreover, a poet may vary the tone within a poem, even within a verse paragraph, and it is easier to make the tonal transition in verse, where a quiet line may serve as a bridge. Finally, the verse translator must consider the question of emphasis and decide "what aspect of any passage is the important one and which words have, consequently, to be brought to the rhyme and stress point in order to get this emphasis right."

Dorothy Sayers's version of Dante illustrated her theories. She was eager to have a sounding-board for her work as it progressed, and in C. Wilfred Scott-Giles she found "the very audience I want—one who will compare my attempts, not with Dante himself . . . but with other translators to see whether I have done any better."[26] Scott-Giles, a Royal Herald who had helped design and draw the arms of the Wimsey family in the 1930s, was now pressed into service to draw the maps and illustrations for this translation of the *Commedia.*

Sayers frequently submitted a very rough sketch of a desired illustration to Scott-Giles, and their discussions toward a final version were based on a close reading of the text. While keen to get visual details correct, she insisted that the exact dimensions of Dante's Hell were unimportant because it was a "vision."[27] Sayers believed the maps and illustrations to be vitally important for an understanding of the geography of Hell, Purgatory and Heaven and of Dante's movements through these three regions. She coaxed and persuaded Penguins into allowing more space and money for the *Inferno* than they had first allotted. Originally projected at about 250 pages, the final book contained 345 pages.[28] She not only translated the poem, but provided a long introduction, commentaries on each canto, and glossaries of proper names. In May 1946 she wrote:

> Why I ever undertook to *edit* this blooming translation I can't think. Not only does one need to be intelligent about Aristotelian philosophy, Scholastic theology, medieval Italian history, classical mythology, political theory; and Ptolemaic astronomy—but also about falconry, medieval painting, witchcraft and other trifles, all with their own technical pitfalls!
> Oh dear! Well, after all it's great fun.[29]

She said this of the *Inferno,* but commented in 1952 of her notes on the *Purgatorio*:

They are *much* harder work than the *Inferno* —so many biographies of obscure
mediaeval people, and such loads and loads of clotted scholastic theology to elucidate
and make palatable.[30]

Dorothy Sayers revelled in this work. The same curiosity and penetrating intelligence that had led her to master campanology in *The Nine
Tailors,* "Bradshawism" in *Five Red Herrings,* and the theological
complexities of the fourth century in *The Emperor Constantine* led her
on from commentator to commentator. She did not do original research
for her notes, but carefully weighed conflicting views, backed up her
choices in the notes, and if she could not resolve a question in her own
mind, sought expert advice.

Let us descend now to the Nether Hell of Cantoes XVIII-XXX of the
Inferno, to the arrangement of which Sayers devoted much thought.
The eighth circle of Hell is divided into 10 concentric trenches or
Bowges, each representing one of the "sins of the wolf." A keenly
observant reader, who was determined to make her own readers feel
the excitement of the poem by thoroughly visualizing it, she noted in
a letter,

> In Hell he [Dante] and Vergil always turn to the left (except once, exceptionally in
> Canto X). Clearly it is much better that, as they go along, they should meet and see the
> faces of the spirits nearest to them. Therefore these spirits *must* be going round on the
> right side of the ditch. Then D. and V. can go up over the bridge and look down at the
> people coming the opposite way because, as Vergil says: "You could not see them
> from the bank, since they were going in the same direction as ourselves."[31]

The Bowges are navigated by a series of bridges beginning at the Great
Barrier and meeting at the Well in the center. Sayers filled many sheets
of paper in writing to Scott-Giles about their number and the point at
which they are broken. With characteristic penetration and insight (and a
clue from Maria Rossetti's *Shadow of Dante,* the knowledge of which is
an indication of how wide she cast her net in searching commentaries)
she worked it out. Maria Rossetti had determined that all the bridges
over Bowge six were broken. Sayers does not merely leave it there,
because she passionately believed that in the *Commedia* even the
smallest detail tells. In Canto XXI the demon Belzecue tells the poets,
"Go in by the bank—near at hand is another spur which forms a path,"
and then says to his Demons, " 'See this pair safe *as far as the crag which
crosses the ditches unbroken.'* Whereupon all the demons exchange
dirty and sinister looks. The point is, I think, that there is *no such*

bridge, and Malacoda's [Belzecue's] 'safe-conduct' is no safe conduct at all. And that is why Vergil is so angry (in Canto XXIII) at having been hoodwinked by Malacoda."[32]

In Canto X Dante meets among the burning tombs the Ghibelline Farinata degli Uberti, whom Sayers describes as "Dante's first great image of pride—the first image of that dark, Satanic facade of nobility that also persuades us to be of the devil's party."[33] Vergil can read Dante's thoughts and urges him to speak to Farinata, but cautions, "In thy speech precision is what's wanted" [X, 39]. Sayers constantly strove for precision in her rendering of Dante's intellectual images, and also of his simplest physical image. In Circle six, the circle of the burning tombs, she asks, What kind of a tomb? How large? Rather large, as several persons seem to occupy it. Not an obelisk, as Dante specifies that the lid was raised.[34] In Canto XI, the two poets take refuge behind one of the tombs or *vaults*—the word she settled on as comprehending various kinds of tombs and monuments which can contain the dead. She discovered that commentators disagreed as to whether the Italian word *coperchio* actually means the "lid" of the said monument, tomb or vault.

Did they take shelter behind the upturned lid or behind the body of the tomb? (and does it matter a hoot one way or the other?) In view of the fact that the whole thing was white hot, I should think that either would be a pretty unpleasant neighbor. Possibly the lid was cooler than the tomb, and this would be an argument in its favor. But it encumbers the line horribly, so I propose not to bother, but merely to say:

. . . and for a screen were forced to shrink

Behind a massive { tomb } where, plain to view
      { vault }

Stood writ, etc. [XI, 6–8]

The Italian reads:

Ci raccostammo dietro ad un coperchio
d'un grande avello, o 'io vidi una scritta
che diceva. . . .

The correspondence demonstrates her refusal to accept a received reading unless her own understanding is convinced by it. She wrote:

I have—stupidly—followed other commentators in describing the sinners in Bowge eight as "givers of 'Fraudulent Counsel.' " Thinking it over, I believe that is a little misleading—it sounds as though they were deceiving the people to whom they gave the counsel. The right title is, I think, "Counsellors of Fraud"—i.e. they did not deceive the people whom they counselled, but counselled *them* to deceive others— the point is subtle, but it seems important.[35]

It was so important to her that the lettering on the already completed diagram of the Bowges had to be changed to reflect this better understanding. The inhabitants of this Bowge include Ulysses and Diomede, the "crafty" Ulysses being, of course, he who advised the stratagem of the wooden horse—a perfect example of a counsel of fraud. Dante, Sayers noted, describes this Bowge as the "thieves fire" [XXVII, 128], which she interprets as meaning that its inhabitants have counselled the taking of other men's property and thus stolen the integrity of those who listened to them.[36]

It is a temptation to extract quotations from Sayers's letters; they sparkle with the delight she took in her work and in the odd bypaths of speculation to which it led her: "I don't know, whether, strictly speaking, Demons require public conveniences. . . ."[37] She liked to castigate her own artistic abilities when she sent rough sketches to Scott-Giles: "Shortage of wings is due merely to my inefficient draughtsmanship. I couldn't manage all that amount of bat's trimmings. . . . Also I omitted to draw him furry—fur not being my strong point." But along with the fun goes her usual care for the esoteric, in this case, a fine point in angelology. "There were quite certainly six wings, because Satan was a fallen cherub. . .,"[38] but his wings have been transformed into those of a bat.

One way in which Sayers coped with the demanding terza rima was to allow herself the "license which English poetic tradition allows in the way of half rhymes . . ., identical, and (if necessary) eccentric rhyme."[39] In difficult passages she also took refuge, as she had with "vault," in words which could summon up varied impressions. This practice, and the addition of a noun or epithet to make an image more vivid in English, a practice she defended in "The Translation of Verse,"[40] are all exemplified in her translation of Canto XXXIV, 46–68. Satan is being described and the Italian reads:

Sotto ciasun uscivan due grand'ali
quanto si conveniva a tanto uccello:
vele di mar non vid'io mai cotali.

A bare prose translation gives:

> Under each shoulder came out two great wings, as well suited such a bird; I never saw
> such on the sea.

Here is Miss Sayers:

> From under each spring two great wings that *well*
> Befitted such a *monstrous* bird as that;
> I ne'er saw *ship* with such a spread *of sail*.

The italicized words are her additions. She has extended the implications of size in the "quanto/tanto" construction and conveyed both the
immensity and quality of Satan by the adjective "monstrous."

While still immersed in details of the *Inferno*, Sayers began "brood-
ing over Purgatory." She felt that all previous illustrations and diagrams
were "hideous and preposterous." She longed for those that would give
"something of the feel of that strange, solitary island, going up to an
impossible height," or at the very least, "something a little more ethereal
than the usual bit of garden rock work is indicated." The great height of
the Mount Purgatory she recognized as a difficulty in making the illustration. [41] The drawing which appears with her translation looks neither like
a "factory chimney" nor an "inverted ice-cream cornet," and, although a
linecut, skillfully conveys the icy nature of the Mount. Only six diagrams were needed, and these were produced with great ingenuity,
especially the Universal Clock, which, when cut out, pasted and attached as indicated, permits the reader to see simultaneously the times
on Mount Purgatory, Jerusalem, Rome, the Ganges, and Morocco.

In the Introduction to his 1891 prose rendering of the *Inferno*,
Charles Eliot Norton had admonished, "It is to be remembered that the
familiar use and subtle associations which give to words their full
meaning are never absolutely the same in two languages." [42] Sayers was
acutely aware of this fact when she was working on Canto XV of the
Purgatorio, which includes Vergil's explanation of the "doctrine of
the increase of spiritual goods by sharing of them" [*Purg.* XV, 52; *et
seq.*]. English gives a double sense to the plural of the word good. Dante
used "i primi ben" and "i secondi" —"meaning no doubt various sorts of
good or goods, —he also uses the singular in the same sense." In Canto
XV, 61–63, he uses the singular where the sense calls for the plural
because he is talking about "how 'ben' can be increased by being shared

by several people. . . ." This example, which Sayers called "tire-some,"[43] may be trivial but illustrates the care she took to convey Dante's sense. Here is the Italian,

> "Com'esser puote che un ben distributo
> i piú posseditor facci piu ricchi
> di sè, che sè da pochi e posseduto?"

and her translation:

> "How can it be that when a greater throng
> Divides the goods, there is more wealth for each
> Than if a few possessed them all along?"

In "The Worth of the Work," the "Postscript" to her book on the creative process, Sayers ventured that ideally work of all kind should be "in itself a sacrament and manifestation of man's creative energy."[44] A work of art, especially, "must be measured by the standard of eternity. . . ." She declared in this 1942 essay that "the activity of creation is a primary human need." Verse translation in the demanding mode of terza rima offered her a tremendous artistic challenge; honoring Dante as she did, she became possessed by the need not to dishonor him by unworthy work. How well did she succeed in this task she so eagerly embraced in 1943? Is there worth in the work?

In the same essay she also maintained, "It is a short and sordid view of life that will do injury to the work in the kind hope of satisfying a public demand."[45] Her unfriendliest critics accused her of doing just this; others found the work excellent in parts but generally unsatisfying.[46] If there was some feeling she had overstressed Dante's humor, there was even more lamenting over her choice of terza rima rather than blank verse or blank tercets. Critics were almost unanimous in praising the layout of the Penguin volumes and the diagrams. Her introductions and notes came in for general praise for their lucid exposition of the allegorical mode and of the political and theological materials necessary for an intelligent understanding of the poem. The Introduction to the *Purgatorio* was sometimes censured for its patronizing tone (there *are* passages which sound as if Uncle Peter was laying out Lord St. George for his failings) and Professor Charles Singleton, then of Harvard, himself an editor of Dante, regretted her adherence to Charles Williams's view of Dante as the poet of the Affirmative Way because, in his view, Williams had done "more to obscure than to illuminate Dante."[47]

With the inaccuracy typical of many passages in *Such A Strange Lady*, [48] Janet Hitchman describes Dorothy Sayers's translation of the *Inferno* as having met with a "storm of disapproval" upon its publication. Evidently there were some snide glances at her past history as a detective story writer in the popular press and she reacted emotionally to them, as she did whenever her theological or dramatic writings were reviewed in the same style, but the "storm" seems to have been no more real a phenomenon than the "booming silence" Ms. Hitchman describes as greeting the *Purgatorio* in 1955. The academic reviews were slow to come in, but when they did, they were, in the main, no unkinder to Sayers than to other contemporary translators of Dante. In general, her work was reviewed, as so many books of all kinds were and are, in terms of the reviewers' prejudices. In the *serious* notices I have found, Dorothy Sayers was not, contrary to the impression given by Janet Hitchman, mocked or castigated as a thriller writer masquerading as a Danteist; but no doubt reviewers' feelings about her other work may have colored their reactions, even if they did not allude to Lord Peter or *The Man Born to Be King*.

The most perceptive of the reviewers of the *Inferno* volume was the "C.F." (perhaps the scholar Cesare Foligno) who contributed a lengthy notice in Italian to *Studi Danteschi*. He paid homage to her "solida preparazione accademica a Oxford," something she always stressed about herself, and correctly associated her with T. S. Eliot, C. S. Lewis, and Charles Williams in matters Dantean. The reviewer sympathized with the desire of the Penguin Classics to "togliere la patina arcaica da opere del passato." Unlike other reviewers, he saw no fault in translators' "padding" a line with phrases of their own to fill out the syllables it needed. Since English is far more of a monosyllabic language than Italian, such "zeppe" will be necessary in even a blank verse translation. What matters is the quality of the "zeppe." "C.F." praised Sayers's attention to the rhythm of Dante's verse and defended her use of half rhymes and eccentric rhymes by pointing out that Byron is never criticized for having used them in *Don Juan*. [49] He did criticize her for having apparently restricted herself to English commentaries on the *Commedia*, when Italian scholarship could have saved her from (unspecified) errors, and for displaying too great a partiality for the views of Charles Williams. Finally, he chided her for grafting a modern English sense of humor onto a medieval Italian poet. Nonetheless, her work "sembra meritare considerazione e rispetto e in più parti ammirazione."

To this comprehensive and balanced review, the other notices supply mainly addenda. For Professor Singleton and the poet Dudley Fitts, Dorothy Sayers's choice of terza rima constituted a fundamental error of judgment which must in itself guarantee an unsatisfactory result. Professor Singleton went further; her use of terza rima and Dante's ten-to-eleven syllable line constituted "the sin of hubris, the wages of which is padding at every turn. . . ." The reviewer in *Comparative Literature* accused her, as well as John Ciardi and Geoffrey Bickersteth, of sacrificing some accuracy to formal ends. In his view, Sayers was "at her best when Dante is at his toughest," thus echoing the reviewer in the *Times Literary Supplement* who found her Dante "swift, exciting and topical." This anonymous critic noted that the Dante of our grandfathers was admired for his "grandeur" and "jewelled precision," and that too many have admired him only from a "reverent distance." Reviewers who found the *Paradiso* volume, half of which at least is the work of Dr. Barbara Reynolds, an improvement in tone and diction over the racy and often colloquial language of the first two *cantiche* failed to mention that 5,000 lines on the subject of heavenly bliss lend themselves to a more chaste diction in the original than descriptions of the torments of Hell and the expiations of Purgatory. The unsigned review in the *New Statesman and Nation* indicted a translation which purported to speak in the language of "our day" but made use of unusual words or esoteric meanings of common ones (e.g., *affright* as a noun), and inveighed even more passionately against Sayers's use of "thou" for familiar address when its use frequently resulted in peculiar verb forms.[50]

The *New Statesman*'s reviewer was one of those who decried the "impurity" of her language, while acknowledging that it occasionally attained "something of the grandeur of the original." His reaction was diametrically opposed to that of Theodore Holmes in *Comparative Literature*, who praised the "admirable flow" of her diction, and her use of "rare" and "antiquated" words. Gilbert Cunningham, in his recent survey of modern translations of Dante and some of their critics, praises these usages as elements which make for a variety "notably lacking" in many terza rima translations.

Various critical judgments can be levelled at the following passage:

> Io m'assettai in su quelle spallacce.
> Si volli dir, ma la voce non venne
> com'io credetti "Fa che tu m'abbrace."
>   [*Inf.* XVII. 91–93]

Laurence Binyon had previously made this translation:

> On those dread shoulders [of the eagle] did I then get hold.
> I wished to say, only the voice came not
> As I had meant: "Thy arms about me fold."

This is an accurate if unexciting rendering of the lines. Sayers differs with the *spirit* of Binyon's version. The difference between his phrasing and hers is the difference between a translator who does not believe Dante is laughing at himself in recollection and one who does. Sayers "believe[s] that he is, and that his treatment of his own character is suffused throughout with a delicate spirit of comedy, which no reverence should tempt the translator to obscure with dignified phrases."[51] Her version reads:

> So I climbed to those dread shoulders obediently;
> "Only do" (I meant to say, but my voice somehow
> Wouldn't come out right) "please catch hold of me."

Her Italian reviewer found the tone of this "too familiar." He might, as he did with some of her other passages, have discussed the following "zeppe": "obediently" and "somehow" are pure interpolations while "wouldn't come out right" and "please catch hold of me" represent her deliberate choice to give a humorous flavoring to quite neutral phrases on the theory that they are being uttered (or thought of) by a poet Dante who is amused at his persona in the poem. Peter Russell, the editor of the elite, conservative English little magazine, *Nine,* reviewed the *Inferno* himself and belabored Sayers for her lack of taste by taking her own example, the passage given above, and crucifying her with it. Compared to Binyon, "her language is a curious confusion of literary stock-in-trade, archaism and slang."[52]

Even this unkind reviewer called her Commentary "really valuable," although he found her Introduction marred by "colloquial words and a sort of hearty old-girlish giggling." Usually, both the commentaries to each canto, and the Introductions received high praise. The poet and translator Dudley Fitts reviewed the *Inferno* and *Paradiso* together in the New York *Times* in 1955 and is representative in his unqualified praise for her historical background and notes. Fitts was biased, as were others, against the mentors to whom she owed her own interpretative bias. Thus he found her "philosophical and theological reflections . . . too unfocused for my taste, too sentimentally patronizing in the homiletic manner of C. S. Lewis." Sentimental, no; homiletic, yes. Fitts displays here that modern dislike for the didactic which a medieval poet or commentator would have found incomprehensible. Fitts did call her "singularly happy" in suggesting the tone changes, the "special nuances" of many passages, but must rate the translation a failure because of her choice of terza rima.

Yet the history of Dante in English demonstrates that avoidance of terza rima is no guarantee that the translation will find the right road. John Ciardi, whose version of the *Inferno* appeared in 1954, found that by working with "dummy" terza rima (which omits the middle rhyme) the translation began to "happen" for him.[53] While this freer form might have been chosen to lessen the translator's need to depart from the text, Ciardi instead rejected the idea of "translation" (which he interprets as the finding of word-for-word equivalents) in favor of "transposition." He regrouped tercets and added and deleted lines. His announced goals are to render accurately "Dante's vulgate," which he regards as "overwhelmingly . . . a spoken tongue," and his pace, "the rate at which the writing reveals itself to the reader." Ciardi's version has been popular, like that of Sayers, and like hers it has been abundantly praised and censured. A review of the critical judgments on the two versions[54] leads to the conclusion that a translator cannot escape charges of inaccuracy, distortion, or even lack of "humility" before the original author from some critical quarter. In a recent brief assessment of John Ciardi and Dorothy Sayers as translators, Joan Ross Acocella focuses on their handling of Ulysses' tale.[55] She dislikes Sayers's combination of colloquialism and "Victorian pomposities," but commends her and Ciardi for having "appreciated something in Dante that had not been adequately appreciated in previous translations: a strength of statement and a range of statement which could include both the high and the low." The use of terza rima to express this vision became an obstacle course for Sayers to struggle over. Interestingly, Acocella rates Ciardi's translation no higher than hers, despite its freedom from the struggle with rhyme which she blames for some of Sayers's failures. Indeed, all critics except her Italian one declared she achieved her good effects *despite* this unfortunate choice. Her view of the matter, as her essays make clear, was that the choice was *responsible* for her best effects.

In my view, Sayers's approach to Dante was not unlike her approach to the life of Christ in *The Man Born to Be King* in its emphasis on the humanness of the Divine and determination not to obscure the poem's (or Gospels') relevance to our own spiritual condition by using received phrases or a grand style. Her radio script, as a reading of it makes clear, must have had its strengths enormously increased by the excellent production Val Gielgud gave it on the BBC. Her Dante, for most readers, will remain a solitary, silent reading experience and for the first two *cantiche,* at least, this is a pity. As Sayers viewed Christian dogma as a great drama in which Christ is the central actor, it is not, perhaps, surprising that her translation stresses the dramatic elements in Dante's presentation of essential Christian concepts. She displays the Dante in the poem as a sometimes self-deprecating, sometimes childishly egotistical, but always humorous, and very English protagonist in a swiftly moving dramatic narrative.

One motif running through *Gaudy Night* is the importance of finding and knowing one's own "job" and doing it honestly, with all the strength of the "feeling intellect." As Miss deVine, who clearly stands for values Sayers admires, puts it: "If there's any subject in which you're content with the second rate, then it isn't really your subject," and, "If you are once sure what you want to do, you find that everything else goes down before it like grass under a steam-roller—all other interests, your own and other people's."[56] The words were prophetic. Dorothy Sayers's letters and essays, as well as the translation and apparatus, reveal that when she discovered Dante, all her other interests were crushed under this particular poetic steamroller. Whatever the reactions of her critics, she herself was never satisfied with the second-rate reading, scansion or image. I can judge her translation only as a reasonably informed reader of Dante's own language; in my view, there is great worth in the work. It mirrors the strong individuality of the mind that produced it, and the strength and variety of critical response evoked are testimony, often unwitting, to its great power.

IV: AESTHETICS

Nancy Tischler

Artist, Artifact, and Audience: The Aesthetics and Practice of Dorothy L. Sayers

GOD is the archetype of the creator; the artist is a type. ". . . the mind of the maker and the mind of the Maker are formed of the same pattern, and all their works are made in their own image."[1] With this conviction central to her thought and her work, Dorothy L. Sayers was able to discover a principle for synthesis and for creativity. In several of her works, notably "Toward a Christian Aesthetic," *The Mind of the Maker, The Zeal of Thy House,* and *Gaudy Night,* she explained her basic aesthetic and demonstrated her theological premises.

Drawing heavily on the first chapter of Genesis for her insights, she notes that the image of God is almost exclusively creative at the point when He created man in His own Image. "The characteristic common to God and man is apparently . . . the desire and ability to make things."[2] Elaborating on this, she notes that this "image" is shared by male and female alike[3] —an insight that was to provide the basis for her own work and for her explorations of womankind in *Purgatorio* and *Are Women Human?*

Thus, if human beings are by nature creators, they are in some limited way both enabled and driven to create. Certainly one of the first commands given in the garden was to work—to keep the garden, thereby reinforcing the idea of work as vocation even prior to the Fall. Dorothy L. Sayers insists that this tending of the garden, seeking to establish dominion over the concrete world, serving and loving it, is a deeply felt human need. For many people, the action takes a literal and physical form; for many women, the shape of creativity is the physical replen-

ishment of the earth, the bearing of children. But for artists, the garden is
the stuff of their craft, and creativity is the spiritual and active process of
bearing forth new life to enrich the earth. Within this theoretical con-
struct, Sayers could never be puzzled about the "mode of existence of the
work of art." The process, moving from artist through artifact to audience, is all part of the work; no segment may live without the others.

Like other moderns, she seeks to discover her own essence by medi-
tating on artists and their creativity. Though she notes the parallels to
potters and farmers, she selects artists, "[men] like other men" (or
women like other women) and considers them within the Wordsworthian
pattern—as a person like others, but with greater sensitivity. Avoiding
the extreme idealism expressed in the Shelley poet-seer, Sayers prefers
the more democratic and realistic Pauline approach—the fallible creature with special "gifts." In all men and women she believes some form of
creativeness dwells as the image of God, our peculiar humanness that
places us slightly above the animals, yet a little lower than the angels.
She would never embrace the attitude of the aesthetes, who see the artist
as a person apart. She, in fact, deplores the current isolation of the artists
from government and church, and society's consequent devaluation of
their gifts. Much of her appeal lies in her refusal to play the intellectual/
aesthetic role. She chooses to acknowledge the kinship between artist
and audience. She enjoys the rich stuff of everyday life.

In her system, the artist's creative urge starts with the "Idea," not a
Platonic vision, but a concept or image which demands expression. In
"Creative Mind," Sayers discusses this image-making process, revealing a rich Christian orientation: "In the Middle Ages," she notes, "the
word 'imagination' meant primarily the faculty of producing mental
images—something more like what we now mean by 'visual fancy.'"
She goes on to explain the term as it relates to creativity: ". . . we
mean, not merely that it is seen vivid and complete like an 'image' or
picture, but that it shows profound insight and intellectual grasp of
the whole subject."[4] In her own experience, she found that the
source of this image was no great mystery: a word, a story, a memory
might trigger a set of responses that gradually shape themselves into
a being that is a new creation. Sayers explains this in terms of
metaphor:

> The poet's imagination creates by metaphor. It perceives a likeness between a number
> of things that at first sight appear to have no measurable relation, and it builds them
> into a new kind of unity, a new universe, that can be handled with power *as if* it

possessed independent existence, and whose power is operative in the world of things that can be observed and measured.[5]

Thus, unlike many moderns who follow the Romantic notion of frenzied artists possessed by their creative urges, Sayers's artists find their path to be a rational and existential road to an ordered vision. Working within inevitable limitations, they use observation, experience, and imagination to build their creations. This respect for experience, for precise observation (for actual cats prior to theories about cats), for reality, individually and particularly perceived, is central to Sayers's aesthetic and practice. As she notes at one point, echoing Aristotle and expanding his brief note on image-making, "Man measures everything by his own experience; he has no other yardstick."[6] Thus, her mode of discovery is analogical, her mode of expression is necessarily metaphoric.[7] Language is an "expression of experience and of the relation of one experience to the other. Further, its meaning is realized only in experience."[8] This statement derived from Sayers's own practice: unlike most aestheticians, she developed her theories after her practice and from her experience. Theories of art, in her case, are therefore rooted firmly in reality.

This emphasis on experience appears to place Sayers squarely in the mimetic tradition, as opposed to the Platonic idealistic tradition. But unlike other "realists" she does not allow her love of the physical and perceived world to deny the metaphysical realm of experience. She has, following the path of Charles Williams, elected the "way of Affirmation," which is a love of this world as an image of the Creator. As she explains this peculiarly Christian concept of the image and the reality, she relates it to the fact of the Incarnation and the doctrine of the Trinity:

> Suppose, having rejected the words 'copy,' 'imitation' and 'representation' as inadequate, we substitute the word 'image' and say that what the artist is doing is *to image forth* something or the other, and connect that with St. Paul's phrase: "God . . . hath spoken to us by His Son, the brightness of this glory and *express image* of His person.'—Something which, by being an image, *expresses* that which it images . . . the Son, who is the express image, is not the copy or imitation, or representation of the Father, nor yet inferior or subsequent to the Father in any way—in the last resort, in the depths of their mysterious being, the Unimaginable and the Image are *one and the same.*[9]

If artists follow this theory of reality, the physical world can never become for them an object of idolatry, an end in itself. As Dante sees the physical world as testimony to God's majesty and as a clue to His nature, so Sayers embraces the flesh that she might have life that transcends the flesh. In fact, she particularly dwells on the combined immanence and transcendence in creativity.

In addition, this zest for experience demands that the artist serve as the synthesizer. The chaos of moment-to-moment experience can emerge into meaning only if the creative mind imposes order.

On the one hand, this means that artists are under the obligation to seek harmony, unity, and meaning in the whirligig of incident. On the other hand, it also means that they must experience life as fully as possible, omitting no experience as alien. They cannot embrace one of C. P. Snow's two cultures and ignore the other. This idea of Sayers's runs counter to the Romantic notion of the artist as a specialist in sensitivity. As Sayers notes, ". . . it is now very difficult for the artist to speak the language of the theologian. But the attempt must be made; and there are signs everywhere that the human mind is once more beginning to move toward a synthesis of experience."[10] This image of the Christian poet as the ideal human creative type helps explain why Dorothy L. Sayers loved Dante: his unified sensibility allowed him to explore theology, physics, politics, or aesthetics with no sense of awkwardness. In a more modest and sequential way, Sayers's own career demonstrates a parallel concern with the multiplicity of human experiences. It is in fact one reason that audiences found her so accessible. She helped them to discover insights and bridge ideas because she shared their concerns. As she expresses this essential relationship between artists and their audience: ". . . what the poet does for himself, he can also do for us. When he has imaged forth his experience he can incarnate it, so to speak, in a material body —words, music, painting—the thing we know as a work of art. . . . In the image of *his* experience, we can *recognize* the image of some experience of our own. . . ."[11]

Seeking to explain the apparent contradiction between materialistic reordering and imaginative creating, Sayers asserts her belief in creation *ex nihilo*. She insists that artists, like God, in a sense create "out of nothing"—not matter, but new and unique entities. And she says, "It is the artist who, more than other men, is able to create something out of nothing. A whole artistic work is immeasurably more than the sum of its parts."[12] This expanding process is the key to her credal affirmation, and in it she appears to accept all of the traditional interpretations of the creation as reconcilable facets of the creative act: the use of matter into which the Creator breathes His spirit; the shaping of chaos into order; and the creation out of nothing. Though the doctrines appear on the surface to be contradictory, Sayers uses her own experience to make sense of them all, finding in one an explanation for our way of knowing and communicating, in another an insight into our merging of spirit and matter, and in the final one the mystery of inspiration. She has said that experience can illuminate problems and suggest solutions while the rational intellect might boggle, and she demonstrates this to be so in her interpretation of God as the archetype of the artist.

In a world dominated by the scientific method, human beings are inclined to value rationality, logical demonstration, and problem-solving. But Sayers is not inclined to settle for one exclusive and tidy explanation of art, especially not one that would identify the artist and the scientist. Just as God the Creator steps above scientific theory to be the Master Artist of Creation, so art itself is more imaginative and exciting than flat rationalism. ". . . the artist does not see life as a problem to be solved, but as a medium for creation. . . . he is well aware that creation settles nothing. . . . his concern is not with death but wife life: 'that ye may have life and have it more abundantly.' "[13] The vocation of the creator is not to solve problems "within the limits imposed by the terms in which they are set, but to fashion a synthesis which includes the whole dialectics of the situation in a manifestation of power."[14] Artists, in Sayers's aesthetic, are to delight in the experience of life, the portrayal of it, and the deepening of it.

And yet, they cannot ignore the tools of their craft. When writing her detective stories, Sayers was very aware of the limits imposed by the terms and by the problems and the solutions. Good artisans understand their craft and approach it with respect. "The business of the creator," notes Sayers, "is not to escape from the medium or to bully it, but to serve it; but to serve it he must love it."[15] This sacramental view of work is a central theme for Sayers, especially explicit in *Creed or Chaos,* which includes such assertions as: ". . . work is the natural exercise and function of man," it is ". . . the thing one lives to do," it is the ". . . medium in which he offers himself to God."[16] In this book she also lashes out at twentieth-century England for its failure to acknowledge this basic need in human beings: "The greatest insult which a commercial age has offered to the worker has been to rob him of all interest in the end-product of the work and to force him to dedicate his life to making things badly which were not worth making."[17] Echoing her predecessor, John Ruskin, in this concern, she pleads for a return to a sense of vocation and a love of craftsmanship. Although her immediate concern is the craft of writing, she acknowledges parallels in other labor, accepting something of the classical Greek theory of art as craft (or *techné*) but expanding it to include the "important contribution that Christianity has made to aesthetics"—i.e., creation.[18]

For the dynamic process to happen, the word must become flesh and dwell among humanity. For the artist, as for God, the tools of creativity are words. Sayers attacks the abuse of the verbal skills, realizing that shabby workmanship dims the image and warps the perception. She argues against the "slatternly habit of illiterate reading" in one book[19] and the "sloppy habit of illiterate writing" in another.[20] Words have specific meanings and functions. They are the rich material that deserves study and care in their use. As a medieval linguist, Dorothy L. Sayers recognized that words have a history and a rich heritage of meaning; as a poet, she knew they have rhythm and sound and shape; as a popular novelist, she knew they can reflect thought or conversation; as a polemicist, she knew they are sharp weapons with great impact. All of these verbal activities, in addition to her work in advertising, her experience as a playwright, working with radio and stage, her lectures and her essays as a literary critic, led her to respect words. It was, after all, by the word that God created: He *said* and it was. The power of the word revealed in Genesis and the miracle of the Word made flesh in John reinforced for her the idea of the word/Word as one marvelous and concrete material with which human beings (like God, and in His image) create. In Sayers's system, this process of making or enfleshing she calls "energy."

In these new creatures they have made, artists find some of the same problems that the Creator found in His creation. Among these is the need to separate the creation from the creator, acknowledging and respecting the creator's independent will. Thus the creature is not a mirror of the artist nor a puppet. As Sayers often noted, she did not share Lord Peter's taste for brandy, though she agreed with his enthusiasm for incunabula. She would not force him into an uncharacteristic conversion experience. Nor, because she incorporated autobiographical detail into the portrait of Harriet Vane, including the illicit affair, need we look in Sayers's past for a murdered lover—except perhaps in a metaphorical sense. Sayers describes the process she used to create and separate a character:

> When making a character he [the artist] in a manner separates and incorporates a part of his own living mind. He recognizes in himself a powerful emotion—let us say jealousy. His activity then takes this form: Supposing this emotion were to become so strong as to dominate my whole personality, how should I feel and how should I behave? In imagination he becomes the jealous person and thinks and feels within that frame of experience, so that the jealousy of Othello is the true creative expression of

the jealousy of Shakespeare. He follows out, in fact, the detective system employed by Chesterton's "Father Brown":

"I mean that I really did see myself, and my real self, committing the murders. . . . I realized that I really *was* like that, in everything except actual final consent to the action."[21]

The extension of a single facet of the author's personality through an act of imagination is not to be confused with the writing of autobiography. Unlike the myriad modern chroniclers of personal experience, Sayers is not interested in portraying the artist as a young woman. Although we catch glimpses of her musings on the nature of the artist, the role of woman, the responses to and problems of physically plain women, the problems of social ostracism, or the experience of unhappy marriages, we are never invited into the inner sanctum of her fascinating life. This would be to dwell unduly on the mind of the human creator and to emphasize the process of creation rather than to recognize and acknowledge the chief end of art—to glorify God. The artist is to transcend the individual, to cull out idiosyncratic detail unless the artifact images forth a richer meaning. Her delight in Dante's use of Beatrice—a real Florentine woman, a combination in her characterization of the qualities of Beatrice and other women he had known, an infusing of that image with symbolic meanings, and a dynamic patterning of responses and insights that result from her role in her dramatic context, culminating in her final bearing of the lover, body and soul, into the hands of the waiting God—this rich critical analysis explains Sayers's own theory of the Way of Affirmation. Harriet D. Vane is not Dorothy L. Sayers. Though authors may use a character to discover the truth within themselves and to communicate that discovery, the character's portrayal should not draw the reader back to a contemplation of the author. From self, the mind should fly to human nature, and from there to God's image in mankind in a modified Platonic progression.

Sayers also sees artists (like God) as active in their creation; not leaving the creature to the will o' the wisp that absolute free will seems to imply. She believes in a God who brings order out of chaos, who creates with a purpose, who is still capable of interfering in human history—and who in fact entered history physically in the Person of Christ. Though she is reluctant to use miracles in her stories, she does occasionally structure a work so that God is an actor on stage (as in *Nine Tailors, The Devil to Pay, The Zeal of Thy House,* and *The Man Born to Be*

King). She obeys the rules of probability in her own structured universe, not permitting gratuitous miracles.

In this insistence on probability, she is Aristotelian. But her defense of Aristotle is modern, scientific, and realistic, not blindly neoclassic. She, in fact, shares much of his mind-set. "What is the use," she demands of her disorderly world, "of saying that twentieth-century playwrights should refuse to be bound by the dictum of an ancient Greek professor? They are bound, whether they like it or not, by the fundamental realities of human nature."[22] Thus, Aristotle's notes on the unities are not rules for neoclassical playwrights to accept or Romantic ones to reject, but insights into human nature that can help the sensitive playwright to create more effectively. Playwrights may expect a positive response in an audience only if their work conforms to certain innate human demands. Artists are not free to select rules or reject them. Their work is to discover them, through a discovery of the nature of the human mind and the means to communicate with it. The rules are not proscriptive, but prescriptive, not regulatory like social laws, but descriptive like natural ones. The effective artist recognizes the limits and potential of the human mind as well as the medium of ideas. Sayers's own description of the process involved in her composition of *The Man Born to Be King* underscores her concern for natural law. (Sir Arthur Eddington is as clear an influence on her work and theory as is Aristotle. She quotes him almost as frequently and makes extensive use of his ideas.)

In all of her concern for craftsmanship, we see her as no mystic viewing herself as an inspired amanuensis for her muse, but as a pragmatist viewing herself as a craftsman. "God," she insists, "is not served by technical incompetence. . . ."[23] She has no patience with worthy ideas clumsily expressed. If the work of artists is a vocation, a means of serving God, then they must serve God by serving the work. Christian artists may not use the work to draw attention to themselves; they must use it to build toward the greater glory of God, not the greater glory of mankind. Nor may they turn the artifact itself into an object of worship —as do many moderns who prefer logology to theology (as J. Hillis Miller has demonstrated). The word does not deserve worship: it must enflesh the idea and communicate it to the reader. This third element of Sayers's scheme she designates the "power."

The long flirtation and alienation between religion and the arts has been a result of this very power, acknowledged to reside in aesthetic products. As Milton so eloquently asserted in the *Areopagitica*, ". . . books are not absolutely dead things, but do contain a potency of life in

them to be as active as that soul was whose progeny they are. . . ."
They certainly can prove "dragon's teeth," giving birth to emotions and
ideas that are only partially predictable. To a certain extent, of course,
the audience's response can be controlled by the artist. Sayers speaks, in
"Toward a Christian Aesthetic," of Collingwood's pseudo-arts, amusement and magic, as opposed to art "proper." These are arts that manipulate the audience toward ends predetermined by the artist. Both pornography and didacticism would be "kinetic," therefore not art proper,
which must be "static," a product of expression and imagination. In
Sayers's aesthetic, this art proper involves an intensification of the joy in
experience, a fullness of life. "Spell-binding" or "entertaining" lead not
to a discovery of our deeper humanity, but a "falsification of the consciousness." As Sayers explains this in terms of the Incarnation and the
Christian idea of the Image, she asserts:

> What they [spell-binding and entertaining] have in common is the falsification of
> the consciousness; and they are to Art as the *idol* is to the Image. The Jews were
> forbidden to make any image for worship, because before the revelation of the
> threefold unity in which Image and Unimaginable are one, it was only too fatally easy
> to substitute the idol for the Image. The Christian revelation set free all the images, by
> showing that the true Image subsisted within the Godhead Itself—it was neither copy,
> nor representation, nor inferior, nor subsequent, but the brightness of the Glory, and
> the express image of the Person—the very mirror in which reality knows itself and
> communicates itself in power.[24]

The role of the artist, then, is to serve the work, not to falsify the
consciousness in order to manipulate an audience.

In her early experience with advertising, as she demonstrates in
Murder Must Advertise, she discovered the means by which the public
may be manipulated. Her estimate of this abuse of her craft is obvious, as
she discovered good writing and serious ideas are less important than
public taste. Truth and beauty are seldom relevant in advertising campaigns. In *The Mind of the Maker,* Sayers asserts that no respectable
artists would alter their form to please their audience (cf. "Scalene
Trinities" and the case of Beddoes's plays). The falsification of the art for
public appeal is a variant of this sin against vocation. And, in a sense, the
"kinetic" arts are related, though didacticism manipulates toward a more
noble end than does pornography or advertising. Such works as *Creed or
Chaos* testify to Sayers's own admission that at times art is less important
than propaganda. In fact, given the significant needs of an audience and
the compassion of an author, a work of didacticism is the proper use of an

artist's talent; but artists must recognize that they are producing a temporary and limited artifact, hardly comparable with true art. As Dante made use of the arts for teaching the penitent, as both whips and goads on various levels of Purgatory, so Sayers also came to accept a sacramental theory of the arts. Thus, her chancel plays and her radio cycle fall within the medieval doctrine of the subordination of Beauty to Truth. Yet, even so, she insists in *The Mind of the Maker* (a book that came after several of these works), that one cannot write with one ear tuned to Rome and the other to Geneva for fear of spreading error. Though increasingly her subject matter demanded a didactic approach, she continued to believe that artists who serve their work also serve their Master. No art "proper" can be a submissive puppet to a doctrine; it must grow naturally out of a belief in a creed, challenging that creed whenever necessary. For Dorothy L. Sayers, such freedom proved a pathway into the discovery of doctrinal truth.

Like Jacques Maritain and other neo-Thomists, Sayers rediscovered the hard-won truths of the schoolmen. She too saw "making" as an ordering toward an end, serving the work and stamping it with the character of man: *animal rationale.* She too considered the mystery of impressing idea on matter, and she too contemplated St. Thomas's aesthetic trinity: integrity, proportion, and splendor. Her study of the Church Fathers demonstrated to her the temptations and limitations of the standard heresies as well as the wisdom and truth of orthodoxy. Her talent was a synthetic one. She could bring together insights from Sir Arthur Eddington and Augustine, Aristotle and Plato, St. Thomas and Johann Wolfgang von Goethe, developing them into a comment on a medieval poem or a modern play. While her experience had convinced her of the validity of ancient creeds, she accepted no limits to exploration. Though she knew the commentaries on creativity by William Wordsworth, Samuel Taylor Coleridge, E. M. Forster, Nikolai Berdyaev, and numerous others, she drew primarily from her own experience. She considered audience response as well as aesthetic theory, trying to discover why certain stories succeeded or failed. Her concept of the "scalene" trinities is an imaginative and useful tool for evaluation of artifacts.

In many ways, Sayers's work seems derivative; she appears to be a popularizer rather than an original thinker. A case might well be made for citing parallels between her creative trinity and that of St. Thomas. Her *idea,* like M. H. Abrams's *author,* [25] is the key to Thomistic *unity.* Her *energy,* like Abrams's *artifact,* provides insights into Thomistic *proportion;* and her *power,* like Abrams's *audience,* would seem to explain the response noted in Thomistic *splendor* or *claritas.* But no one else was so aware (or at least so explicit) as she of the parallels this trinity provided for the greater one. The Christian artist must be grateful for her insights into the correspondence between the *idea* and the Father, the *energy* and the Son, the *power* and the Holy Spirit.

Her emphasis on the harmonious balance of parts solves the problems of creative or critical emphasis on any one of the components to the exclusion of the others: The "autotelic" fallacy,[26] of seeing the work of art as a monad, so common among formalists and those aesthetes who would write only for the delight of the explicators; the "intentional" fallacy, of Romantics who believe that the idea is everything, and of psychological critics who believe that in discovering the intention of the artist they have performed a work of value; and the "affective fallacy" of the impressionistic critics and those who assume that a work is to be judged by the size and enthusiasm of its audience, and by those popular writers who pervert their talent for their bank account. Through her uncommon use of common sense, she avoids the extremes of the artist-as-seer, artifact as idol, and audience as infallible judge.

The fullest demonstration of Sayers's aesthetic and the neatest summary of it appears in her 1937 Canterbury play, *The Zeal of Thy House.* Testifying to the Divine inspiration that reveals the paradigm to her, she allows the full statement to be spoken by the archangel Michael:

> Children of men, lift up your hearts. Laud and magnify God, the everlasting Wisdom. the holy, undivided and adorable Trinity.
>
> Praise Him that He hath made man in His own image, a maker and craftsman like Himself, a little mirror of His triune majesty.
>
> For every work of creation is threefold, an earthly trinity to match the heavenly.
>
> First: there is the Creative Idea; passionless, timeless, beholding the whole work complete at once, the end in the beginning; and the image of the Father.
>
> Second: there is the Creative Energy, begotten of that Idea, working in time from the beginning to the end, with sweat and passion, being incarnate in the bonds of matter; and this is the image of the Word.
>
> Third: there is the Creative Power, the meaning of the work and its response in the lively soul; and this is the image of the indwelling Spirit.
>
> And these three are one, each equally in itself the whole work, whereof none can exist without the other; and this is the image of the Trinity.

Look then upon this Cathedral Church of Christ: imaged by men's minds, built by the labour of men's hands, working with power upon the souls of men: symbol of the everlasting Trinity, the visible temple of God.[27]

Dorothy L. Sayers's primary contribution to aesthetics must be her imaginative and convincing interpretation of the creative process in terms of Augustinian doctrine. Christians, by virtue of their experience of the Incarnation, have insights unavailable to the pagan—even to so wise a pagan as Plato. "This word—this idea of Art as *creation* is, I believe, the one important contribution that Christianity has made to aesthetics. . . ."[28] The Incarnation thus serves as the archetypal pattern for every new creation. Working with the dynamic triad of the artist, the artifact, and the audience, Sayers discovered in the Trinity a magnificent synthesizing principle for aesthetics.

Richard T. Webster

The Mind of the Maker: Logical Construction, Creative Choice and the Trinity

THE MIND OF THE MAKER, the most philosophical of Dorothy Sayers's writings, proposes an analogy between the Mind of God, the Creator of all things, and the minds of human beings, the makers of works of art, an analogy which, while bold and simple, is at the same time ingenious, and despite a certain logicality, not without an element of mystery. The puzzle consists in how anything so downright and unequivocal as Dorothy Sayers's interpretation of the Trinity—for both God and humanity are "makers" in virtue of their triunity—can fit in with the tangled web of speculation on such triunities, or how, if it cuts across the generally recognized views, it is nonetheless compelling and unforgettable.

Comparisons between the human mind and the Mind of God have seldom been pushed very far in the English-speaking world where, since the Middle Ages the emphasis has usually been on the impossibility of knowing anything of God otherwise than morally or affectively, and the human mind has been thought properly adapted only to this world. But it has been otherwise in the Graeco-Latin and related traditions, where Mind has often enjoyed a kind of transcendental status, in which something of this Mind can be attributed in the first place to God, and then, by derivation or illumination, to human beings. This is not the immediate problem, however, since Dorothy Sayers makes it abundantly clear that she is talking specifically about the mind of the artist or writer, not any sort of mind, or Mind in the philosophical sense, unless it be by tacit implication.

165

For the particular aspect of the matter considered by Dorothy Sayers there are, however, classical precedents. Aquinas says that "God's knowledge stands to all created things as the artist's to his products" [S.T. 1a, 14, 8]; and Giambattista Vico, the anticipator of German Idealism, is celebrated for the principle on which he based all his work, that "the truth is something *made*" —*verum est factum*—i.e., human knowledge is creative, and creative, as Vico thought, on the analogy of God's creation in the first place. Yet while both *The Mind of the Maker* and Vico offer a new message of prophetic intensity for a world split in two by scientific rationalism, Vico himself did not influence Sayers—his name gets lost among the Idealists.

In any case, whereas the philosophers were dealing with such general principles as "knowledge" and "truth," in the case of Dorothy Sayers, we have to deal with a temperament—and what a temperament!—morally concerned with truth indeed, but preoccupied in all things with artistic *making*. With or without her religious views, she burns to make! To make with words rather than with other materials, but with sympathy toward other makers, toward architects and painters, for instance. It is this personal experience of the processes of making that becomes for her an analogy of the Divine Mind; but while this analogy is worked out as a clearcut doctrine with considerable logical precision, it is not actually a comprehensively philosophical sort of doctrine. "For other minds, other analogies," she remarks [ch. IX]. This is fair enough; but since the subject happens to be God, one might want to ask: what other analogies?

This problem of extension is further illustrated by the following consideration. In Chapter V and in the Note to Chapter IX, Sayers draws a very sharp distinction between the business of literary creation and the personal experience of the writer outside it—she will have nothing to do with the notion that good art has to be somehow autobiographical, for that would not be "making"—but at the same time the justification for her doctrine, apart from the element of religious faith, lies in the appeal to experience, i.e., to the experience of the literary creator. Yet in connection with such a universal theme one might want to bring in more "personal experience" of other kinds. One feels that Dorothy Sayers, in her aversion from sentimentality, was not much concerned with all this. In this sense she is an intellectualist, but not in the sense in which the term would be used in metaphysics, although what she is doing in this book, is, after all, metaphysics.

No doubt the notion that aesthetic experience is qualitatively separate from any other (so that Dorothy Sayers speaks of "the writer's experience" as something peculiar that is not accessible to the average person) is a notion inherited from the age of aestheticism and professional caste. Yet it would be unfair to suggest that she exaggerates the distinction since, while in Chapter III "the poet is . . . his own society" mentally, in Chapter VIII, "Pentecost," "The Power—the Spirit—is thus a social power, working to bring all minds into its own unity, sometimes by similarity and at other times by contrast. There is a diversity of gifts, but the same spirit." And the Postscript, "The Worth of the Work," deals with creativity in all work. It is just that she is so very much concentrated on her chosen theme.

To obtain a general perspective of the possible relations which may be postulated between God considered as a Trinity and the human mind, or the human being as a whole, it must be recalled that for St. Augustine (whom Dorothy Sayers quotes with enthusiasm as pointing out the inevitability of natural components in all our conceptions of the Super-natural) there was an analogy between the Holy Trinity of Father, Son, and Holy Ghost on the one hand, and on the other, as he put it, the natural triunity of Memory, Understanding, and Will. The natural triunity could also be stated as that of Body, Mind, and Soul, which is usually accepted, and in fact survives, I should say, the notorious onslaughts of philosophers like Gilbert Ryle; or it could be stated in any of the many ways in which it has been suggested throughout the history of thought from Hinduism to Jacob Boehme or Georg Hegel. For all these alternatives Dorothy Sayers substitutes the triunity of what she calls Idea, Energy (or Activity), and Power, corresponding to (i) the primary artistic conception—"Idea" in that sense, (ii) the energy or activity of its material execution or embodiment, and (iii) its subsequent power of communication. For the artist this is a plain matter of experience, and at the same time it gives us a firm grasp of what, she finds, is too often ignorantly treated as a mere mystery, or even an absurdity, the Trinity of Father, Son and Holy Ghost.

Now it may be objected that for St. Augustine, as explained in *De Trinitate*, XV, as also for Aquinas, if the natural triunity of the human mind can give us the notion of a three-in-one in a general way, it is not supposed to come anywhere near the reality of the Holy Trinity, which is set at an awe-inspiring distance from the human mind, so that the analogy is only very faint. Thus, although a modernizing theologian like Richard Acland refers to *The Mind of the Maker* as "the first book I read which made the doctrine of the Trinity seem real and sensible"

[*Nothing Left to Believe?*, London: Longmans, Green, 1949], a representative orthodox Trinitarian such as Eric Mascall emphasizes the transcendence of God and the view that the analogy from any natural triunity is "partial and incomplete." "The doctrine of the Trinity falls outside the proper sphere of natural theology," and "the discernment of a trinitarian structure in creation is not the product of natural theology at all, but arises from a deliberate reflection upon the created world from the standpoint of Christian revelation" [*He Who Is, a Study in Traditional Theism,* corrected ed., London: Longmans, Green 1962]. Mascall does not mention Sayers. Since Sayers claimed to be orthodox, and very orthodox, I do not think that there is necessarily a contradiction between the two positions, which are rather a matter of different emphases within the same framework. But we have to consider that Dorothy Sayers's concern, rather than being with theoretical discussion for its own sake, was with the fact that religion has become for many in these days so very unreal. Western civilization, perhaps more especially in Europe, has come to suffer more and more from an appalling dualism whereby what is known to be real in this world has next to nothing to do either with "religion," or indeed, one may say, with any official philosophy, both of which appear in the light of unreal abstractions. As she aptly puts it in the Introduction to *The Man Born to Be King,* religion has become a matter of stained-glass-window decorum. "I did not know that Christ was really a human being" someone said after hearing the broadcast of *The Man Born to Be King,* although the doctrine had always been that Christ was Man: yet only abstractly Man, it would seem, not any particular real man such as one might meet in the street. The language, as it does in so many instances, gets stereotyped and meaningless. The result is often an iconoclasm that, instead of trying to understand, merely seeks to destroy. The process of bringing things down to earth, but with understanding, which in *The Man Born to Be King* some people found refreshing and others very shocking, is the process which in *The Mind of the Maker* is applied to the doctrine of the Trinity. The Trinity is in one sense not on earth, but the earth, having been created by the Trinity, must always have some relation to it; and if there has been revelation of it, then it must be to some extent comprehensible.

There have always been two somewhat conflicting views about the relations between human knowledge and the transcendence of God, which is supposed to lie outside the possibility of human knowledge except on faith or authority. The one view stops short at these limits, thus maintaining its distance from the world, or at any rate treating the world as *only* "the world." The other view finds in nature, in human experience of various kinds, or in the needs of the world, certain transparencies such that God, or some aspect of God, becomes the object of almost direct vision. As a matter of fact, both views are found in the Middle Ages, which were not only authoritarian, but were capable of seeing numerous images of the Trinity, and capable of realistic religious drama as well, not to mention the visions of St. Francis and St. Bonaventure. But in modern times the stained-glass-window syndrome has become everywhere more marked, and has been called "alienation."

Among the few geniuses who have effectively seen a way of breaking down this barrier, but have not always met with official approval, I should be inclined to place Vico, Friedrich von Schelling, Pierre Teilhard de Chardin, the contemporary Catholic theologian Hans Urs von Balthasar, the new French physicist Jean Charon—and Dorothy Sayers. For, although her vision is on philosophical terms a comparatively narrow one, it is precisely the sort of vision which overcomes the usual abysmal separation between theology and real life. This also appears in her play *The Emperor Constantine*, which deals in a very human way with the formulation of orthodox Christian belief about the Trinity at the Council of Nicaea. I do not know what a historian, or Eric Mascall, would have to say about this play, but the general principles of Sayers's metaphysical thinking, as set forth in *The Mind of the Maker*, lend themselves to philosophical discussion.

The central principle is that all problems connected with the Trinity point in two directions at once, toward an orthodox Trinitarianism and toward the most balanced construction of the human mind and character, so that "heresies" in the first case correspond to intellectual or other constitutional defects in the second case, and vice versa. For instance, there is the phantasmal Christ represented by the Docetic heresy, which maintained that Christ was not a real human being at all. On the other hand, there is the view that Christ was only a human being, and nothing more, although no doubt a model human being, a view represented by the much-fought-over Arianism, and in modern times by Unitarianism. To this antithesis there correspond two opposed sorts of human mind or character: that which seeks comfort in religion as a faraway stained-glass-window world, and that which, materialistically, would know of nothing outside the immediately given. In any case, while men and women are each virtually "one" in the midst of the inevitable triune structure, in human beings the three aspects are never perfectly combined as they uniquely are in the Holy Trinity. In Chapter X, "Scalene Trinities," we are given examples of a variety of types of unbalanced relationship between the three aspects of the human being, most of them drawn from the field of literature. William Blake, for instance, is shown as being Idea-ridden, but relatively weak when it comes to the incarnation of his Ideas. Swinburne is shown as being perfectly in control of the verbal media, but weak in Ideas. Others unnamed are put down as Spirit-ridden, easily carried on and on by an emotional impetus, yet devoid of either worthwhile Ideas or properly formed expression. In these matters there could be found endless variations and gradations, as also in the corresponding Christological heresies, to some of which she alludes.

If, however, no human triunity is actually perfect, then, by the requirement for self-reference, which is all too often overlooked in universal pronouncements, we are entitled to ask what are the specific peculiarities of Dorothy Sayers's own theory of "Idea, Energy, and Power."

> For every work (*or act*) of creation is threefold, an earthly trinity to match the heavenly.
>
> First, (*not in time, but merely in order of enumeration*) there is the Creative Idea, passionless, timeless, beholding the whole work complete at once, the end in the beginning: and this is the image of the Father.
>
> Second, there is the Creative Energy (*or Activity*) begotten of that idea, working in time from the beginning to the end, with sweat and passion, being incarnate in the bonds of matter; and this is the image of the Word.
>
> Third, there is the Creative Power, the meaning of the work and its response in the lively soul: and this is the image of the indwelling Spirit.
>
> And these three are one, each equally in itself the whole work, whereof none can exist without other: and this is the image of the Trinity.

Having quoted this passage from her play, *The Zeal of Thy House*, she then goes on to say: "Of these clauses, the one which gives the most trouble to the hearer is that dealing with the Creative Idea. (The word is here used, not in the philosopher's sense, in which the 'Idea' tends to be equated with the 'Word,' but quite simply in the sense intended by the writer when he says: 'I have an idea for a book.'") Dorothy Sayers's "Idea" is thus one particular kind of Idea, and to get an overall balance we have to pay more attention to the throwaway remark she has placed in parentheses. The point is, finally, that the question concerns not only the strength or weakness of a human capacity as giving rise to the greater or less perfection of a work of art, but also, if God is to be included, its range or scope, its breadth or narrowness. I think therefore that we have to say that Dorothy Sayers's "Idea," so far as she makes it explicit, is a narrow one, and for being a narrow one, is all the more vivid; and that if it is not at all weak, it nevertheless appears to be circumscribed. One might want to know what happens to the philosopher's Ideas, or for that matter what happens to the remarkable Ideas of William Blake. Because of his alleged deficiencies as a literary artist, which is admittedly a problem, are they not supposed to count? This I must stress, first of all because it helps to explain the puzzle of the relationship between Sayers's natural triunity and all the other possible natural triunities, and secondly because it seems to me to be a widespread fundamental error of modern times (with an exception I will note later) to be incapable of seeing the transcendental force of philosophical Ideas as they used to be.

Ideas in modern times are usually empirical, critical or negative; or else, if they are positive and creative, are apt to settle for a rootless aestheticism. But the transcendental status of certain philosophical Ideas, of the very Idea of Truth, for instance, or of Goodness or Value, or of the individual rational subject, means that, as for St. Augustine, all such Ideas, in their disembodiment, lie in the first place in the Mind of God, and only in the second place in the minds of human beings or philosophers, or in embodied "words" of any kind. The absence of the very notion of a transcendental means that modern philosophy leaves us with the choice between materialism or analytical reductionism on the one hand, and a wild existentialism or an erratic impressionism on the other. Yet since Dorothy Sayers, not unlike Vico, gives us a creative Idea that makes sense, it would be unfair to hold against her the relative narrowness of her "disembodied Idea," which would be capable of expansion and is not actually confined to its function as producing visible works of art. "The creative act," she goes on, "does not depend for its fulfilment upon its manifestation in a material creation." Hence, "the glib assertion that 'God needs his creation as much as His creation needs him' is not a true analogy from the mind of the human creator." To which she adds: "Nevertheless, it is true that the urgent desire of the creative mind is towards expression in material form." And there, surely, we have it: "the urgent desire of the creative mind," which is the urgent desire of the mind of Dorothy Sayers in particular.

All this implies that there is a certain narrowness also on the side of the Power of communication. Obviously Dorothy Sayers is not lacking in this. Who has more strength in this way than she? But it is communication of the literary sort, and not of the sort which might be called that of "personal experience" in all its variety, some of which she might have been inclined to call "sentimental." (In this connection one would have to consider above all the story of Harriet Vane, as well as Dorothy Sayers's own life.) In any case, in view of the whole truth, I must put it that if the triunity be expressed as that of (i) Thinking, (ii) Actual Making in embodied form, and (iii) Loving, then for Dorothy Sayers, with her emphasis on a special kind of *making*, the thinking is, so to say, a *making* sort of thinking, and the loving has even to be called a *making* sort of loving. But there are kinds of thought and kinds of love which elude this precise pattern. Characteristically, she finds that Dante is primarily a storyteller; but this is not what an Italian would say.

Having said all this, however, it must also be admitted that her philosophical acumen is very considerable, and that it chimes in well enough with the one wholly modern school of philosophy that has maintained the necessary transcendental Ideas, namely, the phenomenological school of Edmund Husserl, eminently represented in the United States by the World Phenomenology Institute—with which is associated the International Society for Philosophy and Literature—at Belmont, Massachussets. If *The Mind of the Maker* is a meeting place between literature and philosophy, these institutions are likewise largely dedicated to the principle of human creativity. Unfortunately, *The Mind of the Maker* has not yet received the attention it deserves; even to the comparatively few who know the author as a religious writer, as well as for her novels, the book does not seem to be known for its precise philosophical significance. In working out her theory, Dorothy Sayers displays an instinctive grasp of important phenomenological principles, especially those of exact definition as preceding proof, and the appeal to experience in its givenness. As for the first, the "bracketing" principle, it is not only necessary that we should say whether or not we believe, or whether or not something has been proved, but first of all exactly what it is that is being said, with or without the assumption of reality. This might be thought obvious, yet how often, as she notes, do people vociferously deny or affirm without bothering to ascertain what it is that is actually being said. Thus she begins by telling us in the Preface that the book is not "an expression of personal belief" or "an apology for Christianity," but, as is in due course explained, a statement of what the Trinity *means*. The doctrine can then *either* be affirmed as a plain matter of fact on the basis of a certain kind of human experience, *or else* affirmed as a matter of theological belief regarding the integral structure of the universe and the nature of God—or possibly both. At the same time, the human experience in question is, as already shown, carefully demarcated. Other philosophical points well explained are (i) the distinction between natural law as regularity in nature and conventional law as depending on stipulation [ch. I], and (ii) the distinction between the use of the word 'problem' as meaning 'logical problem' and the use or misuse of it as referring to value judgments or social predicaments such as that of unemployment [ch. XI]. But here she overdoes it, since she will scarcely allow us to use the word 'problem' at all outside the logical context, whereas there are metaphysical problems that are really problems without being strictly logical ones. In fact, we continue to use the word in all sorts of contexts, and it cannot be denied that *The Mind of the Maker* presents us with a good many problems.

Not everything is dealt with that would ultimately need to be dealt with. On the other hand, we are given metaphysics as well as phenomenological method, and the fundamental metaphysical suggestion would appear to be susceptible of much more development than it has received so far. I must also say that I have never read such a trenchant and convincing metaphysical exposition of the problem of evil as that offered in Chapter VII, "Maker of All Things, Maker of Ill Things." The distinction between metaphysical negation or merely relative evil (if there is any x, there must also be a not-x) and moral evil as the willful opposition of a destructive spirit (not only not-x, but maliciously anti-x) is very simply and clearly drawn; and the conclusion is no less persuasive: "We must not . . . try to behave as though the Fall (of Man) had never occurred nor yet say that the Fall was a good thing in itself. But we may redeem the Fall by a creative act." This actually gives to "creative act" a much wider scope, after all, than that which seemed to have been implied in her concentration on the artistic experience. As already suggested, it is not her intention to exclude other people's experience, but, wisely, to talk about the experience which she herself has had. To this it can be added that while in *The Mind of the Maker* she expresses the sensitive person's revolt against the analytic reductionism of scientific language as it is often recommended, she can be as alive to the realities of scientific experience as to any of her own. The incidental scientific inaccuracies in *The Documents in the Case* do not diminish the significance of this.

At the Week-End Course on Dorothy Sayers held at Moor Park College, Farnham, England in April 1977, one of the speakers observed that Dorothy Sayers shows a tendency to be carried away by the fascination of patterns, further instanced by her fondness for knitting. This is a serious matter since the charge preferred against the older metaphysics has usually been that it was a kind of artificial patterning, and phenomenology has sought to maintain the necessary transcendental ideas or principles without falling into the traps of patterning, but adhering to experience. On the same occasion I was asked by someone whether *The Mind of the Maker* was not, after all, a piece of intellectual structuring imposed *a priori* on actual experience: the same question put in other words. The answer I would suggest is that *The Mind of the Maker* might indeed be considered patterning in that unacceptable sense if one tried to push the theory too far without adequate consideration, or if one wanted to make use of it on all occasions; and apart from that there is no doubt some excess of patterning in, say, *The Five Red Herrings*. But with these provisos, and with the caution required in all theoretical procedures, I do not think that the objection applies. The point is, I should say, that it is not only metaphysical system-building but *music* that is patterning, and the great musician makes it expressive. It is a question of what the particular given person happens to find the most moving given experience, and so potentially a divine analogy, which might in some cases be more obviously intellectual, and in others less so. How carefully patterned, and how well-knit, is *The Divine Comedy*! Yet it has proved more time-resisting than the critics of its intellectualism.

In any case, there is an intimate connection between the author of the famous detective novels and the author of *The Mind of the Maker*, which, far from being *a priori*, belonged to her later career, when she had given up novel-writing, and was the result of reflection on that past, as well as of her religious conversion. And the connection is even more profound than that which is suggested by her plain declaration that everything she has to say about the natural triunity is based on her experience as a novelist or writer. For in the novels there are hints of mystic insight that take us into that strange realm of transparencies where the world which is outside this world, and yet somehow at the same time within it, becomes the object of more or less direct vision. The excitement of the pattern might be taken as either poetical or metaphysical. This would take too long to illustrate, and it is for individual readers to say what they themselves find. But we may notice here, as an example of the undercurrent connecting the two different periods of her writing, what she writes in *The Mind of the Maker* about the novel *Murder Must Advertise*. In this book, she says, "I undertook . . . to present a contrast of two 'cardboard' worlds, equally fictitious—the world of advertising

and the world of the post-war 'Bright Young People.' . . . I mentioned
this intention to a reader, who instantly replied: 'Yes; and Peter Wimsey,
who represents reality, never appears in either world except in disguise.'
It was perfectly true; and I had never noticed it. With all its defects of
realism, there had been some measure of integral truth about the book's
Idea, since it issued, without my conscious connivance, in a true
symbolism." In particuar, the fantastic and poetical incidents in this
novel between Lord Peter Wimsey and Dian de Momerie are already
suggestive of the Invisible Reality, first disguised—by an ancient rite—
as Harlequin, and then, later on, when he is whistling that traditional
tune in the dark . . . "'It's too *stupid*,' said Dian. The sound was so
bodiless that it seemed to have no abiding-place." The incident of the
chess set in *Gaudy Night* is also mentioned by Dorothy Sayers as having
been at the time a piece of unconscious patterning. This particular image
is of a rather intellectual kind, but the motions of her spirit, as with any
great poet, are partly unconscious. Incidentally, in the short story "The
Unsolved Puzzle of the Man with no Face" we already find the same
distinction between the logical and the creative solution expatiated on in
Chapter XI, "Problem Picture," of *The Mind of the Maker*. We thus
have to say, altogether, that she was by nature poetically logical, or
poetically metaphysical. The metaphysics of *The Mind of the Maker*
has its own poetic inevitability. No wonder she was drawn to Dante!

Richard L. Harp

The Mind of the Maker: The Theological Aesthetic of Dorothy Sayers and Its Application to Poetry

DOROTHY SAYERS'S *The Mind of The Maker* is not a systematic treatise of any kind. Its purpose is not to propound aesthetic or theological dogma. Rather, it is to make suggestions about the nature of artistic creativity which are based on analogies between statements in the Christian creeds about the Trinity and the creative experience of writers. Because the book does not pretend to be rigorous or definitive in the elaboration of its statements, one would have expected that in the great many years since its appearance numerous other critics would have added to its theoretical structure or would have applied its insights in the work of practical criticism. But this has not been done to any appreciable degree, and therefore it is my purpose in this essay to examine *The Mind of the Maker* both theoretically and practically. I must necessarily be less complete about these matters than I would like, but I shall at least give examples of the book's relevance for both the theoretical and the practical critic. First, though, let me summarize the book's argument.

Sayers writes that "the characteristic common to God and man is . . . the desire and the ability to make things."[1] Poets are known through their work as God is known through His creation. The poets' minds are revealed through their poems, which communicate the content of their minds and of their experiences to readers, and evoke a response from them. This is analogous to the workings of the Trinitarian Godhead. The Father is the *Idea,* the generative form of the poem; the Son is the *Energy* by which the Idea is incarnated in a work of art; the Spirit is the *Power* responsible for the communion between the poet's mind, the poem, and the audience. Such an intimate connection between the parts of the creative act is necessary for poetry to be communal and not isolated in its own uniqueness. The poem or story cannot be a thing-in-itself, but must, through selection of a proper plot, artistic medium, etc., reveal the intent of the author. In a mystery story, for example, if the arrangement of the circumstances does not permit one to believe in the possibility of the crime's occurring, the story has failed to fulfill the requirements of the form in which it was written. Or, perhaps, the author was not a good seer. In either case, the story depends on something beyond itself, but which is not extrinsic to its nature. The nature of the work is not to be in and for itself. Neither, however, can the work be didactic; to the contrary, communication of an Idea demands a specific form of expression and produces a response only when a reader recognizes the faithful rendering of images in that form. The Power or Spirit of the work is increased when an individual's response is then added to all the critics, actors, and other readers who have also experienced that work. The histories of words and metaphors are important here, for "each new work should be a fresh focus of power through which former streams of beauty, emotion, and reflection are directed" [p. 119]. Hence, the intrusion of anything truly extrinsic (i.e., didactic) to this three-part activity would destroy the creation.

Any elaboration of the theoretical foundation of this aesthetic must begin by locating and examining the biblical sources which relate to it. There are many scriptural passages which could be fruitfully discussed; I shall be able to look at only a few but I can thereby suggest the kind of discussion that is most productive. We must begin with the beginning: the Genesis account of creation. The following three verses will serve as a model for our discussion of this Hebrew description of God's creative activity in the foundation of the world: "In the beginning God created the heaven and the earth. . . . And God said, Let there be light; and there was light. And God saw the light, that it was good" [Gen. 1.1, 3–4]. In these lines is the ultimate source for the Christian understanding of divine creativity, and consequently for Sayers's application of it to literary creation. Creation is in Genesis at one and the same time: 1) an Idea: "In the beginning," for an Idea is necessary before anything can begin; 2) the Energy or execution of that Idea: "And God said, Let there be . . .," which tells us that God performs creation by fiat, by a simple giving of a word; and 3) the Power or love of that Idea and Energy: "And God saw . . . that it was good." Although the text, because it is a literary narrative, distinguishes three parts to this creative action, we must remember Sayers's insistence, repeated throughout her book, that all such action is essentially simple and simultaneous. God would never have begun to create, would never have had the Idea of creation or have executed that Idea, had He not also known that the whole process would be full of love and Power: Power is both the effect and the cause of creation. Similarly, a writer simultaneously conceives and delights in the Idea for a book. And neither the conception nor the delight is possible without a concurrent embodiment of them in imagery or narrative action through creative Energy. Thus, all parts of the creative trinity are distinct but unified, all are both cause and effect of one another. The statement in the Athanasian Creed in respect of the Christian Trinity is quite specific on this point: "In this Trinity none is afore or after other, none is greater or less than another; but the whole three Persons are co-eternal and co-equal."[2]

It should also be remembered that creation and re-creation is the profoundest theme that runs throughout the whole Bible. For it is God's loss of delight in humanity, His seeing that "the wickedness of man was great in the earth, and that every imagination of the thoughts of his heart was only evil continually" [Gen. 6.5], that leads Him to repent that He had made man and to determine to send the flood upon the earth. But simultaneous with this decision to destroy creation is God's determination to make a new creation: for He says to Noah: "Behold I, even I, do bring a flood of waters upon the earth, to destroy all flesh, wherein is the breath of life. . . . But with thee will I establish my covenant" [Gen. 6.17–18]. And after the flood the rainbow, that most delightful of all symbols, is shown to Noah as a sign that God loves His creation and that He will indeed "remember my covenant, which is between me and you and every living creature of all flesh" [Gen. 9.15]. In this event of the flood, then, God's three-fold creative action is made especially clear. He sees human wickedness and as a result conceives the Idea of the flood; and He establishes His new creation by means of His spoken word to Noah, which is validated, given Power, through the gift of the rainbow.

Nearly the whole of the Psalms also testifies to the richness and pervasiveness of God's creativity. The Psalmist frequently finds himself cut off from God and hence from life itself; he calls to God *"de pro-fundis,"* "out of the depths," [130.1] or cries, "My God, my God, why hast thou forsaken me? why art thou so far from helping me" [22.1]. The Psalmist recognizes overwhelmingly that without God there can be no vitality of any kind, so he implores God to re-create his mind and heart and to show him wisdom in his inward parts: "Create in me a clean heart,

O God; and renew a right spirit within me. Cast me not away from thy presence; and take not thy Holy Spirit from me" [51.10–11]. If this is done, the Psalmist is quite definite what the result will be; his tongue "Shall sing aloud of thy righteousness," for God will have opened "my lips and my mouth shall show forth thy praise" [51.14–15], and he will be able with all the righteous to "Be glad in the Lord, and rejoice . . . and shout for joy" [32.11]. This is over and again the pattern of the Psalms: the Psalmist is afraid, or even experiences the absence of God's creativity and vitality, because of his own or others' wrongdoing, he then prays for a renewal and a remaking of his broken and contrite heart, and he finally experiences the power and delight of this new creation as he sings songs of praise, blessing, and thanksgiving. It is the same pattern we have noticed in Genesis and it contains the same basic three parts: 1) the awareness of the need for a creative action, whether because of the formless void of Genesis 1.2, or of the world destroyed by flood, or of the shattered heart of a contrite sinner; 2) the creative Energy, which God may execute by a simple spoken word, or by the making of a covenant, or by, in the case of the Psalmist, a washing, cleansing, or purging (he uses any number of verbs); 3) the response to or the Power of this creative Energy, which may be the simple perception of creation's goodness, or the forming of the rainbow, or the rejoicing of the sinner's renewed heart.

The Old Testament contains a particularly rich description of the second part of Sayers's creative triad, that which she calls "the Energy revealed in creation." In discussing this Sayers remarks: "The mind is not the sum of its works, though it includes them all. . . . Before it made them, it included them all, potentially, and having finished them, it still includes them. It is both immanent in them and transcendent" [p. 63]. She then adds an important qualification to this statement: although authors' personalities do include all their works, "as soon as they are expressed in material form they have a separate reality *for us*"—works do have a reality apart from their author's mind [p. 63]. The book of Proverbs describes the activity of Wisdom, God's agent in creation, in similar terms. Wisdom declares that "The Lord possessed me in the beginning of his way, Before his works of old. I was set up from everlasting, from the beginning, Or ever the earth was" [8.22–23]. She further proclaims that during the work of creation, "Then was I by him, as one brought up with him: And I was daily his delight, Rejoicing always before him" [8.30]. Let us see how this is analogous to what Sayers tells us of creative Energy.

The major point of the first nine chapters of Proverbs is that Wisdom contains all the knowledge a person needs to lead a happy and productive life on earth. She herself shows the way to, and indeed embodies, riches, strength, beauty, understanding, all the things that normal human life seeks and desires. But in the remarkable passages cited above she quite clearly implies that she provides the needs of practical life precisely because she has been with the Lord from the beginning—indeed, even before the beginning began—that she is, in effect, co-eternal with Him. Nothing could more specifically comment upon what Sayers has said of creative Energy. For Wisdom, too, Proverbs tells us, is both "immanent" in the works of creation and also "transcendent" of them. And, furthermore, Wisdom's incarnation in the material forms of the world does assure us, as does an author's Energy, that the ideas in the creative mind of the maker will have a "separate reality for us." Proverbs speaks of Wisdom having "builded her house" and "hewn out her seven pillars"; of having "killed her beasts," "mingled her wine," and "furnished her table" [9.1–2]. To know Wisdom fully, then, one must know her in two different but complementary ways: as she is in herself, which is to know her as she reveals herself in practical, daily experiential events, and as she is recognized as a reflection of her divine maker.

The Power or love of creation is also noted in these passages about Wisdom in Proverbs. During God's creative action she says, if I may repeat, that she "was by him, as one brought up with him: And I was daily his delight, Rejoicing always before him: Rejoicing in the habitable part of his earth; And my delights were with the sons of men" [8.30–31]. Here again, then, the community that creation establishes between God, His creative Wisdom, and the begotten creation is declared, and it is stated that this community is characterized by "rejoicing" and delight ("my delights were with the sons of men"). Indeed, it is because of this community that Wisdom can command human beings, in the very next verse, to "hearken unto me, O ye children: For blessed are they that keep my ways." Her Power, to use Sayers's word, over her listeners is established because she is the intermediary, the active bridge between God and humanity, as she reflects in her words and in her playfulness the divine Idea of creation, which she has possessed "from the beginning, Or ever the earth was."

Of the many passages in the New Testament that reflect the trinitarian nature of divine creativity, I shall speak of only one: the Prolog of St. John's Gospel. In these verses we have both a recapitulation and a profound intensification, because of their imaging the whole creative process through the incarnate Word, Jesus Christ, of the accounts in Genesis, Psalms, and Proverbs of the founding and sustaining of the world. The following verses from this marvelous Prolog will serve as the focus for our discussion of this text in relation to *The Mind of the Maker:*

> In the beginning was the Word, and the Word was with God, and the Word was God. The same was in the beginning with God. All things were made by Him; and without Him was not any thing made that was made. In Him was life; and the life was the light of men. . . . He was in the world, and the world was made by Him, and the world knew Him not. He came unto His own, and His own received Him not. But as many as received Him, to them gave He power to become the sons of God, even to them that believe on His name: Which were born, not of blood, nor of the will of the flesh, nor of the will of man, but of God. And the Word was made flesh, and dwelt among us, (and we beheld His glory, the glory as of the only begotten of the Father,) full of grace and truth. [vss. 1–4, 10–14]

The first words of this Gospel are the same as those of Genesis: "In the beginning." Now, however, a more specific description of the circumstances of that beginning is provided: there was a Word which was with God, which in fact was God, and through Whom all things were made. This is the clearest statement the Bible makes concerning the union of God's creative Idea and the Energy which brings that Idea into being. After speaking about those who reject this Word—"He was in the world, and the world was made by Him, and the world knew Him not"—St. John proclaims the effect for humanity of the divine creative act: "As many as received Him, to them gave He power to become the sons of God" [v. 12]. It is this "power" which Christ tells about to His disciples in some of His long discourses that St. John records and which is fully transmitted to them at Pentecost.[3] This power embodies the new creation that the Gospels state is Christ's mission to bring, and as such it is of equal importance with the creation recorded in Genesis. For the new creation, like the old, comes "not of blood, nor of the will of the flesh, nor of the will of man, but of God" [v. 13]. And, further, this Word and the power that it brings will not be transient, nor subject to the weakness of those to whom it is spoken; to the contrary, It will bring into Its life all those who accept It: "If ye abide in me, and my words abide in you, ye shall ask what ye will, and it shall be done unto you" [Jn. 15.7]. Christ will make manifest what the Old Testament "words" of creation could only declare; namely, glory, "the glory as of the only begotten of the Father" [v. 14].

I have no further room to discuss the way in which the New Testament has helped Sayers establish and make vital her notion of aesthetic creativity, but obviously much more could be done. Throughout St. John's Gospel Christ refers to the community of His Father, Himself as the bearer of His Father's Word, and the disciples who are empowered by that Word. And of course there are St. Paul's many discussions of the subject, as, for example, his Letter to the Colossians in which he speaks of Christ as the "image of the invisible God, the firstborn of every creature: For by Him were all things created" [1.15–16] and who can therefore give us the Power to be reconciled with that invisible God. But I must now turn to the one other text to which *The Mind of the Maker* owes a major debt: the *De Trinitate* of St. Augustine.

This great treatise, which Augustine worked on for sixteen years, influenced both the method and the content of Sayers's book. About one-half of *De Trinitate,* as one of Augustine's best commentators points out, is concerned "to *show* us the Trinity, as it were, by means of various images and analogies which do in some way represent it. But none of these is developed with the rigor and method of the Scholastics. It would seem that the author is less concerned with satisfying the mind with a rigorous demonstration than with gradually leading souls to God in Three Persons by means of a series of ever simpler images of divine activity."[4] Augustine's basic theological purpose was always confessional; that is, he searched both nature and the human soul for the traces of their divine authorship and he then declared the fruits of his search. He never, in his major works, put forth a body of thought or doctrine which could be judged apart from his own soul's spiritual inquiry or from God's supernatural creativity. When he discusses the Trinity, therefore, he is most concerned that it be seen not only as a transcendental dogma but also as an existential reality known in the daily lives of men and women. And it is just such an approach to God, an approach based on His trinitarian nature—"one substance, three persons"—as it is reflected in the world and in the individual soul that Sayers uses for her own book.

One of the trinities that Augustine discovers within the human mind relates especially well to Sayers's discussion of artistic creativity. This trinity is composed of memory, understanding, and will (*memoria, intelligentia, voluntas*), and it is the burden of Augustine's exegesis of them to show how they are three distinct faculties which nonetheless comprise only one single act: they have, he says, "not three lives but one life, not three minds but one mind, [so] it follows that they are certainly not three substances, but one life, one mind, and one essence. . . . But they are three in that they are mutually referred to each other."[5] Augustine then becomes quite specific about the way in which each of these is separate yet also simultaneously contains all the others: "For I remember that I have memory, understanding, and will; and I understand that I understand, will, and remember; and I will that I will, remember, and understand; and at the same time I remember my whole memory, understanding, and will" [*De Trin.* 10.18].

It is illuminating to compare this trinity to Sayers's artistic trinity of Idea, Energy, and Power.[6] Sayers notes quite often that the last member of this triad is the most difficult to elucidate, a fact testified to by the traditional English word for it, 'ghost,' but I have found that many readers regard Sayers's notion of Idea similarly difficult to grasp. For it is as hard for all but the most confirmed idealists to understand a pure idea as it is to understand pure spirit. (What sense is one to make, for example, of Croce's statement that a Raphael without hands would still have been a great painter?) The Judaeo-Christian God always made Himself known through material creation; before His human incarnation He had filled the Hebrew world with concrete signs of His presence: manna, quail, cinders burning a prophet's lips, or a "still, small voice" speaking to another prophet after fire, earthquake, and hail. We understand Sayers best, then, when she speaks of the Energy, the Word, of creation; St. Augustine, however, can aid us quite specifically in understanding the first and last terms of the creative trinity, Idea and Power.

For Augustine suggests that the first act of the intellect is one of memory, and some of the greatest poets in the world have echoed his statement when they composed their own works. The epic poet always began his work with an invocation of one of the nine muses, who, as the daughter of Mnemosyne, Memory, knew "of the things that are and will be and were before this."[7] Homer, for example, begs the Muse to help him tell the tale of "that resourceful man," Odysseus, just as Virgil asks her to help him remember the reasons why Aeneas was pursued across the seas by the vengeful goddess Juno. Milton brings these classical daughters of memory into the Christian world by declaring that the muse whom he invokes (whose name he gives as Urania, the muse of astronomy, rather than Calliope, the muse of epic poetry) converses with "Eternal Wisdom" and did with

Wisdom thy Sister . . . play
In the presence of th' Almighty Father, pleas'd
With thy Celestial Song. [*Paradise Lost,* VII, 9–12]

Such lines, of course, recall to us the words of Proverbs about Wisdom.

This traditional notion of the muse is astonishingly analogous to what Augustine tells us of the trinity of the mind and to what Sayers says about artistic creation. For the epic poet's Idea must come from the muse, as she is the one who knows all things; nothing escapes her, as she is in her own nature memory itself. Further, the muse accompanies the poet throughout the incarnation of the creative act: Milton refers to her presence in the beginning of four of the twelve books of *Paradise Lost,* as she "inspires/Easy my unpremeditated Verse" [IX, 23–24], and Hesiod says that "The sweet music flows from their lips effortlessly." Finally, the effect or Power on the affections of their songs, Hesiod says, is to "delight the heart of their father Zeus on Olympus."

Some great poets, then, would agree with Augustine that the mind's first act is one of memory; and I think we may also conclude that such an act leads, still employing Augustine's terminology, to engaging the understanding—the writing itself of the poem, in which what was before only remembered may now be seen in a material form—and to moving the affections and the will.

We are now prepared, I believe, to summarize how Sayers's aesthetic is correlative to some major biblical and Augustinian texts and how it is illuminative of the most significant poetic convention—the Muses— that the poets themselves have used about creativity. Sayers suggests that the knowledge of the Idea of a book is always with the writer, "while writing it and after it is finished, just as it was at the beginning" [p. 49]. The Idea, then, presides over the entire composition, although it cannot be perceived apart from Energy and Power. This same organizing function is given by Augustine to memory in respect to the trinity within the mind ("I remember simultaneously the whole of my memory and understanding and will") and it is also the role given by the poets to the muses, the daughters of memory. The Energy of the work, which Sayers describes as "the sum and process of all the activity which brings the book into temporal and spatial existence" [p. 49], is what Augustine calls understanding and may be likened to the role the epic poet himslf plays when inspired by the muse. The poet, filled with the muses' knowledge of "the things that are and will be and were before this," gives material form to this inspiration. And it is this creative Energy which is also most conspicuous in the biblical texts that I have cited.

Finally, there is what Sayers calls the creative Power, the activity by means of which both author and reader are aware of and respond to the completed book. And here Sayers does not sufficiently emphasize, I think, the delight, enjoyment, or love which comprise this Power of the work. We are all familiar with the delight of discussing a favorite book with our friends, and such delight is the most characteristic element of the third part of the trinities we are discussing. God declares to Job, for example, that when the foundations of the earth were laid, "the morning stars sang together, And all the sons of God shouted for joy" [38.6–7]. Also, Augustine notes that "in memory and the understanding, the knowledge and science of many things are contained; but the will is present by which we may enjoy or use them" [De Trin. 10.13]. The will leads us to desire and love what we have remembered and understood, and thus there is an affective faculty as well as recollective and cognitive ones within the Trinity. Etienne Gilson remarks that for Augustine the will, which is love, is not only effect but also cause of the word's generation by the mind: "What we produce we want to have and possess; what we have produced we cling to and delight in. Love, then, is doubly interested in every generation; it caused it and after causing it clings to the thing produced."[8] This of course reminds us specifically of the comforting powers which Christ promised would come from the Spirit, of the delight which Proverbs says that Wisdom effects when she plays before the Lord, and which Hesiod says is given to the gods by the songs of the muses. Indeed, I will soon suggest that celebration is by no means too strong a word to describe the operation of the creative Power in poetry.

One has a great interest, naturally, in seeing how Sayers's trinitarian aesthetic might illuminate the literature that one knows and loves. *The Mind of the Maker* contains many examples, drawn from greatly diverse texts, that illustrate the author's arguments, but Sayers does not take any one text or author and thoroughly and consistently apply her principles to it. Since this is the test that is required by most of today's practicing academic critics of any critical theory, I want to set forth some of the ways this might be done.

The great virtue of Sayers's aesthetic is that it does not depend upon categorical formulations; it sees literature as both deriving from and continuing to embody, for as long as it is heard or read, creative Energy: literature, that is to say, is never an artifact to be dissected, a fact that will surely lighten the hearts of students and "common readers." For Sayers, theory is never an end in itself; it is rather a means, a conductor by which we may be led into the dynamic life of literature, and theory most emphatically will not be permitted by her to destroy that life with its sterile tentacles. Thus it is possible to view literature as religious in the profoundest sense: as that which, recalling etymology, "ties us together." No theological framework need be imposed upon a poem, nor need we even search for theological elements or references in it in order to understand it as exhibiting and communicating an experience that is analogous to the divine.

Given such an approach, I am convinced that one of the best ways to use it in conducting the work of practical criticism of poetry is through the study of the words of the poem. Most modern rhetoricians, while writing what seem necessarily mechanical and superficial textbooks on "how to write," find special delight in giving advice on choosing correct diction. Organization, coherence, unity, these are all finite and manipulable subjects: but finding the right word—there is a matter both mysterious and inexhaustible. Words can give us access to the life of our subject in a way that "strategies" of sentence structure or analyses of paragraph organization can never approach. We have already seen the importance of the divine Word to Sayers's aesthetic, but we can never be fully persuaded of that until we also see how that primal Word is reflected in each particular word, phrase, and statement that compose a literary work. And poetry will serve this purpose best, as it demands the economical and sensitive use of language.

Sayers herself notes, in discussing the Power of created works, that "words and phrases become charged with the Power . . . by passing through the minds of successive writers" [p. 116], and throughout the book she gives brief examples from Shakespeare, Keats, Tennyson, or her own fiction of the way in which words, as writers make use of their accumulated history and themselves add to that history, may take us into the life of the creative trinity. Words come to poets with a life of their own, but it is a life they are free to reshape and extend in their own particular fashion: "the words of the common poet—the creator in words—must never be interpreted absolutely, but only in relation to their context."[9] And it is new and complete contexts that poets are free to create—not out of nothing, to be sure, but using materials they have inherited, refashioning them so that both their lineage and their singularity are recognizable. To use Sayers's words: "Creation proceeds by the discovery of new conceptual relations between things, so as to form them into systems having a consistent wholeness corresponding to an image in the mind, and consequently, possessing real existence."[10] Words, then, and the contexts which they build, are the tools which discover these "new conceptual relations" and which thus do the work of creation.

I have chosen, for a number of reasons, to look first at two poems of Ben Jonson as a test case for this aesthetic. Jonson is still much underrated as a poet. Some critics, those who fall victim to the occupational hazard of pigeonholing, have attacked him as a merely learned man, full of classical wisdom but with little of the poet's natural lyricism.[11] If they were to use Sayers's terms, they would say Jonson's imagination was a "scalene trinity,"[12] with a surplus of creative Ideas and a deficiency of Energy and Power. But the balance, depth, and emotion of Jonson's mind are apparent, and perhaps only apparent, when one is specifically aware of the various parts of the creative act and the ways in which they are interdependent. For Jonson's classicism, while it did provide him with a vocabulary and a poetic diction that was heavily Latinate, did so with effects opposed to those conventionally cited. Latin was not a dead or learned language for Jonson; its words contained even in their English derivatives real Energy and Power, and Jonson's extensive use of them in contexts both conventional and personal is a testimony to his understanding of the dynamic nature of poetic creation.

Further, Jonson is not generally considered a religious poet; that is, few of his poems have religious subjects. But I shall try to make clear that his poems are profoundly religious when judged by Sayers's standards of Idea, Energy, and Power, and I hope to show thereby that the brilliance both of Sayers's aesthetic and of Jonson's poetry is their mutual concern, not with formulas, schemes, or categories, but with life and its abundance.

Interestingly enough, Jonson, one of several great English poets who was also a significant literary critic, made a few remarks about poetic creation that are strikingly similar to those of Sayers. In his prose work *Discoveries* he distinguishes three separate parts of the poetic act: the poet, the poesy, and the poem. His discussion of poesy is especially crucial for us, for it is the agent by which creation takes place and is therefore analogous to Sayers's Energy, Proverbs' Wisdom, and St. John's Word. Jonson's "poet" and "poem" only very roughly correspond to Sayers's Idea and Power, but his remarks about "poesy" are illuminating. It is, he says, "the habit, or the art . . . which had her origin from Heaven, received thence from the Hebrews, was held in prime estimation with the Greeks, transmitted to the Latins and all nations that professed civility. The study of it . . . offers to mankind a certain rule and pattern of living well and happily."[13] Poesy is the means, the *tekhné,* the craft through which poetry is written and it can be nowhere better grasped than through the poem's words. Let us now apply Sayers's and Jonson's aesthetic to one of Jonson's secular poems and see what illumination of the creative act may be discovered in it.

TO WILLIAM CAMDEN

Camden, most reverend head, to whom I owe
    All that I am in arts, all that I know.
(How nothing's that?) to whom my countrey owes
    The great renowne, and name wherewith shee goes.
Then thee the age sees not that thing more grave,
    More high, more holy, that shee more would crave.   5
What name, what skill, with faith hast thou in things!
    What sight in searching the most antique springs!
What weight, and what authoritie in thy speech!
    Man scarse can make that doubt, but thou canst teach.   10
Pardon free truth, and let thy modestie,
    Which conquers all, be once over-come by thee.
Many of thine this better could, then I,
    But for their powers, accept my pietie.

This is an especially good poem for us to consider here; most of the readers of this essay are students and scholars, and this poem is a tribute from a student to his old teacher who also happened to be one of Renaissance England's greatest scholars.

The structure of the poem as seen through Sayers's aesthetic is this: *Idea:* Jonson's memory of his teacher; *Energy*: the words of the poem, which give rise to the *Power*: the community of praise and gratitude which the poem establishes between poet, subject, and audience. This Power is inspirational, as it arises from a celebration of Camden's very nature, and all of us as readers may participate in it since we have either known teachers like Camden or may aspire to be such ourselves. The key element in Sayers's poetic, I think, is the creative Energy, those words and other material elements by which the Idea is turned into fact and by means of which Power is loosed, so let us look at a few of the words in the poem as examples of this process.

"Camden, most *reverend* head" (l. 1). To revere means "to feel again respect or awe." Here, then, Jonson's memory of his teacher, which is the Idea of the poem, is immediately incarnated in a word, "reverend"; and such a word stirs not only the poet who utters it but also all those who hear it: their own memories recollect, and pass on to the understanding and the will for their cognition and assent (using Augustine's terms), what it means to be a teacher and a scholar. Such a response to this word, and to the poem as a whole, is the Power of the poem, a Power, let it be stressed, that forms a community and that can make of the poem an act of communal celebration. The poem, that is to say, can be read in the same way as the biblical texts cited earlier. Camden, like Wisdom in Proverbs, may through this poem be "daily our delight," and Jonson's ability to make him such derives from the very nature of creativity, as it was ordained and described in the first chapter of Genesis and of St. John's Gospel. In looking at the Energy of this poem as manifested in its words (e.g., "reverend") we are made aware simultaneously of its Idea (memory of a teacher) and its Power (an act of gratitude and thanksgiving); just as, when we hear of St. John's "Word," we must also think of the Father who generated Him and of the light and life that He communicated to the whole world. Through Sayers's poetic, then, poems such as this can be seen as one unified creative act, deeply analogous to divine creation but without a hint of dogma or theological formulation.

Jonson next says that he owes to Camden "All that I am in arts, all that I know/(How *nothing's* that!)" [1.3]. Here Jonson acknowledges, as do all students to their great teachers, Camden's major formative influence upon him, but says that even so his art and skill are on the brink of "nothing." And here again a word, "nothing," in this context takes us to the heart of the creative trinity. For what could be more biblical or more in accord with what Sayers tells us of creativity? That is, the best evidence that Jonson can present that he is indeed "something" is this poem itself, this act of creation, this Energy, which has at its heart gratitude and thanksgiving. And the power of the poem is our similar praising of those who have formed or made us out of "nothing."

England itself, Jonson says, owes to Camden "The great *renown* and *name* wherewith she goes" [1.4]. Here Jonson suggests that Camden has uttered the "words" about England (he was a historian) which results in making its past available as a present inspiration to its citizens. Again, then, through Jonson's choice of words to express the poem's controlling Idea, a community is established for the poem. For we all know that to name is to give real being to a created object, to actualize its existence as a distinct thing. Camden has named Britain; Jonson names, gives renown to Camden; the reader then could, perhaps, praise Jonson but it is clear that the pattern which is here established should lead to that ultimate place where names were given: the garden of origins and creations: Eden. There Adam named all the animals of the earth as soon as God had created and brought them before him. The word, the Energy of Jonson's poem, then, "renown" or "name" (they are etymologically the same) reflects the Idea of the poem while at the same time providing the Power which establishes the poem in a wider communal context.

Then consider Jonson's unusual tribute to Camden's abilities in line 7: "What name, what skill, what faith hast thou in *things.*" The Latin word for "thing" is *res,* from which English derives the words "real" and "reality." Reality is of course precisely what the divine act of creation makes, and human creation, Sayers continually reminds us, imitates that divine act. Jonson praises, then, Camden's "faith" in reality, for it is this which makes any achievement possible and which gives man the knowledge that he may re-create through his own faculties what God has put before him. But, let us repeat, it is not only Camden that is praised here. The Idea of the poem, gratitude to a maker, and the words of the poem make clear that its Power, and the power of Camden's deeds themselves, a Power that we as readers participate in, reside in the mind of the maker.

Finally, notice the last word of the poem, which Jonson chose to denote the nature of the act he has rendered to Camden by writing this poem: "Many of thine this better could then I;/But for their powers accept my *piety.*" "Piety": it is a modest word in this context, one that Jonson uses to help depreciate his own poetic "powers" in comparison with those of Camden's other students, but besides its decorousness it is also a word that perfectly reflects the Idea of the poem and helps transmit its Power. Piety is an act of homage that we make to those, be they gods or human beings such as parents or other ancestors, who existed prior to us and to whom our very nature, our being, owes a debt. This is, we now recognize quickly, the essence of Jonson's whole poem; but we also recognize the unusually public and traditional nature of the word piety, and we then realize that Jonson did not want to choose a word to state his devotion to his teacher that was private or personal to himself. Rather, in this word, as in nearly all the significant words, the Energy, of the poem, he chose one that would immediately allow his readers to share, through their own experience of piety, in his act of praise.

Jonson's deep and persistent awareness throughout his poetry of his poetic craft and of the wellsprings of his creative inspiration make him an especially good poet to examine through Sayers's aesthetic trinity. However stately and uncluttered Jonson's poetry may appear to be, it is consistently informed by an unusual sensitivity to, and sometimes a direct statement about, ·the creative process which generates, develops, and fixes a poem in the hearts of readers. This does not mean that he criticizes or analyzes his poems while he is writing them, but rather that his choice of subject, theme, and diction permit him to make clear the ultimate source of his poetry. In Jonson's poetry, that is to say, we not only find human creativity working parallel or analogously to the mind on the divine maker, but also at the same time expressly recording its debts to Him. Jonson's famous eulogy of the death of his first son is a good further example of this.

ON MY FIRST SONNE

Farewell, thou child of my right hand, and joy;
    My sinne was too much hope of thee, lov'd boy,
Seven years tho'wert lent to me, and I thee pay,
    Exacted by thy fate, on the just day.
O, could I lose all father now. For why   5
    Will man lament the state he should envie?
To have so soone scap'd worlds, and fleshes rage,
    And, if no other miserie, yet age?
Rest in soft peace, and, ask'd, say here doth lye
    Ben Jonson his best piece of poetrie.   10
For whose sake, hence-forth, all his vowes be such.
    As what he loves may never like too much.

The Idea of this or any poem about death is to say something to the bereaved that is consoling without being either sentimental or unfeeling. This can be carried out in Power only if the statement is not overly particular; something of the general human experience of death and consolation must be manifest in the poem. So many epitaphs and elegies fail because the author's deep involvement produces one of Sayers's scalene triangles: the extreme grief either leads the poet into an elaborate but far too general and diffuse consideration of the subject (Shelley's "Adonais") or a densely-packed catalog of words and phrases that have no controlling Idea at all (perhaps Dylan Thomas's "A Refusal to Mourn the Death, by Fire, of a Child in London," with the exception of its last line). The wonder of Jonson's poem is that his overwhelming personal involvement in its subject does not in the least hinder, does in fact promote, the harmony of Idea, Energy, and Power.

In these 12 powerfully condensed lines we never once forget the Idea of the poem: the deep emotion and sense of tragic loss over the death of the poet's eldest son, a lad who was only seven years old when he died. But we also experience in each of its lines, in each instance, that is, of the creative Energy's manifestation of the Idea, the hardening of that personal loss into an expression of the more general human experience that

is involved and of the consolation that is available to all who suffer such a
loss. The result of such a successful incarnation of Idea into Energy is
the Power the poem has to make nearly every reader participate in the
experience that is described. For example, the first word of the poem,
"Farewell," tells us immediately that the boy is gone and that the poet
will not try to pretend that death is anything other than it really is: that
which utterly destroys all the "hope" [l.2] that a father always fondly
holds for his eldest son. It is not, then, a sentimental word that denies the
reality of death; but neither is it a word of embittered or frustrated anger.
"Farewell" means "go according to one's wish or will"; thus Jonson
signifies at the very beginning that while this death is a loss, it is not an
end, and this way of considering the subject is maintained throughout the
poem. For in the second line Jonson again chooses a word which makes
impossible any emotional indulgence of his own mere private loss; he
says his desire that the boy should have realized his own ambitions for
him was his "sin," and in line 3 he acknowledges the universal truth that
children are "lent" to us in, as it were, trust for purposes which we do not
dictate.

But lest we think that he is being too resigned to fate, Jonson reasserts
in line 5 the Idea of the poem, a father's bereavement, when he cries:
"Oh, could I lose all father now!" The tug toward pathos and agony is
always very strong—as Othello cries when considering Desdemona's
"necessary" sacrifice: "O, Iago, the pity of it, the pity of it"—but even in
expressing this Jonson reaches outside himself. For he asks to lose his
fatherhood so that he may see what this death means for his son and not
just for himself. The thought recalls that of Christ when He tells the
disciples that those who lose their lives for His sake will be given a new
life that is eternal. This is exactly what Jonson, by the "loss" of his
fatherhood, is freed to understand in lines 6–8: his son has escaped
"world's and flesh's rage" and the misery of "age." Hence, again the Idea
of the poem is expressed through words in such a way that its readers may
share in, may receive Power from the experience described because of
the general truths which are maintained.

But it is in line 10 that Jonson best reveals in this poem his exceptional
ability to talk about the things of creation while at the same time showing
us how he embodies in his own craft the creative source from which those
things come. He says that the tombstone should declare, if asked, "here
doth lie/Ben Jonson his best piece of poetry." This touching statement,
the most beautiful in the poem, expresses Jonson's knowledge that while
a poet is a maker, he is not a divine maker: the best poem of Jonson's life

is his son, who was not created by him but rather "lent" to him. But the magnificence of the line is found in something else: it reveals perfectly the poem's integration of the creative triad. The Idea is reflected in Jonson's having this statement come, literally, from the grave, a sign that he never forgets the real situation out of which the poem has grown. But the Idea is incarnated in a statement which connects this experience to the most important things in Jonson's continuing life: his poetic creativity and his ability to father children. The very act of writing the poem inspires Jonson to know what is the profoundest human creation— namely, children—and such knowledge gives in turn to the poem, the mere human artifact, its beauty. The Power of the line, then, is simply the readers' awareness that they as much as Jonson are genuine creators; if they have begotten children, then they too have written great poems, have known the mind of the maker in as intimate a way as the poetic creator.

Because Ben Jonson was a poet who was quite conscious of his craft and because he so firmly was a part of and believed in the classical-Christian legacy concerning poetry's proper subjects and their treatment, his poetry is a fine example of how Sayers's aesthetic might be concretely applied. This, again, emphatically does not mean that either Jonson or Sayers is proposing doctrines or dogmas, conventions or traditions; rather, they propose to us, and their very writing gives us an example of, the dynamics, the fecundity of creativity. Their subject matter and their mode of treating that subject matter both point to that end. The poet must be a critic and the critic (a much harder task!) must also try to be a poet. But now let us turn to another poet, Robert Frost, who is far removed from Ben Jonson in time and temperament.

Frost's poetry is informal and conversational in tone, apparently quite different from Jonson's ordered classicism. But as we have seen with Jonson, for whom "classicism" does not begin to get to the heart or express the power of his poetry, one must be careful with conventional tags and descriptions. For a reader whose mind was uncluttered with the categories of literary history might find one striking similarity in reading the poetry of Frost and Jonson: they both possess an easy and supple mastery of their craft. They seldom make their poems needlessly complex and they can convey both sound and sense in straightforward statements. Their language is lucid and controlled without sacrificing metaphor or emotion. They are similar, that is, in none of the externals of literary taxonomy, by which handbooks and literary histories are constructed; but they are very interestingly alike in the way in which they develop and communicate the creative Ideas by which poetry is constructed.

"Two Tramps in Mud Time" illustrates many of the characteristic qualities of Frost's poetry, and it will also permit me to apply Sayers's poetic to a text in a way different from that used for Jonson. Therefore, although the poem is somewhat lengthy for this essay, the full text must be given:

TWO TRAMPS IN MUD TIME

Out of the mud two strangers came
And caught me splitting wood in the yard.
And one of them put me off my aim
By hailing cheerily 'Hit them hard!'
I knew pretty well why he dropped behind   5
And let the other go on a way.
I knew pretty well what he had in mind:
He wanted to take my job for pay.
Good blocks of oak it was I split,
As large around as the chopping block;   10
And every piece I squarely hit
Fell splinterless as a cloven rock.
The blows that a life of self-control
Spares to strike for the common good
That day, giving a loose to my soul,   15
I spent on the unimportant wood.

The sun was warm but the wind was chill.
You know how it is with an April day
When the sun is out and the wind is still,
You're one month on in the middle of May.   20
But if you so much as dare to speak,
A cloud comes over the sunlit arch,
A wind comes off a frozen peak,
And you're two months back in the middle of March.

A bluebird comes tenderly up to alight   25
And turns to the wind to unruffle a plume
His song so pitched as not to excite
A single flower as yet to bloom.
It is snowing a flake: and he half knew
Winter was only playing possum.   30
Except in color he isn't blue,
But he wouldn't advise a thing to blossom.

The water for which we may have to look
In summertime with a witching-wand,

In every wheelrut's now a brook,   35
In every print of a hoof a pond.
Be glad of water, but don't forget
The lurking frost in the earth beneath
That will steal forth after the sun is set
And show on the water its crystal teeth.   40

The time when most I loved my task
These two must make me love it more
By coming with what they came to ask.
You'd think I never had felt before
The weight of an ax-head poised aloft,   45
The grip on earth of outspread feet.
The life of muscles rocking soft
And smooth and moist in vernal heat.

Out of the woods two hulking tramps
(From sleeping God knows where last night.   50
But not long since in the lumber camps).
They thought all chopping was theirs of right
Men of the woods and lumberjacks,
They judged me by their appropriate tool.
Except as a fellow handled an ax,   55
They had no way of knowing a fool.

Nothing on either side was said.
They knew they had but to stay their stay
And all their logic would fill my head:
As that I had no right to play   60
With what was another man's work for gain.
My right might be love but theirs was need.
And where the two exist in twain
Theirs was the better right—agreed.

But yield who will to their separation,   65
My object in living is to unite
My avocation and my vocation
As my two eyes make one in sight.
Only where love and need are one,
And the work is play for mortal stakes,   70
Is the deed ever really done
For Heaven and the future's sakes.

Jonson's poetry is notable for the way in which the words, the creative Energy, focus the meaning of the poem; Frost's poetry, I think, is primarily a poetry of Power, a poetry in which the author is especially concerned to share with us the knowledge, delight, or love which has come to him through describing and understanding a particular experience. This is not to say that he ignores Idea and Word—Frost at his best, such as in this poem, does not suffer from Sayers's scalene trinity — but only to suggest that he is gifted in revealing the social and affective dimension of poetry. His great popularity is of course immediate evidence of this fact but since such a once-reputable standard of criticism finds no vogue among today's judges, let us examine this poem itself to find evidence of Frost's genius.

The poem's Idea concerns the mysterious pleasure Frost (and I shall not use in this discussion the jargon of the "speaker" or "persona" in referring to the poem's protagonist) finds in chopping wood. Mysterious pleasure or wonder or puzzlement at the ordinary things or activities in nature is in fact the Idea of the majority of Frost's poetry, and it frequently leads him, as it does here, to other apparently random observations which are then united in a final statement. The incarnation of the Idea in "Two Tramps" is done in two different ways: first, through the encounter with the tramps and Frost's considering what is his proper relation to them; and second, in stanzas 3–5, through considering "how it is with an April day" [l. 18], that is, through noticing the poise and balance which has penetrated nature. The poem's last stanza then brings together these two parts of the poem's development and makes a statement which makes the whole experience one of Power, that is, of delight and love for both Frost and his readers.

What saves the last stanza from being discursive and exhortative, from being merely prose in verse, and what therefore establishes its poetic nature, is the way in which its wisdom comes directly from the description of springtime at the poem's center. For in those stanzas the creative Energy has its most profound manifestation and thereby gives to the concluding declaration its persuasiveness. Now let me here stress how carefully I am following Sayers and am not merely imposing upon the poem an abstract personal reading. For the persuasiveness, the Power of Frost's final speech is analogous to that which the apostles possessed after the great deed of Christ's Resurrection and after the descent of the dove at Pentecost. To take one example of many from the Acts of the Apostles: Peter, who is the common fisherman and shamed denier of Christ in the Gospels, becomes in Acts one who is able to heal a lame man and, perhaps even more remarkable, declare exactly and straightforwardly by what means this was done: "Ye men of Israel, why marvel ye at this? or why look ye so earnestly on us, as though by our own power or holiness we had made this man to walk? . . . . faith in his [i.e., Jesus'] name hath made this man strong" [3.12, 16]. Now what is perhaps most fundamental to Sayers's aesthetic is that a poet's embodiment of particular Ideas in creative Energy does have a power analogous to that which Peter exemplified and proclaimed, and which he also derived from the Energy in creation. And therefore I am suggesting Sayers helps us to understand how Frost in this poem can take a perception of nature's activity, which his poetic Energy makes into concrete images, and transform it into a statement of Power.

For at the beginning of "Two Tramps," Frost is neither very energetic nor powerful. He knows what the tramps want—"to take my job for pay" [l. 8]—but he gives no evidence that he knows how to answer them. He also knows why he is chopping the wood; it is a diversion, a recreation to release the frustration "that a life of self-control/Spares to strike for the common good" (ll. 13–14). But there is no assurance that Frost has any idea what to say to the tramps when they will inevitably challenge him that theirs is the right to do this work because of their greater competence and their need for the money. But then come the three stanzas of exceptionally fine poetic Energy. Frost describes in them three things: the sun, a bluebird, and the water on the ground, and they all testify to the same quality: poise, balance, equilibrium. "The sun was warm but the wind was chill" [l.17] but look out: if you dare to speak,

> A cloud comes over the sunlit arch
> A wind comes off a frozen peak
> And you're two months back in the middle of March [ll.22–24]

The bluebird and the water also know this thing: there is more here than is apparent; in springtime things are neither completely one way or another; "it is snowing a flake," so the bird "half knew" (for with created things is any more complete knowledge ever possible?) that "Winter was only playing possum" [ll. 29–30]. Similarly with water: its plentifulness, so different from the summertime scarceness, is deceptive: it won't evaporate but a March chill might freeze it again, so it is best not to take it, either, as a sign that good weather is at hand.

After these stanzas, then, the Power of the poem begins to be felt, although of course this is not separate from the presence of the Idea or continued flow of Energy. But there is now a new assurance and conviction in Frost's tone and the appearance of a new word: love. He has at least now the will if not the words to answer the tramps' intimidating stares: "The time when most I loved my task/These two must make me love it more" [ll. 41–42]. And he now recognizes that his wood-chopping is something more than sublimation of his aggressive passions; it begins to have an intrinsic satisfaction, its own reason for being, as he feels "The life of muscles rocking soft/And smooth and moist in vernal heat" [ll. 47–48]. Hence, Frost is finally prepared to complete the first of the poem's major incarnations, that of the encounter with the tramps. He need now in no way minimize their challenge to him: he freely acknowledges that "They thought all chopping was theirs of right" and that they were critically judging his ability with an ax [ll. 52–56]. Further, he knows that their arguments for allowing them to finish the job are in a way compelling and that they expect him to bow to them:

> My right might be love but theirs was need.
> And where the two exist in twain
> Theirs was the better right—agreed. | [11. 62–64]

This is only to say, of course, that Frost does no violence to the creative trinity, as he gives every element and character of the poem its due. The tramps do not go away in the last half of the poem simply because Frost's attention had shifted from them to the spring day around him. Rather, the Idea of the poem, which we might now state as the paradox, "How an amateur does better what a professional does best," is manifested progressively in deeper and more varied ways, and the professional woodchoppers' limitations are fully revealed by Frost in a way that we had not originally foreseen. They are allowed to make their case the best that it can be made but they fail to persuade Frost because he takes the matter in the last stanza into a realm they cannot enter. Energy completely expresses Idea in this poem but it does so in freedom and unpredictability, just as the Son is the adequate and complete yet totally unexpected revelation of the Father.

And what then is the Power of this last stanza and hence of the poem as a whole? We can see it, as always, only in the context of Idea and Energy. For in these lines Frost finds in himself that poise and balance, which comes from uniting his avocation and his vocation as his "two eyes make one in sight" [ll. 67–68], that he has earlier discovered present in nature. The tramps are vagrants, have no purpose beyond doing a job of work, have no experience of uniting need with love. But Frost understands that just as an April day balances life and death, sun and clouds, rain and snow, so his own life, in activities such as this very one of chopping wood, balances love and need, work and play, present and future without preferring either. Such direct and general statements make audacious poetry because they can so easily fail and degenerate into moralizing (witness the end of "The Rime of the Ancient Mariner") but here they do not. They communicate with Power because they are essentially linked to Frost's other incarnations of his poem's Idea and hence in no way make lopsided the poem's own balance.

The Mind of the Maker, then, may direct our reading of poetry in many different ways. And, of course, not only poetry: the epic, romances, novels—all works of the imagination—are constructed within the creative framework which Sayers sketches. She is not prescriptive and hence I can see no kinds of literary works to which her book could not apply. Basically, Sayers provides us a starting point for any work of criticism, and it is the most liberal and generous imaginable: the heart of the creative act. Critics are then free to relate to it whatever works their own imaginations can discover or, if they are more historically or theoretically inclined, to render a fuller and more complete account of that creative act itself. Sayers's book communicates in Power: we are not asked to be medievalists or modernists, Johnsonians or Arnoldians; we are only asked to remember that literature has a purpose, that it means something, and that its purpose and meaning derive from and depend upon a Power not its own.

Robert Paul Dunn

"The Laughter of the Universe":
Dorothy L. Sayers and the Whimsical Vision

> The aesthetic view of life is not, however, confined to those who can create or appreciate works of art. It exists wherever natural senses play freely on the manifold phenomena of our world, and when life as a consequence is found to be full of felicity. —HERBERT READ, *Annals of Innocence and Experience.*[1]

DOROTHY L. SAYERS was one of those authors of whom the gods have decreed that her first books would be better known and loved than her last. Many have come to enjoy her carefully written detective fiction, but relatively few are aware of her delightful religious plays, of her popular but penetrating theological essays, and of her spirited translation and criticism of Dante. This is a shame because the same witty realism and attention to the details of the plot or argument that readers find so compelling in the detective novels are also present and rendered themat-ically significant in the author's later works. What is especially signifi-cant about Sayers's nondetective work is that it was written to show that the Judeo-Christian aspect of our heritage has something to tell "modern" men and women. This meant that it was necessary for the author to graft onto the comedy-of-manners approach that she had primarily employed in the detective fiction a fully spiritual vision of life.

Sayers began to write her religious work toward the end of the 1930s in England. This was a time when it was becoming increasingly clear to many that philosophies based on science and strict, rational inquiry were insufficient for dealing with the crises of a society that was beginning to expect the possibility of another major war. In literary criticism, too, people were beginning to question the historically-oriented scholars who were endeavoring to approach a text in the spirit of a scientist, analyzing it and cataloging it as though it were a dead body. The "New Criticism" in America and similar schools in Europe began to suggest that art spoke one language and science another. Science, these literary critics thought, was analytical: it was problem-oriented and progressive. Once a particular fact was discovered, once a particular problem was solved, that fact and that solution could be added to the store of scientific knowledge. Then science could move on to something else. But art was synthetic: it was experience-oriented and circular. Here knowledge was not thought to be cumulative, as it was in science, and one expected to see the same themes treated by different people and different ages. A vital work of art never could be "put on a shelf": it was a dynamic entity that continually remained "current" and continually reached out to change readers.

As a writer and loyal citizen, Dorothy L. Sayers could be expected to be interested in the relation of her work to society. But as a Christian she might be inclined toward silence. For as she looked about she could see that people everywhere felt that Christianity had had its chance and had failed to solve the moral problems of Europe. If science had anything to teach in this situation it was that once a hypothesis has failed, it should be discarded and the researcher should move on to try other approaches.[2] Furthermore, she observed that biblical scholars themselves, working then (as very often today) in a historical and analytical manner, had succeeded in dissecting the canon and uncovering the layers of textual tradition, but had not seen a way to reconstruct the text as a literary unity. She saw that ordinary people gagged on the miracles and supernatural interventions in the Bible when they read it—as they had been conditioned to do—with the scientist's or historian's eye for fact.[3]

In *The Mind of the Maker*, her most profoundly original book, Dorothy L. Sayers showed that there was a way to reconcile the Christian tradition with the contemporary ethical situation. She suggested that the way of the artist, who lovingly accepts the limitations of the medium as an opportunity for creation, is the way of the Christian religion and of human and social reintegration. She went back to the trinitarian and incarnational analogies of Augustine to suggest that the mind commonly relates the "Creative Idea," the "Creative Energy," and the "Creative Power."[4] In other words, there is a synthesis between an artist's plan for a work (the "Creative Idea"), the material or artistic form in which that plan is given expression (the "Creative Energy"), and the effect of the embodied plan upon the reader or viewer (the "Creative Power"). Sayers also suggested that this seemingly remote Augustinian theory touched upon the average person in the realm of the ethical.

But, although Sayers accepted the basic doctrines of Christianity, she believed that they were not simply religious. She proposed that the doctrines of creation, incarnation, and the trinity were correct statements of universal reality. In this way she took the stand of a Christian poet and asked how her view of the world might reveal a pattern of integration in mankind and in society. She insisted that she was not a Christian propagandist. What she sought to do was to integrate the ordinary language of ordinary men and women with the language of religion by showing that they both operate according to common "laws" or assumptions. The result of this synthesis for her was a comprehensive comic view of the universe, a view which I call the "whimsical vision."

Briefly, I would describe the whimsical vision as a paradoxical recognition of human limitation within historical existence and of human access to a transforming spiritual reality that revalues and (if allowed) reshapes all one's endeavors. The recognition of human limitation corresponds to the artist's acceptance of a material medium in which to work. The transforming spiritual reality corresponds to the artistic idea that governs the work and that also judges the final product in the light of itself.

The whimsical vision of which I speak goes beyond the humorous realism of the early detective works. Nevertheless, it is firmly rooted in that realism. The whimsical vision suggests, of course, Dorothy L. Sayers's famous detective investigator, Lord Peter Wimsey, and it is possible to see in his development a movement toward the fuller spiritual vision of the later works. There is a significant continuity, seen especially in Lord Peter, between the early and later stages of Sayers's writing. What happens in the later works is that grace comes to perfect nature. In this the traditional Thomistic understanding of the relation of Christ and culture is shown. But even before the religious works, we see the development of the whimsical vision.

In the early works there is little of the comic synthesis that Sayers would later develop. There the comic realism serves mainly to make the characters more appealingly human, although from time to time it seems to rise above this function and to anticipate its more complex uses in the later writings. Readers will readily recall such humorous scenes as Lord Peter's cheerful unflappability during the trial of his brother before the House of Lords in *Clouds of Witness,* the jocular exhumation "party" in

The Unpleasantness at the Bellona Club, and the swinging de Momerie crowd in *Murder Must Advertise.* Throughout the detective novels the dialog and action, in cooperation with the basic setting, often humorously work to reveal specific types of English character and behavior. But the characters appear only to add variety to the plot and to play their assigned roles within the detective action. Almost never, then, does their humor illuminate an ethical situation; it is there mainly for entertainment. Occasionally, however, the humor points beyond the level of a superficial comedy of manners. Such is the case when Sergeant Lumley in *Murder Must Advertise* asks why "Godamighty wanted to put such a lot of bones" in Kippers, and his assistant, P. C. Eagles, in shocked indignation, warns him not to question the ways of God.[5] But the significance of Lumley's question is, of course, never pursued.

The humor in each of these examples seems to derive from the general predictability of a character's actions when he is placed in a new or interesting situation. It is as though the author had said, "Let us conduct a psychological experiment. What would happen, given what we know of his character, if we were to place Lord Peter in the House of Lords during the trial of his brother for murder? How would he behave? How would the House behave toward him?" The answer, of course, is clear that he would continue to act and speak as Lord Peter always acts and speaks — competently, convincingly, but significantly for the humor, not always decorously. So, too, the House would continue to act as we have been led to believe it always acts — with grave and dispassionate demeanor. Flexibility is given to the author in that she may develop the particularities of the setting and assign the precise words spoken and the actions performed. In this way she is able to keep "one jump ahead" of us. Nonetheless, the humor is (at least retrospectively) perfectly predictable. This is because just as Sayers has told us that "The detective problem is solved in the same terms in which it is set,"[6] so, too, the humorous "problem" is solved in the same terms in which it is set.

Since no genuinely new element is introduced into the picture, it is no wonder that the author eventually grew weary of Lord Peter and her other creations and called them "cardboard" characters.[7] There is an inexhaustible potential for new situations into which a stock character may be placed, but one eventually will tire of watching predictable responses.

Yet there is some indication that Dorothy L. Sayers wanted to change. At least as early as the *The Documents in the Case* (1930, written with Robert Eustace), Sayers seems to be growing restless with the limitations of the conventional detective novel and endeavoring to expand the form. This novel is different from most of the other detective novels in that it emphasizes an idea, in this case the idea of causation. The humor does from time to time help to underscore the meaning of this theme; however, the beginnings of that comprehensive comic vision of the universe that I call the whimsical vision did not come until 1935.

In 1935 Dorothy Sayers published *Gaudy Night,* her penultimate Wimsey novel and a book that clearly marks a change in her attitude toward her responsibilities as a writer.[8] *Gaudy Night,* like *The Documents in the Case,* has an important theme, viz. the duty of workers to be faithful to their work. Furthermore, there is a genuine development of the characters of the principals, Harriet Vane and Lord Peter, who during the course of the novel come to a new understanding of themselves and of one another and, in the end, become engaged. But what is most significant is that for the first time in Sayers's writings there is a clear indication that the humorous inanities of a person might, if looked at from the right angle, constitute a part of a comprehensive comic vision of the universe. That indication comes toward the end of Lord Peter's long courtship of Harriet. There, protesting that he had never wanted Harriet to sacrifice herself to him out of a sense of gratitude for favors received, he observes, "I have nothing much in the way of religion, or even morality, but I do recognise a code of behaviour of sorts. I do know that the worst sin—perhaps the only sin—passion can commit, is to be joyless. It must lie down with laughter or make its bed in hell—there is no middle way."[9]

This is a brief but basic statement of the whimsical vision. Even in this concise form it reveals a paradoxical pattern of integration based upon the recognition and laughing—or, alternatively, the creative—acceptance of reality. The vision rests on man's perception of unity in diversity. On the one hand, a duality really exists at one stage of development or from one point of view. Man encounters his body and, as an extension of his body, the world itself as in some sense "opposed" to him, i.e., to his conscious will. This is seen in Harriet's perception of her restlessness and of the uncertainty of her own identity after the notoriety she had gained during the trial that took place in *Strong Poison.* Furthermore, during much of the novel Lord Peter represents a threat to the security she is coming to rediscover in Oxford. She sees him as "swift, rattling, chattering, excitable and devilishly upsetting" like London in contrast to quiet Oxford with its grey stones [Ch. 11], as "something explosive from the outside world to break up the ordered tranquility of the place" [Ch. 14]. And, for his part, Lord Peter found Harriet opposed to him in spite of all his efforts to take the sting out of her rejection through rationalization: "I told myself that you were only afraid of the social consequences of marriage. I comforted myself with pretending that it showed you liked me a little. I bolstered up my conceit for months, before I would admit the humiliating truth that I ought to have known from the beginning— that you were so sick of my pestering that you would have thrown yourself to me as one throws a bone to a dog, to stop the brute from yelping" [Ch. 23].

On the other hand, although this duality can never be completely abolished, a genuine unity may tenuously be established by one possessed of sufficient imagination to make creative use of the diversity of reality. A reconciliation is possible only by accepting reality and respecting its integrity, and then by living creatively within the limits of that reality. This fact is pointed up by Miss de Vine, who tells Harriet that "If you ever find any kind of repose with him [Peter Wimsey], it can only be the repose of very delicate balance" [Ch. 22]. Indeed, Harriet finally comes to see that Peter experiences such a balance within himself, that he can "hear the whole intricate pattern, every part separately and simultaneously, each independent and equal, separate but inseparable. . ."; it is significant, too, that he likes his music polyphonic [Ch. 23]. Thus, even though there is a resolution to the paradox, to the human "problem," still the resolution, like everything human, can only be temporary at best.

What I have been describing is, of course, a comic attitude, one that in itself need not contain much in the way of humorous words and action. *Gaudy Night,* to be sure, is a more serious and solemn novel than most that Sayers wrote, but it contains a good deal of her usual sparkling humor. One recalls Harriet's midnight prowls about the grounds and buildings of Shrewsbury College, the strange but (in their own perverted way) humorous pranks that Harriet first investigates, her encounters with young Mr. Pomfret and with Peter's nephew Lord Saint-George, the surprisingly placed but apt allusions to various literary texts, and, above all, Lord Peter's own scintillating conversations. It is just this sort of comedy that the reader of Dorothy L. Sayers has come to expect from her. And yet although the humor is as appropriate to the characters as ever, there is an important difference: here the humor derives not from the predictability of a stock character, but from a reflection of the wide range of choices that human beings can actually make.

A good example of this sort of humor is Harriet's first glimpse of Peter in Oxford. It is funny to see Harriet and the Dean come upon "a group of gowns, chatting with animation," and to watch one of them turn suddenly and lift his mortar-board [Ch. 14]. We, as well as Harriet, were not prepared to see Peter at just that moment, and our humorous response to this unexpected situation is intensified when we see how casually the debonair lord fits into a scholastic robe. This scene is based on more than comedy of situation; it reveals as well that people can make choices about the kind of man or woman they would like to be, and that they can rise above stereotypes. Furthermore, Harriet's nightly prowls and her encounters with people like Pomfret and Saint-George, who force her to recognize that certain good-natured compromises owing to ethical differences in people are necessary if society is going to run smoothly, help her come to understand that in a marriage with Lord Peter both sides in the relationship can joyfully maintain their individual outlooks and yet be enriched by their associations together.

Sayers's move from detection to theology reflects her increasing concern over the moral crisis facing Europe during the period. In particular, she was much concerned over the economic and political problems that were becoming increasingly ominous during the years just before the war, and these problems gave added point to her reflections. As a writer she liked to consider the human predicament by analogy with the problems facing the artist. "The re-integration of society," she wrote in the early days of World War II, "is not a kind of detective problem, for which a single, final, and complete solution can be found. It is a work, like a work of art, which has to be imagined with vision, and *made* with intelligence and unremitting labor."[10] Indeed, just as Peter and Harriet in *Gaudy Night* learned that they must joyfully come to accept the integrity of one another, so artists must learn to respect the individuality of the very characters that they have created: "The only way of 'mastering' one's material is to abandon the whole conception of mastery and to co-operate with it in love"; the true creative artist "does not see life as a problem to be solved, but as a medium for creation."[11] Furthermore, the integration of society must recognize the individuality, the integrity, of all the individual people composing the social whole. Society is a product of diverse but complementary choices, of a delicate balance.

This fundamentally comic insight into life is clearly expressed in *The Zeal of Thy House,* Sayers's first Canterbury Festival play. It is the story of William of Sens, the thoroughly human architect hired to repair the choir of Canterbury Cathedral. William's greatest strength—and paradoxically his tragic weakness—is his complete dedication to his work, his feeling that he is indispensable. He makes many mistakes: he has not been forthright in his estimates of the project's cost; he has lusted after food, drink, and women; he has shown wrath. All these sins he recognizes and eventually confesses. But these are, in a sense, offset by the fact that he looks on his work as of supreme importance and labors with unremitting zeal and attention to complete it; he does not consider the repairs simply a "job," but looks upon his work in the loving way of the true artist. Yet he thinks that he is indispensable to the work, not remembering that God the Son was Himself willing to be dispensable. The "comic" insight comes to William toward the end, when he understands that just as God completed His work after the death of Jesus, so, too, the work on the church will go forward only after he has given it up to another to finish.

The use of the Christian myth—that God Himself, incarnate in Jesus the man, was willing to give up Himself in order that His own work on humanity's behalf might be completed—underscores the "whimsical" vision in the play and gives it a cosmic and thematic depth that we have not yet seen in Dorothy Sayers's comic attitude toward life. The basic pattern discovered in *Gaudy Night*—that of passionate lying down with laughter—is here, too, but it is clarified because it is shown to operate on several interrelated levels of discourse. On the human level we see it in William's eventual willingness to give up his work, to make a virtue out of necessity. We see it also in the ordinary conversations and the coarse jokes of the pilgrims: "Ah, the poor, dear, martyred Archbishop! Such a charming man. I saw him when he came back from France—yes, really, he was as close to me as I am to you. . . . Have you heard the one about the three fat friars and the tinker's widow?"[12] It is seen, too, in the dogged insistence of Ernulphus on William of Sens when Gabriel wakes him up in time to cast the deciding vote for the architect [pp. 31–32], and in everything else that proclaims the joyful acceptance of our own humanity, and of all the limitations that recognition involves.

On the divine level we see a joy in work equal to William's in Cassiel's fussy attention to his accounts and in the alacrity with which Michael, Gabriel, and Raphael perform their own duties. It is not only humorous to see Gabriel matter-of-factly break off one of his feathers for Cassiel to use as a pen [p. 29], or to hear Cassiel muttering, "Put down four and carry eight" as he tried to put in order the accounts of men's sins as a human accountant might deal with his ledger [p. 7], but such humor reveals how serious, and yet at the same time how insignificant, work really is. More important still, the divine comedy of this play completes what would otherwise be a human tragedy: William's fall and the necessity that he should give up his work would be tragic for him if God were not by William's acceptance of the limitations of fallen human nature able to complete His own work in him.

Finally, on the level of the creative artist, we see more precisely yet the nature of the whimsical vision. Raphael's final speech [pp. 114–15] adapts the Augustinian idea of a universal trinitarian structure to explain the mystery of creative work, whether human or divine.[13] There is first (not in time, but only in order of enumeration) the eternal Creative Idea, then the incarnate Creative Energy that develops the Creative Idea in the time-space world, and, finally, the Creative Power which is "the meaning of the work and its response in the lively soul." This suggests that the joyful response of workers to the limitations of their materials is not only characteristic of Christians who must in the "work" of salvation first come to accept themselves as in need of grace, but of all workers in whatever line of endeavor who must also come to know the limitations and possibilities of their art.

Furthermore, because we see that there is a basic trinitarian and incarnational pattern underlying all creative work, we see more clearly than we did in *Gaudy Night* that the delicate balance on which life rests is established from the "outside," by means of a special "gift." Just as the "solution" to the "problem" confronting Harriet and Peter could not be found, as it can be in a simple detective puzzle, "in" the Harriet and Peter seen at the beginning of the novel, so, too, William's fall and election are both "outside" himself, both come from God's "whimsical" decree. And yet, of course, God does not compel William, but allows him to make his own choice: William accepts his limitations and allows the Divine Architect to complete His work in him even though William cannot complete his own work.

But one wonders, does the use of essentially the same formal pattern in both the novel and the play indicate that there is no essential difference in outlook either? That is, is Peter Wimsey a Christian in spite of himself? Sayers says explicitly that Lord Peter was not a Christian, but that he was "'an eighteenth-century Whig gentleman, born a little out of his time.'"[14] Further support can be found indirectly in her critical essays. In discussing Dante's comic vision, she noted, "The vision of the whole, without diversity or contradiction, is a divine gift. It does not belong to human nature—not even to human nature in its original perfection—but is something superadded. Nature must not indeed be lost in order to attain vision, but it must be 'transhumanised'. "[15] She also writes that Vergil missed heaven through a failure of his imagination to conceive such a plane of existence: "faith is imagination actualised by the will. What was lacking in the heathen philosophies was precisely the imagination of bliss. They had not, so to speak, sufficient faith in the good intentions of the universe."[16]

Now the Peter Wimsey seen in most of the novels is a man of an impressive but limited imagination. He does well at solving detective puzzles, is pleasing, witty, and ideal in nearly every respect. But Peter's "scientific," problem-oriented imagination was limited in just this way: he could not devise a satisfactory way of dealing with human guilt. Still he does achieve the "whimsical vision" in his relationship with Harriet Vane at the end of *Gaudy Night*. Consequently the pattern of reality symbolized in the whimsical vision of Sayers is a universal, and not a narrowly Christian, one. It is above all human, and it is accessible to all who possess a strong imagination. Dante, she notes, placed the pagans Rhipeus and Trajan in Paradise because of their strong commitment to justice.[17] Thus, even an imaginative Rationalist like Wimsey might be able to gain a helpful insight into the structure of the universe.

Nonetheless, Dorothy L. Sayers especially prized the Christian vision because it more than any other pattern shows how to deal with moral and spiritual evil. The Christian vision, she observes in her "Introduction" to *The Man Born to Be King*, a series of radio plays on the life of Christ, is a comedy because it shows that man's "worst sins are redeemable by his worst suffering; his evil is not merely purged—it is in the literal sense made good. The iron necessity that binds him is the working of the divine will—and lo! the gods are friendly."[18] Even very ordinary people like Matthew, who in his "oily black hair" is "as vulgar a little commercial Jew as ever walked Whitechapel," or like Philip, who is "An ingenuous young man . . . of an engaging and puppy-like simplicity" [pp. 99–100], were able to perceive this vision.

The reason that the whimsical vision can be enjoyed even by very ordinary people is that it is based on physical reality and expressed in concrete images. Sayers speaks of it as "The Poetry of the Image" and "The Mysticism of the Affirmative Way."[19] Here again her Catholic theology of the incarnation affected her aesthetic. The universe is transparent to the image. Always she strives to be realistic and down-to-earth. She has no desire to leave physical reality and make a Gnostic leap for the spiritual.

But could a Christian writer who at one point implied that she held a

"Platonic ideal philosophy"[20] really fulfill her own program of affirming the divine only in the mode of time-space existence? It would appear that she had some difficulty in doing this.

Sayers herself recognized that she faced a different problem in her second Canterbury play, *The Devil to Pay*, which was based on the Faustus legend, from the one she had faced in her first play. "In my previous Canterbury play, *The Zeal of Thy House*, the problem was to supply a supernatural interpretation of a piece of human history. In the present play, the problem is exactly reversed: it is a question of a supernatural legend."[21] No longer, then, does the supernatural element affect only the moral aspect of the play (as she says, "take away the visible angels, and the course of William of Sen's [*sic*] fall and repentance remains essentially unaltered"), but now "the supernatural element *is* the story" of Faustus.

Again, as in the previous play, Sayers attempts to make her lead characters believable human beings. Marion B. Fairman described Faustus as "a twentieth century man, oversensitive to suffering, eager to set the world right," and Mephistopheles as bringing "to his task of buying a man's soul a brisk and business-like manner, an everyday casualness."[22] She adds that the function of Mephistopheles is to externalize "Faustus' internal struggle with the hopelessness of his life." This suggests that the usual humor and tension between actors and audience found in *The Zeal of Thy House* is still present.

The difference is that the dialectic now operates on a quasi-realistic level. The machinery is still in place: the recognizability of the characters is enforced by the typicality of the speeches and actions assigned to them; the settings are (until Faustus appears before the Judge) more or less historical. The difference is primarily that the issues and sympathies of the author are now more abstractly theological or sociological, less essentially down-to-earth. Faustus himself is a reformer whose sympathies are all abstract. Lisa and Wagner serve him well and love him, but there is little indication that he can recognize genuine love when he sees it, or that the subject really interests him. This is true not only before his conversion in heaven, but afterwards as well. In the end he and the Judge have a good theological discussion on evil and responsible choice that succeeds in reclaiming Faustus for orthodoxy.

This desire to fly from immediate issues to the far reaches of the speculative intellect is one of the dangers of the Christian (or, indeed, any other type of religious or philosophical) imagination. Even Dante, whom Dorothy Sayers thoroughly loved as a consummate storyteller, was not exempt from this. The entire structural movement of the *Comedy* is away from the physical and concrete toward the spiritual heights. Sayers asserts that Dante gains Beatrice again on the spiritual level after she dies, but that does not negate the hard fact that he has lost her physically. Dorothy L. Sayers in *The Devil to Pay* and also in *The Emperor Constantine* and *The Just Vengeance* finds it difficult to avoid the abstract issues.

Still, the contribution made by Sayers to aesthetics cannot be negated. The advantage of her aesthetic theory is that it shows how to bring together the intellectual and the practical. In *The Mind of the Maker* and also in a little essay entitled "Towards a Christian Aesthetic,"[23] she suggested something that still has not carefully been studied: that only a truly creative and truly Christian aesthetic can avoid the Platonic reduction of art to the status of a metaphysical and moral cheat or the Aristotelian reduction of it to a moral cathartic. On the contrary, a genuinely Christian aesthetic can help us to appreciate how art can create something new. It is through the Creative Idea of artists, the Creative Energy of their style, and the Creative Power of the literary work itself that something absolutely new appears in the world, something so compelling that the lives of readers everywhere can be illuminated and changed. Each member of this trinity must be in place for a proper aesthetic and moral balance. The implications are not only for the artist, but for the citizen as well.

In the best of Sayers's fiction one feels a warm, witty, earthy presence. This is true in both her religious and secular work. Perhaps this presence can be felt as well in a little poem I discovered in the William Andrews Clark Library of the University of California at Los Angeles as in any of her great efforts. This poem, "Lord, I Thank Thee,"[24] was written early during World War II when material things were becoming scarce. It may take on a new significance in this day when the finitude of our own natural resources is once again becoming apparent. Among the things for which Sayers was thankful was that she liked to knit her own stockings:

> I need not shiver in silk stockings; —
> I had a hunch about wool before it was rationed;
> Now I have knitted myself woollen stockings
> That come a long way up.
> They are warm and admirable,
> They do not ladder or go into holes suddenly.
> I can boast quietly about them
> And smirk while others admire my industry;
> As it happens, I like knitting

And nothing gratifies one more
Than to be admired for doing what one likes.

Nowhere is it clearer in the writings of Dorothy L. Sayers than here how practical, how perfectly adequate the "whimsical vision" is for the ordinary person, and how easily he or she may share in that universal response to the basic friendliness of the universe toward man that Dante called *un riso dell'universo*, "the laughter of the universe."

V: BIBLIOGRAPHY

*Joe R. Christopher, E. R. Gregory, Margaret Hannay,
and R. Russell Maylone*

Dorothy L. Sayers's Manuscripts and Letters in Public Collections in the United States

THE MATERIAL in the following annotated checklists is arranged in this sequence:

1. Manuscripts in the Marion E. Wade Collection, Wheaton College (Wheaton, Illinois)
2. Manuscripts at the Humanities Research Center, The University of Texas at Austin
3. Letters in the Marion E. Wade Collection, Wheaton College (Wheaton, Illinois)
4. Letters at the University of Michigan, Ann Arbor
5. Letters in the Houghton Library, Harvard University
6. Letters at the Humanities Research Center, U.T.
7. Letters in the Special Collections Department, Northwestern University Library

For the sake of clarity, each of these divisions has been started on a separate page, as well as been given a running headline.

These checklists are intended as guides for Sayers scholars and enthusiasts. So far as we compilers know, they contain all of the manuscripts and letters which are available in public collections in the U.S. —but this is an area which it is difficult to check thoroughly. At least, while we would not be surprised to learn of a few scattered letters given to other libraries, we hope these are the major collections.

There is some minor variance in forms of annotations and of bibliographic information. For example, the smaller letters in Section 4 have their dimensions given because the librarian at the University of Michigan had already prepared the information; since we had intended works closer to finding-lists than formal descriptive bibliographies, we had not planned to include such information —but we did not turn it down when it was available. Likewise, call letters are given for the materials in the Houghton Library because they will speed a student's work; no such letters are used at the Wade Collection or the Humanities Research Center.

The following abbreviations are used in these descriptions:

A = autograph
cc = carbon copy
From London [on letters by Sayers] = from 24 Great James Street,
    Bloomsbury, London
From Witham [on letters by Sayers] = from 24 Newland Street,
    Witham, Essex
H & B = Robert B. Harmon and Margaret A. Burger, *An Annotated Guide to the Works of Dorothy L. Sayers* (New York:
    Garland Publishing, 1977)
H.R.C. = Humanities Research Center
I = initialed
L = letter
lf./lvs. = leaf/leaves
ms./mss. = manuscript/manuscripts
nd = no date
n.p. = no place
p./pp. = page/pages
pub. = published/publication
S = signed
T = typescript
[Title] = a title supplied by the editor
WC:C&BS = Dorothy L. Sayers, *Wilkie Collins: A Critical and Biographical Study*, ed. E. R. Gregory (Toledo, Ohio: The
    Friends of The University of Toledo Libraries, 1977)
WColl = Wade Collection

The distinction between leaves and pages has been made only where necessary —that is, where Sayers wrote on both sides of the same leaf.

Although the quantity of papers we describe may seem substantial, Sayers's son still has a number of papers which will eventually (no doubt) find their way into collections. The largest group of these is that of Sayers's Dantean mss., which are currently available for purchase as a unit. In addition, there are at least a few other single mss.: three which were once offered and then withdrawn are "The Priest's Chamber" (a complete, unpublished, early short story), "Cat O'Many: The Biography of a Prig" (about 250 pp. of a nondetective novel, which Sayers once announced she was going to publish under the pseudonym of Johanna Leigh), and "My Edwardian Childhood" (the first 33 pp. of an autobiography). So the following listings of materials, while basic in the areas of Sayers's detective fiction, dramas, and research on Collins, may be considered an interim report on the full range of Sayers's literary activities.

J. R. C.

1. Manuscripts in the Marion E. Wade Collection, Wheaton College (Wheaton, Illinois), ed. E. R. Gregory

The Dorothy L. Sayers papers at Wheaton College were purchased by Clyde S. Kilby, Curator of the Wade Collection, on 26 September 1975, after having been offered for sale by the Sayers estate for some years. The London agent for the sale was David Higham. The checklist in H & B, pp. 249–63, was prepared by Professor and Mrs. Joe H. McClatchey of Wheaton College in the summer of 1975 in conjunction with Wheaton's possible purchase of the papers. Although it was in no sense intended as a scholarly guide, Harmon and Burger reproduce it *verbatim* down to and including the most obvious misreadings. "Striding Folly," for example, is reproduced as "Stitching Folly."

The following bibliography is limited strictly to the papers covered in this sale, except for the final division on signed copies of books. Sayers's letters are listed in Section 3. In all instances, I have examined the original documents and not the Xerox copies that the Wade Collection encourages scholars to use.

The materials are organized in this manner:

    A. General Notebooks
    B. Mystery Novels, Dramas, and Collaborative Works, with Letters Relating to the Novels
    C. Mystery Short Stories
    D. Nonfiction Dealing with Mystery Fiction and True Crime
    E. Noncriminous Fiction, Drama, and Christmas and Easter Cards
    F. Nonfiction on Religious, Social, and Aesthetic Topics
    G. Translations of Romance Literature
    H. Inscribed Books in the Wade Collection

In addition to brief descriptions of the manuscripts and later publication information, I have given a brief précis if the work is nonfictional prose and unpublished, and comments, at times, on factual and bibliographical matters, including dating.

As always with good writing, Sayers's is very difficult to précis. One feels that her wording is really the only adequate way of saying what she said. I have, however, resisted the temptations and relied entirely on paraphrase. I have not, perhaps, distinguished as sharply as I might between précis and summary, having resorted to summary in instances where I could not précis the work, or found that to do so would take an inordinate amount of space. In any event, I have provided the material necessary to understand the unpublished, expository prose in the collection. With regard to the unpublished imaginative literature, any kind of summary seemed inadequate and undesirable.

I have put down in my comments every piece of information that could conceivably help in dating the works. In the future, it should be possible to pinpoint most of the works' dates more precisely through examination of internal evidence (works and events referred to, editions used, etc.), and through questioning of Sayers's friends and associates. Such work should be carried out as soon as possible. The likelihood of complete and accurate dating constantly diminishes. According to Colleen B. Gilbert, the examination of the files of Victor Gollancz, whose business relation with Sayers began in 1927, and those of David Higham, whose firm, founded in 1935, served as Sayers's literary agent, is not fruitful in dating the bothersome minor materials. I have sometimes assumed on the mystery fiction, where being up to date is a commercial virtue, that internal dates indicate the approximate date of composition; all of these assumptions are clearly indicated in my commentary.

In classifying the works, I have used the classifications that Sayers herself indicated wherever available. Where not available, I tried to follow her wishes as I understand them. For many of the mystery short stories, since they are classified by the division in which they appear, I have added no further notation. When an element of detection was actually present, I added the subclassification of "detective story." In giving measurements, I have always given the vertical measurement first.

The final division, of inscribed copies of books, has nothing to do with the 1975 purchase of mss. from Sayers's son, but it seems worth including because Christopher, in Section 2, has described the inscribed books at the H.R.C. Most of the work on it was done by Christopher, with the assistance of Barbara Griffin, former secretary-librarian of the WColl.

I wish to thank the University of Toledo Graduate School for grants in 1977 and 1978 which enabled me to work on this project at the WColl.

E.R.G.

A. General Notebooks

A.1. *Lord Peter Wimsey Amateur Sleuth*. Ams, nd [c. 1927–28], 59 lvs. (20 x 15½ cm.).

The title is given by Sayers on p. 1 of this red-covered Exercise Book, which is of the same manufacture as D3 in Section 2. The notebook, which is in poor condition, consists of 117 lvs., 58 of which are completely blank. Selections described under *Recto* read from front to back of the book and have occasional corrections on facing versos. Selections described under *Verso* read from back to front with the notebook upended, and with additions on the recto facing 1f. 10.

Recto:

a. "The Adventure of the Cat in the Bag." 35 pp. Detective story; complete. The manuscript includes a title page. *Publication:* See *Lord Peter Views the Body* (item C.18), where it appeared under the title of "The Fantastic Horror of the Cat in the

Bag." The story was written prior to November 1927, when its publication was discussed with Gollancz.

    b. "The Tooth of Time." 4 pp. Familiar essay; complete; unpublished. *Précis:* Though dental hygiene is definitely better than in Sayers's youth, it is sad to think that the large, mechanically moving dentures seen in display windows when she was a child are now gone forever.

    c. "N or M." 4 pp. Familiar essay; complete; unpublished. *Précis:* Shakespeare notwithstanding, names are important, whether for characters in fiction, titles of books, or children. *Comment:* Despite the similarity in title to Agatha Christie's *N or M?* (1941), a Tuppence and Tommy novel about a Nazi spy with the code name of either N or M, the cause is not Christie's borrowing from Sayers, but a common borrowing from the English *Book of Common Prayer.* The response to the first question in the Catechism is the person or persons' names. In the 1928 Protestant Episcopal *Book of Common Prayer*, the response printed for "What is your Name?" is "N. or N.N."; but in the English *Book*, the plural of N. is given as M.: "N. or M." For further details, *Brewer's Dictionary of Phrase and Fable*, rev. ed. (New York: Harper and Row, 1965), p. 630, may be consulted. (I would like to thank Charles E. Noad for this information.)

    d. "Wilkie Collins: List of Letters etc." 4 pp., including title page. A list.
Verso:

    e. [Secondary Materials on Collins.] 4 pp. (lvs. 1-4). This list may be dated as c, 1928 because the Oxford University Press edition of *The Moonstone* and the Ley edition of John Forster's *Life of Charles Dickens* both appeared in 1928, and they are here listed.

    f. "Obituaries" [of Collins]. 2 pp. (lvs 4–5). A list.

    g. "Articles &c." 5 pp. (lvs. 5–9). A list.

    h. "Articles &c in H.W." [*Household Words*]. 2 pp. (lvs. 10–11). A list.

    i. [Articles, etc., in] "A.Y.R." [*All the Year Round*]. 2 pp. (lvs. 11–12). A list.

A.2. *Lord Peter Wimsey —Unprofessional Sleuth.* Ams, nd [before July 1929], 69 lvs. (20½ x 16½ cm.)
A dark-green covered notebook titled by Sayers. Selections described under *Recto* read from front to back; selections described under *Verso* and *Verso and Recto* read from back to front with the notebook upended.
Recto:

    a. "The Fascinating Problem of Uncle Meleager's Will." 37 pp. Detective story; complete. *Publication: Lord Peter Views the Body* (item C.18). This story is numbered "5" in this ms., and "The Horrible Story of the Missing Molar" (immediately below) is numbered "6"; this suggests that *Lord Peter Wimsey — Unprofessional Sleuth* was a working title for what became *Lord Peter Views the Body* (in which, however, "The Fascinating Problem of Uncle Meleager's Will" is the third story, not the fifth); further, this suggests that *Lord Peter Wimsey Amateur Sleuth* (item A.1) is another working title for the same book, since it contains the story which appeared in *Lord Peter Views the Body* as "The Fantastic Horror of the Cat in the Bag."

    b. "The Horrible Story of the Missing Molar." 6 pp. Detective story; incomplete; unpublished. Numbered "6" in this ms.; see the discussion of the item immediately above.

c. [Fragment of a personal letter.] 2 pp. In pencil. The letter has to do with the translation and publication of *Tristan in Brittany*.

Verso:

d. [A quotation from *The History of Fortunatus*.] 1 p.

Verso and Recto:

e. [Notes for a Lord Peter novel.] 17 pp. This does not seem to be a novel which Sayers completed, for it involves characters named Angus McDongal, Peter Brandon, Elizabeth Pendred, Vera Hastings, and John Gurney; the plan calls for a time scheme running, with a chapter per hour, from 7 p.m. on a Tuesday until 6 a.m. on a Wednesday; and the collection of epigraphs all involve a reference to time.

Verso continued:

f. *The Romance of Tristan*. 38 pp. Translation; unfinished. This constitutes the first four chapters of *Tristan in Brittany,* which was published July 1929.

g. [Instructions for knitting.] 2 pp. Jottings.

A.3. Dark green notebook (20 x 16½ cm.). Ams, nd [c. 1927], 51 lvs.

This notebook contains two writings: the incomplete play, *The Mousehole* (item B.12), and the first chapter of *The Unpleasantness at the Bellona Club* (item B.21). See those items for fuller details.

A.4. *The Song of Roland:* Notebook 13. Besides some notes on *The Song of Roland,* this notebook pad also contains a page of notes for a detective story and a page with two jottings about a paper on Charles Williams. See items G.2.d and G.2.e for fuller details.

A.5. Combined manuscripts. These are not notebooks, but it should be observed that the versos of some of Sayers's manuscripts have partial or complete works on them, thus being similar to the notebooks in their multiple contents. See the descriptions of *The Just Vengeance* ms. (item E.10), with a letter and with part of [Translating Dante], and *The Man Born to Be King* ms. (item E.11), with parts of "Blood Sacrifice," "Holmes' College Career," and an interesting title page. (For the fullest information about [Translating Dante], see item F.15; and about the title page, see the discussion under item D.9). *Note:* Although they are not on the verso of a page, two drafts of a prefatory paragraph for what seems to be "The Learned Adventure of the Dragon's Head" are filed with the *Thrones, Dominations*—ms. (item B.19).

B. Mystery Novels, Dramas, and Collaborative Works, With Letters Relating to the Novels

B.1. *Ask a Policeman*. Ams, nd, 63 pp. Collaborative detective story. *Publication:* London: A. Barker, 1933; New York: William Morrow, 1933. The following works by Sayers are included:

a. "The Conclusions of Mr. Roger Sheringham." 59 pp.

b. "NOTE [Explanation to be included in final chapter]." 4 pp.

Sayers's collaborators in the volume were Anthony Berkeley, Milward Kennedy, Gladys Mitchell, John Rhode, and Helen Simpson; but the WColl does not have all of their contributions. These are the other items at Wheaton:

c. Pen-and-ink drawing. 1 p. (25 x 20 cm.) The floor plan and map of Hursley Lodge which appeared as the frontispiece to *Ask a Policeman*.

d. [Synopsis of Part I.] Tcc/ms, nd, 11 pp.

e. John Rhode, "Death at Hursley Lodge." Tcc/ms, nd, 71 pp. Rhode's contribution is Part I of the book; included in the 71 pp. are a page of "Proper Names" and a title page.

B.2. Barton, Eustace Robert. Two letters to Sayers. Barton, who collaborated with Sayers on *The Documents in the Case* under the pseudonym of Robert Eustace, also collaborated with other mystery writers of the time —e.g., with L. T. Meade on *The Brotherhood of the Seven Kings* (1899) and *A Master of Mysteries* (1898), with Edgar Jepson on "The Tea Leaf" and "Mr. Belton's Immunity" (the latter 1926). Since, as various historians of the detection genre have noted, Dr. Barton was a mysterious figure, the bits of information about him that can be gleaned from the following letters are of interest in their own right.

a. TLS, 13 November 1930, 1 p. From the County Mental Hospital, Gloucester. Barton encloses a copy of notes from recent literature on hemophilia, sent to him by a young friend at Edinburgh University; he returns two letters from a London physician, Dr. George MacDonald, about synthetic thyroxine (see item B.11); Barton wishes to know whether he should return the form to an agent with details of his life on it, since he is supposed to be a mystery (this is presumably connected with publicity for *The Documents in the Case*, published in this year); his friend at Oxford is working on the muscarine problem.

b. TLS, 2 June 1931, 2 pp. (1 1f.). From St. Swithams, Carbis Bay, Cornwall. The letter contains more information about hemophilia and "the final and authoritative dictum" about muscarine. Barton feels that her work in *The Documents in the Case* was very good, and he regrets his blunder. (The reason for the apology, and the reference to the muscarine in the previous letter, is because the variety of mushroom used in *The Documents in the Case* does not have the scientific attributes there credited to it. Barton's references to hemophilia are probably part of Sayers's preparation for writing *Have His Carcase* [1932]. See item B. 10.)

B.3. *Behind the Screen.* Ams, nd, 52 pp. Collaborative detective story, broadcast over the BBC 28 June 1930–19 July 1930 (source: H & B, p. 133); unpublished. For the relation of this work to *Have His Carcase*, see item B.10. The WColl has the following work of Sayers:

a. Table of Contents. 2 pp.
b. Suggested Solutions. 5 pp.
c. Alternative Solution. 1 p.
d. Synopsis. 5 pp.
e. Fragment of Chapter III. 4 pp.
f. Chapter III. 17 pp.
g. Part III. 18 pp.

Sayers's collaborators were Hugh Walpole, Agatha Christie, Anthony Berkeley, E. C. Bentley, and Fr. Ronald Knox; the WColl has Tcc's of some of the rest of the work.

B.4. *Busman's Honeymoon: A Detective Comedy in Three Acts* (collaboration with M. St. Clare Byrne). Ams, nd [c. 1936], 45 pp. (43 lvs.). Detective comedy. The ms. consists of prefatory matter prepared for the publication of the play and pieces of various scenes; no scene is present in its entirety. Not all the ms. is in Sayers's hand; the other hand is, presumably, that of Muriel St. Clare Byrne. *First perfor-*

mance: 16 December 1936. *Publication:* Gollancz, February 1937. (*Note:* H & B, p. 127, fail to list this first publication of the drama.)

B.5. *Busman's Honeymoon: A Love Story with Detective Interruptions.* Ams, nd [c. early 1937], 548 pp. + Tms, nd, 2 pp. + Tcc/ms, nd, 2 pp. Detective novel, originally subtitled "A Murder Theme with Sentimental Variations." The Ams is complete; the Tcc/ms's are duplicates of the first two pages, Tms, of Chapter 3. *Publication:* Gollancz, June 1937. Presumably the novel was written between December 1936, when the play opened, and June 1937, when the novel was published. One variation between the plots of the play and the novel is the hanging of the guilty party in the latter; cf. *The Documents in the Case* (item B.6), where such a hanging was also an afterthought.

B.6. *The Documents in the Case* (collaboration with Robert Eustace [pseudonym]). Ams, nd, 383 pp. Detective novel. The Ams includes a title page for the entire work and title pages for Sections 1 and 2; complete (but see below). *Publication:* E. Benn, July 1930. The story is conceived as happening between 9 September 1928 and 18 March 1930. Ordinarily, one would presume that the novel was written after the last date in the novel; but since Lathom's hanging on the last page of the first edition is dated 30 November 1930 and since the book was originally published in July 1930, this cannot be. However, the last document, *"Extract from the 'Morning Express' of November 30th, 1930,"* was not part of the original ms., which ends with Sir Gilbert Pugh's line, "Get me the Chief Commissioner on the phone." Since Janet Hitchman has noted in *Such a Strange Lady* (London: New English Library, 1975, p. 76; New York: Harper and Row, nd [1975], pp. 55–56) that this and *Busman's Honeymoon* are the only novels in which Sayers specifies that the murderer is hanged, perhaps it is worth further noting that in this instance, whether the idea was Sayers's or that of her editor or publisher, it was definitely an afterthought. For additional information about Sayers's collaborator, see item B.2.; for related correspondence, see B.11. *Comment:* No doubt can exist that Sayers got the idea for this novel from the Thompson-Bywaters case. The victim, Percy Thompson, was stabbed to death on 4 October 1922; his wife, Edith, and her lover, Frederick Bywaters, were hanged 9 January 1923. Sayers's library contained a copy of Filson Young's *Trial of Frederick Bywaters and Edith Thompson* (Notable British Trial Series, 1923). Although her copy contains no evidence, like marginalia, to indicate that she actually read it, her notes for a talk, "Where Do Plots Come From?", provide conclusive evidence that the case was her source; for she lists *Documents* along with other novels based on actual cases and writes "Thompson Bywaters case" beside it. (The preceding information was supplied to me by Anthony Fleming in a letter of 17 December 1977.) The year 1923, then, is an absolute *terminus a quo* for the work, but there is no reason to assume that Sayers did not write it within a year of its publication. The story of Thompson and Bywaters has been retold numerous times. A first-hand account of the investigation was given by Frederick Porter Wensley in *Forty Years of Scotland Yard* (Garden City: Doubleday, 1933), pp. 231–46. Another fictional handling is F. Tennyson Jesse's *A Pin to See the Peep Show* (London, Toronto: Heinemann, 1934).

B.7. *Five Red Herrings.* Ams, nd, 512 pp. Detective novel. The ms. includes a title page, table of contents, and foreword; it is complete except for a few pages of Chapter 24. *Publication:* Gollancz, 1931.

B.8. *The Floating Admiral*. Ams, nd, 128 pp. (127 lvs.) + Tms, nd, 1 p. + Tcc/ms, nd. 13 pp. A collaborative detective story. *Publication:* London: Hodder and Stoughton, 1931. The WColl has the following work of Sayers:

    a. Summary of the story, being a rough draft of "Story according to Dorothy L. Sayers." Ams, 25 pp.

    b. "The Story according to Dorothy L. Sayers." Ams, 28 pp.

    c. "The Story according to Dorothy L. Sayers." Title page typed; Tcc/ms, 13 pp.

    d. Notes on Chapter 7. Ams, 7 pp.

    e. Chapter 7, "Shocks for the Inspector." Ams, 52 pp.

    f. Notes and queries. Ams, 16 pp. (15 lvs.).

Sayers's collaborators on the published book were G. K. Chesterton, Canon Victor L. Whitechurch, G. D. H. and M. Cole, Henry Wade, Agatha Christie, John Rhode, Milward Kennedy, and Fr. Ronald Knox.

B.9. *Gaudy Night*. Ams, nd [probably 1934–35], 640 pp. Detective novel. The ms. includes the title page; complete. *Publication:* Gollancz, 1935. If, as Sayers indicated, a speech at Oxford was the origin of the novel, and if, as I think, this particular speech was given in 1934, then the novel was written between 1934 and its publication in 1935 (see "Toast of the University of Oxford," item F.12, for a dating of the speech).

B.10. *Have His Carcase*. Ams, nd [late 1930 through 1931], 242 pp. (238 lvs.). Detective novel. *Publication:* Gollancz, 1932. The letters from Eustace Barton and John Rhode listed in this section (items B.2, B.16) relate, at least in part, to this book; the approximate time of writing can be judged from the continued interest in hemophilia, extending from the first letter from Barton, 11 November 1930, through the last letter from Rhode, 26 October 1931. The WColl has the following materials by Sayers:

    a. Notes. 12 pp. (8 lvs.). The leaves are of various sizes. One page, working out the genetics of hemophilia with regard to the Romanoffs, is on the verso of the last page of Rhode's letter of 7 October 1931 (item B.16.h).

    b. About one-third of the novel. 230 pp. The manuscript includes the first 12 chapters, with a title page, a page with an epigraph "'You must produce the body. . . .'—*Habeas Corpus Act*," and a leaf (13 x 20 cm.) containing an earlier version of parts of two paragraphs in Chapter XXI. *Comment:* J. I. M. Stewart writes the following in *D. N. B., 1951–1960*: "Monsignor Ronald Knox, himself a writer of detective stories, told a story illustrating this [Sayers's continuing alertness for new ideas]. A group of writers was discussing a proposed collaboration in a play for broadcasting, and one was in favour of beginning with a river of blood flowing from under a curtain and surrounding a group of intent bridge players. Another declared that blood would not behave in such a way, 'unless it were from a haemophiliac,' and the idea was abandoned. Dorothy Sayers did not contribute to the discussion at this point, but was observed to make an entry in a notebook. From this she evolved one of her cleverest novels." The play to which Knox refers was *Behind the Screen* (item B.3), which was broadcast between 14 June and 19 July 1930.

B.11. MacDonald, George. Two letters. *Note:* This is not the author (who died in 1905), but an osteopathic physician in London.

    a. To Sayers. TLS, 31 October 1930, 1 p. From 62 Harley Street, London.

MacDonald has a vegetarian patient who refuses to take anything of animal origin. She badly needs thyroid hormone. From reading *The Documents in the Case*, he has inferred that gland extracts can be prepared synthetically, and he wishes to know more about this.

b. To Dr. Eustace Barton. TLS, 10 November 1930, 1 p. (13 x 20 cm.) From 62 Harley Street, London. MacDonald was referred to Barton by Sayers. Since writing her, he has discovered that synthetically prepared thyroxine is on the market. (See the brief reference to these letters in item B.2.a.)

B.12. *The Mousehole*. Ams, nd [probably before 1928], 12 pp. Play (labeled by Sayers "A Detective Fantasia in Three Flats"). The manuscript includes a title page; incomplete; unpublished. This fragment is written on the versos of the last leaves in a 20 x 16½ cm. notebook, which also contains Chapter I of *The Unpleasantness at the Bellona Club* (item B.21.a); the notebook has to be reversed and upended to read its alternate contents. *Comment:* This work was written during the same general period as *The Unpleasantness* (which probably was written in 1927—see the annotation to B.21.a).

B.13. *Murder Must Advertise*. Ams, nd, 497 pp. Detective story (so labeled by Sayers). The manuscript includes a title page, two pages of the floor plan at Pym's (one in pencil, one in ink), three pages of fictional advertising slogans with preliminary bits of dialog, and one page of possible titles for the novel. Complete. *Publication:* Gollancz, February 1933.

B.14. *The Nine Tailors*. Ams, nd, 525 pp. + 1 water-color board. Detective novel. *Publication:* Gollancz, 1934. The materials fall into these categories:

a. Red-covered Exercise Book (20½ x 16 cm.). 63 pp. Some physical details fit the notebook described under *Lord Peter Wimsey —Amateur Sleuth*. Printed material on the verso of the front cover of *LPW —AS* is the same as the recto of the back cover of *The Nine Tailors* notebook; the verso of the back cover is the same on both notebooks. The notebooks are not identical, however: their size, number of leaves, and other details differ. This notebook contains 81 leaves; some leaves have been torn out; 45 are completely blank. In keeping with her usual practice, Sayers has written from front to back and, with the notebook upended, from back to front. The material in the notebook falls into three general, though overlapping, categories: notes on bells: the mathematical working out of changes; notes on the plot.

b. 1 lf. (20½ x 16 cm.) with printed grid markings on it. Pencilled notations and calculations.

c. Three drawings. 2 lvs. + 1 water-color board. A pen-and-ink sketch of the Church at Fenchurch St. Paul; 1 lf. (25½ x 20 cm.). A pencilled map of Fenchurch St. Paul; 1 lf. (31½ x 20½ cm.) with printed grid markings on it, drawn so that each square = 60 ft. A pen-and-ink map of Fenchurch St. Paul; 1 Water-Color Board (30 x 25 cm.).

d. Preparatory matter. 23 lvs. Notes on the plot, sketches, quotations, and a title page.

e. The novel. 436 pp. Complete. The page count includes title pages where they are separate; most pages are 25 x 20½ cm. No leaf is written on both sides.

B.15. [Notes for an unwritten Lord Peter Wimsey novel.] See A.2.e.

B.16. Rhode, John [pseudonym for Cecil John Charles Street], 1884–1964. Ten letters to Sayers. Unless otherwise indicated, the letters are mailed from North Brewham, Nr. Bath, Somerset.

    a. ALS, 31 March 1931, 4 pp. Freeman Wills Crofts and Rhode concur that Sayers's idea for *Have His Carcase* is excellent, and Rhode makes a number of suggestions about locale and includes information about tides.

    b. ALS, 2 June 1931, 4 pp. (3 lvs.). Rhode expresses great interest in Sayers's story; he quotes *The Encyclopaedia Britannica* on hemophilia; he suggests a character's descent from Paul I, whose amours were notorious, attaching a genealogical table, with imaginary personages in pencil; he makes observations about how the body might be gotten to the rock.

    c. ALS, 5 June 1931, 4 pp. (2 lvs.). More about hemophilia and a plausible ancestry for the victim.

    d. ALS, 29 July 1931, 4 pp. More about the same subjects, including a family tree for the Spanish Bourbons.

    e. ALS, 25 August 1931, 2 pp. (1 lf.). Rhode comments about the Devonshire dialect; he says the bleeding taint is probably traceable to the British royal family; he suggests that the Playfair Cipher be used; he compliments her on her introduction to the new *Great Short Stories of Detection, Mystery and Horror* and says that he agrees with all she says except her admiration for *Masters of Mystery* (Sayers, in a footnote in her introduction to her *Second Series* of *GSSDMH*, calls H. Douglas Thompson's book "a valuable work of reference for the student").

    f. ALS, 17 September 1931, 6 pp. Five pages are instructions on how to work the Playfair Cipher; if he sends her a message in code, the code word will be "Excalibur."

    g. ALS, several dates, 3 pp. (2 lvs.). From several places. The letter is divided into three parts: (i) S. S. Britannia at sea, nd; (ii) still at sea, 25 September 1931; (iii) back home, 2 October 1931. Rhode says the Playfair Cipher is quite the best for Sayers's purposes; he sent her a message (presumably in code) from Gdynice. He gives his estimates of Poland, Czechoslovakia, and Hungary; he is glad she liked *The Hanging Woman*, and thinks *The Fire of Greycombe Farm* will baffle her (the latter title is the American title—and possibly Rhode's manuscript title—for his 1932 *Mystery at Greycombe Farm*); he congratulates her on decoding with the Playfair Cipher on her first try.

    h. ALS, 7 October 1931, 3 pp. (2 lvs.). More about the Playfair Cipher and how to use it in the novel. See item B.10.a for Sayers's Ams on the verso.

    i. ALS, 26 October 1931, 4 pp. (2 lvs.). More about royal genealogy. *Comment:* It is perhaps not entirely gratuitous to note about this series of letters that Janet Hitchman devotes a couple of pages to showing that John Cournos "most certainly . . . would have provided the medical [information about hemophilia] and [the] technical details" for "the Playfair cipher" (*Such a Strange Lady* [London: New English Library, 1975], pp. 102–03; [New York: Harper and Row, nd (1975)], pp. 80–81). It is true that Hitchman could not have access to these letters, but Sayers left a quite adequate clue as to her source—if indeed one may speak of a direct statement as a clue—in her prefatory note: "My grateful acknowledgments are due to Mr. John Rhode, who gave me generous help with all the hard bits."

B.17. *The Scoop.* Ams, nd, 30 pp. + Tms with A note and corrections, nd, 32 pp. + Tcc/ms with A corrections, nd, 30 pp. A collaborative detective story given as a serial on the BBC, 10 January 1931–4 April 1931 (H & B, pp. 136–37), and envisaged as a novel although never so published. The following works by Sayers are included:

a. Chapter I, "Over the Wire." Tms with A corrections, 18 pp. The broadcast version, read by Sayers over the BBC on 10 January.

b. Chapter XII, "The Final Scoop." Tms with A note, 14 pp. The broadcast version, read by Sayers over the BBC on 4 April; the first page has a request by Sayers (presumably to her typist) for a rustle-proof copy, which is to be sent to Witham.

c. Chapter XII, "The Final Scoop." Ams, 16 pp.

d. [Synopsis of Chapter V.] Ams, 3 pp. A chapter by Anthony Berkeley, "Tracing Tracy," broadcast on 14 February.

e. [Rough outline of the story.] Ams, 7 pp.

f. [Descriptions of the characters.] Ams, 1 p.

g. [Pencilled notes for chapters.] Ams, 3 pp.

h. Chapter I, Expanded Version Tcc/ms, 10 pp.

i. Chapter I, Broadcast Version. Tcc/ms with A corrections and deletions, and with some duplicates of pages in B.17.h, 20 pp.

Sayers's collaborators were Agatha Christie, E. C. Bentley, Anthony Berkeley, Freeman Wills Crofts, and Clemence Dane; in addition to Sayers's mss., there are various copies of the other authors' work, both broadcast and novel version, many synopses, notes, queries, maps of the murder site, etc. —all, in Professor Mac-Clatchey's words, "horribly jumbled and confus[ed]."

B.18. *Strong Poison*. Ams, nd [c. 1928–1930], 370 pp. Detective novel. The manuscript includes the title page and a page with the quotation from "Lord Randall" used as an epigraph to the novel; complete. Some of the material is contained in writing pads. *Publication:* Gollancz, 1930. *Comment:* The novel was written between 1928 and September 1930, for the second writing pad has a notation: "?Ley J.W.T. / *The Dickens Circle*." Ley's book was published in 1928.

B.19. *Thrones, Dominations* —. Ams, nd [after 1937?], 177 pp. (176 lvs.). Detective novel. The manuscript includes a title page, a sketch of the seating at a dinner party on the verso of one leaf, a page of notes in pencil on *Mourning Becomes Electra* and *Night Must Fall*, and a page with two versions of a paragraph introducing a Lord Peter story, probably "The Learned Adventure of the Dragon's Head"; incomplete. The description in the sale catalog of this manuscript as being the first five or six chapters of an unfinished sequel to *Busman's Honeymoon* is inaccurate; rather, one has a series of scenes which Sayers has worked and reworked —and these scenes are not in sequence. The novel is set precisely at the time of the death of George V and the accession of Edward VIII. *Comment on the dating:* Presumably the novel was begun after the completion of *Busman's Honeymoon* in 1937. *General comment:* Despite the above label of "detective novel" because Wimsey appears, the book is described this way in Alzina Stone Dale's *Maker and Craftsman:* "Very much a comedy of manners, and in nearly two hundred pages it has no corpse" (Grand Rapids, Michigan: Wm. B. Eerdmans Publishing Co., 1978, p. 102).

B.20. *Unnatural Death*. Ams, nd, 333 pp. Detective novel. The manuscript includes the title pages for Parts Two and Three; one or more pages from Chapter V and the last two chapters are missing. *Publication:* E. Benn, 1927.

B.21. *The Unpleasantness at the Bellona Club*. Ams, nd [c. 1927], 257 lvs. Detective novel. Incomplete. *Publication:* E. Benn, 1928. The manuscript —some of whose pages are so badly faded and stained as to be illegible —exists in two parts:

   a. Dark-green notebook with 51 lvs. (20 x 16½ cm.) The rectos of the first 47 lvs. contain the first three chapters of *The Unpleasantness*; the verso facing lf. 12 contains a correction. The verso of the last 12 lvs. contains a fragment of a play entitled *The Mousehole* (item B.12). Here, as with other notebooks, Sayers upended the notebook before writing on the versos of leaves. *Comment:* The title page in this notebook reads "The Unpleasantness at / the Bellona Club / by / Dorothy L. Sayers / Author of / 'Unnatural Death.'" Since *Unnatural Death* was published in 1927, Sayers presumably wrote this title page either after the publication of *Unnatural Death* or shortly before, when she was assured of the novel's appearance under this title; therefore, this notebook probably dates from 1927.

   b. Chapters 4 to 18. 210 pp. Incomplete.

B.22. *The Wrecker.* Ams, nd [c. 1928], 22 pp. Film scenario (labelled by Sayers *"Preliminary outline only"*). The manuscript includes a title page, a cast of characters, and an alternate version of one scene. Despite a normal tendency to associate this scenario with the one movie with which Sayers is generally known to have provided a "theme" —*The Silent Passenger* (Phoenix Films, 1935)—this is incorrect, according to Colleen B. Gilbert. *The Wrecker* was written for Gainsborough Pictures, but was not used for the 1928 film.

C. Mystery Short Stories

C.1. "Absolutely Elsewhere." Ams, nd, 26 pp. A detective story with Lord Peter. The manuscript, which includes the title page, is complete. *Publication: Mystery: the Illustrated Detective Magazine,* 9:1 (January 1934), 19–21, 104, 106, 108, under the title of "Impossible Alibi" (*source:* H & B, p. 64). *Collected: In the Teeth of the Evidence* (item C.13).

C.2. "An Arrow o'er the House." Ams, nd [probably late 1930s], 20 pp. The manuscript, including the title page, is complete. The date of composition may be suggested by Mr. Podd's use of "Time has an Arrow—see Eddington," which refers to Sir Arthur Eddington's *The Nature of the Physical World* (New York: Macmillan; Cambridge, England: Cambridge University Press, 1928), pp. 68–69. Sayers's reading of Eddington accords, on the whole, better with her intellectual interests in the late 1930s than the late 1920s —she refers to this Eddington book again in *The Mind of the Maker* (London: Methuen, 1941), p. 15, for example. That the story was collected in *In the Teeth of the Evidence* (1939)—item C.13 —and not in *Hangman's Holiday* (1933) also suggests the late 1930s. But neither of these indications is solid evidence, of course.

C.3. "Blood Sacrifice." Ams, nd, 45 pp. + Tms, nd, 6 pp. The autograph manuscript, including a title page, is complete. A partial Tms exists: pp. 15, 17, 18, 19, 22, and 23 were reused, becoming the reverse of pages of the seventh play, "The Light and the Life," of *The Man Born to Be King* (item E.11). *Collected: In the Teeth of the Evidence* (item C.13).

C.4. "The Cyprian Cat." Ams, nd, 20 pp. Thriller. The manuscript, including a title page, is complete. An early publication: in *My Best Thriller: An Anthology of*

Stories Chosen by Their Own Authors (London: Faber and Faber, 1933). (*Source:* H & B, p. 63.) *Collected: In the Teeth of the Evidence* (item C.13).

C.5. "Dilemma." Ams, nd [before 6 April 1934], 25 pp. The WColl has two versions, both complete:

    a. 13 pp. This version has "Dilemma" written at the top of the first page.

    b. 12 pp. This version includes a title page, and it is the version published in *In the Teeth of the Evidence* (item C.13). The story, in some form, existed prior to 6 April 1934, when a radio adaptation was broadcast in a "Short Story" series on the BBC (H & B, p. 239); if the text of this broadcast could be found—if, indeed, it is not just the first of these versions—it might establish whether the second version was written before or after that date.

C.6. "The Fantastic Horror of the Cat in the Bag." For the ms. version, "The Adventure of the Cat in the Bag," see item A.1.a. *Collected: Lord Peter Views the Body* (item C.18).

C.7. "The Fascinating Problem of Uncle Meleager's Will." For the ms. version, see item A.2.a. *Collected: Lord Peter Views the Body* (item C.18).

C.8. "The Fountain." Ams, nd, 22 pp. Two-thirds of p. 7 is missing; otherwise complete. Collected under the title "The Fountain Plays": *Hangman's Holiday*.

C.9. *Hangman's Holiday.* A collection of short stories published by Gollancz and Harcourt Brace in 1933; the earliest review listed in H & B is in *The Times Literary Supplement* on 11 May 1933 (H & B, p. 205). The WColl has the following stories only:

    a. "The Fountain." collected as "The Fountain Plays" (item C.8).

    b. "The Image in the Mirror" (item C.12).

    c. "The Man Who Knew How" (item C.21).

    d. "The Queen's Square" (item C.25).

For additional information, see the entries on these stories.

C.10. "The Haunted Policeman." Ams, nd [1937], 33 pp. + Tcc/ms, nd, 32 pp. Detective story with Lord Peter. Both manuscripts include title pages; complete. *First publication: Harper's Bazaar*, 73 (February 1938), 62–63, 130–35 (H & B, p. 60). *Collected: In the Teeth of the Evidence*, rev. ed. (item C.13); *Lord Peter* (item C.18). Since this story opens immediately after the birth of Lord Peter's first son, it presumably was written after *Busman's Honeymoon*; it could have been completed before the publication of *Busman's Honeymoon* in June 1937, but was more likely completed between then and its publication early in 1938. Cf. "The Master Key" (item C.22).

C.11. "The Horrible Story of the Missing Molar." Incomplete detective story; see item A.2.b.

C.12. "The Image in the Mirror." Ams, nd, 45 pp. Detective story with Lord Peter. The manuscript, complete, includes a title page. *Collected: Hangman's Holiday* (item C.9).

C.13. *In the Teeth of the Evidence, and Other Stories.* A collection of short stories published by Gollancz in 1939; the earliest review listed in H & B is in *The Times Literary Supplement* on 18 November 1939 (H & B, p. 207). The WColl has manuscripts for the following stories only:

    a. "Absolutely Elsewhere" (item C.1).

    b. "An Arrow o'er the House" (item C.2).

    c. "Blood Sacrifice" (item C.3).

    d. "The Cyprian Cat" (item C.4).

    e. "Dilemma" (item C.5).

    f. "The Leopard Lady" (item C.16).

    g. "Nebuchadnezzar" (item C.23).

    h. "Scrawns" (item C.26).

    i. "Suspicion" (item C.32).

In 1972 Gollancz issued a revised edition of *In the Teeth of the Evidence* with the following additional stories, for all of which the WColl has manuscripts:

    j. "The Haunted Policeman" (item C.10).

    k. "Striding Folly" (item C.30).

    l. "Talboys" (item C.32).

For additional information, see the entries for these stories.

C.14. [Introducing Lord Peter.] Ams, nd, 48 pp. An unfinished short story; unpublished. This is very early work, and is listed as such in the sale catalog. Some evidence: Bunter is not mentioned; Inspector Sugg, who appears in *Whose Body?*, is a character; Lord Peter is introduced with a long paragraph of exposition, which is not only amateurish, but which also suggests that this may be the very first work about him that Sayers wrote.

C.15. "The Learned Adventure of the Dragon's Head." Ams, nd, 1 p. + 1 color-board. Detective story with Lord Peter. WColl has these items only:

    a. Two versions of a prefatory paragraph. This is presently with the manuscript of *Thrones, Dominations* —(see item B.19).

    b. 1 piece of a Water-Colour Board (18 x 14½ cm.) with an old-style map, etc., on it. This is the illustration which accompanies most, perhaps all, printed versions of the story. The story is collected: *Lord Peter Views the Body* (item C.18).

C.16. "The Leopard Lady." Ams, nd [1930s], 32 pp. The manuscript, with a title page including "SMITH & SMITH—Removals II," is complete. *Collected: In the Teeth of the Evidence* (item C.13). This story was most probably written during the 1930s because a document in the story is dated 193–. *Comment:* Together with "The House of the Poplars," which is labeled "SMITH & SMITH —Removals I," this was conceived as part of a series of short stories of the supernatural. For "The House of the Poplars," see under "Smith and Smith, Removals" below (item C.28).

C.17. *Lord Peter: A Collection of All the Lord Peter Wimsey Stories*. A collection compiled by James Sandoe and published by Harper and Row in 1972. For the WColl holdings of manuscripts of stories appearing in *Hangman's Holiday* (item C.9), *In the Teeth of the Evidence* (C.13), and *Lord Peter Views the Body* (C.18), see the lists with those titles. In addition to the Wimsey stories from these three collections, *Lord Peter* includes the following stories —the first two in the first printing, all three in the second printing (not so identified on the copyright page):

    a. "The Haunted Policeman" (item C.10).

    b. "Striding Folly" (item C.31).

    c. "Talboys" (item C.33).

For additional information, see the entries for these stories.

C.18. *Lord Peter Views the Body*. A collection of detective stories published by

Gollancz in 1928. The WColl has the following stories, or material related to them, only:

    a. "The Adventure of the Cat in the Bag," collected as "The Fantastic Horror of the Cat in the Bag" (item A.1.a).

    b. "The Fascinating Problem of Uncle Meleager's Will" (item A.2.a).

    c. "The Learned Adventure of the Dragon's Head" (items B.19 and C.15).

    d. "The Piscatorial Farce of the Stolen Stomach" (item C.24).

    e. "The Undignified Melodrama of the Bone of Contention" (item C.34).

    f. "The Unsolved Puzzle of the Man with No Face" (item C.35).

For additional information, see the entries for the individual items. According to a letter from Livia Gollancz, Governing Director of Victor Gollancz, to this editor on 7 September 1976, Sayers had written nine of the stories for *Lord Peter Views the Body* by November 1927, of which five were published in *Pearson's Magazine*, one in *Twenty-Story Magazine*, and three were not published elsewhere; four more were written by 30 Janaury 1928; and a final story was written by 11 August 1928. Since this is a total of 14 stories and only 12 appear in *Lord Peter Views the Body*. Sayers must have decided not to publish two stories, or she was optimistic in her letters about some stories she did not actually finish (cf. "The Horrible Story of the Missing Molar," item A.2.b). No doubt additional information will be available about the stories published in magazines before this checklist appears in print: Colleen B. Gilbert's descriptive bibliography of primary materials, *A Bibliography of the Writings of Dorothy L. Sayers*, is scheduled for publication by Archon Books (The Shoe String Press) in the fall of 1978.

C.19. *Lord Peter Wimsey Amateur Sleuth*. A notebook listed above as item A.1; the title was probably an early version of *Lord Peter Views the Body* (see the discussion in item A.2.a). It contains:

    a. "The Adventure of the Cat in the Bag," collected as "The Fantastic Horror of the Cat in the Bag" (item A.1.a).

For additional information, see the entries indicated.

C.20. *Lord Peter Wimsey —Unprofessional Sleuth*. A notebook listed above as A.2; the title was probably an early version of *Lord Peter Views the Body* (see the discussion in item A.2.a). It contains:

    a. "The Fascinating Problem of Uncle Meleager's Will" (item A.2.a).

    b. "The Horrible Story of the Missing Molar" (item A.2.b).

For additional information, see the entries indicated.

C.21. "The Man Who Knew How." Ams, nd, 25 pp. The manuscript, which is complete, has a notation of "6000 words" at the top of the first page. *Collected: Hangman's Holiday* (item C.9).

C.22. "The Master Key." Ams, nd [probably 1937], 15 pp. Unfinished; unpublished. The manuscript includes a title page. The story was written in the late 1930s; the most likely period is between June 1937 and February 1938. In the story, Harriet and Peter are married and living in Audley Square, but no mention is made of their having any children. Therefore, the likeliest period of composition is after the publication of *Busman's Honeymoon* (item B.5) and before the publication of "The Haunted Policeman" (item C.10).

C.23. "Nebuchadnezzar." Ams, nd, 16 pp. The manuscript, which includes a title page, is complete. *Collected: In the Teeth of the Evidence* (item C.13).

C.24. "The Piscatorial Farce of the Stolen Stomach." Ams, nd, 33 pp. Detective story with Lord Peter; complete. *Collected: Lord Peter Views the Body* (item C.18).

C.25. "The Queen's Square." Ams, nd, 24 pp. Detective story with Lord Peter; complete. *Collected: Hangman's Holiday* (item C.9).

C.26. "Scrawns." Ams, nd, 21 pp. The manuscript, including a title page, is complete. *Collected: In the Teeth of the Evidence* (item C.13).

C.27. "The Situations of Judkin: I. The Travelling Rug." Ams, nd, 35 pp. Detective story; unpublished. The manuscript, including a title page and two pages rewritten, is complete. This story was apparently designed as the first in a series featuring as detective Judkins, an astute serving girl, each story describing one of her "situations" or jobs.

C.28. "Smith and Smith, Removals: I. The House of the Poplars." Ams, nd [1930s], 27 pp. The manuscript of this supernatural short story, which includes a title page, is complete; unpublished. Since a document in the story is dated 17th Dec. 193–, the story was presumably written in the 1930s. Further, it was written in conjunction with "The Leopard Lady," published in *In the Teeth of the Evidence* (1939). (For the relationship of this story with "The Leopard Lady," beyond the question of the date, see item C.16).

C.29. *Song of Roland:* Notebook 13. Listed as items G.2.d and G.2.e; one page of notes for a detective story is included.

C.30. "Spick and Span." Ams, nd, 9 pp. Unfinished; unpublished. The story concerned an unscrupulous lawyer who preys on authors whose work may possibly bear some remote resemblance to a living person. The situation involved is familiar to most writers. After the publication of *Gaudy Night* (1935), a Miss M. L. Barton wrote to Gollancz and accused Sayers of basing the character of Miss Barton in *Gaudy Night* on her. In the rough draft of her letter to Gollancz, Sayers made the same offer that the author in this short story does—to insert in any future edition an explicit statement that the character is not based on her. (The rough draft of the letter, crossed through, is included with the notes on *The Just Vengeance* [item E.10].) It is more likely than not that this story should be dated after *Gaudy Night*; but, since life sometimes imitates art, it is still possible that the story preceded the letter.

C.31. "Striding Folly." Ams, nd, 20 pp. + Tms, nd, 22 pp. Detective story with Lord Peter. Complete; the Tms includes a title page and two versions of p. 8. *Publication:* in *Detection Medley,* ed. John Rhode (London: Hutchinson, 1939). *Collected: In the Teeth of the Evidence,* rev. ed. (item. C.13) and *Lord Peter* (item C.17). *Comment:* Instructions on the first page are "top / 2 carbons / to Curtis Brown." Brown was Sayers's literary agent before David Higham set up office independently in 1935, and this might help in dating the story more precisely than the first publication does. On the other hand, it is possible that Brown was John Rhode's agent and hence was involved in the preparation of *Detective Medley —* after 1935.

C.32. "Suspicion." Ams, nd, 29 pp. The manuscript, including a title page, is complete. *First American publication: Mystery League Magazine,* 1:1 (October 1933), 102–09 (H & B, p. 64). *Collected: In the Teeth of the Evidence* (item C.13).

C.33. "Talboys." Ams, 1942, 33 pp. + Tms, nd, 37 pp. Lord Peter story including a detective aspect. The Ams includes a title page, as does the Tms; complete. The Ams has a notation "(Talboys 1942)" on it in Sayers's hand. The story appeared in three editions in 1972, and no attempt has been made for the purposes of this manuscript checklist to establish which of these is the true first edition:

    a. *In the Teeth of the Evidence,* rev. ed. (item C.13).

    b. *Lord Peter,* second printing (item C.17).

    c. *Extra! A brand-new, long-lost, Dorothy L. Sayers story —about Lord Peter Wimsey and Harriet and their three sons. Just discovered!* New York: Harper and Row, 1972. The third page of this item, a pamphlet, has a regular title page, giving the story's title. The publisher's note on the fifth page is a brief history of the story, and the text begins on the seventh page, which is numbered 431 so as to continue the first printing of *Lord Peter.* This pamphlet was published to supply purchasers of that printing with the missing story, and it was not intended for separate sale. *Note:* H & B. p. 50, list *Striding Folly, Including Three Final Lord Peter Wimsey Stories* (London: New English Library, 1973) as appearing in 1972, which would add a fourth publication of "Talboys" in that year; but, while the paperback volume is copyrighted as of 1972, it first appeared in May 1973.

C.34. "The Undignified Melodrama of the Bone of Contention." Ams, nd, 83 pp. + 1 water-color board. Detective story with Lord Peter. The manuscript, with four substantial lacunae in it, is incomplete; some of the pages are faded and badly stained. The 27 x 19 cm. water-color board has a pen-and-ink sketch on it of the map which appears in most, perhaps all, printed versions of the story. *Collected: Lord Peter Views the Body* (item C.18).

C.35. "The Unsolved Puzzle of the Man with No Face." Ams, nd, 34 pp. Detective story with Lord Peter. Incomplete; the ms. ends with the sentence, "I shouldn't have thought that mattered much to a man of Crowder's ability" (which is said by Lord Peter during his lunch with Miss Twitterton at the Savoy). *Collected: Lord Peter Views the Body* (item C.18).

C.36. ". . . Who Calls the Tune." A supernatural story, more religious than sensational, listed below as E.14.

C.37. "The Wrecker." A film scenario whose shortness —only 22 pp. —justifies a cross-reference from this short-story section; see item B.22.

D. Nonfiction Dealing With Mystery Fiction and True Crime.

D.1. "Arsenic Probably." Ams, September 1926, 4 pp. Topical article; unpublished. The manuscript includes a title page and an attached rejection slip from the *London Daily News*; complete. The date on the rejection slip is 21 September 1926, and the editor comments on the dispatch with which Sayers submitted the article. Therefore, the item to which this article refers cannot have appeared much earlier. *Précis*: A Mr. Gay, whose goldfish have died by the thousands, blames arsenic poisoning on the part of some wicked rival. Possibly the number of famous "arsenists" is responsible for his assumption. As a poison, however, arsenic has disadvantages as well as advantages.

D.2. Collins, Wilkie (materials on). Although most of Sayers's Collins mss. were sold to the H.R.C. at the University of Texas at Austin, and are listed in Section 2 of these checklists, a few items are in Sayers's *Lord Peter Wimsey Amateur Sleuth* notebook:

    a. List of letters (item A.1.d).

    b. Secondary sources (item A.1.e).

    c. Obituaries (item A.1.f).

    d. Articles, etc. (item A.1.g).

    e. Articles in *Household Words* (item A.1.h).

    f. Articles in *All the Year Round* (item A.1.i).

For slightly more information, see the entries on these items.

D.3. "The Comedy of Horror." Ams, nd [c. March–June 1937]. 12 pp. Speech; unpublished. The manuscript is notes, not a written-out version of the speech as delivered. A *terminus a quo* is established by the date of Desmond MacCarthy's reply to her, to which she alludes. Their exchange appeared in the *New Statesman,* 13. His original review appeared on 13 February 1937, pp. 241–42; her criticism, "Chekhov at the Westminster," on 27 February 1937, p. 324; and his reply on 13 March 1937, p. 399. Also, Sayers's comments about *Busman's Honeymoon* in the speech are limited to the play, and this may indicate a date before the publication of the novel in June 1937. *Précis*: Since detective stories emphasize thinking rather than feeling, they are basically comic though they deal with horrible matters. If the detective has feelings as well as thoughts, however, the possibility of a stronger work that is both comic and horrid opens up. One finds this commingling—not juxtaposition—in Chekhov, Shakespeare, and Dickens. The Lord Peter works, especially *Gaudy Night* and *Busman's Honeymoon,* also attempt this commingling, the "comedy of horror."

D.4. "The Craft of Detective Fiction" (I). Ams, nd [after 1937], 13 pp. Speech; unpublished. The manuscript is an outline for a speech, not the full text of the speech; further, it is not an outline for the speech of the same title listed immediately below—Sayers gave two speeches of this title. This outline was made after *Busman's Honeymoon,* to which reference is made. *Précis*: Sayers takes up the technical problems of detective fiction, such as the choice of a detective, the hiding of the murderer's identity, the denouement, and the unity of atmosphere. Detective-story writers need constantly to experiment with their craft.

D.5. "The Craft of Detective Fiction" (II). Ams, nd [after 1939], 9 pp. (6 lvs.) + Tms with A corrections and completion, nd, 12 pp. Speech; unpublished. The address was given after 1939 because Sayers refers to the 20 years between the wars. The manuscript falls into two divisions:

    a. An incomplete rough draft. Ams, 6 pp. (3 lvs.).

    b. The finished version. Tms with A corrections, 12 pp. (the twelfth page being completed in A) + Ams, 3 pp.

The Tms is not Sayers's work, because it contains such mistranscriptions as *Vidacgon* for *Vidocq*. *Précis:* Sayers distinguishes between the thriller and the detective story, traces the history of the genre to the period between the two world wars, and concludes with speculations on its popularity. The detective story is basically a literature of escape. During the nineteenth century, it represented escape from prosy reality into a world of excitement; during the twentieth, escape from a problematic reality into a world of security.

D.6. "Detection Club Speech." Ams, nd [c. 1929–1931], 6 pp. Speech; complete;

unpublished. A reference to a book by Clemence Dane and Helen Simpson dates this work around 1930–31; the book in question was published in London under the title of *Printer's Devil* (Hodder and Stoughton, 1930) and in New York under the title of *Author Unknown* (Cosmopolitan Book Corporation, 1930). The American edition has a note on the last page indicating the book's composition in February–March 1929. *Précis:* A witty survey of the conventions of the detective story, this speech makes the sarcastic observation that the writing of detective stories is a minor British industry and develops it at length.

D.7. "Detectives in Fiction." Ams, nd. 6 pp. Speech or essay; complete; unpublished. *Précis:* The detective in fiction is not conceived in realistic terms. He has tended in recent years to be almost completely cerebral. This style, however, is passing, though it is still acceptable in some continental detectives. The individualistic detective, like Lord Peter, is irritating; and yet he must have mannerisms if he is to be remembered at all, for lack of space precludes the development of characterization which could make him similarly memorable. Other possible variants include the psychologist and the scientific detective; but the determining factor in what will succeed is economic: short novels mean specialization; long novels mean a greater opportunity for verisimilitude.

D.8. "Dr. Watson, Widower." Ams, nd, 26 pp. Satire (in Monsignor Ronald Knox's tradition of pseudoscholarship). Complete except for the second note—"Note on the Date of 'Lady Frances Carfax'"—of the printed version. *Collected (and probably first published): Unpopular Opinions* (item F.16). *Comment:* This item is labelled "IV" on the ms.; perhaps it was the fourth written of Sayers's Holmesian studies, even though it appears in the third position among the four such essays in *Unpopular Opinions*. But see item D.9.

D.9. "Holmes' College Career." Tcc/ms, nd, 1 p. Satire (of the type in D.8). On the back of one of the pages of *The Man Born to Be King* (item E.11) is the carbon typescript of a page of this essay: probably the second page of the typescript, as it begins in the second quotation Sayers gives—that from "The Musgrave Ritual"—with the words "of these cases" and continues through *G* of the questions to be answered about Holmes. *First published: Baker-Street Studies,* ed. H. W. Bell (London: Constable, 1934). *Collected: Unpopular Opinions* (item F.16). But the interesting aspect of the re-use of pages for *The Man Born to Be King* is a title page which is also a Tcc/ms: "STUDIES / IN / SHERLOCK HOLMES / BY / DOROTHY L. SAYERS. M.A./sometime Scholar of/Somerville College in/the University of Oxford/——— oOo ———". This title page, together with the numbering of the item immediately above, indicates that at some point in her career Sayers planned a volume (or chapbook) of Holmes studies.

D.10. "The Importance of Being Vulgar." Ams, 12 February 1936, 23 pp. Speech, headed "Red X 12.2.36" (with "Red X" meaning "read on"?); complete; unpublished. A *terminus a quo* is provided by an article—a review of 10 books by "G. O."—in the *New English Weekly*, 8 (23 January 1936), 295–96, to which Sayers refers. (The reviewer was George Orwell, and about half of his review—including his discussion of the snobbery in *Gaudy Night*—is reprinted in *An Age like This: 1920–1940*, ed. Sonia Orwell and Jan Angus—Vol. I of *The Collected Essays, Journalism and Letters of George Orwell*—[New York: Harcourt, Brace and World, 1968], pp. 160–62.) *Précis:* Reviewers who have criticized Sayers's work as vulgar and snobbish, albeit cleverly written, are correct. Though her novels are not great, their vulgarity—their appeal to sentiments widely held by the common man—is a trait possessed by all really great writing, which takes commonly held feelings and articulates them uncommonly well. Their snobbishness is a trait shared with commoners, whose attitude toward the nobility is a blend of respect for the title and amusement at the person. So long as literature expresses his sentiments, the common man does not mind its being well written. Unfortunately, those who can write well are increasingly taking as their subject matter the uncommon—the queer and perverse. The danger is that if the common man is left exclusively to bad writers, he will lose the ability to distinguish between bad and good writing. The opportunity for writers like Sayers is to keep alive a literature that appeals to high- and low-brows.

D.11. "The Modern Detective Story." Ams, February 1936, 8 pp. Speech; incomplete; unpublished. According to a note in Sayers's hand on the first page, this paper was read to the Sesame Imperial Club on 27 October 1936. According to Anthony Fleming, this was also given as a talk to the English Club, Cambridge, on 14 February 1936, and to the English-Speaking Union, Oxford, on 27 October 1936. He has the date for the Sesame Club as 26 October 1936. The discrepancy of one day is not important, but it is worth noting that the speech, in one form or another, had been written in February. *Précis:* In the years following World War I, the paper shortage and the expensiveness of printing made short books easier to place than long ones. The increasingly morbid and pornographic nature of serious literature encouraged many professional persons to look to detective stories for recreation. The detective story did some good in reminding the public of virtue's superiority to vice; and the skill with which writers handled plot and technical matters increased greatly. Still, the detective story lost contact with life and with literary tradition, and by 1929, some were saying that it must reroot itself or die. The most disturbing symptom of its malaise was the distinction made between novelists and detective novelists, the latter, however brilliant, being considered technicians rather than artists.

D.12. "Les Origines du Roman Policier." Ams, nd [during World War II], 12 pp. Speech in French; complete; unpublished. Statements in the speech indicate it was given during World War II. *Précis:* The speech is largely a rehash of ideas that Sayers had given earlier. She surveys the history of the genre and suggests ways that it can continue to develop, feeling, for example, that Gladys Mitchell's use of Jungian and Freudian psychology to solve the problem of analyzing character in depth without giving away the solution is promising.

D.13. [The Profession of Murder.] Ams, nd, 15 pp. Speech; complete; unpublished. *Précis:* Murder should be considered as an agreeable pastime rather than a full-time occupation. Great care should be given to such matters as choice of victim and means; but despite all precautions, one must note that there are certain unavoidable drawbacks, like the difficulty of disposing of a body. Indeed, when we consider the matter carefully, the only successful murderers are the ones we do not know about.

D.14. *Studies in Sherlock Holmes.* See the discussion under "Holmes' College Career" (item D.9) for this projected title.

D.15. *"Trent's Last Case."* Ams, 1934, 5 pp. Essay; complete. The BBC broadcast a version of *Trent's Last Case* on 24 January 1934; Sayers's essay appeared in the

Radio Times as an accompaniment, in the issue for the week of 21–27 January. More recently the essay was reprinted from ms., with a note indicating the essay was probably written for radio broadcasting, as the introduction to E. C. Bentley, *Trent's Last Case* (New York: Harper and Row [Perennial Library, P440], 1978). (I wish to thank Miss Challice B. Reed, Assistant Programme Information Officer, BBC, for the information about the original publication.)

D.16. *Unpopular Opinions*. A collection of essays, listed below as item F.16, which contains "Dr. Watson, Widower" (item D.8) and "Holmes' College Career" (item D.9).

E. Noncriminous Fiction, Drama, and Christmas and Easter Cards

E.1. *Cat's Cradle*. Ams, nd, 130 pp. Play (labeled by the author "A Comedy in Three Acts"). The manuscript, which includes a title page, is complete; unpublished. A review in the London *Times*, 10 April 1940, p. 6, makes clear that this is the play which was performed under the title *Love All*.

E.2. *The Days of Christ's Coming*. Ams, nd, 6 pp. Christmas card; complete. Published as a Christmas card in London: Hamish Hamilton, 1953, 1960; as a small book in New York: Harper and Brothers, 1960.

E.3. *The Emperor Constantine: A Chronicle*. Ams, nd [1949–1951], 276 pp. (272 lvs.) + printed prompt text with A marginalia, nd [c. July 1951?], 120 lvs. Play. *Publication:* Gollancz, 1951. The dates of composition are from c. July 1949 to c. July 1951. In an interview with the Colchester newspaper before the play's opening there on 3 July 1951 (the date from H & B, p. 130), Sayers said she "was commissioned to write the play about two years ago" (clipping from a Colchester paper in the WColl, nd [but after Sayers addressed the Summer School of Italian Studies at Oxford]). The WColl has the following materials:

a. Black notebook (25 x 20 cm.). Ams, 15 pp. (11 lvs.) + a note on the recto of the back cover. The notebook actually contains 78 lvs., but most are blank. The manuscript has largely to do with the establishment of a historical chronology.

b. The play in a prolog, three acts, and an epilog. Ams, 239 pp.

c. Preface. Ams, 9 pp.

d. Program note. Ams, 2 pp.

e. Notes. Ams, 11 pp. These notes are on stage directions and on the Biblical quotations used by Arius and Athanasius.

f. Green promptbook (31 x 20½ cm.). Printed text with A marginalia, 120 lvs. The book contains 155 lvs., but 35 are blank. The text looks like galley proofs which have been pasted in, with marginal notes and other material, most of it not by Sayers. *Note:* The WColl also has the following materials, none of which contain Sayers's hand:

g. Notes. Ams, nd, 20 pp. (18 lvs.). Notes on costumes, cast, and scenery.

h. Inventory. Tms, nd, 2 pp. Scenery from preceding plays.

i. Blue notebook: "CAST: Names, addresses, measurements, etc." (20 x 12½ cm.)

E.4. "The Enchanted Garden." Ams, nd [late 1950s?], 14 pp. + Tms, nd, 12 pp. Text for a Christmas (?) card; complete; unpublished. After the above title on the title page, Sayers continues: "adapted by / Dorothy L. Sayers / from the 'Orlando Innamorato' / of / BOIARDO / The picture painted by / *Fritz Wegner*." The general period in which Sayers wrote this work was probably close to that when her Christmas and Easter cards with illustrations by Fritz Wegner were first appearing: *The Days of Christ's Coming* (1953), *The Story of Easter* (1955), *The Story of Adam and Christ* (1955), and *The Story of Noah's Ark* (1956). Sayers also shows an interest in Boiardo in two letters to T. H. White in 1954 (listed in Section 6, items Q.3 and Q.4.) Of course, the 1950s are also the period of her translation of *The Divine Comedy*. Anthony Fleming, in a letter of 3 December 1978, indicates that an examination of Sayers's correspondence with her publisher at the time of the above cards shows no mention of this work, and so believes it probably postdates them.

    a. Ams, 14 pp. This manuscript includes a title page, 10 pp. of text, and 3 pp. of *"Boiardo's Descriptions"* —the latter intended as instructions to the artist.

    b. Tms, 12 pp. This manuscript includes a title page, 9 pp. of text, and 2 pp. of *"Bioardo's Descriptions"*. The typing is poor and may be Sayers's own.

E.5. [Encounter with Dante.] Ams, nd [1944?], 14 pp. (7 lvs.). Short story (a fantasy or dream vision); unfinished; unpublished. Lf. 4 and lvs. 5-7 are alternate versions of the same material; the fuller version, lvs. 5-7, is probably the second or later version. The story is a fantasy in which a soldier near Ravenna in World War II finds himself, after a shell attack, in the fourteenth century, where he has a long conversation with Dante. Thus, the story was written after Sayers's first reading of Dante in the summer of 1944; also, reference is made in the text to the present year being 1944. The inclusion of this story with the other mss. which were published in *Unpopular Opinions* (item F.16) might suggest that it was written before 1946.

E.6. *Even the Parrot; Exemplary Conversations for Enlightened Children.* Ams, nd, 42 pp. (24 lvs.) + 12 galley proofs with A corrections, 1944 + page proofs, nd, 24 pp. (20 lvs.). Satire (of didactic, edifying books for children). *Publication*: Methuen, 21 September 1944. *Comment:* Some of the prefatory material omitted from the published version makes clearer Sayers's satiric aim and was probably omitted as needlessly explicit. The WColl has these materials:

    a. Ams, 42 pp. (24 lvs.). Complete. 24 pp. recto, including the title page; 18 pp. verso. Verso of the title page has a fragmentary title on it; verso of lf. 8 is crossed out.

    b. 12 galley proofs with A corrections. First galley proofs; the hand of the corrections is that of Sayers. The earliest date marked on the galley proofs is 22 March 1944.

    c. Page proofs, 24 pp. (20 lvs.). Proofs of prefatory material and illustrations. The illustrations are pasted onto scrap paper. (The name of the illustrator is given in the book as Sillince.)

E.7. [Griselda and Her Cat.] Ams, nd, 7 pp. Children's story; unfinished; unpublished.

E.8. *He That Should Come.* Ams, nd, 25 pp. "A Nativity Play for Broadcasting." The manuscript includes a title page and a list of characters; incomplete. *First broadcast:* Christmas Day, 1938. *Publication:* Gollancz, November 1939. The WColl also has a copy of the music by Robert Chignell, 24 pp. As a cover letter from Margery Vosper Ltd. to Anthony Fleming, 20 December 1960, makes clear, this is a copy and not the original score.

E. 9. *Herod the Great.* Ams. nd [c. 1938], 85 pp. (84 lvs.) + Tms, nd, 33 pp. with A corrections. Dramatic trilogy; unfinished; unpublished. The work was done around 1938: the pages of the Bookseller's Catalogue, from W. Heffer, lists several books published in 1938—most importantly, A.H.M. Jones's *The Herods of Judaea*–but none later. The WColl has the following materials:

a. Miscellaneous materials, Ams. 35 pp. (34 lvs.) + Tms. 2 pp. + bookseller's catalog, 2 pp. (1 lf.). The bookseller's catalog, not by Sayers of course, was mentioned above. The Tms belongs to an intermediate version between "A" and "C" below; see the comment after E. 9.c.

b. Act I, "A" version. Ams, 24 pp.

c. Act I, "B" version. Ams, 26 pp. + Tms. 8 pp. The Ams and Tms are not consecutive but interfiled. The pages of the Tms belong to an intermediate version, which also includes the two pages of Tms listed in item E.9.a. This intermediate version generally follows "A" but with some exceptions.

d. Act I, "C" version. Tms with A corrections, 23 pp. The general descent of the versions can be established by internal changes.

E. 10. *The Just Vengeance.* Ams, nd, 87 pp. (68 lvs.). Verse play. This Lichfield Festival Play for 1946 was first presented at the Lichfield Cathedral, 15 June 1946 (H&B, p. 131). *Published:* Gollancz, 1946. *Comment:* Nowhere does Sayers's thrifty habit of saving paper and recycling it produce more interesting results than in this manuscript. On the recto of one leaf is a crossed-out passage of dialog; on the verso, a crossed-out draft of a letter to Victor Gollancz about a threatened lawsuit involving a Miss M. L. Barton and the character. Miss Barton, in *Gaudy Night* (for a fictional version of a similar incident, see "Spick and Span" [item C. 30]). Other leaves have part of a lecture on translating Dante on the versos (cf. item F.15). The size of the leaves varies from 32½ x 20½ cm. to 5 x 19½ cm. The WColl has the following materials:

a. The play. Ams, 63 pp. (53 lvs.). The rectos include a title page, a "Dramatis Personae," and a coherent version of the play, lacking only the last 36 ll, of the published work. The versos of 10 leaves have alternate versions of some passages, most of which have been crossed through.

b. Miscellaneous material. Ams, 24 pp. (15 lvs.). Notes, casts of characters, stage diagram, bits of dialog.

E. 11. *The Man Born to Be King.* Ams, 1940-1942, 633 pp. + Tms, 18 pp. + music scoring, 1 p. + pencilled diagram (of the seating at the Last Supper), 1 p. (406 lvs. overall). Play cycle (for radio broadcast), consisting of 12 episodes. Incomplete: some scenes and smaller pieces of the work are missing. The Introduction, e.g., is complete except for the last paragraph and a few words from the next-to-last. Some material appears in differing versions. Some material does not appear in the printed version (London: Gollancz, 1943)—e.g., a charming note to the actors at the beginning of the ninth play, "The King's Supper," adjuring them not to be afraid of the material just because it is very sacred and important. The writing of the play cycle can be dated with fair exactitude. According to J. W. Welch's "Foreword" to the printed text, he wrote Sayers proposing the series in February 1940 (second paragraph); by the time the first play, "Kings in Judaea," was broadcast on 21 December 1941, Sayers had finished 5 plays (fourth paragraph). Therefore, the last 7 plays were completed during 1942, before the final play, "The King Comes to His Own," was broadcast on 18 October 1942. *Comment*: In counting pages, I included any page that had any writing or typing on it whatever, regardless of whether it had been crossed through and of whether the writing or typing had anything to do with the play cycle. Sayers's habit of saving paper and recycling it produces some curious juxtapositions. The typed pages of the seventh play, "The Light and the Life," for example, are on the back of a partial Tms of "Blood Sacrifice" (item C.3). Two of the typed pages in the eleventh play, "King of Sorrows," are typed on the back of a page of "Holmes' College Career" and a title page of a projected collection of studies of Sherlock Holmes (both described in item D.9).

E.12. *The Story of Easter.* Ams, nd, 9 pp. Easter card; complete. *Published* as an Easter card in London: Hamish Hamilton, 1955. I want to thank Anthony Fleming for a letter of 3 December 1978 in which he indicated the publication of this work (H & B do not list it), and Coleen Gilbert for checking the publisher in her forthcoming Sayers bibliography.

E.13. *The Tale of Adam and Adam.* Ams, nd, 21 pp. Text of an Easter card. 27 short poems on Biblical subjects; complete. *Publication*, as *The Story of Adam and Christ:* London: Hamish Hamilton, 1955; illustrated by Fritz Wegner. The manuscript consists of a title page, a list of poems (1 p.), the poems themselves (14 pp.), and suggestions for the artist (4 pp., one suggestion per poem). I want to thank Anthony Fleming for correcting the date of this work's publication in a letter of 3 December 1978 (H & B, p. 179, date it in 1953 as a Christmas card).

E.13A. *Thrones, Dominations* —. See item B.19; an unfinished novel with Wimsey but without a mystery.

E.14. ". . . Who calls the tune." Ams, nd [before 1917], 10 pp. Short story; complete. According to Colleen Gilbert, basing her information on correspondence with a Mutual Admiration Society member, this story was published in that Society's *Blue Moon*, c. 1917. According to Anthony Fleming (letter of 17 December 1977), he has another ms. version of what appears to be the same story in an exercise book that includes material clearly dating from Sayers's teens. There is a substantial possibility then that the story may be very early work indeed.

E.15. *The Zeal of Thy House.* Ams, nd, 158 pp. (156 lvs.) + Tms with A corrections, nd, 33 pp. + Tcc/ms, nd, 16 pp. + drawings, nd, 5 lvs. Play in verse and prose; incomplete. First produced at Canterbury for the Canterbury Festival: 12 June 1937. *Published:* Gollancz, June 1937. Some of the manuscript material postdates the publication of the Gollancz edition; Sayers added extra lines to serve as "bridges" in Act III (pp. 68, 70, of the published text). Also, there are duplications between pages of the Ams, Tms, and Tcc/ ms. Although the holdings of the WColl may be distinguished in the following manner, the materials are not consecutive but interfiled; the pages do not follow seriatim.

    a. Ams, 158 pp. (156 lvs.). Eleven of the pages are less than full-sized—e.g., 12 x 20 cm.

    b. Tms with A corrections, 33 pp. Twenty-three of the pages have A corrections.

    c. Tcc/ms, 16 pp.

    d. Four sketches. These sketches are difficult to describe; Sayers's comments (not really titles or clear descriptions) are autograph.

    i. "Floor of Chapter House" (sketch of the choir area?).

    ii. "Something to link up with Festival of Arts, Crafts, Music &c" (aisle, steps, choir area?).

    iii. Two elaborately costumed figures, one with censer. The page also lists colors of various tones: e.g., "Jasper—red or green."

    iv. Diagram of stage positions for members of the chapter and for angels in Act I.

    e. Card (11½ x 14 cm.). 1 lf. *Recto:* an invitation from Nelsons to Sayers for a sherry party. Wednesday, 24 February. (The year, not given, is 1937.) *Verso:* a pencil sketch of stage positions of Michael, Raphael, Gabriel, and Cassiel. Also the WColl has the following item in with these papers, which is not technically part of Sayers's manuscript:

    f. One leaf, cut from a book (21 x 14 cm.). A photograph of the "Seal of the Norman Cathedral" by Fisk-Moore.

F. Nonfiction on Religious, Social, and Aesthetic Topics

F.1. "Arsenic Probably." A topical article, listed above as D.1.

F.2. "Creative Mind," Ams, February 1942, 21 pp. (20 lvs.). (The final leaf has writing on recto and verso.) Speech; complete. The heading on the manuscript states this was given at "Humanities Club Feb. 1942"; the note with its publication in *Unpopular Opinions* (item F.16) indicates the Club was in Reading. The manuscript varies slightly from the published version. It contains some authorial corrections in pencil, but the published version agrees with the original text in each case. Perhaps Sayers planned to publish a revised version of the text as printed.

F.3. *Even the Parrot.* Social satire, listed above as E.6.

F.4. "The Gulf-Stream and the Channel." Ams, 1943, 11 pp. Essay; complete. The date is given on the first page of the essay as published in *Unpopular Opinions* (item F.16).

F.5. "If You Want War." Ams, nd [between the World Wars], 4 pp. Article (so referred to by Sayers); but the item is signed by Sayers at the end so it *may* have been intended as a letter to some newspaper or journal. Complete. Unpublished? *Précis:* Excessive commentary on the need for peace makes war inevitable. Instead of vague talk about the desirability of peace, we need hard-headed exchanges on substantive issues like the Saar and the Polish corridor. Democracy, open diplomacy, politicians, the newspapers, and the public —all will share in the blame if war comes.

F.6. "IN ENGLAND—NOW: Rambling meditations on the subject of 'Christian Duty.'" Ams, nd [late 1943-early 1944?], 36 pp. + galley proofs with A corrections, 17 pp. Article in two parts. Complete? Unpublished? The galley proofs are of the first part of the article, and the distinction between parts may be made in this way:

    a. First part. Ams, 22 p. + galley proofs with A corrections, 17 pp. The galleys are dated 25 April 1944 and printed by Sherratt and Hughes.

    b. Second part. Ams, 14 pp. Possibly incomplete. The second part refers to Charles Williams's *The Figure of Beatrice*, and so was written after its appearance in 1943. (The only review of Williams's book listed in Lois Glenn's *Charles W. S. Williams: A Checklist* [Kent, Ohio: The Kent State University Press, 1975] is one of 11 September 1943 in *Notes and Queries* [Glenn, p. 97].) Thus a date of late 1943 to early 1944 is likely. Despite its subtitle, this article is really too closely reasoned to précis. It is Sayers's definitive statement on anti-Semitism and should be required reading for all who facilely brand her as an anti-Semite. She does find the pro-Semitic stance of some liberals and nominal Christians distasteful, but her point is that it is insulting to Jews as well as Christians. Only when Jews and Christians fully accept their differences can they come to terms with each other both ideologically and practically. Even where ideological differences remain, she feels that much can be done on the practical level, advocating, among other things, the establishment of a Jewish state in Palestine.

F.7. *The Mind of the Maker.* Ams, nd, 207 pp. + Tms with A corrections, nd, 36 pp. + Tcc/ms, 1 p. Aesthetic theory. The manuscript is complete except for one page of Chapter X, the last pages of Chapter XI (although the last pages of the "A" version of that chapter correspond with the printed text), and the postscript, "The Worth of the Work." *Publication:* London: Methuen, 1941. The WColl has these items:

a. "Preface." Ams, 6 pp.

b. Ch. I, "The 'Laws' of Nature and Opinion." Ams, 15 pp.

c. Ch. II, "The Image of God." Ams, 10 pp. + 1 slip of paper (20 x 13 cm.) attached to the fourth page of the Ams.

d. Ch. III, "The Trinity of Man the Maker." Ams, 12 pp. The published title of this chapter is "Idea, Energy, Power."

e. Ch. IV, "The Energy Revealed in Creation." Ams, 12 pp.

f. Ch. V, "Free Will and Miracle." Ams, 23 pp.

g. Ch. VI, "The Energy Incarnate in Self-Expression." Ams, 6 pp.

h. Ch. VII, "Maker of All Things —Maker of Ill Things." Ams, 14 pp.

i. Selected quotations. Tms, 2 pp. These are the passages quoted to indicate the "sources" of a descriptive passage in *The Nine Tailors*; used in Ch. VIII of *The Mind of the Maker.*

j. Ch. VIII, "Pentecost." Ams, 16 pp.

k. Ch. IX, "The Love of the Creature." Ams, 22 pp.

l. Ch. X, "Scalene Trinities." Ams, 32 pp. A page is lacking between pp. 29 and 30 of this chapter.

m. Ch. XI, "Problem Picture." Ams, 38 pp. + Tms with A corrections, pp. 34 + Tcc/ms, 1 p. This chapter consists of two versions:

i. "A" version. Ams, 30 pp. A complete earlier version.

ii. "B" version. Ams, 8 pp. + Tms with A corrections, 34 pp. + Tcc/ms, 1 p. An incomplete later version, consisting of a Tms made from the "A" version, corrected, and intercalated with new pages of Ams material. One page of the Tms has been cut into two parts, with each placed where it falls in the revision; one typed page is a carbon instead of an original.

F.8. "N or M." Familiar essay, listed as item A.1.c.

F.9. "The Proserpina Image in Dante and Milton." See [Translating Dante] (item F.15).

F.i0. "They Tried to Be Good." Ams, 1943, 12 pp. (7 lvs.). Political essay. Complete; the twelfth page (seventh leaf) contains a cancelled addition. The date given above comes from the first page of the essay on its publication in *Unpopular Opinions* (item F.16).

F.11. *A Time Is Born.* Ams, 1944-1945, 6 pp. (4 lvs.). An introduction to Garet
    Garrett's book of the above title (London: Basil Blackwell, 1945); complete. Sayers
    refers to incidents in 1944 in her text, so she wrote her introduction between then
    and publication.

F.12. [A Toast of the University of Oxford.] Ams, nd [probably 1934], 11 pp. Speech;
    complete. The dating and publication of this speech present problems which can,
    however, be solved. In the sale catalog, this was listed as a speech on the
    retirement of Mildred Pope, a fair assumption since Pope is the honoree of the toast
    of the university. The fact is, however, that she did not retire from Oxford but
    became Professor of Romance Philology at Manchester University in 1934. Either
    her leaving Oxford in that year or her being made an honorary fellow of Somerville
    College the following year could be the occasion of the speech. On the assumption
    that this is the speech to which Sayers refers in her essay "Gaudy Night" (1937) —"I
    was asked to go to Oxford and propose the toast of the University at my College
    Gaudy dinner" —the publication of her novel *Gaudy Night* in 1935 would indicate
    the earlier date, for she says the thematic use of intellectual integrity in the novel
    was subsequent to her discussion of it in the toast. In her essay, Sayers also states
    that the substance of her toast was later published in the magazine of the Oxford
    Society; Sayers's "What Is Right with Oxford?" appeared in *Oxford*, summer 1935,
    pp. 34–41. *Précis:* Many object to Oxonian education because it is irrelevant to the
    largely commercial needs of the age. Sayers's experience at Benson's suggests that
    an Oxonian education can help in business through teaching orderly habits of the
    mind, the ability to use words, and the attitude that knowledge is to be shared. Still,
    Oxford's primary purpose is to promote scholarship. Scholars have a difficult time
    when young; but as they grow older, the knowledge that intellectual matters endure
    affords a consolation for the burdens that life imposes on all. Though nothing in the
    world is secure, the intellectual beauty that Oxford represents can never wholly be
    destroyed.

F.13. "The Tooth of Time." Familiar essay, listed as item A.1.b.

F.14. "Toward a Christian Aesthetic." Ams, nd, 14 pp. (14 lvs.). Essay. Complete; the
    manuscript includes crossed-out material on the versos of lvs. 4 and 14. Originally
    given as one of the Edward Alleyn lectures for 1944, this essay was first published in
    Our Culture: Its Christian Roots and Present Crisis, ed. Vigo Auguste Demant
    (London: S.P.C.K. [The Society for Promoting Christian Knowledge], 1944).
    Collected: Unpopular Opinions (item F.16). Since, as Sayers's introductory note
    in *Unpopular Opinions* acknowledges, she draws on ideas in R. G. Collingwood's
    Principles of Art (1938), 1938 is the *terminus a quo* for the essay's composition.

F.15. [Translating Dante.] Ams, nd, 6 pp. Lecture? Incomplete. The six pages are
    legal-sized sheets, surviving as the versos of pages of *The Just Vengeance* (item
    E.10), where they are not in sequence; all six are crossed through with one or two
    lines each. The material begins and stops in mid-sentence. The substance is
    concerned with the translation of three passages in the *Divine Comedy*. The first of
    these is the simile appearing in the *Inferno*, xxii. 130–32, in which one of the
    damned and a devil chasing him are compared to a wild duck and a falcon; Sayers
    comments on Dante's style and her translation of the passage (she also seems to be
    commenting on someone else's translation of it in the passage which begins the
    page, but the fragmentary material is not completely clear). She turns to something

"less plain & simple," involving Dante's imagery. What follows [pp. 1-4], covers essentially the same material, in often the same words, as "The Proserpine Image in Dante and Milton," which is Note B to "Dante and Milton," *Further Papers on Dante* (London: Methuen, 1957), pp. 178–82. One conclusion about this fragmentary paper is possible from this version: since Sayers gives the Italian in English translation here but cites the Italian in the published version, this paper seems to have been intended for a nonacademic audience. The conclusions of the two versions are different, since in this manuscript Sayers turns back to the question of how the passage is to be translated (for the last 4 ll. of p. [3] and most of p. [4]), after the comparisons to Milton's similar materials and Shelley's translation. The final passage discussed—"our third example"—is the Hymn of St. Bernard which begins the last canto of the *Paradiso*. Sayers compares Dante's handling of the material with Chaucer's paraphrase of Dante in "The Second Nun's Tale" (p. [5]); she also quotes this passage from Chaucer in "The Art of Translating Dante," *Nottingham Mediaeval Studies*, 9 (1965), 15. On p. [6], she uses the terms "hammer-rhyme" and "anvil-rhyme" which she explains more fully in "On Translating the *Divina Commedia*," *The Poetry of Search and the Poetry of Statement* (London: Victor Gollancz, 1963), p. 112. The basic discussion of rhyme possibilities and choices of phrasings is much like that in "On Translating the *Divina Commedia*," except for the use of different examples of course.

F.16.   *Unpopular Opinions.* A collection of essays published by Gollancz in 1946. The WColl has manuscripts (or partial manuscripts) for the following essays only:

   a. "Creative Mind" (item F.2).
   b. "Dr. Watson, Widower" (item D.8).
   c. "The Gulf Stream and the Channel" (item F.4).
   d. "Holmes' College Career" (item D.9).
   e. "They Tried to Be Good" (item F.10).
   f. "Toward a Christian Aesthetic" (item F.14).

For further information, see the entries for the individual items. In addition to these manuscripts, the WColl has 72 galleys (65½ x 16½ cm.). This is a complete set of galleys for the book. Seventeen of the galleys have authorial corrections; these constitute the third section of the book, "Critical." *Comment:* As late as the galley stage, "Christian Morality," "Forgiveness," and "Living to Work" were untitled, the last designated as "B.B.C. Postscript (untitled)." *Re* the specimens of handwriting which appear in "The Dates in *The Red-Headed League*," the printer wrote, "Please supply blocks;" Sayers replied, "I have no blocks —I have supplied photographs badger Mr. Gollancz I hope to God he has not lost them." The only galley lacking is for the Foreword, which was written after Sayers had given titles to the previously untitled essays.

G. Translations of Romance Literature

In additon to the following translations, one example of Sayers's critical writings on romance literature is in the WColl, the incomplete [Translating Dante] (item F.15); of related interest is [Encounter with Dante] (item E.5). As noted in the general introductory note to these checklists, Sayers's Dantean papers have not yet been sold by her son; what follows is from non-Dantean areas.

G.1. "The Enchanted Garden." An adaptation from Boiardo's *Orlando Innamorato*, listed as E.4 because it was intended as a Christmas card.

G.2. *The Song of Roland*. Ams, nd, 433 pp. + Tms, nd, 3 pp. Translation; published by Penguin Books in 1957. The manuscript is in 13 notebook pads and one folder; the material may be classified as follows:

a. Introduction (in one notepad). Ams, 42 pp. This part of the introduction includes a title page.

b. Introduction (in a folder). Ams, 28 pp. + Tms, 3 pp. The material in the folder belongs with the material in Notebook I. Between the two, they constitute most of the introduction. Some of the pages in the folder obviously have been torn out of a notebook pad of the same manufacture. The sections of the introduction are out of order, and a few parts, like the opening paragraphs, are not present.

c. Translation. Ams, 352 pp. The bulk of the notebook pads.

d. Notes (or jottings). Ams, 11 pp.

The thirteenth notebook, which contains these jottings, also has the following:

e. Unrelated material. 2 pp. These consist of one page of notes for a detective story and one page with two jottings on Charles Williams; the latter: (i) "Fr Mascoll (Ch. W. Paper p. 25 note)"; (ii) "Retype last page of C.W. paper." The former does not seem to be a story Sayers wrote, since it involves arsenic poisoning in a Varnimoter (?) family; the notes are a family tree and a chart of where people (or their glasses) were—presumably at the time of the poisoning.

G.3. *Tristan in Brittany*. A translation of *The Romance of Tristan* by Thomas, listed as item A.2.f; note also the related letter (item A.2.c).

H. Inscribed Books in the Wade Collection

H.1. *The Emperor Constantine*. London: Gollancz, 1951. First edition, in dust jacket. On the recto of the front free endpaper: "To the Bishop of Colchester, the onlie begetter of this play, with all good wishes from Dorothy L. Sayers." (The allusion in "onlie begetter" is to the dedication of the first edition of Shakespeare's *Sonnets*.)

H.2. *He That Should Come: A Nativity Play in One Act*. London: Gollancz, 1936. First edition. On the cover: "With love and best wishes, from Dorothy L. Sayers."

H.3. *The Just Vengeance*. London: Gollancz, 1946. First edition. Signed, without inscription, on the recto of an extra, blank page between the front free endpaper and the half-title page.

H.4. *Papers Relating to the Family of Wimsey*, ed. Matthew Wimsey [pseudonym for Helen Simpson and Sayers]. Privately printed for the family: Humphrey Milford, nd [1936]. Only edition. On the recto of the front free endpaper: "Victor Gollancz, with all good wishes from Dorothy L. Sayers[.] Christmas 1936."

2. Manuscripts in the Humanities Research Center, University of Texas at Austin, ed. Joe R. Christopher

In 1960 the Humanities Research Center ordered Sayers's manuscripts and letters which dealt with her work on Wilkie Collins, and in 1961 the materials were delivered. A statement, with more precise dates, the name of the agent for Sayers's son, and other details, is quoted in Gregory's introduction to WC:C&BS, pp. 15–16. For the background of Sayers's work on Collins, the same introduction should be consulted. Gregory dates the writing of the five chapters of the actual study from 1931 to 1933 (p. 8). Although he does not mention it, the last two letters from A. May Osler, Sayers's research assistant in 1933, refer to some domestic problem which was causing Sayers to stop her work at that time. Of course, Sayers later published the Collins bibliography in *The Cambridge Bibliography of English Literature* (1941), as the materials below show. She also wrote the introduction to the Everyman Library edition of *The Moonstone* (1944), using a number of the ideas which occur in the critical notes below. (The H.R.C. does not have a draft of the introduction.)

The following materials are organized into 10 divisions. First are materials which have been published—the CBEL listing and the five chapters of WC:C&BS:

A. "Bibliography / William Wilkie Collins / 1824-1889" (pub. 1941).
B. "Wilkie Collins / A Critical and Biographical Study" (pub. 1977).

Next are five divisions of Sayers's manuscripts compiled during her work on Wilkie Collins:

C. Outlines of WC:C&BS.
D. Notebooks and File Cards on Collins.
E. Substantial Autograph and Typewritten Manuscripts on Collins.
F. Brief Items, Notes, and Jottings on Collins.
G. Copies of Materials Related to Collins.

Finally are three divisions of contracts and books signed, initialed, or inscribed by Sayers:

H. Sayers's Signatures and Initials on Albatross Contracts.
I. Sayers's Signature and Inscription in Two of Her Books.
J. Sayers's Signatures and Inscriptions in Collins's Books.

These final three divisions were not part of the purchase of Sayers's manuscripts and letters, of course, but they have some biographical interest so far as the student of Sayers is concerned.

In addition to the materials listed here, a substantial amount of material on Collins presumably prepared by Sayers's research assistants or secretaries is in the H.R.C. There is one large binder folder with copies of reviews of Collins's works, Collins's death notices, and extracts from newspapers and journals on his life (the first two groups are typed, the third is handwritten —but not by Sayers). There are seventeen Amss done by A. May Osler (from the handwriting) —mainly copies of wills and census reports involving Collins's family. And there are 28 other items: a consideration of Collins's legal position under his father's will, not signed but done by Dorothy Scott Stokes (cf. her letter to Sayers in the H.R.C.); 4 other Amss (some more notes than mss. proper) in non-Sayersian hands; 7 Tmss copying census reports, letters, wills, etc.; one Tms of 5 pp. listing actors and actresses who appeared in Collins's plays; a photostat of Collins's will (this was obtained by Osler, and sent to Sayers in a letter of 8 April 1933); and 14 bills or receipts for Sayers's purchase of Collins's books or AL's.

The letters by Sayers in the H.R.C. largely (not wholly) deal with her research on Collins: see Section (6) following. Also, in Section (1) immediately preceding, an exercise book in the Wade Collection titled *Lord Peter Wimsey Amateur Sleuth* (item A.1) has lists of Collins's letters, and of obituaries, articles, and other materials. I wish to thank the Research Committee of Tarleton State University for the grant which took me to the H.R.C. in the summer of 1977 and allowed me to prepare this checklist, and that in Section (6); I also wish to thank Charlotte Carl-Mitchell and Lois Bell Garcia for their helpfulness in the reading room of the H.R.C.

J. R. C.

A. "BIBLIOGRAPHY / WILLIAM WILKIE COLLINS / 1824-1889" (pub. 1941)

A.1. Ams, nd, 25 pp.
A.2. Tms, nd, 20 pp., + 2 Tcc/ms. Both carbon copies have a few identical corrections in ink, but one has a number of additions—for example, four short story titles added to the list of magazine stories not republished in book form (this page is out of sequence in the ms.). The original copy has been extensively revised for publication in the *Cambridge Bibliography of English Literature,* Vol. III (1941), 480-82. For example, all places of publication and names of publishers have been crossed out with ink. These and other revisions are explained by an extra title page at the front of the ms. which has written on it in blue pencil, "Re-arranged or rejected— 725." The number presumably is that of an editor of the *Cambridge Bibliography of English Literature,* and the words presumably are elliptical for "This must be re-arranged or rejected." Also the pp. are numbered in blue pencil in sequence (Sayers's numbering starts over with each section); dates of unreprinted materials in *Household Words* and *All the Year Round* are crossed out in blue pencil (this is due to their style, not the information, which was included in the *Cambridge Bibliography of English Literature);* two notes on identifications of unsigned items are combined by a blue-pencil arrow (this re-arranged note is unchanged in

The New Cambridge Bibliography of English Literature, Vol. 3 [1969], 927);
the secondary materials are reorganized in blue pencil. Since Sayers would presumably have followed *Cambridge Bibliography of English Literature* style if she had started the bibliography for that publication, the obvious assumption is that she intended the bibliography for her study of Collins and submitted it to *Cambridge Bibliography of English Literature* later.

A.3. Two sets of galley proofs of the *Cambridge Bibliography of English Literature* version. These contain slight variations from the *Cambridge Bibliography of English Literature* —spaces left for the dates of some stories are not yet closed up, etc.

B. "Wilkie Collins / A Critical and Biographical Study" (pub. 1977)

For Gregory's discussion of these mss., see WC:C&BS, pp. 16–17, 24. Chapter I covers pp. 25–44 in WC:C&BS; Chapter II, pp. 45–58; Chapter III, pp. 59–74; Chapter IV, pp. 75–94; and the incomplete Chapter V, pp. 95–117. Since the content is available in published form, the following notes avoid any summarizing.

B.1. Chapter I. Ams, nd, 28 pp. Pp. 17 and 21 have pasted extensions to them, containing footnotes; p. 22 is a half page. Various notes are added, such as on p. 2, about a coat of arms, in red. This and each subsequent chapter has a small slip of paper at the front with a picture or another illustration for the chapter indicated. None of these autograph chapters have page numbers.

B.2. Chapter I. Ams, nd, 34 pp. This seems to be a fair copy, with many minor revisions, of the draft of Chapter I listed immediately above.

B.3. Chapter I. Tms, nd, 22 pp., + 2 Tcc/ms. The typed version of B.2. There are a few lacunae in the footnotes, waiting the checking of page numbers or other matters. No corrections appear on any of these typed copies.

B.4. Chapter II. Ams, nd, 23 pp. P. 18 has a pasted extension for a footnote. This and the subsequent chapters listed immediately below are parallel to B.1.

B.5. Chapter III. Ams, nd, 22 pp. Pp. 1 and 17 have footnotes pasted onto them; pp. 5 and 13 are pasted together from several sources (one passage on p. 13 is typewritten), with footnote extensions; p. 18 is two partial sheets pasted together. Although this chapter, like its parallel Amss, is written in dark ink, it has a few pencilled queries and revisions, two X's in red pencil, and one crossing out in red ink; these revisions are typical of the autograph chapters (except B.2) though this one may have more of them than most.

B.6. Chapter IV. Ams, nd, 28 pp. Pp. 5 and 8 are each made of 2 pp. pasted together; p. 6 is a short page made of 2 pp. pasted together; and pp. 17 and 18 each have long, pasted on footnotes.

B.7. Chapter V. Ams, nd, 31 pp. Pp. 1 and 21 are each made of 2 pp. pasted together, and in the case of p. 1, a draft of a sentence is cut off at the bottom (the upper loops, etc., are visible); pp. 10 and 17 have pasted on footnotes.

C. Outlines of WC:C&BS

C.1. Ams, nd, 2 pp. A listing of eight chapters, with some indications of the content of each.

C.2. Ams, nd, 2 pp. A listing of 19 chapters, with an indication of the contents of each—such as one on Collins and women (ch. 16) and one on Collins and the development of the detective novel (Ch. 15).

C.3. Ams, nd, 3 pp. A listing of 22 chapters, with an indication of content. As with C.2, the content is chronological at first with some general chapters near the end. In this outline, for example, the chapter on Collins and women becomes Ch. 18, while the next-to-last chapter is on the construction of the sensational novel (a history of the mystery novel was promised earlier, as part of Ch. 7).

D. Notebooks and File Cards on Collins

D.1. A small, black, snap-top notebook with Ams notes on the first 8 pp. only; c. 1930. This notebook belongs with the Collins materials only because of the first page of notes. On this page Sayers discusses Collins's treatment of women in his novels, as being in advance of his times: he does not want them educated so they will be good companions for men, as did Tennyson and Meredith; he sees women as independent. The next two pages are taken up with names of mystery writers and novels — three authors on the first and six on the second of these pages. The fourth page has the name of an author of a novel about Basque life and a list of (Basque?) names; the fifth page has further names. These fourth and fifth pages seem to be part of Sayers's preparation for writing "The Incredible Elopement of Lord Peter Wimsey"; the last name of a small boy in that story, Etcheverry, appears in the list of names on p. 4. The last 3 pages of notes, pp. 6–8, contain the list of the contents of an artist's satchel—the large compartment on p. 6 and the small compartment on pp. 7–8. This seems to be part of the preparation for writing *The Five Red Herrings* (1931), so 1931 provides a *terminus ad quem* for the notebook.

D.2. A small notebook with black covers and a red spine; the paper inside is indexed with the alphabet. Ams, nd, 98 lvs. of which 44 are blank on both sides. Sayers entered (usually in ink) the names of Collins's books in the appropriate alphabetical sections; some short stories and other works are entered in pencil. Notes appear under most of these titles —sometimes very full notes, some even being continued elsewhere in the notebook, but sometimes very brief; sometimes in pencil, in several different colors, and sometimes in ink; often with page numbers, presumably as Sayers had ideas while reading the books. Some of the notes on the early books are crossed out with red pencil or dark ink, not with an X but with a shape like half of a bracket:]. In addition to these notes on Collins's works, there are a few personal notes (e.g., opposite the listing of *The Queen of Hearts*, on somebody with tonsillitis). The last four pages, including the back free endpaper, contain drawings, presumably by Sayers: 4 are landscapes; 3 are of the same man in an armchair, reading a book (he seems to have a moustache; Sayers's husband?).

D.3. A red-covered Exercise Book with Collins's name and dates printed in ink on the cover. Ams, nd, 124 lvs. There is water damage to the back portion of the book. The first 3 pages are introductory: the first page is a title page, indicating this volume deals with the life of Collins; the second is primarily a list of the residences of Collins; the third has a Collins family tree. The rest of the book is divided into a chronological table of Collins's life from 1824 through June of 1854; 3 months are covered on each set of facing pages, with events in Collins's life entered on the right side and societal events on the left. Sayers usually gives her source for the events she enters; many of the pages have no events entered on them.

D.4. An Excelsior Jotter, being a notebook stapled at the top, with perforated pages. Ams, nd, 96½ lvs. remaining (orig. 100). The originally blue cover is waterstained and loose; the first page is loose. Pp. 2, 3, 4, and 8 have bibliographic notes on them. For example, one of the 3 notes on p. 2 describes the title page of *The Evil Genius*, and the note on p. 4 describes the title page of *The Yellow Tiger and Other Tales*; the note on p. 8 is a memorandum to copy all entries in the British Museum Catalogue under Collins's name except for translations (cf. Sayers's correspondence in 1930 from Elizabeth D'Oyley and J. F. Fenn, now in the H.R.C.). Pp. 9 through 36 have Collins's books entered alphabetically, with information about editions of the books entered beneath the titles; in the case of *The Moonstone*, the list of editions is on both sides of the leaf. The rest of the pages are blank.

D.5. A small, leather notebook, identical to D.6, with a simulated leather cover; the paper of the pastedown and free endpapers has a marbled design in brown and gold. Ams, nd [some material c. 1933], 32 lvs. The 32 lvs. have notes on a variety of subjects, almost all of them connected with Collins; most of the leaves have notes on both sides. Some examples: a list of what the 1870s thought coarse (pp. 1–2); 2 observations on Collins: his men *vs*. his women, his coarseness on one topic (p. 3); Collins's understanding of intellectual women, and his feminism compared to Meredith's (p. 5); a note on the possible Pre-Raphaelite influence on Collins (p. 21); 6 citations of the aesthetic beauties in Collins's writings (p. 33); a paragraph comparison of Collins's characterizations with those of Dickens—to Collins's advantage (p. 35); a citation of a critic who calls Collins a master of suspense, with Sayers's comment that this was Collins's main contribution to literary technique: the use of delayed action (p. 53). Some of the pages—such as pp. 54–61—are blank. The 2 items not connected with Collins are a sketch of a woman in a bustle (upside down, p. 64) and 2 lists of (bell) names (p. 62)—this latter obviously dates from the period of planning *The Nine Tailors* (1934).

D.6. A small, black notebook, identical to D.5, but with Sayers's name and London address ink-stamped on the verso of the front free endpaper. Ams, nd [some material c. 1929], 50 lvs. Some of the more interesting notes: Sayers observes that Collins's method of characterization, by a few outstanding traits or catchwords, is very useful for serial publication (p. 47); the Victorian writers had an eagerness to do types beyond any plot necessities—the blind man, the deaf man, the Jew, the artist—but Collins also had a journalist's instinct to be the first to describe a certain group or aspect of society, as in *Poor Miss Finch* (pp. 47–49); the use of diaries in fiction can be defended in two ways: as a literary convention for baring thoughts, like the soliloquy in Renaissance drama, or as a literary tradition, for Collins is in the Richardson tradition just as Dickens is in the Fielding-Sterne-Smollett tradition; indeed, Collins is at his best in the first person (as in diaries), for he does not vary his style enough in the later books (p. 61); Sayers's husband, in reading *The Woman in White*, noticed the frequent use of a phrase which said that something was "of the last importance"—Sayers adds a citation of the phrase's use in *The Fallen Leaves* (p. 71); Sayers copies down a long passage from Aldous Huxley's *Point Counter Point* about structuring fiction through counterpointed multiplicity, and then she comments that this is the method of melodrama, a crude way of writing a story but one which is immediately impressive (pp. 87–88); Sayers discusses the Victorian tendency to have ideas or subjects behind novels, with examples from Dickens — this also applies to some of Collins's works, but not to *The Woman in White* and *The Moonstone*, which are pure stories —unless the detection *is* the idea; further, Dickens has no followers in his thematic tradition, while Collins has many in his non-thematic practice (pp. 90–91). Perhaps it should be added that the Huxley comment is typical of several in which Sayers is attempting to place Collins in light of modern fiction: for example, she refers to Virginia Woolf's *To the Lighthouse* (p. 56) and Percy Lubbock's *The Craft of Fiction* (p. 61). Also, it is obvious that Sayers was to some degree trying out ideas in these notebook comments: her discussion of the thematic novel in her introduction to *The Moonstone* in the Everyman Library (London: J. M. Dent and Sons, 1944), p. ix, is not as negative. The non-Collins material is brief in this notebook: there are 2 pages of names and addresses, including that of H. G. Wells—these are probably persons to whom Sayers was writing at the time (possibly, but not necessarily, about Collins), for Sir Fredric Pollock is listed and E. S. P. Haynes is mentioned (see their letters in the H.R.C.) (pp. 76–77); there is a note (p. 80) about the occupational effect of hairdressing on a hairdresser's wristwatch —intended for a detective story? Sayers also has a note to herself to ask Tom Darlow about Dickens's accordion-playing (p. 89); the reply to this specific question in Darlow's letter (in the H.R.C.), dated 10 March 1929, helps to date this notebook.

D.7. Two hundred forty-four 3x5 file cards, containing autograph notes on materials connected with Collins; these are not alphabetized as they currently are held by the H.R.C. The content of most, but not all, of these is that of citations of others' opinions on, or facts about, people connected to Collins, Collins's works, his characterizations; a number of cross references appear. One example of a card giving Sayers's opinions: on that for *Hide and Seek*, Sayers comments that if Collins had lived today —i.e., in the time of *Elmer Gantry* (her example)—he might have produced a better book on early sexual repression, its consequences, and later guilt feelings.

E. SUBSTANTIAL AUTOGRAPH AND TYPEWRITTEN MANUSCRIPTS ON COLLINS

The handwriting of items 2 through 8 seems to be that of Sayers.

E.1. "Love-Affairs of Wilkie Collins." Tms with A revisions, nd, 8 pp. The style and the handwriting of the corrections indicate this is by Sayers. The manuscript begins with seventeen references to Collins's love affairs in biographies, letters and other sources; on p. 4 "Queries and conclusions" begin, with four subpoints (A-D), which in turn are subdivided by numbers. The essay sets up very clearly the possibilities about both Martha Rudd and Caroline Graves, tracing what is known of both their careers, with comparisons to the novels. The corrections are mainly of typos (done in red ink), but there is a typed revision pasted over a passage on p. 2 and three handwritten revisions of the text (two in dark ink, one in red).

E.2. [Wilkie Collins and Opium.] Ams, nd, 4 pp. A fragmentary manuscript. Part way down the first page appears point three, so the pages missing at the first include all of a first point and part of a second. At the end of these pages, presumably the end of the original essay, Sayers outlines the effect of opium on Collins's writing, finding the novels of 1866 through 1870 to be Collins's best —*Armadale, The Moonstone, Man and Wife; Poor Miss Finch* in 1872 is nearly as good, but with *The New Magdalen* of 1873 there is a clear falling off; the books after this through 1880 are very poor; after 1880 there is a slight recovery, but Collins never reaches his greatest level again —and this pattern is attributed, in this manuscript, to the effects of opium.

E.3. Ams, nd, 3 pp. These pages have been torn from a notebook; the first two list Collins's books in chronological order, and the third lists his plays in chronological order.

E.4. Tms with A corrections, nd, 4 pp. A list of Collins's movements and residences, 1851–1889; there are two handwritten notes, which seem to be by Sayers.

E.5. Ams, nd, 10 pp. The first page is titled "Appendix 1"; the pages list Collins's books, with notes on variant editions and other matters. The pages are stained, and the final page is torn in half, with only the bottom half remaining with the manuscript.

E.6. Ams, nd, 10 lvs. A list of the contents of Collins's library, written in ink, usually on one side of a sheet, but with some items on versos.

E.7. Ams, nd, 4 pp. A pencilled list of Collins's possible contributions to *All the Year Round* (with a large number of question marks).

E.8. Ams, nd, 26 pp. Small sheets of various sorts of paper, containing information mainly on Collins's letters, arranged chronologically.

F. Brief Items, Notes, and Jottings on Collins

All of the materials seem to be in Sayers's handwriting; it is possible that there might be disagreement about a few items, since their brevity does not always give enough evidence for certain judgment.

F.1. Drawing with A marginalia, nd, 1 p. A drawing in pencil of Collins's grave, with notes in one color and other details; the notes seem to be in Sayers's hand, and presumably the drawing is also by her.

F.2. "Original Manuscripts of Wilkie Collins." Ams, nd, 1 p. A list.

F.3. Ams, nd, 1 p. A genealogy of William Collins's descendants.

F.4. Ams, nd, 1 p. Another genealogy of William Collins's descendants.

F.5. Ams, nd [c. 1933], at the end of a T copy of an 1871 census report on Collins's daughter's home. Sayers indicates that if Collins's daughter were alive at the time, she would be 88; since the daughter was born in 1845, this suggests the date of 1933 for the note.

F.6. Ams, nd, 1 p. A genealogy of David Geddes's descendants.

F.7. Ams, nd, on the back of an envelope addressed to Sayers. The notes are mainly on Alexander Geddes.

F.8. Ams, nd, 1 p. Notes on Elizabeth Harriet Bartley, with records of places checked for information.

F.9. Ams, nd, 1 p. A note on Ferrucio Busoni's interest in Collins's works.

F.10. Ams, nd, 1 p. A note on Collins's play *The Evil Genius*.

F.11. Ams, nd, 2 pp. Notes about Collins-related paintings.

F. 12. Ams, nd, 1 p. A note about a catalog.

F.13. Ams, nd, 1 p. A note on Miss Emily Mooney, who thought *Blind Love* to be based on her story.

F.14. Ams, nd, 2 pp. A copy of selected verses from Lord Neaves's "The Tourists' Matrimonial Guide through Scotland" — verses on Scottish marriage laws —keyed to *Man and Wife*. As a copy perhaps this item should be classified in G, but the keying to a Collins novel seems to give it special significance.

F.15. Ams, nd, 1 p. A note on half a small sheet of paper on Collins's tour of Switzerland and Italy with Dickens and Egg.

F.16. Ams, nd, on the back of a frayed envelope which held the copy of *Miss Gwilt* sold by Maggs Brothers. A note of the original production and the first London production of *Miss Gwilt*, with a list of characters and some of the names of actors and one name of an actress.

F.17. Ams, nd, at the top left of the first page of a TL/copy from Collins to William D. Booth on 20 September 1870. The note lists 3 performances of *Man and Wife* in an unauthorized version, including the New York performance which Collins is writing about in this letter. For the source of this copy, see F.18.

F.18. Ams, nd [c. 31 March 1933], 1 p. A note giving information from Morris L. Parrish, a Philadelphia, Pennsylvania, stockbroker, about 2 performances —3 January and 16-17 December 1874 —of the dramatic form of *Man and Wife* and about the play's publication in book form in Ohio in 1873. There are 2 TLS from Parrish to Sayers in the H.R.C.; the second, of 20 May 1929, enclosed copies of 2 Collins letters —one of them presumably the TL/copy listed in F.17. But there seems to have been a third letter from Parrish, for the 2 in the H.R.C. —the first, 23 April 1929 —do not match Sayers's dating of the information in this ms. as being from Parrish on 31 March 1933. (There are also 26 T 4x6 cards from Parrish in the H.R.C., but they are related to the first letter and do not affect this point.)

F.19. Ams, nd, 1 p. A list of pseudo-memoirs of private detectives and policemen, 1859–1863. Here included with the Collins material since it was presumably intended as a background for the discussion of Sergeant Cuff.

F.20. Ams, nd, 1 p. Notes summarizing aspects of *Memoirs of a Picture*, a picaresque novel by Collins's grandfather.

F.21. Ams, nd, on an envelope. A list of items on the large envelope which currently holds two of the outlines of the study of Collins (C.2 and C.3)—none of the items listed, being playbills, letters in facsimile, and other materials, are currently in the envelope.

F.22. Ams, nd, 1 sheet. One side has a note on the sale of Collins mss. at Sotheby's; the other has doodling.

F.23. Form with A inserts, S. A receipt to Mrs. A. M. Osler, Sayers's research assistant in 1933.

F.24. Ams, nd [c. 4 July 1928], on the face of a postcard. This postcard, from Edmund Sidney P. Haynes, is dated 4 July 1928; Sayers's jottings may date from her reception of the card, but this is not certain.

F.25. Ams, nd [c. 15 March 1933], on one page of a 2 page letter. A. May Osler writes on 15 March 1933, enclosing the death certificate of Mary Ann Graves, whom she identifies as the mother of Caroline Graves; the brief, pencilled note suggests she may have been Caroline Graves's mother-in-law.

F.26. A notes, nd [c. 19 July 1933], on a list of Collins's books. With a letter of 19 July

1933, [H.] Graham Pollard sends a list of American and English first editions of Collins's titles; the list itself was prepared by I[sidore] R[osenbaum] Brussel, as part of the preparation for *Anglo-American First Editions 1826–1900: East to West* (London: Constable and Co.; New York: R. R. Bowker Co., 1935). Sayers's bibliographic notes were presumably for her reply, for which Pollard thanks her in a letter of 21 July 1933.

F.27. Ams, nd [c. 2 August 1933], on a letter. Sayers and Pollard are still involved in bibliographic information (cf. F.26). Pollard passes on from Brussel the contents of *Alicia Warlock* and the place and date of the original publication of "Miss or Mrs.?" Sayers adds marginalia.

F.28. Ams, nd [c. 24 August 1934], 1 p. This small separate note summarizes Pollard's information about *The Devil's Spectacles*; in the H.R.C., it is filed with Pollard's letter of 24 August 1934, in which he mentions sending her a proof from the (then) forthcoming *New Paths in Book Collecting*, ed. John Carter (London: Constable, 1934), with information on *The Devil's Spectacles*.

F.29. Ams, nd, 1 p. In the H.R.C. file with 4 letters from William Seymour (of South Duxbury, Massachusetts), but not clearly related to them, is a 2x4 card with three names and addresses written on it.

F.30. Ams and A crossouts, nd [c. 16 December 1932], 1 p. Michael Sadleir, in a letter of 16 December 1932, says he is adding 5 items to the Collins bibliography (presumably one which Sayers had drawn up); some items are crossed out—presumably by Sayers, after checking them—and one bibliographic comment is added. (*Note:* In a letter without a date from Sadleir—the only one of Sadleir's letters to Sayers in the H.R.C. sent from Surrey—he gives a reference to a Collins story in *The National Magazine;* this is crossed out in pencil, presumably by Sayers— this hardly seemed worth listing separately.)

F.31. Ams, nd [c. December 1923], in a catalog. *A Catalogue of Modern Books from the Library of the late Frederic Harrison* [etc.], issued by Hodgson and Co., No. 7 of 1923-24, for a sale on 6-7 December 1923. On pp. 15–19 are "Original Mss. of Novels and Plays by William Wilkie Collins"; Sayers's pencilled initials are opposite five items, a note in what seems to be her hand appears on p. 17, and another note, perhaps in her hand, on p. 15. There are a number of other initials and financial amounts (presumably for bids) in the catalog. *Note:* According to E. R. Gregory, in WC:C&BS, p. 7, Sayers was planning her study of Collins before the publication of *Whose Body?* (1923); thus it is probable that Sayers's markings were made at the time of the sale.

F.32. Ams, nd, in a catalog. *Catalogue of Autograph Letters and Manuscripts . . . of the Late Wilkie Collins*, issued by Sotheby's for a sale in 1891; a newspaper paragraph about the sale is pasted on the front cover. Sayers's pencilled initials appear on pp. 4 and 5, the latter with a brief note; another name, in what looks like Sayers's script, is on p. 4. Since Sayers could hardly be bidding in 1891—two years before her birth—perhaps these marks indicate AL's and Amss which she had traced or owned.

F.33. Ams, nd, on a catalog page. A page from a Raphael King catalog; there is a line opposite the Collins items, and a dealer's name is written at the top of the page in what seems to be Sayers's script.

F.34. Ams, nd, on a catalog page. A page from a Dobell's catalog with pencilled notes on the published editions of a number of Collins's mss. offered for sale.

F.35. Ams, nd [c. 1923-1924], on a printed page. A page from the 1923-1924 printed book-auction records, with an addition in ink, at the bottom of one side, of the sale of *No Name*.

F.36. Ams, nd, on a catalog page. A page of association books from Foyle's Rare Book Catalogue; there are x's on either side of a book with Collins's annotations in it, "Foyle's Rare Book Catalogue" written at the top of the page, and a footnote (with Sayers's characteristic asterisk, an *x* with dots between its arms) commenting on the phrasing of the book-owner's career.

F.37. Ams on the back of *The Bookman*, June 1912. An address (with no name); the hand is not certain. A list at the H.R.C. includes this item as part of the Sayers collection, but there are A changes of the price on the cover of the magazine — so the issue is a second-hand copy and the address need not have anything to do with Sayers. (The reason that this magazine was part of Sayers's possessions is that it contains an article on Collins by A. Compton-Rickett.)

G. COPIES OF MATERIALS RELATED TO COLLINS

Note: A copy of a poem keyed to *Man and Wife* is listed in F.14. The following items seem to be in Sayers's hand.

G.1. Ams, nd, 2 pp. Excerpts from William Powell Frith's *My Autobiography and Reminiscences*.

G.2. Ams, nd. 4 pp. Collins's death notice, from *The Critic*.

G.3. Ams, nd, 1 p. A note about Sydenham trousers, from *The Critic*.

G.4. Ams, nd, 3 pp. Notes from James Payn's *Some Literary Recollections*.

G.5. Ams, nd, 2 pp. Notes from Charles Knight's *Passages of a Working Life*.

G.6. Ams, nd, 1 p. Notes on Collins from an unidentified source, given as Haut, vol. II.

G.7. Ams, nd, 1 p. Notes from *The Hibbert Journal*, comparing Thomas Hardy's *Desperate Remedies* and Collins.

G.8. Ams, nd, 1 p. Notes from a sale catalog.

G.9. Ams, nd, 1 p. Two notes from *Punch*.

G.10. Ams, nd, 2 pp. A copy of a letter from George Augustus [Henry] Sala to Collins, with a pencilled notation at the top about the source and the disposal of the original.

G.11. Ams, nd, 2 pp. Notes from Alfred T. Story's *The Life of John Linnell* (2 vols., Bartley?, 1892), mainly about Collins's father although one letter from Collins to Linnell (about painting) is copied without page reference after the main notes.

G.12. Ams, nd, 1 p. An extract from a letter from David Wilkie to his brother (in 1882) about meeting Collins's wife, a former Miss Geddes from Edinburgh. (*Note:* This is filed at the H.R.C. with a letter from A. May Osler to Sayers, 25 February 1933; besides the 1 page letter, there is a 1 page extract from Joseph Foster's *Men-at-the-Bar* [1885] in Osler's hand — but with notes in pen and in pencil below in two different hands, one of which may be Sayers's.)

H. SAYERS'S SIGNATURES AND INITIALS ON ALBATROSS CONTRACTS

Note: Filed with these 3 contracts is a TccL, 24 May 1938, 1 p., from "Editor" to Jan Collins of Glasgow, saying that the Albatross Crime Club did not realize that he had the rights on the 3 books it had taken an option on, so £ 20 is being sent him as the usual advance on a royalty of 3 percent.

H.1. Printed agreement with T inserts, S, 13 March 1934, 2 pp. Two pages of heavy, legal-sized paper in a red folder with a green ribbon at top; on the back of the folder is a sticker with "109 [handwritten] / Agreement / between / Dorothy L. / Sayers [the name is handwritten] / and the / Albatross." This sticker is decorated around the edges by a design of forty, repeated, stylized birds; they look more like small birds pulling worms from the ground than like albatrosses. The actual contract is a "Memorandum of agreement" between Sayers and The Albatross Verlag of Paris for the publication of an English-language edition of *The Nine Tailors* on the continent of Europe, with various terms, £30 on publication. Sayers's name is typed in red; the other typed inserts are in black. Sayers has signed the contract on the second page.

H.2. Typed agreement/cc, I and S, 2 December 1937, 2 pp. A 2 page, onion-skin copy of a "Memorandum of agreement" between Sayers and The Albatross Verlag of Paris for the publication of an English-language edition of *Gaudy Night* on the continent of Europe, with various terms. £40 on publication; Clause 7 allows for an edition of *Busman's Honeymoon* under the same terms within a year. Initialed by Sayers on p. 1; signed by her on p. 2.

H.3. Printed agreement with T inserts, I and S, 17 July 1946, 1 sheet. A "Memorandum of agreement" between Sayers and Messrs Albatross Ltd of London for a Portuguese edition of *The Nine Tailors,* with various terms. £50 on publication. Initialed twice on the front side of the page by Sayers; signed by her on the back.

I. Sayers's Signature and Inscription in Two of Her Books

I.1. *Whose Body?* New York: Boni and Liveright, 1923. This volume is not signed, but it is inscribed to Sayers's parents by Sayers. For the background of the volume (before it came to the H.R.C. in the Ellery Queen collection), see Ellery Queen's *In the Queen's Parlor* (New York: Simon and Schuster, 1957), p. 164. *Note:* This is the first edition of *Whose Body?*; according to Colleen Gilbert, the book was published in the U.S. in May 1923, and in Britain by T. Fisher Unwin in October 1923.

I.2. *Lord Peter Views the Body.* London: Victor Gollancz, 1928. The card catalog in the H.R.C. says this volume is signed, but actually Sayers's name has been cut from some paper and it was at one time attached to the front of the front free endpaper with one of those small gummed hinges used on stamps (there is a slight discoloration where it was attached); currently, this signed slip of paper is laid between the front free endpaper and the half-title page. (Part of the Ellery Queen collection.)

J. Sayers's Signatures and Inscriptions in Collins's Books

All of the following items are in the Ellery Queen collection; since Sayers died on 17 December 1957 and the Queen collection at the H.R.C. was officially opened on 16 January 1959, Frederic Dannay (the bibliophile of the two cousins who wrote under the name of Ellery Queen) presumably purchased the books from Sayers's son and then sold them with his other books to the H.R.C. In addition to the volumes listed below, Hans Sehlbach's *Untersuchungen über die Romankunst von Wilkie Collins* (Jena, 1931), also part of the Ellery Queen collection, is signed by Sayers. (Presumably purchased directly from Sayers's son by the H.R.C. is a letter from Sehlbach to Sayers, 21 July

1930, in German.) The following listing of signed or annotated volumes in the H.R.C. may be incomplete, for not all of Collins's books have been examined and books on Collins —despite the example of Sehlbach's volume —were not searched. It does, however, contain all Collins volumes identified in the card catalog of the H.R.C. as signed or stamped with Sayers's name —as well as two others which have annotations by Sayers. (I wish to thank E. R. Gregory for calling my attention to two of these books —one of them being an annotated volume which I would have otherwise missed— in a letter of 22 April 1977, before I started my investigation of the papers at the H.R.C.)

J.1. *Antonio; or, The Fall of Rome: A New Edition*. London: Chatto and Windus, n.d. Stamped with Sayers's name and London address (in purple ink, as are the other 4 stamped books); since the front free endpaper and the half-title page are missing, this volume is stamped on the front pastedown endpaper. There are pencilled notes, in what seems to be Sayers's hand, on pp. iii, 8, 25, 26, 31, 39, 54, 59, 130, 132, and 139. All of the comments are fairly brief, and most simply note aspects of style or authorial biases —3 of them note pictorial passages, such as Sayers discusses in WC:C&BS, pp. 69–70.

J.2. *Basil*. London: Sampson Low, Son, and Co., 1862. Signed on the front free endpaper and dated 1929. This copy, running 314 pp. of text, has been rebound with blank white sheets between the printed leaves. Sayers begins a comparison of this edition with the "Editio Princeps of 1852" (opposite p. ii); because of the major variants, the notes on the Letter of Dedication are particularly full. Sayers's notes, including variants in punctuation, continue through p. 55 of the text.

J.3. *Basil: A New Edition*. London: Smith, Elder and Co., 1874. Stamped with Sayers's name and London address on the front free endpaper. As the volume is currently held in the H.R.C., it has a program for "Witham and District / War Weapons Week / . . . / July 6–12" laid into the book (between pp. 110–11). Sayers is not mentioned in the program.

J.4. *The Frozen Deep and Other Tales: A New Edition*. London: Chatto and Windus, n.d. Stamped with Sayers's name and London address on the front free endpaper. On p. 205, in the part of the volume containing "The Dream Woman," appears a reference in ink to Sheridan Le Fanu's "Sir Dominck's Bargain"; the note seems to be in Sayers's script.

J.5. *"I Say No": A New Edition*. London: Chatto and Windus, 1886. Stamped with Sayers's name and London address on the front free endpaper.

J.6. *Little Novels: A New Edition*. London: Chatto and Windus, 1889. No signature or stamp. On the title page, in ink, is a list of alternate titles for the stories in the volume, with, in one case, two extra titles. Presumably Sayers was listing for most of the stories the magazine titles, or other titles under which the stories had appeared. Oddly, the information on alternate titles is fuller here than in Sayers's note on *Little Novels* published in her Collins bibliography in *Cambridge Bibliography of English Literature*.

J.7. *Miss or Mrs.?* Title page (with the publisher's name) missing. Stamped with Sayers's name and London address on the front free endpaper. Brief pencilled notes appear on pp. 17 and 60; the latter seems to be Sayers's script, while the former, consisting only of the numeral *56*, is both obscure in meaning and too brief to be certain in authorship.

J.8. *Poor Miss Finch*. Vol. I. London: Richard Bentley and Son, 1872. Signed (below

another signature and the date 1872) with the date 1928. The original owner has also
signed the other two volumes, but Sayers has not.

J.9. *Rambles beyond Railways; or, Notes in Cornwall Taken a-Foot.* London:
Richard Bentley, 1851. No signature or stamp. Two notes appear in what seems to
be Sayers's hand: on p. 34 an adjective is added to a description of an education, and
on p. 37 the geographic name with a bishop's title is corrected (the latter is copied
from the errata list on p. x). *Note:* This volume is Queen 5531, in H.R.C.'s Ellery
Queen collection; another copy of this same edition, Queen 5532, has only the
correction on p. 37 and the script is not Sayers's.

J.10. *The Two Destinies: A Romance: A New Edition.* London: Chatto and Windus,
1878. Signed by Sayers on the front free endpaper. Notes appear on pp. 194 and
207, and a list of five page numbers with notes by three of them appears on the back
pastedown endpaper. These seem to be in Sayers's hand.

3. Letters in the Marion E. Wade Collection, Wheaton College (Wheaton, Illinois), ed. Joe R. Christopher

Thirteen of the letters in this section were listed and briefly annotated several years ago; the lists appeared as half of "A Sayers Bibliography, Part 5" in *Unicorn: A Miscellaneous Journal,* 3:2 (May 1975), 51. They have been revised, with fuller bibliographic information and more details about the content; to them have been added notes on letters subsequently gained by the WColl. I would like to thank Karen Rockow, editor of *Unicorn,* for permission to reprint that early material here, and the Research Committee of Tarleton State University for a grant in the summer of 1973 which enabled me to visit the WColl and, among other things, to list those thirteen letters. Further, I would like to thank Barbara Griffin, former secretary-librarian of the WColl, for telling me of the new letters, and Barbara Hendershott for help when I revisited the collection in December 1977. For a number of letters *to* Sayers in the WColl, see items B.2 (Eustace Robert Barton), B.11 (George MacDonald), and B.16 (John Rhode) in Section 1.

J.R.C.

A. To Miss [Margaret] Douglas.

A.1. ALS, 16 May 1945, 2 pp. (1 lf.). From Witham. About Charles Williams's death: Sayers feels the loss personally; her present work owes much to him. (Evidently Douglas had been working for, or with, Williams in some way and had written Sayers immediately after his death, 15 May 1945. For her first name, see A. M. Hadfield's *An Introduction to Charles Williams* [London: Robert Hale, 1959], p. 203.)

B. To Everybody's Weekly.

Note: The second of these letters is addressed to Kenneth Hopkins at *Everybody's;* it is uncertain if both letters went to him, since the first is just addressed to the editor.

B.1. To the editor. ALS, 23 January 1952, 1 p. From Witham. Sayers has written the story of *Christ's Emperor* while dealing with rehearsals, etc. (This refers to "Constantine—Christ's Emperor," *Everybody's Weekly,* 16 February 1952, pp. 15, 20. The rehearsals are of *Christ's Emperor,* the shortened version of *The Emperor Constantine,* which was presented at St. Thomas's Church, Regent Street, London, on 5–26 February 1952. See H & B, p. 128, for the production; they miss this retelling of the story for *Everybody's.*) The manuscript is too long, but she has no time to cut it or to get it typed at the moment; would the editor please make the cuts in the first four pages? She asks that the *L.* appear in her name, that business communications go through her agents, and that she see proofs. (*Note:*

The letter has written at the top "Being Typed" —crossed out —and other notations, presumably all by the editor at *Everybody's.*)

B.2. To Kenneth Hopkins. TLS, 7 April 1952, 1 p. From Witham. Sayers indicates he must work out the fee with her agents. (There is no indication in the letter of what the fee is for.)

C. TO THE BISHOP OF LEICESTER.

C.1. TLS, 22 November 1950, 1 p. From Witham. A refusal of an opportunity to speak at Leicester in 1951; Sayers explains she has given up almost all public speaking, for she is working on the Festival Play at Colchester (*The Emperor Constantine: A Chronicle*) and her next volume of the *Divine Comedy.* (*Note:* The letter has a pencilled price in the lower left and "A tiny Christian offering" in the upper right; presumably a purchased letter given to the WColl.)

D. TO FRED[ERIC]K MASON.

D.1. ALS, nd, 1 p. (a postcard). N.p. Not a full sentence: a thank-you for his best wishes, and season's greetings to him. (*Note:* The other side of the postcard has a reproduction of Melchior d'Hondecoeter's "Peacock and Poultry," a picture in the British Museum.)

E. TO S. C. ROBERTS.

E.1. TLS, 23 December 1937, 1 p. From Witham. A Christmas and New Year's good wishes, with a gift of a pamphlet on an ancestor of Lord Peter Wimsey. (Presumably this pamphlet was *An Account of Lord Mortimer Wimsey, the Hermit of the Wash,* which, according to H & B, p. 177, was delivered from the printer on 21 December 1937.)

F. TO SIR RONALD STORRS, HALSTEAD, ESSEX.

F.1. TLS, 25 January 1950, 1 p. From Witham. Sayers writes to Sir Ronald about a prospective review of her translation of the *Inferno* in *The Observer* (an unsigned note by Storrs at the bottom of the sheet refers to his review's appearance): she does not know why editors get upset over terza rima; the *Sunday Times* refuses to allow letters answering Kennet's review. She adds that her husband is not yet quite well and spends a paragraph on a fire in a neighbor's yard early that morning.

F.2. TLS, 11 April 1953, 1 p. From Witham. Sayers responds to Sir Ronald's letter in which he had commented on her published letter on her relationship to Edwardian poets (Sayers's published letter, not listed in H & B, is "Binyon's Dante," in *The Times Literary Supplement,* No. 2669 [27 March 1953], 205, in which Sayers discusses the rhyming patterns in Laurence Binyon's translation of *La Divina Commedia;* she is replying to a review article, "Edwardian Poets," *T.L.S.,* No. 2668 [20 March 1953], 186, which says Binyon avoids "the deceptive smoothness and regularity which informs such a work as Miss Dorothy Sayers's subsequent version of the *Inferno*"); she wrote a gentle reply and was lucky to have Foligno write an attack (this does not seem to have been published in the *T.L.S.*). She is finishing up the introduction and notes to the *Purgatorio,* and can return Sir

Ronald's Dante dictionary now if he wishes; she will give a dinner party for fellow Dantists when the *Purgatorio* is finished; she has been further delayed by collecting her Dantean lectures for Methuen.

G. TO MICHAL AND MICHAEL WILLIAMS. "Michal" (actual name, Florence) was the wife and Michael the son of Charles Williams, the English poet and critic whose death is discussed in A.1.

G.1. To Michael Williams. ALS, 2 December 1947, 2 pp. (1 lf.). From Witham. Sayers is glad that Charles Williams was her guide to Dante, for he left the authors he discussed alive and relevant. She mentions the two basic questions of all good criticism: what did this writer mean to say to his readers and what does his work mean today? She is glad that the book (presumably *Essays Presented to Charles Williams* [London: Oxford University Press, 1947]) is nearing publication.

G.2. To Michael Williams. ALS, 24 May 1948, 1 p. From Witham. Sayers thanks him for giving her name to a friend in Milwaukee, who is sending her aid parcels; she can always give the gifts to the more deserving (this refers to food and clothing parcels sent to Britain after World War II). She is sorry that Michael and his mother could not come to the Detective Club dinner; the rain which bothered him at the Steiner Hall did not affect the dinner. She adds thanks for a copy of (Charles Williams's) plays (probably *Seed of Adam and Other Plays* [London: Oxford University Press, 1948]); she will send a copy of the misprints in *The Figure of Beatrice* (by Charles Williams [London: Faber and Faber, 1943]).

G.3. To Michal Williams. ALS, 28 June 1948, 2 pp. (1 lf.). From Witham. Sayers thanks Michal for the inscribed copy of Charles Williams's plays; she says it does no harm to throw a controlled fit about (Charles Williams's) followers; she will order a copy of *Arthurian Torso* (by Charles Williams and C. S. Lewis [London: Oxford University Press, 1948]).

G.4. To Michael Williams. ALS, 29 September 1948, 2 pp. (1 lf.). From Witham. A thank-you note for a gift copy of Charles Williams's *Shadows of Ecstasy* (probably not the first edition, of 1933, but the Faber and Faber edition of 1948) and for some sugar, with a comment or two about each; Sayers is happy about the money he, and his mother, received from sales of *Essays for Charles Williams;* she regrets not being able to hear a speaker—Pat McLaughlin (the rector of St. Anne's Church, Soho)—on the third (of October?), but on the seventh she has a business meeting in connection with St. Anne's Church in the day and a Detection Club meeting in the evening; she regrets his heart problems and trouble with his plumbing and dry rot; the previous day she read the manuscript of a German translation of *The Man Born to Be King*.

G.5. To Michal and Michael Williams. ALS, 5 May 1950, 2 pp. (1 lf.). From Witham. Sayers thanks them for a copy of Charles Williams's *The Greater Trumps* (London: Gollancz, 1932); she had had a copy previously, but it vanished from her book-shelves; she comments about a Harvard inquirer about Charles Williams, Mr. Lock, who made her feel frivolous with his seriousness.

G.6. To Michal Williams. ALS, 23 December 1953, 1 p. From Witham. Having sent the Christmas cards early, so the doors could be opened on the appropriate days, Sayers now sends her a bed jacket.

G.7. To Michal Williams. ALS, 4 January 1956, 2 pp. (1 lf.). From Witham. Sayers is happy the cushion was useful and sorry about Michael's problems. She and Pat McLaughlin enjoyed the meeting on Charles Williams's works organized by Miss Coupland —for reading and study are what literary works are for; but she thinks no biographies should be written until 50 years after an author's death; she has been bothered by critics wanting her help to study her works; she thinks Cavaliero is the proper sort of critic (presumably Glen Cavaliero, who has two articles on Charles Williams's writings listed in Lois Glenn's *Charles W. S. Williams: A Checklist* [Kent, Ohio: Kent State University Press, 1975], p. 60; the earlier appeared in 1956, and Sayers may have seen the manuscript before publication).

H. To Miss Hilda M. Wilson, Reigate, Surrey.

H.1. TLS, 27 July 1951, 1 p. From Witham. Sayers apologizes for not replying earlier —she had been busy with her Festival Play at Colchester; she has not heard of any opera based on the *Paradiso* and thinks there would be dramatic problems — but she is not a musical expert.

I. To Canon A. Linwood Wright, St. Mark's Vicarage, Leicester.

I.1. TLS, 21 March 1946, 2 pp. (1 lf.). From Witham. A humorous letter about a misleading article in the *Daily Sketch:* Sayers explains what she is actually involved in —a study program at St. Thomas's Church, Soho.

4. Letters at the University of Michigan, Ann Arbor, ed. E. R. Gregory

Most of the materials in this collection were given to the University of Michigan by the theatrical producer, Maurice Browne (1891–1955). It includes presentation copies of *The Heart of Stone,* sent as a Christmas card in 1946, and *The Zeal of Thy House* (New York: Harcourt, Brace, 1937). Sayers's correspondence with Browne is important. Some of the letters are short and perfunctory, but others deal at length with substantive matters like the structure of her detective stories and her ideas about Christian orthodoxy.

The increasingly sharp tone of the letters after World War II and the absence of any further letters after 17 February 1947 suggest that the friendship deteriorated because of religious differences. The correspondence appears to be a complete file of Sayers's correspondence and is probably the most important single file of letters currently available to scholars. (I wish to thank Margaret Berg, manuscripts cataloger at the University of Michigan, Ann Arbor, for her help in preparing this checklist. She had prepared a list of these letters for the collection with briefer indications of content.)

E.R.G.

A. To Maurice Browne.

A.1. TLS, 17 February 1936, 1 p. From Witham. Sayers discusses the changes involved in transforming *Busman's Honeymoon* from a play into a novel.

A.2. TLS, 2 May 1936, 1 p. (5 x 9 cm.) From Witham. Sayers encloses tickets for Browne and (Marjorie) Morris for a Detection Club Dinner.

A.3. TLS, 4 May 1936, 3 pp. From Witham. The letter focuses on the structure of *Busman's Honeymoon,* but also comments on *Whose Body?, Unnatural Death,* and *Gaudy Night.* Sayers disclaims that Peter is ruthlessly logical, referring to Ogden Nash's famous couplet on Philo Vance—Vance exemplifying the unwavering bloodhound type of detective. Peter's method is to look at the facts until they effortlessly arrange themselves into the truth. She refers to the real-life case of William Herbert Wallace as an example of how motive without method is valueless, and suggests that what is to the detective writer primarily a matter of method must always be disguised to the audience as a matter of motive. [Important.]

A.4. ALS, 31 December 1936, 4 pp. (2 lvs.). From Witham. An invitation to lunch, with references to the success of *Busman's Honeymoon,* and with the observation that some had found allusions to the Abdication Crisis in some of Harriet and Peter's lines.

A.5. TLS, 12 March 1937, 1 p. (5 x 9 cm.) From Witham. Sayers says that she is not leaving Gollancz as her publisher.

A.6. TLS, 6 October 1937, 2 pp. From Witham. Sayers refers to her receipt of author's copies of *The Zeal of Thy House* from her American publisher, one of which she had promised Browne. (The University of Michigan has the copy of the first American edition of this that Sayers presented to Browne.) She describes how some of the play's features originated in the architectural arrangements of the Chapter House at Canterbury.

A.7. ALS, 11 October 1937, 1 p. (5 x 9 cm.) From Witham. Sayers regrets that Browne's show (Arthur Reid's *People in Love?*) has folded: its consciously artificial structure was a part of its charm to her, but this may have precluded its being popular.

A.8. ALS, nd [c. 25 October 1937], 1 p. N.p.; as a postcard. Written on the verso of a photograph of a scene from *The Zeal of Thy House*. Sayers plans to visit Browne in Gipping. (For the dating of this item, see item B.1.)

A.9. ALS, 30 October 1937, 2 pp. (1 lf.). (5 x 9 cm.) From Witham. Sayers expresses thanks for hospitality at Gipping, then passes on to theatrical matters. She suggests Lady Colefax as a possible *entree* to the Cecil family and encloses a notice of a Charles Williams play, which she intends to see. (Williams's play was *Seed of Adam*, which was produced for three days at the Rudolf Steiner Hall in London in November 1937. *Source:* Alice Mary Hadfield, *An Introduction to Charles Williams* [London: Robert Hale, 1959], p. 134.)

A.10. ALS, 5 March 1938, 2 pp. (1 lf.). From London. The letter is taken up with problems of *The Zeal of Thy House* in rehearsal.

A.11. TLS, 10 October 1941, 1 p. (5 x 9 cm.) From Witham. Sayers sends a play of Muriel Byrne's, which Miss Byrne asked her to send him. (According to a letter of 18 January 1978 from Miss Byrne to this editor, the play was probably, but not certainly, an unproduced work titled *Paul*. This date is too late for the play to be *Busman's Honeymoon*, which Browne also looked at and took an option on, but was not able to produce; since Miss Byrne has a note from Sayers praising *Paul*, she believes it to be the likeliest possibility.)

A.12. TLS, 28 October 1946, 1 p. From Witham. Sayers comments on the production of *The Just Vengeance*. She expresses her belief and desires that its doctrine be orthodox and, therefore, sound. She states that, in her view, he has fallen into the Gnostic heresy in his book (*The Atom and the Way* [London: Gollancz, 1946]).

A.13. TLS, 22 November 1946, 3 pp. From Witham. Sayers affirms the importance of orthodoxy in determining whether a person or belief is Christian; she states her oft-reiterated conviction that the Church does not send people to Hell, that they go there because they choose to, that much in Christian doctrine which has been taken as prescriptive is actually descriptive only. She devotes several paragraphs to showing that from Apostolic times on, Christians have been more interested in the Person-hood of Christ than in His teachings. From this, she passes on to human person-ality, which in Christian thought is always unique and distinct from God. Even con-sidered in its totality, the Church is not a body of doctrine, but a society of persons, the Body of Christ. She closes by asserting again that what she is saying is not her thought, but Christian thought. [Important.]

A.14. TLS, 27 January 1947, 2 pp. (1 lf.). From Witham. Sayers refers back to *The Mind of the Maker*, which Browne had said he was rereading; she distinguishes, again, between her opinions and the Church's; she devotes a paragraph to the possiblity of creation of new matter *ex nihilo,* which is allowable in Church doctrine, although she thinks most physicists would reject it. Sayers refers to his receipt of *The Heart of Stone,* sent as a Christmas card in 1946 (University of Michigan has the copy she sent Browne), saying that she is primarily working on her translation of the *Commedia* and that she indulged herself by doing the *canzoni* in *The Heart of Stone.*

A.15. TLS, 11 February 1947, 1 p. From Witham. Sayers dismisses his statement that he is more interested in her opinion than in Church doctrine as frivolous. She states she does not feel strongly about whether the universe is finite or not, though it seems philosophically sounder to proceed on the assumption that it is until science proves otherwise; modern pamphlets ("Mr. Edward's little pamphlet"?) merely confirm what Aristotle and Aquinas taught about matter and motion. She concludes with a brief comment that other than her translation of Dante, she has written no verse in years.

B. To M[ARJORIE] MORRIS.

B.1. TLS with A corrections and postscript, 19 October 1937, 4 pp. From Witham. Sayers writes about the production of *The Zeal of Thy House,* although she does refer to the prospective visit to Browne at Gipping and thus, with her subsequent letter of 30 October 1937 to Browne (item A.9), provides grounds for dating the postcard described above as c. 25 October 1937 (A.8).

5. Letters in the Houghton Library, Harvard University, ed. Margaret Hannay

A. To [Elkin Nathan] Adler, 1861–1946. [Autograph file.]

A.1. ALS, 7 January 1928. From London. Sayers mentions the endorsement on the Collins ms. of "The Evil Genius" which establishes its authenticity; she is grateful for the loan of the manuscript. See "The Evil Genius" ms. available at Houghton Library, MS Eng 968.1. *Note:* There is a letter from E. N. Adler (of Adler and Perowe, Solicitors and Privy Council Agents, London) to Sayers, 27 June 1928, in the H.R.C., in which he makes an appointment to show Sayers his "Evil Genius." The date on this letter from Sayers therefore may be an error (common enough in early January) for 1929.

B. To John Cournos, 1881–1966. [Autograph file.]

B.1. Eleven ALS, 1924–1925. Restricted; these letters may be consulted only with permission of the Librarian. *Note:* The background of these letters is given in a letter to editor by Alfred W. Satterthwaite, "'Such a Strange Lady,'" *The Times Literary Supplement,* No. 3812 (28 March 1975), 338. "Cournos's liaison with Dorothy Sayers occurred in 1921 and 1922. It was terminated by Cournos, not by Dorothy Sayers, as a series of letters written by Dorothy Sayers to Cournos in 1922 and 1923 clearly demonstrate. . . . Cournos sold these letters to the Houghton Library at Harvard University, to be kept under seal until the death of Dorothy Sayers." Despite the difference in dates, there can be little doubt that these eleven letters are those Satterthwaite refers to.

B.2. ALS, 18 October 1925. From London. Responding to a book by G. K. Chesterton on detective fiction which Cournos had sent her, Sayers discusses problems of plot, love interest, denouement; she mentions *The Moonstone, Trent's Last Case,* "The Invisible Man," and the work of Baroness Orczy, Austin Freeman, Conan Doyle, and Freeman Crofts; she mentions her new book (presumably *Clouds of Witness* [1926]), which is attempting to combine appeal to emotions with appeal to reason. [Important.]

C. To Edgar H. Wells. [bMS Am 1160 (288)]

C.1. ALS, nd, From London. Sayers is looking forward to reading "Stories in Murder"; she accepts a lunch date for herself, and for her husband if he is free.

D. To Alexander Woollcott, 1887–1943. [bMS 1449 (1473)]

D.1. ALS, 7 November 1930. From Witham. Sayers expresses an interest in the Dickens-Collins correspondence, which was never published in England because of the Dickens family; she is working on a preface for Woollcott. (The latter reference is obscure; possibly Sayers was to suggest some critical reading on Collins for Woollcott's "Foreword" to Random House's Modern Library edition of *The Moonstone* and *The Woman in White*. But, if so, there was a delay in publication, for Woollcott's foreword appeared in 1937. He does refer to her projected biography—as well as Lord Peter Wimsey—in his foreword.)

D.2. ALS, 16 May 1931. From Witham. An amusing apology for neglecting to thank him for the Dickens-Collins correspondence. Sayers likes the preface (to the correspondence?—or the one mentioned in the previous letter?); she quotes a Dickens letter to show that he had changed his mind about *The Moonstone*, probably from jealousy; she attributes nasty allusions to Collins to Percy Fitzgerald; and she mentions finding someone whose mother was Collins's first cousin. (This latter refers Mrs. Bertha Long. Sayers learned about Mrs. Long through a 29 April 1931 letter from R. F. Halcomb—which is in the H.R.C.; she did not actually communicate with Mrs. Long and another second cousin, Miss Katherine Linsell, until after this letter to Woollcott. One letter from Miss Linsell and three from Mrs. Long are in the H.R.C.)

D.3. TLS, 1 November 1936. From Witham. Sayers is hoping to finish the Collins biography, but she is currently involved in a Wimsey play, another novel, and a play for the Canterbury Festival.

D.4. TLS, 22 October 1941. From Witham. Sayers is sorry that an acquaintance was disappointed that her latest book was not a detective story, and glad that Woollcott appreciated it.

6. Letters in the Humanities Research Center, The University of Texas at Austin, ed. Joe R. Christopher

The following annotated list is of the letters *by Sayers* in the H.R.C.; also, when the other side of the correspondence is available there, it has been included. In addition to these annotated letters, other letters *to Sayers* are available there: from E[lkan] N[athan] Adler, Frederick Wilse Bateson, Charles J. Bennett, Frank W. Bennett (to Payson and Clarke), Francesco Berger (2 letters), Helen Brown, Montague Bull, Muriel [St. Clare Byrne], Cyril Clemens, Arthur Compton-Rickett (2 letters), John Cournos, Tom Darlow, William H. Dierkes, Jr., Elizabeth D'Oyley (2 letters), J. F. Fenn, Alick Fletcher, H. Haines, R. F. Halcomb, Hugh Harting, W[illiam] Harvey (to A. May Osler; 2 letters), Edmund Sidney P. Haynes (4 letters), the Rev. Canon W. Henderson-Begg (to A. May Osler; 2 letters), Henry Ellinton Humphries (3 letters), the Rev. C. Jones-Bateman (to A. May Osler), Alice Lehmann (3 letters), R. Lercombefiwith (2 letters), Katherine Linsell (to A. May Osler), Bertha Long (to A. May Osler; 3 letters), the Rev. Harry Q. Macqueen, Edward Harry William Meyerstein (2 letters), W. Miller, The Montmartre Gallery, Maurice Newfield, A. May Osler (21 letters), Edwin C[harles] Parker (to A. May Osler), Morris L[ongstrath] Parrish (2 letters and 26 file cards), Frank Lester Pleadwell (3 letters), [H.] Graham Pollard (14 letters), Sir F. Pollock (to E. S. P. Haynes), Myles Radford (6 letters), John S. Rake (2 letters), Michael Sadleir (7 letters), Charles J[ames] Sawyer, Paula Schörke, Hans Sehlbach, William Seymour (4 letters), Squire Sprigge, Dorothy Scott Stokes, Ralph Straus (described in Section 7), F[rederick] Moy Thomas, the Rev. J. E. Tomlinson (to A. May Osler), J. Doman Turnel, Hugh Wheeler (3 letters), Mary Wooten, W. G[reville] Worthington, and an unidentified writer of Bath, England (2 letters). Most of these letters are related to Sayers's research on Collins —A. May Osler worked as Sayers's research assistant, hunting for information about Collins's family, from at least 18 February 1933 to 2 October 1933 —which explains her letters and correspondence with others during that period. But a few of the letters are unrelated to Collins: Maurice Newfield writing about detective stories, for example, or the last two letters, which are largely illegible, personal letters of 1929. For reasons of space, all of these items solely to Sayers are omitted, except for this brief indication of their existence. For further information about the Sayers collection at the H.R.C., see the introductory note to Section 2. I want to thank Professor Robert R. Hodges, of the English Department at California State University at Fullerton, for drawing my attention to Timothy d'Arch Smith's *Love in Earnest,* cited in the note to F.1.

J.R.C.

A. To Mrs. [Marie Adelaide] Belloc Lowndes, 1868–1947.

A.1. ALS, 20 February 1934, 1 p. From London. Sayers thanks her for a copy of a Harcourt, Brace advertisement (presumably for *The Nine Tailors*); Sayers is glad she likes *The Nine Tailors,* an experiment—generally approved—in combining serious writing and the mystery story. Sayers will be happy to meet her for lunch on 27 (February?); it will be nice to see her again.

B. To Ernest Bramah [Smith], 1868–1942.

B.1. TLS with A footnote, 30 January 1931, 1 p. From London; with envelope. Sayers asks Bramah to choose a Max Carrados story for inclusion in the second series of *Great Short Stories of Detection, Mystery and Horror;* she is having the authors choose the stories this time, when possible, and is offering the same British terms as before; in a footnote she asks if he received the money for the first series.

B.2. ALS, 2 February 1931, 1 p. From London; with envelope. Sayers hopes he will be able to disentangle a Carrados story from his jumble of agents and publishers; she suggests dealing directly with him but sending the check to whomever he names; she promises a slight raise in the payment for the second series.

B.3. ALS, 14 April 1931, 2 pp. (1 lf.). From Witham; with envelope. Sayers apologizes for causing him to write twice: the poisoned mushroom story arrived in London safely, but she had come to Essex without his address and could not acknowledge it after arrival; she accepts his suggested title. (The Bramah story which appears in *The Second Omnibus of Crime* is "Who Killed Charlie Winpole?," reprinted from *The Eyes of Max Carrados* —where it is titled "The Mystery of the Poisoned Dish of Mushrooms.")

C. To John Chamson.

C.1. TLS, 14 May 1952, 1 p. From Witham. A two-sentence thank you for a letter praising *The Man Born to Be King.*

D. To The Civil List Pension Fund (Trustees of), London.

D.1. Mimeographed form L/S, Summer 1951, 1 p. n.p. The mimeographed letter recommends John Metcalfe for the Board's consideration. *Note:* This item seems to have come to the H.R.C. through the T. I. Fytton Armstrong collection.

E. To T[ERENCE] I[AN] FYTTON-ARMSTRONG ("JOHN GAWSWORTH"), 1912–1970.

Note: Fytton Armstrong's last name is not usually spelled with a hyphen, and the H.R.C. alphabetizes him under *Armstrong,* but Sayers uses a hyphen in the second letter and presumably, therefore, thinks of the name as compound.

E.1. ALS, 23 December 1930, 1 p. From Witham; with envelope. On a card with a Christmas message printed on the verso. Sayers says that she does not remember where the quotation from A. M. (Arthur Machen?) came from, as she had several books by her at that time; but if she finds it again when she returns to London, she will send the information.

E.2. ALS, 27 January 1931, 1 p. From London. Sayers wishes to borrow a copy of Arthur Machen's *The Great Return* for use in the second volume of her *Great Short Stories of Detection, Mystery and Horror.* ("The Great Return," a seven-chapter novelette or novella, does appear in that volume; it was previously published as a separate volume, 1915).

E.3. TL, July 1957 [added in pencil], 1 p. From Witham. Sayers thanks His Majesty Juan I for an honor bestowed (*Note:* In the bookplate appearing in some of his books in the H.R.C., John Gawsworth has the words "Realm of Redonda," a crown, and, in parenthesis below his name, "H. M. King Juan 1 [*sic*], 1947–   "; further, in a note in a copy of *Great Short Stories of Detection, Mystery and Horror* in the H.R.C., he refers to Sayers as a duchess; thus the likely assumption is that this note from Sayers is in reply to her elevation to Gawsworth's private ranks of nobility); she says she remembers John Gawsworth (before he became King Juan?); she hopes to finish her biography of Collins in her leisurely old age. This final passage is quoted in WC:C&BS (Gregory's Introduction), p. 7. *Note:* An explanation of the Realm of Redonda is offered in *Who's Who in Horror and Fantasy Fiction,* compiled by Mike Ashley (New York: Taplinger, 1978), p. 162, in a listing on M. P. Shiel: "Born in the West Indies, his father conferred on him the title of King of Redonda—an uninhabited islet near Antigua—in 1880. Britain never recognized this and a legal wrangle continued for years. Shiel regarded it as binding, since he later made his friend and biographer, John Gawsworth, his successor." Matthew Phipps Shiel died on 17 February 1947; Fytton-Armstrong seems to have waited ten years before exercising his power to create Sayers a duchess (at least, if the pencilled date is to be trusted).

F. To [LEONARD] GREEN, 1885–1966.

F.1. ALS, 29 August 1919, 2 pp. (1 lf.). From Christ Church Rectory, Disbech, Cambridgeshire ("Cambs"). Sayers replies to a prospectus of a magazine and a request for a contribution on the topic of friendship. She mentions she is just about to leave for France to be a secretary (the date of this letter disagrees by 11 or so days with that given in Janet Hitchman's *Such a Strange Lady* for Sayers's and Eric Whelpton's departure for France; Hitchman gives 18 August 1919 [London: New English Library, 1975, p. 53; New York: Harper and Row, n.d. (1975), p. 36]); Sayers discusses friendships between women, between men, and between a man and a woman for a paragraph; she refers in passing to her contribution to the forthcoming *Oxford Poetry* (Sayers helped edit both *Oxford Poetry, 1918* —which appeared in 1919—and *Oxford Poetry, 1919;* both volumes have works by her;

therefore, unless the former volume can be established as appearing before August 29, either volume is a possibility for this reference); in a postscript, Sayers mentions a mutual acquaintance, D. Bradford. (Probably the magazine in question is the 1920 single issue of *The Quorum: a Magazine of Friendship,* which has a nonpornographic, homosexual bias; Green has two short stories in it, and Sayers — despite this letter, a contributor, and the only female contributor — has a poem, "Veronica." Green is said in Timothy d'Arch Smith's *Love in Earnest* [London: Routledge and Kegan Paul, 1970], p. 140, to be one of the financial backers of the magazine.)

G. TO THE EDITOR OF **The Hornsey Journal** (LONDON).

G.1. TccL, 12 March 1929, 2 pp., n.p. Sayers asks the editor if any of his readers can suggest the private school at Highbury which Collins attended — at which he probably boarded — sometime before 1841. (Sayers did not find an answer to this question; cf. WC:C&BS, p. 45, and Gregory's Introduction, p. 13.)

H. TO EDGAR JEPSON, 1863–1938.

H. 1. TLS, 15 February 1928, 1 p. From London. With an envelope addressed to T. Fytton Armstrong, on which, in pencil, is written Sayers's name and the date 27 January 1931. Sayers requests permission to include Jepson's "The Tea-Leaf" in *Great Short Stories of Detection, Mystery and Horror* and tells him the financial arrangement offered. (Jepson's story is actually a collaboration with Robert Eustace [pseudonym of Dr. Eustace Robert Barton]; it appears in the British edition of the anthology, but in the American version, *The Omnibus of Crime*, "Mr. Belton's Immunity" by the same two authors is substituted.)

I. TO AND FROM RAPHAEL KING, A LONDON RARE-BOOK DEALER.

I.1. From King. TLS, 21 January 1936, 1 p. King sends Sayers typescripts of two letters from Collins to his American publisher; the letters themselves King recently sold.

I.2. To King. TccL, 20 February 1936, 1 p. n.p. Sayers thanks King for the transcripts; she has been too busy to work on her book recently, but hopes to get back to it. This passage is quoted in WC:C&BS (Gregory's Introduction), p. 8.

J. TO AND FROM H[OWARD] S[EAVOY] LEACH, 1887–1948, LIBRARIAN OF LEHIGH UNIVERSITY, BETHLEHEM, PENNSYLVANIA.

J.1. From Leach. TLS with A corrections, 3 July 1928, 1 p. Leach writes in reply to Sayers's letter in *The Times Literary Supplement*, 21 June 1928; he reports an autograph letter in the Lehigh University Library by Collins, and gives a summary of its reference to a story, "The Devil's Spectacles," and offers either a typewritten transcript of all but three illegible words, or a photostat.

J.2. To Leach. TccL, 16 July 1928, 1 p. n.p. Sayers thanks Leach for offering a facsimile of the letter, which seems to refer to a previously unknown story by Collins; she thinks she can probably decipher the three obscure words in the ms., knowing Collins's handwriting.

K. To The Richards Press Ltd.

Note: Sayers sometimes addresses the company as Richards, Grant Ltd. and sometimes as Grant, Richards Ltd., in addition to the form used above.

K.1. TLS, 29 February 1928, 1 p. From London. Sayers explains her purpose in *Great Short Stories of Detection, Mystery and Horror* as that of collecting the basic representative examples; the book has been accepted by Gollancz; she wishes permission to include Arthur Machen's "The Novel of the Black Seal." (Three obscure numbers are written in pencil at the bottom of the page, presumably at the publisher's.)

K.2. TLS, 7 March 1928, 1 p. From London. Sayers acknowledges their letter; Gollancz has abandoned the American edition due to copyright complications; Sayers asks if they will reconsider their fee for an English edition alone; if not, she will seek a shorter Machen story.

K.3. TLS, 2 May 1928, 1 p. From London. Sayers has been waiting to see if there was to be room in the anthology for a story of the length of "The Novel of the Black Seal"; there is, and she agrees to their terms; payment will be on publication, probably mid-September. (There is a pencilled line through the letter and a pencilled notation for the price of the English edition alone—presumably these were added at the publisher's.)

K.4. TLS with A correction, 5 May 1928, 1 p. From London. Sayers asks permission to reprint Ernest Bramah's "The Ghost at Massinham Mansions," explaining her slowness is due to there being a confusion over who published the story; she has already made financial arrangements with Bramah. (There is a pencilled note at one edge of the price to be asked.)

K.5. TLS with A corrections, 10 May 1928, 1 p. From London. Sayers agrees to their fee; payment will be on publication, probably mid-September. (A pencilled line is through the letter; a pencilled note at the bottom indicates none of the fee is to go to the author.)

K.6. TLS with A correction, 24 March 1931, 1 p. From London. Sayers, now preparing the second series of *Great Short Stories of Detection, Mystery and Horror* for Gollancz, asks permission to reprint M. P. Shiel's "The Primate of the Rose" (the story title is not given until the next letter; here Sayers refers to a story about Mr. Smythe in *Here Comes the Lady*—see Ch. VIII of that book).

K.7. TLS, 31 March 1931, 1 p. From London. Sayers, with reference to a phone call and a letter, agrees to their terms, which include the author's fee; she thanks them for offering to send her John Masefield's *A Tarpaulin Muster* for consideration.

K.8. TLS with A correction, 17 April 1931, 1 p. From London. Sayers asks permission to reprint John Masefield's "Anty Bligh" in her anthology; since it is short, she offers a smaller amount than for Shiel's story. (About these 1931 letters: M. P. Shiel's "The Primate of the Rose" appears in the British anthology but not in the American version, *The Second Omnibus of Crime*; John Masefield's "Anty Bligh" appears in both editions.)

L. To J[ohn] H. S. Rowland, 1907–

L.1. ALS, 31 March 1931, 2 pp. (1 lf.). From London; with envelope. Sayers agrees to Rowland using her distinction between a thriller and a detective story; she also agrees to his quoting her analysis of *Trent's Last Case* from *Great Short Stories of Detection, Mystery and Horror*, but, since the passage is fairly long, asks him to also get permission from the publisher. *Note:* The essay or book in which Rowland was planning to use (or did use) these materials has not been identified. In the front of *Criminal Files* (London: Arco Publications, 1957), there is a list of 19 crime novels; it is possible that one of these has an introduction on mystery fiction; but even more likely is an essay published in some journal. Further, it is possible that the journal is Irish, for this letter was sent to Rowland in County Donegal; according to his autobiography, *One Man's Mind: An Autobiographical Record* (London: SCM Press, 1952), Rowland was teaching in a secondary school there at the time (Ch. III; no reference to Sayers appears).

M. TO AND FROM JAMES SANDOE, 1912– , THEN OF BOULDER, COLORADO.

Note: Since letters 4 through 6 below refer to Sandoe's bibliography of Sayers's works (see letter 4 for a full citation), it may be added that the manuscript of this work, as "Bibliography of Dorothy L. Sayers' Works," is available in the Archives and Manuscripts Department of the Harold B. Lee Library, Brigham Young University, Provo, Utah (Mss 317, Box 15, Folder 4). Also in the Sandoe Collection at Utah are about a hundred 4x6 review notes of reviews of Sayers's works, giving information on where they can be found and some information on Sayers herself. (I wish to thank Dennis Rowley, Curator, for these details.)

M.1. To Sandoe. TLS with A corrections, 6 January 1944, 1 p. From Witham; with envelope. Sayers thanks Sandoe for the copies of the Collins letters he sent, commenting that Collins was not as good a letter-writer as Dickens; her Collins mss. are in bank storage due to the war; she would like to see *Ellery Queen's Mystery Magazine*; she may start writing about Lord Peter again after the war. A passage indicating she hopes to return to writing her life of Collins is quoted in WC:C&BS (Gregory's Introduction), p. 8.

M.2. From Sandoe. TccL, 2 February 1944, 2 pp. (1 lf.). Sandoe sends the fifteenth issue of *Ellery Queen's Mystery Magazine*, commenting on Lillian de la Torre's pastiche of Dr. Johnson in it, and indicating he has ordered the earlier copies of *Ellery Queen's Mystery Magazine* for her; he has read P. M. Stone's copies of the spoof pamphlets (*Papers relating to the Family of Wimsey* [1936] and *An Account of Lord Mortimer Wimsey, the Hermit of the Wash* [1938]—there is a typed copy of the first, probably made by Sandoe, in the H.R.C.), noting a variation in the Wimsey motto from the books and an error in when Justice Fielding served in Bow Street; admitting he is working on a bibliography, he asks about *Thrones, Dominations*, mentioned by P. M. Stone to him, and about the use of Johanna Leigh as a pseudonym, mentioned by Anthony Boucher; Sandoe comments on Boucher's *The Case of the Baker Street Irregulars*; he sends a list of fourteen Collins letters.

M.3. To Sandoe. TLS with A corrections, 20 March 1944, 1 p. From Witham; with envelope. Sayers thanks him for the information about the Collins letters, which she promises to file; she comments on the two forms of the Wimsey motto, one older than the other. (She says nothing about *Thrones, Dominations* or Johanna Leigh.)

M.4. From Sandoe. TccLS, 12 April 1944, 1 p. Sandoe thanks her for her note on the motto; he has sent the back issues and current issue of *Ellery Queen's Mystery Magazine*; he praises Anthony Boucher's, and H. H. Holmes's, mysteries, mentioning their single authorship and Boucher's Holmesian criticism; he refers to the notes he encloses (presumably a draft of his bibliography, "Contribution toward a Bibliography of Dorothy L. Sayers," *Bulletin of Bibliography*, 18:4 [May-August 1944], 76–81), apologizing for sending her a carbon.

M.5. From Sandoe. TccL, 28 June 1944, 2 pp. (1 lf.). Sandoe reports that James Keddie has a ms. of "Obsequies for Music" (as described in Sandoe's bibliography, p. 78) and inquires about its publication; he mentions having sent her the bibliographic notes, hoping she will note omissions and observing he has just discovered the variations in the contents of the English and American editions of the *Omnibuses of Crime;* he continues to send her *Ellery Queen's Mystery Magazine* issues and praises Hake Talbot's *Rim of the Pit* as much like and equal to the supernatural-flavored mysteries of John Dickson Carr.

M.6. To Sandoe. TL/copy with T note on verso, 8 August 1944, 2 pp. (1 lf.). From Witham. Sayers thanks Sandoe for his letters and the copies of *Ellery Queen's Mystery Magazine*; she thinks that "Obsequies for Music" may have appeared in *The London Mercury,* but she is not much interested in a work once it is published and so is not good at her own bibliography; she comments (without bibliographic details) on a French edition of *Unnatural Death* with a fox-hunt pictured on the cover and a Spanish, abridged edition of *Murder Must Advertise* with a Spanish-looking Lord Peter; she apologizes for not knowing more about "Obsequies for Music." (Sayers says nothing about the bibliographic notes of Sandoe's letter of 12 April 1944.) The note on the back of this copy of Sayers's letter indicates that the original was sent to James Keddie on 15 September 1944; a copy was sent to P. M. Stone; a search of *The London Mercury* did not reveal "Obsequies for Music." (The search must not have been thorough, for, according to H & B, p. 151, "Obsequies for Music" appeared in *The London Mercury*, vol. 3 [January 1921], 249–53.)

M.7. From Sandoe. TccL, 17 February 1945, 1 p. Sandoe sends an item from the December *Atlantic Monthly* which refers to Lord Anthony Wimsey and a Duke of Dover, and has sent another issue of *Ellery Queen's Mystery Magazine*. (The reference is to Emily V. Wedge, "Title Tale," *The Atlantic Monthly*, 174:6 [December 1944], 117, 119; the Duke of Dover is mentioned twice on p. 119, the second time with reference also to his grand-nephew, Lord Anthony Wimsey — these appear in a biography of an imaginary John Cleveland Cotton, who was invented by Stephen Vincent Benét; since the biography is invented, Benét is presumably alluding to Sayers's fictional world — despite the use of Dover instead of Denver. The issue also contains Raymond Chandler's "The Simple Art of Murder" [pp. 53–59], with its attack on *Busman's Honeymoon* and other references to Sayers; but it is not clear from Sandoe's letter if he sent the whole issue.)

N. TO R[OLFE] A[RNOLD] SCOTT-JAMES, 1878–1959, AT THE LONDON MERCURY.

N.1. TLS, 22 November 1938, 1 p. From Witham. Sayers thanks him for his letter praising the company production of *The Zeal of Thy House*; she gives credit to Harcourt Williams and Frank Napier; she hopes the play can return to London near Christmas but is having troubles finding a theater; for the sake of such noncommercial productions, she wishes the National Theatre were built.

O. TO P. M. STONE, OF WALTHAM, MASSACHUSETTS.

O.1. TLS with A correction, 3 March 1928, 1 p. From London. Sayers thanks Stone for his praise of *The Dawson Pedigree* and for ranking her with Austin Freeman and Freeman Wills-Croft; she says she is not the author of the Van Dine books.

P. TO SIR HUGH WALPOLE, 1884–1941.

P.1. ALS, 24 April 1933, 2 pp. (1 lf.). From Witham. Sayers writes about the seating arrangements at a Detection Club dinner, saying guests may be seated either with their hosts or with a writer they wish to meet. (She has some fun with the his/her reference to a single, unknown guest.) She asks for his guest's preference. (Sayers puts the abbreviation for Honorable Secretary beneath her name.)

P.2. ALS, 30 April 1933, 1 p. (on a card). From Witham. Sayers acknowledges that Walpole's guest, whichever person he brings, will be seated at his table.

P.3. TLS, 3 January 1940, 1 p. From Witham. Sayers gives Sir Hugh permission to use her name—with an L. in it—on his books-and-manuscript committee; she can attend committee meetings, but cannot contribute money or knowledge; she mentions her wartime propaganda; she would like to meet him for lunch in London one day.

Q. TO T[ERENCE] H[ANBURY] WHITE, 1906–1964.

Q.1. TLS, 29 October 1954, 2 pp. From Witham. Sayers says that she had been telling a friend a good defense of the medieval bestiary could be made, and the next day she found, and purchased, White's *The Book of Beasts*; she suggests, tentatively, that the "scutulatus" horse may be dapple-grey (cf. *The Book of Beasts* [New York: G. P. Putnam's Sons, 1954], p. 88, where White identifies it with a question mark as checkered or roan); she appreciates the plausible explanation of the amphisbaena (she refers to the footnote on pp. 177–78); she adds a brief comment about having enjoyed *The Goshawk* (1951).

Q.2. TLS, 15 November 1954, 2 pp. From Witham. Sayers thanks White for his reply, which included the Latin passage she mentioned in her first letter; she doubts that reviewers make much difference in sales, commenting on three reviews of *The Book of Beasts*; she adds some light-hearted comments on the translation of *scutulatus*; she conjectures the manticora's teeth were suggested by a shark (cf. p. 51), with a comment on the makara (p. 252) and an obscure one on Richard Strachey; she quotes from Konrad Lorenz's *King Solomon's Ring*, in which he shows it was not only in the medieval period that writers copy from each other without checking their materials first hand.

Q.3. TLS, 7 December 1954, 1 p. From Witham. Sayers refuses to be badgered about
      detective stories —she had originally meant to write some more, but was so
      badgered by people that the idea nauseates her and she cuts off correspondence with
      those who write her about them; she discusses a passage in Boiardo's *Orlando
      Innamorato* (II.vi.8) where his *fulicetta* is not a heron (this seems to refer back to
      the Physeter and the Pistris in *The Book of Beasts* and the footnote on p. 107); she
      refers to an antimedieval review (probably of *The Book of Beasts*), in which the
      writer makes an error about photography.

Q.4. TLS, 13 December 1954, 2 pp. From Witham. Sayers expands on material in her
      previous letter, particularly the passage in Boiardo which she quotes, giving
      information about the edition she is using.

7. Letters in the Special Collections Department, Northwestern University Library, ed. R. Russell Maylone

The Ralph Straus Collection at Northwestern contains the following three letters and solitary postcard from Sayers; Northwestern does not have the other side of the correspondence. The interest in Dickens expressed in the first two letters is reflected in Straus's earlier and later studies, *Dickens: A Portrait in Pencil* (1928) and *Dickens, the Man and the Book* (1936); and the discussion of the Sala letter prepares one for *Sala: The Portrait of an Eminent Victorian* (1942). The reference in the second letter to the third chapter of WC:C&BS tends to confirm Gregory's dating of the writing of that work (WC:C&BS, p. 8).

In connection with his work on Section (6), Christopher has located one letter from Straus to Sayers in the H.R.C., predating those below, which may be recorded here: ALS, 5 March (?) 1931, 1 p. Straus sends information about a meeting (unidentified) at which he will say a few words, someone named Elwin will speak, and then Sayers will speak; after which Straus will close the meeting; Sayers is invited to eat with Straus before or after the meeting. (Gregory suggests that "Elwin" may be Malcolm Elwin, whose "Wilkie Collins: the Pioneer of the Thriller" appeared in *The London Mercury* in 1931.)

The letters following are clearer than the references in Straus's letter, but the postcard rivals it for obscurity.

R. R. M.

A. ALL TO RALPH STRAUS (1882–1950).

A.1. ALS, 16 March 1932, 2 pp. From Witham. Sayers thanks Straus for an enjoyable evening, says that as she left she remembered all the details of the Sala letter to Collins, and has made a copy of it for her work and he is welcome to the original; she will probably want to refer to it in her book by saying that it was often rumored that Collins was going to finish *The Mystery of Edwin Drood*, and a French "translation" purported to be his completion was published. She asks about some of the obscurities in the letter, jokes about the plumbing associations of the initials of G. A. Sala and W. Collins, and gives an approximate date for the letter (from the publication date of the French "translation").

A.2. ALS, 22 March 1932, 2 pp. From London. Sayers is happy that Straus likes the Sala letter; she mentions a French doctor, Dr. Dorosae, who published Dickens' last book in France under his own name, and who also borrowed a Scottish family motto for his own; she turns down an offer of a first edition of *Heart and Science*, for her own copy is in equal condition—but she mentions several first editions she does need; she closes with a statement that she is wrestling with Chapter Three of WC:C&BS (cf. the first paragraph of the introductory note to this section).

A.3. ALS, 27 April 1934, 2 pp. From Witham. Sayers writes that the plans for the Detection Club Dinner have fallen through because the speakers, all police and lawyers, cannot attend: the Honorable Secretary (i.e., Sayers) is quite distracted and wonders if Straus can participate in a literary panel—to give a five-minute reply on behalf of reviewers to a toast to literary agents, publishers, reviewers, and literary subscribers—even though it is on such short notice.

A.4. ALS, 12 December 1939, 1 p. (a postcard). From Witham. Sayers thanks Straus for an excellent evening; she suggests that an anonymous book might work if it combined a saeva indignatio with strict factualness.

Notes

CRIME AND PUNISHMENT IN THE DETECTIVE FICTION OF DOROTHY L. SAYERS

1. Of course, in *Have His Carcase* (1932), we have a murder case generally perceived as a suicide, but this is not a relevant consideration here. It is interesting, though, that this case is just the reverse of the situation in *Clouds of Witness*.
2. "IV, A Full Peal of Kent Treble Bob Major, The Third Part."
3. "IV, A Full Peal . . . The First Part."
4. "IV, A Full Peal . . . The Third Part."
5. Sayers, *Introductory Papers on Dante*, p. 68.
6. Sayers, *The Mind of the Maker*, p. 78.
7. Ibid., p. 79.
8. Ibid.
9. Sayers, "Creed or Chaos?" Sec. 7 "Society."
10. "Post Mortem."
11. "Epithalamion, 1."
12. "Epithalamion, 3."

THE AGENTS OF EVIL AND JUSTICE IN THE NOVELS OF DOROTHY L. SAYERS

1. See her *Poetry of Search and the Poetry of Statement*, pp. 237–38, 240.
2. *Unpopular Opinions*, p. 180. Some years before, in *Strong Poison*, ch. 12, Lord Peter exclaims: "Damn it, [Harriet Vane] writes detective stories, and in detective stories virtue is always triumphant. They're the purest literature we have." See also Sayers's radio broadcast of 29 December 1931 (reprinted in *The Listener* [6 January 1932], p. 26): "Do you realise that, as a class, we are the only novelists who have ever really succeeded in making the virtuous characters more interesting than the wicked ones? From that point of view, Conan Doyle is a much better influence than Milton. Satan is undoubtedly the hero of 'Paradise Lost,' but Sherlock Holmes is not merely more virtuous, but infinitely more interesting and exciting than Professor Moriarty."
3. On the difference between great literature and that which is merely edifying or propagan-

distice see Sayers's "Towards a Christian Aesthetic," in *Unpopular Opinions,* and also her *Mind of the Maker,* p. 53.

4. See *Mind of the Maker,* pp. 130–32.

5. Dorothy L. Sayers, ed., *The Omnibus of Crime* (New York: Payson and Clarke, 1929), p. 38.

6. This development in the form as a whole Sayers herself predicts in *The Omnibus of Crime,* p. 43.

NINE TAILORS AND THE COMPLEXITY
OF INNOCENCE

An earlier version of this paper was read before the Houghton English Colloquium in February 1974; I should like to thank Professor Eugene Warren, University of Missouri–Rolla, who responded to the paper at that meeting, for his helpful observations.

1. Sayers stated her intentions for these novels in a 1937 essay, "Gaudy Night," usefully reprinted in Howard Haycraft's *The Art of the Mystery Story* (New York: Simon and Schuster, 1946), pp. 208–21.

2. "The Great Detective Stories," in Haycraft, *Art,* p. 35.

3. All quotations are from the first American edition (New York: Harcourt, Brace, 1934), and are annotated by chapter; "The Bells Are Rung Up."

4. G. K. Chesterton, *Generally Speaking* (New York: Dodd, Mead, 1929), p. 6; Sayers, "Emile Gaboriau 1835–1873: The Detective Novelist's Dilemma," *Times Literary Supplement,* 1761 (2 November 1935), 678; "Introduction," *The Omnibus of Crime* (New York: Payson & Clarke, 1929), p. 37.

5. *The Nine Tailors,* "The Bells in Their Courses."

6. *Ibid.,* "The Quick Work."

7. *Ibid.,* "Lord Peter Follows Course Bell."

8. *Ibid.,* "The Bells Are Rung Up."

9. First American edition (New York: Harcourt, Brace, 1941), p. 118.

10. *The Nine Tailors,* "The Bells in Their Courses."

11. *Ibid.,* "The Waters Are Called Out."

12. *Ibid.,* "The Waters Are Called Home."

13. *Ibid.,* "The Slow Work."

14. *The Dyer's Hand, and Other essays* (New York: Random House, 1962), pp. 146–58.

15. *The Nine Tailors,* "The Waters Are Called Home."

16. Auden, *Dyer's,* p. 157.

HARRIET'S INFLUENCE ON THE CHARACTERIZATION
OF LORD PETER WIMSEY

1. "A Sport of Noble Minds," *Life and Letters,* IV(Jan. 1930), p. 47. This is nearly identical with her introduction to *The Omnibus of Crime.*

2. On Sayers's debt to E. C. Bentley's Philip Trent, see Barbara Reynolds, "The Origin of Lord Peter Wimsey," *Times Literary Supplement,* 22 April 1977, p. 492.

3. John Strachey, "The Golden Age of English Detection," *The Saturday Review,* 7 January 1939, p. 13. Comparing Sayers with Marjorie Allingham, Strachey declares: "She [Allingham] too, has a preposterous young aristocrat as her detective hero. But her love . . . for her paramour of the imagination is more controlled, less wild, less ecstatic than that of Miss Sayers for her Lord Peter. I can express the difference, perhaps, by saying that whereas Dorothy Sayers has endowed her hero with a title and monocle, Marjorie Allingham makes hers merely the nephew of a duke, and gives him horn-rimmed spectacles." See also W. W. Robson, *Modern English Literature* (London:

Oxford University Press, 1970), p. 146, who claims that Sayers "began with some excellent detective stories, which deteriorated when she fell in love with her aristocratic detective and wrote, in *Gaudy Night* (1935) the worst readable novel in the English language, with the exception of its successor, *Busman's Honeymoon* (1937)."

4.   "Craft of Detective Fiction," unpublished notes for an address, n.p., in the Wade Collection, Wheaton College. Although the manuscript is undated, it mentions the play *Busman's Honeymoon*.

5.   Q. D. Leavis, "The Case of Miss Dorothy Sayers," *Scrutiny* 63 (December 1937), pp. 334–35.

6.   W. H. Auden, "The Guilty Vicarage," *The Dyer's Hand, and Other Essays* (New York: Random House, 1962), p. 154. See also G. Legman in *Love and Death: A Study in Censorship* (New York: Hacker Art Books, 1963), p. 72, which calls Lord Peter "the most disgusting snob in English literature."

7.   "Gaudy Night," *Titles to Fame*, ed. D. K. Roberts (London: Thomas Nelson and Sons, 1937), p. 75.

8.   *Whose Body?* (1923), ch. 1.

9.   *Clouds of Witness*, ch. 4.

10.   *The Unpleasantness at the Bellona Club* (1928), ch. 1.

11.   "Gaudy Night," pp. 77–78.

12.   *The Mind of the Maker* (1941; rpt. Westport, Connecticut: Greenwood Press, 1970), p. 69.

13.   "Gaudy Night," p. 91. Note that within the novel *Gaudy Night* Harriet attempts to justify her continued detective writing by economic realities: "Writers can't pick and choose until they've made money. If you've made your name for one kind of book and then switch over to another, your sales are apt to go down, and that's the brutal fact" [ch. 2]. As her unpublished letter to Woollcott makes clear, Sayers realized that many readers would be disappointed when she wrote something other than detective novels (letter dated 11.5.31, in the Houghton Library at Harvard University). Note also that Harriet is pressured by Peter to "abandon the jig-saw kind of story and write a book about human beings for a change" [ch. 15]. This is, of course, what Sayers herself is attempting.

14.   "Gaudy Night," p. 81.

15.   *Whose Body?*, ch. 7.

16.   *Unnatural Death* (1927), ch. 19.

17.   *Strong Poison* (1930), ch. 10.

18.   *Gaudy Night* (1936), ch. 2. Note that this discussion leads into the value of work done for enjoyment—an important theme in Sayers's prose and drama. Thus the problem of the amateur detective who investigates murders as a hobby is fitted into the larger question of whether one should work for money or for the love of the work itself.

19.   "Craft of Detective Fiction." Critics have been irritated with just how thoroughly despicable this criminal is. See, for example, Ralph Partridge, "Gaudy Night," *New Statesman and Nation*, 16 November 1935, pp. 740–41, who complains that "the criminal betrays himself at once by Miss Sayers' dislike of him, in striking contrast to her maternal affection for her other characters."

20.   *Busman's Honeymoon* (1937), "Epithalamion," ch. III.

21.   It is interesting to compare this impersonal passion with Mary's description of Cathcart's lovemaking in *Clouds of Witness*: "Frightfully hot stuff, but absolutely impersonal" [ch. 9].

22.   *Busman's Honeymoon*, "Epithalamion," ch. II. Contrasting this account of Bunter's arrival with that given by Peter in *The Unpleasantness at the Bellona Club* [ch. 7], demonstrates the added depth that Sayers has given to her character.

23.   In "Gaudy Night" Sayers mentions an indignant letter from a reader who was upset that Peter had lost "all his elfin charm." Sayers replied "any man who retained elfin charm at the age of forty-five should be put in a lethal chamber. Indeed, Peter escaped that lethal chamber by inches" [pp. 80–81]. But the character himself must, of course, resent the loss of his youth.

24.   Edith Hamilton, "Gaudeamus Igitur," *The Saturday Review,* 22 February 1936, p. 6. Hamilton observes that "if Miss Sayers does intend to take to another sort of fiction . . . she will have to give us a different Lord Peter—and oh, what a loss."

25.   *Gaudy Night,* ch. 19. Sayers clearly meant this incident to show weakness, not strength. In "Gaudy Night" she mentions "his resentment of his small stature and its compensating outbursts of childish exhibitionism" [p. 86].

26.   "Gaudy Night," p. 22. By contrast, Harriet is intended to portray "the creative artist; her make-up is more stable than his, and far more capable of self-dependence. On the surface he is a comedian; his dislocation is at the centre; she is tragic externally, for all her dissatisfactions are patent, but she has the central unity which he has not."

27.   *Thrones, Dominations,* unpublished holograph manuscript in the Wade Collection, Wheaton College. No pagination.

28.   With the publication of *Gaudy Night,* Sayers's loss to the detective novel had already been bewailed by critics who disliked the intrusion of the novel into the detective story. Mary McCarthy declared that "Her venture into the novelist's field is exactly as regrettable . . . as the stage debut of a drawing-room mimic" ("Highbrow Shockers," *Nation,* 8 April 1936, p. 458). Gilbert Norwood regrets that in *Gaudy Night* "the detection part has dwindled, while the strictly novelistic side has been vastly enlarged. But neither element has been improved. . . . As a result, our delightful friend Lord Peter himself is almost crowded out, which is calamitous." Unaccountably, Norwood finds *Busman's Honeymoon,* with even less emphasis on detection "Miss Sayers' finest book," ("Peter and Harriet," *The Canadian Forum,* April 1937, p. 30).

WILKIE COLLINS AND DOROTHY L. SAYERS

1.   Some of the following material I draw from the introduction to my edition of Sayers's *Wilkie Collins* (Toledo: Friends of the Univ. of Toledo Libraries, 1977).

2.   Letter from Ellen S. Dunlap, Research Librarian, HRC, 11 November 1976, to me.

3.   The date, which is penciled in, is not in Sayers's handwriting, so it may be erroneous.

4.   Letter from Livia Gollancz, 7 September 1976, to me.

5.   The description of the manuscript and extracts from it were included in a letter to me from Anthony Fleming, 15 October 1977.

6.   Letter of 12 July 1948, in possession of Mr. Ashley.

7.   The files of Everyman Library contain a letter from Sayers's agents—Pearn, Pollinger, and Higham—that is so dated and confirms Everyman's offer to her. Jocelyn Burton, Everyman Editorial Manager, conveyed this information to me in a letter of 15 December 1976.

8.   (London: J. M. Dent, 1944), p. viii.

9.   These facts I gleaned from Professor Christopher's description of the notebook in the bibliography that appears with this collection of essays (Item II, B, 1), p. 247.

10.   *Unpopular Opinions,* p. 182.

11.   The incident referred to occurs in the Fourth Narrative of the Second Period, pp. 380–81 in the Everyman Library edition. One example of Munting's self-deprecation is his comment that a manuscript of his "could write its memoirs by this time: *Pigeon-holes I Have Lived in*" [section 17].

12.   *Unpopular Opinions,* pp. 29–43. In this essay, she expresses her conviction on this point in a number of ways: "even if you get an exact representation of something—say a documentary film about a war, or an exact verbal reproduction of a scene at the Old Bailey—that's not the same thing as *Coriolanus* or the trial scene in *The Merchant of Venice*" [p. 33]; the *Agamemnon* "is not the copy or imitation of something bigger and more real than itself. It is bigger and more real than the real-life action that it represents" [p. 36]; "the true work of art . . . is not primarily the copy or representation of anything" [pp. 36–37].

13.   On p. 42 of her introduction to the *Purgatory,* for example, she quotes with approval Sir

Arthur Quiller-Couch's observation that the greatest art is "seraphically free/from taint of personality" [Penguin edition, 1955].

14. Introduction to *The Omnibus of Crime* (New York: Harcourt, Brace, 1929), p. 22.

15. William H. Marshall, *Wilkie Collins* (New York: Twayne, 1970), pp. 81, 85.

16. Sayers's notebooks in the HRC indicate that during this period, she was very much aware of point of view in fiction. See Professor Christopher's summary of the notebook described under II, B, 6 (p, 247). Some of her notes, still in the possession of Anthony Fleming, indicate that she got the basic idea for the plot from the famous Thompson-Bywaters trial of the early 1920s. Her library contained Filson Young's *Trial of Frederick Bywaters and Edith Thompson* (Notable British Trial Series, 1923), and Mr. Fleming has suggested that the importance of the letters in the trial may also have been a factor in Sayers's use of the documentary form (letter of 17 December 1977).

17. Curiously enough, despite the care she took, she and her collaborator (Dr. Eustace Robert Barton) got their chemistry wrong after all. See Harold Hart, "Accident, Suicide, or Murder? A Question of Stereochemistry," *Journal of Chemical Education*, 52 (1975), 444. Miss Sayers and Dr. Barton knew about the blunder. The Wade Collection contains a letter from Barton to Sayers, 2 June 1931, in which he gives "the final and authoritative dictum" about muscarine and apologizes for his error. Sayers touched lightly on the matter in "Trials and Sorrows of a Mystery Writer," *The Listener*, 6 January 1932, p. 26.

18. Janet Hitchman, *Such a Strange Lady* (London: New English Library, 1975), p. 76.

19. Mary Ellen Chase, "Five Literary Portraits," *Massachusetts Review,* 3 (Autumn 1961–Summer 1962), 514.

20. "The Poetry of the Image in Dante and Charles Williams," *Further Papers on Dante*, p. 190.

21. *"Gaudy Night," The Art of the Mystery Story*, ed. Howard Haycraft (New York: Simon and Schuster, 1946), p. 219.

22. The first quotation appears in chapter IV of the unfinished biography; the second in her essay,"' . . . And Telling you a Story': a Note on *The Divine Comedy,"* in *Essays presented to Charles Williams* (London: Oxford Univ. Press, 1947), p. 7.

23. John G. Cawelti, *Adventure, Mystery, and Romance* (Chicago: Univ. of Chicago Press, 1976), p. 121.

24. "The Eighth Bolgia," *Further Papers on Dante*, p. 102.

25. Hesketh Pearson, *Dickens* (New York: Harper, 1949), p. 210.

26. This and the above letter are both in the possession of Mr. Robinson.

27. Professor Reynolds told me this in private conversation last summer (1976).

THE WORD MADE FLESH: THE CHRISTIAN AESTHETIC OF DOROTHY L. SAYERS'S THE MAN BORN TO BE KING

1. Cf. "Problem Picture," in *The Mind of the Maker* (New York: Meridian Books, 1956), pp. 175 ff. where Sayers discusses the simplistic view of the world detective fiction provides.

2. "Creed or Chaos?" in *Creed or Chaos* (New York: Harcourt, Brace, 1949), p. 28. Dr. J. R. Welch, in his Foreword to Sayers's *The Man Born to Be King: A Play-Cycle on the Life of our Lord and Saviour Jesus Christ* (London: Victor Gollancz, 1944), cites an army recruit who believed one of the Gospel writers to be Karl Marx.

3. "Playwrights Are Not Evangelists," *World Theatre*, I (Winter, 1955–56), pp. 61–66.

4. In *Unpopular Opinions* (London: Victor Gollancz, 1946), pp. 29–43.

5. The concluding speech of St. Michael in *The Zeal of Thy House* as quoted by Sayers in "Idea, Energy, Power," *The Mind of the Maker*, p. 47.

6. *The Man Born to Be King* (Eerdmans), Introduction, p. 4. Citations to the Introduction will be made from this edition.

7. The Lord Chamberlain, to whom a BBC religious advisor, Dr. Welch, appealed, exempted

the radio play from the general prohibition applicable to stage plays on the grounds that since no audience would be present, the situation was analogous to a minister's recitation of the Gospels from the pulpit and therefore no impersonation would be implied.

8.   Welch, p. 15.

9.   "The Faust Legend and the Idea of the Devil," *Poetry of Search and the Poetry of Statement* (London: Victor Gollancz, 1963), p. 229.

10.   *The Man Born to Be King,* Intro., p. 2.

11.   *The Man Born to Be King,* Intro., p. 7.

12.   Unlike the ironies in Greek tragedy, the historical life of Christ needs no *deus ex machina:* "By no jugglings of fate, by no unforeseeable coincidence, by no supernatural machinations, but by that destiny which is character, and by the unimaginative following of their ordinary standards of behavior, the Roman and Jewish leaders were led, with ghastly inevitability, to the commission of the crime of crimes." *(The Man Born to Be King,* Intro., p. 5).

13.   "The Greatest Drama Ever Staged," *Creed or Chaos,* p. 3.

14.   "The Greatest Drama Ever Staged," *Creed or Chaos,* p. 3.

15.   "The whole effect and character of the play depend on its being played in an absolutely natural and realistic style. Any touch of the ecclesiatical intonation or of 'religious unction' will destroy its intention. The whole idea in writing it was to show the miracle that was to change the whole course of human life enacted in a world casual, inattentive, contemptuous, absorbed in its own affairs and completely unaware of what was happening: to illustrate, in fact, the tremendous irony of history," [*He That Should Come.* London: Victor Gollancz, 1939, p. 9.] Though this play is predominantly in the realistic mode, its verse form and use of songs elevate it above strict theatrical realism.

16.   *The Man Born to Be King,* Intro., p. 16.

17.   The Roman centurion appearing in Matt. 8:5-13 serves as one certain, though skeletal, source for Proclus.

18.   "Kings of Judea," *The Man Born to Be King,* iii.

19.   "The Heirs to the Kingdom," *The Man Born to Be King,* ii.

20.   Notes to "Royal Progress," *The Man Born to Be King.*

21.   "King of Sorrows," *The Man Born to Be King,* ii, seq. 5.

22.   Cf. Matt. 10.4; 26.25; John 6.71; 12.4; and Luke 6.16.

23.   Matt. 26.14-16; Mark 14.10-11; John 12.4-6.

24.   Luke 22.3-6; John 13.2; 27.

25.   John 12.6.

26.   Matt. 27.3-5.

27.   Notes to "The King's Herald," *The Man Born to Be King.*

28.   Notes to "The Heirs to the Kingdom," *The Man Born to Be King.*

29.   "Kings in Judea," *The Man Born to Be King,* i.

30.   "The Bread of Heaven," *The Man Born to Be King,* i.

31.   "The Feast of Tabernacles," *The Man Born to Be King,* ii, seq. 3.

32.   "The King's Supper," *The Man Born to Be King,* i.

33.   "The Heirs to the Kingdom," *The Man Born to Be King,* ii, seq. 2. Note that there is more than a hint of medieval caricature in this assessment of Judas.

34.   "The Bread of Heaven," *The Man Born to Be King,* i.

35.   "The Princes of this World," *The Man Born to Be King,* ii, seq. 3.

THE MAN BORN TO BE KING: DOROTHY L. SAYERS'S BEST MYSTERY PLOT

1.   Barbara Reynolds, "Lecture Series on Dorothy L. Sayers As Translator and Interpreter of Dante," (Wheaton College, Wheaton, Illinois: 26 July, 2 August, and 9 August 1976).

2.   "The Translation of Verse," *Poetry of Search and Poetry of Statement*, p. 128.

3. *The Man Born to Be King*, Introduction, p. 3.

4. Roderick Jellema, compiler, *Christian Letters to a Post-Christian World*, p. viii.

5. *The Man Born to Be King*, Introduction, p. 15.

6. Papers in the Marion Wade Collection, Mss. *The Man Born to Be King*, "The King's Herald," (Wheaton College, Wheaton, Illinois: © Anthony Fleming, 1978).

7. *The Man Born to Be King,* "The King's Herald," Scene III, p. 73.

8. *The Man Born to Be King*, "The Heirs to the Kingdom," Notes, p. 101.

9. "Divine Comedy," *Unpopular Opinions*, p. 22.

10. *The Man Born to Be King*, "The Heirs to the Kingdom," Notes, p. 99.

11. *The Man Born to Be King*, "The Heirs to the Kingdom," Scene I, p. 108.

12. Papers in the Marion Wade Collection, Mss. *The Man Born to Be King*, "The Heirs to the Kingdom," Scene I.

13. *The Man Born to Be King*, "The Bread of Heaven," Scene 5, p. 145.

14. Papers in the Marion Wade Collection, Mss. *The Man Born to Be King*, "The Feast of Tabernacles," Scene I, Sequence 2.

15. *The Man Born to Be King*, "The Princes of This World," Scene II, p. 266.

16. *The Man Born to Be King*, Introduction, p. 21.

Dorothy L. Sayers and the Drama of Orthodoxy

1. Roderick Jellema, compiler, *Christian Letters to a Post-Christian World: A Selection of Essays by Dorothy L. Sayers* (Grand Rapids, Michigan: William B. Eerdmans, 1969). Dorothy L. Sayers, *The Man Born to Be King*.

2. "The Devil to Pay," in *Four Sacred Plays* (London: Victor Gollancz, 1948), p. 7.

3. "Creed or Chaos," in Jellema, *Christian Letters*, p. 31.

4. *Ibid.*, p. 32.

5. "The Dogma Is the Drama," in Jellema, *Christian Letters*, p. 26.

6. *The Man Born to Be King*, p. 8.

7. "He That Should Come," in *Four Sacred Plays*, p. 225. Subsequent references will be placed in the body of the essay.

8. "The Zeal of Thy House," in *Four Sacred Plays*, p. 31. Subsequent references will be placed in the body of the essay.

9. Charles Moorman, *The Precincts of Felicity* (Gainesville: University of Florida Press, 1966), p. 126.

10. "The Devil to Pay," in *Four Sacred Plays*, p. 113. Subsequent references will be placed in the body of the essay.

11. "The Faust Legend and the Idea of the Devil," in Jellema, *Christian Letters,* p. 233.

12. *Ibid.*, pp. 225–26.

13. *Ibid.*, p. 226.

14. "The Just Vengeance," in *Four Sacred Plays*, p. 280. Subsequent references will be placed in the body of the essay.

15. Moorman, *Precincts of Felicity*, p. 131.

16. *The Emperor Constantine: A Chronicle* (1951; rpt. Grand Rapids, Michigan: William B. Eerdmans, 1976), p. 6. Subsequent references will be placed in the body of the essay.

Dorothy L. Sayers as a Translator of *Le Roman de Tristan* and *La Chanson de Roland*

1. "Miss Lydgate's manner was exactly what it had always been. To the innocent and candid eyes of that great scholar, no moral problem seemed ever to present itself. Of a scrupulous personal

integrity, she embraced the irregularities of other people in a wide unquestioning charity. As any student of literature must, she knew all the sins of the world by name, but it was doubtful whether she recognized them when she met them in real life. It was as though a misdemeanour committed by a person she knew was disarmed and disinfected by the contact. So many young people had passed through her hands, and she had found so much good in all of them . . ." [*Gaudy Night*, ch. 1.].

2. "The English tutor's room was festooned with proofs of her forthcoming work on the prosodic elements in English verse from Beowulf to Bridges. Since Miss Lydgate had perfected, or was in process of perfecting (since no work of scholarship ever attains a static perfection) an entirely new prosodic theory, demanding a novel and complicated system of notation which involved the use of twelve different varieties of type; and since Miss Lydgate's handwriting was difficult to read and her experience in dealing with printers limited, there existed at that moment five successive revises in galley form, at different stages of completion, together with two sheets in page-proof, and an appendix in typescript, while the important Introduction which afforded the key to the whole argument still remained to be written. It was only when a section had advanced to page-proof condition that Miss Lydgate became fully convinced of the necessity of transferring large paragraphs of argument from one chapter to another, each change of this kind naturally demanding expensive over-running on the page-proof and the elimination of the corresponding portions in the five sets of revises; so that in the course of the necessary cross-reference, Miss Lydgate would be discovered by her pupils and colleagues wound into a kind of paper cocoon and helplessly searching for her fountain-pen amid the litter' [*Gaudy Night,* ch. 3].

3. *Op. I*, p. 59.

4. *Op. I*, p. 29.

5. *Op. I*, p. 35.

6. E.g., the fact that he makes Mark King of Cornwall and of England, and that he praises London so highly, 2651-63.

7. Claude Luttrell, *The Creation of the first Arthurian Romance: a Quest* (Arnold, 1974), p. 32.

8. Ernest Muret suggested 1165 to 1170 for the main part of Béroul's *Le roman de Tristan* and 1190-91 or later for the continuator: see the introduction to his *C.F.M.A.* edition, 1903, reprinted in 1922, p. ix; and the introduction to his *S.A.T.F.* edition, 1903, pp. lxiv-v.

9. Cil qui fist . . .
    Del roi Marc et d'Ysalt la blond, . . . *Cligés,* 1 & 5.

10. *Tristan in Brittany*, p. xxxiv.

11. *Ibid.*, p. xxxii.

12. *Ed. cit.*, II, p. 94.

13. In her lecture "The Translation of Verse," given to the Oxford University English Club on 6 March 1957 and published posthumously in *The Poetry of Search and the Poetry of Statement*, Gollancz, 1963, pp. 127–53, she tells how she had prepared a rhymed translation of *La chanson de Roland* "shortly after going down" [p. 127]. She then goes on to say that *Tristan in Brittany,* which was "begun not very much later, took a less unconscionable time in being born. It was actually done [i.e., completed?] and published in 1929. It brought no great financial reward and is now hopelessly out of print" [*ibid.*].

14. There is some significance in the fact that *Whose Body?* (1923), *Clouds of Witness* (1926), *Unnatural Death* (1927) and *Tristan in Brittany* (1929) were published by Ernest Benn, while *The Unpleasantness at the Bellona Club* (1928), *Lord Peter Views the Body* (1928) and all the later novels were published by Gollancz. All Benn's records were destroyed by enemy action in 1940.

15. *Tristan in Brittany*, p. xxxiv.

16. *Ibid.*, p. xxx.

17. *Ibid.*, 2535-71.

18. *Ibid.*, 3011-42.

19. *Ibid.*, p. xxx.

20. *Ibid.*, pp. xxx-xxxi.

21. *Ibid.*, pp. 92–93. Cf. the same passage in Bédier, *op. cit.*, Vol. I, pp. 203–04.

22. *Ibid.*, pp. xxix-xxx.

23. *Ibid.*, p. xxx.

24. *Ibid.*, 179–214.

25. *Ibid.*, 2651–52.

26. *Ibid.*, p. xxix.

27. *Ibid.*

28. Later on I prepared the index for *Further Papers on Dante*, which Methuen published in 1957.

29. On 30 July 1956, for example, she wrote: "Looking forward very much to seeing you and chewing it all over."

30. See note 13 above. The quotation is from p. 127.

31. *The Song of Roland*, p. 45. Mildred Pope died in September 1956 and so did not live to see the finished work. In a letter dated 23 August 1956, Dorothy Sayers wrote: "I am afraid that there is no hurry about it, as I hear from Miss Kempson that Miss Pope's progress has not been maintained, and they fear that she cannot now hope to make any sort of recovery. This is sad, though I suppose that she could not in any case have lived very long."

32. *La chanson de Roland, publiée d'après le manuscrit d'Oxford et traduite par Joseph Bédier*, Piazza, Paris, first published 1922.

33. *The Song of Roland*, p. 39.

34. *Ibid.*, p. 8.

35. *The Song of Roland*, 1152–64.

36. *Ibid.*, pp. 16–17.

37. *The Song of Roland*, p. 19.

38. Gaston Paris, *Extraits de la chanson de Roland*, Paris, first published in 1887, p. xxviii.

39. G. Lytton Strachey, *Landmarks in French Literature*, first published Home University Library, 1912, p. 10.

40. *The Song of Roland*, p. 27.

41. *Ibid.*, 2259–70.

42. *Ibid.*, 2366–96.

43. It was in this periodical that I published "The Beatrician Vision on Dante and other poets," "On translating the *Divina Commedia*," (Volume II, 1958), "The art of translating Dante" and "The 'Terrible' Ode" (Volume IX, 1965). The first two were reprinted in *The Poetry of Search and the Poetry of Statement*, Gollancz, 1963.

44. This was printed in *The Poetry of Search and the Poetry of Statement*, pp. 127–53.

DOROTHY L. SAYERS, INTERPRETER OF DANTE

This article is a digest of lectures originally delivered at Wheaton College, Illinois, in August 1976.

1. "And Telling You a Story," *Further Papers on Dante*, p. 1.

2. *Ibid.*, p. 2; my italics.

3. Letter dated 5 January 1955.

4. *Further Papers*, p. 2.

5. *Ibid.*, p. 2.

6. Penguin Classics, *Divine Comedy,* I, 9.

7. *Further Papers*, p. 6.

8. *Ibid.*, p. 7.

9. *Ibid.*, p. 10.

10. *Ibid.*, p. 15.

11. *Ibid.*, p. 19.

12. *Ibid.*, p. 20.

13. *Ibid.*, p. 21; parenthesis in the original text. See also the masterly article "The Comedy of the *Comedy*" in *Introductory Papers on Dante*, pp. 151–78.

14. *Further Papers*, p. 22.

15. Letter dated 22 October 1947.

16. *Further Papers*, p. 102.

17. At the summer School of Italian organized at Jesus College, Cambridge in August 1946.

18. See for instance "The Fourfold Interpretation of the *Comedy*," in *Introductory Papers*, pp. 101–26.

19. "The City of Dis," *Introductory Papers*, p. 128.

20. *Ibid.*, p. 129.

21. "The Fourfold Interpretation of the Comedy," *Introductory Papers*, p. 112.

22. *Ibid.*, pp. 119–20.

THROUGH A DARK WOOD OF CRITICISM: THE RATIONALE AND RECEPTION OF DOROTHY L. SAYERS'S TRANSLATION OF DANTE

1. Chaucer retells the story of Count Ugolino in the Tower [*Inf.* XXXIII] in about 60 lines in *The Monk's Tale*; the Hymn to Our Lady appears in the Prolog to *Second Nun's Tale* and is modelled on *Paradiso* XXXIII, 1–21. Miss Sayers points out these parallels in "The Art of Translating Dante," *Nottingham Medieval Studies*, ed. Lewis Thorpe, 9 (1965), 15ff, where she discusses Gray and alludes to Huggins.

2. Of this translation, Sayers comments that it is in "very blank" verse and "its author displays a mastery of the split infinitive which can seldom have been equalled." *Ibid.*, p. 19.

3. William J. DeSua, *Dante into English: A Study of the Translation of the Divine Comedy in Britain and America* (Chapel Hill: University of North Carolina Press, 1964), p. 23ff for much of the information in this and the next three paragraphs. The statistics on the number and kinds of translations have been compiled from DeSua's bibliography by the present writer.

4. Dorothy Sayers thought that the neoclassic critics found Dante "wild" and "wanting in connection" because "they had completely lost that eschatological tradition which had been a common-place of literature since the second century," "Art of Translating Dante," p. 21.

5. DeSua, *Dante into English*, pp. 16ff. He quotes Carlisle's translation of this passage as a vivid example of this sort of thing [p. 10].

6. *Ibid.*, p. 28.

7. *Ibid.*, pp. 37–38.

8. "Art of Translating Dante," pp. 21–22. Cary's translation of the inscription over Hell-Gate contains a line which has become almost a saying in English: "Abandon hope, all ye who enter here" (*Inf.* III, 9).

9. DeSua, *Dante into English*, quotes Norton's introduction on p. 66.

10. *Ibid.*, p. 69, summarizing Norton.

11. *Ibid.*, p. 92.

12. "The Translation of Verse," 1957; rpt. in *The Poetry of Search and the Poetry of Statement*, pp. 129–30.

13. *Ibid.*, p. 130.

14. ". . . And Telling You a Story," in *Essays Presented to Charles Williams* (London: Oxford University Press, 1947), rpt. in her *Further Papers on Dante*, pp. 1–2.

15. "Introduction" to *Hell* by Dante Alighieri (Harmondsworth: Penguin Books, 1949), pp. 62–63. The *Purgatory* appeared in 1955 and Dr. Barbara Reynolds published the completed *Paradise* in 1962. Although Sayers entitled her translation "Hell," in her essays and in references to it in the *Purgatory*, she always cites it as "Inferno." Consequently, I have followed Dr. Reynolds in using the Italian titles unless I am specifically quoting from Sayers's Introduction to the first book of the *Commedia*.

16.   Letter to C. Wilfred Scott-Giles (23 January 1946). All citations to Letters refer to Sayers's letters to him. I am deeply indebted to Mr. Scott-Giles for lending me these letters and allowing me to make copies of them for my own uses. He has informed me that Dr. Barbara Reynolds of the University of Nottingham is preparing to write about Sayers's work on Dante. Dr. Reynolds, who completed the *Paradiso* after Miss Sayers's death, is in possession of her notes for the commentaries and of trial versions for various passages; her account of Miss Sayers's work on Dante will be definitive.

17.   "The Comedy of the *Comedy*," in *Introductory Papers on Dante*, pp. 151–54.

18.   *Ibid.*, p. 157.

19.   "Introduction" to *Hell*, p. 10.

20.   Sayers, Letter (12 April 1946).

21.   *Ibid.*, p. 137, where she gives a fine example.

22.   "Introduction" to *Hell*, p. 56.

23.   *Ibid.*

24.   "The Translation of Verse," pp. 138–39. The subject of "paragraphing" Dante deeply interested Sayers and "The Art of Translating Dante" contains several examples by other translators that she considers misparagraphing.

25.   "The Translation of Verse," p. 145.

26.   Letter (23 January 1946).

27.   There is written evidence for this view in a letter dated 5 March 1946, and other letters contain very rough sketches.

28.   Her hopes and fears in this regard are expressed in the letter of 5 March 1946.

29.   Letter (16 May 1946).

30.   Letter (26 September 1952).

31.   Letter (25 February 1946).

32.   Letter (27 March 1946).

33.   "The City of Dis," in *Introductory Papers on Dante*, p. 140.

34.   Letter (28 March 1946).

35.   Letter (2 April 1946).

36.   *Ibid.*

37.   Letter (28 March 1946).

38.   Letter (2 April 1946).

39.   "Introduction" to *Hell*, p. 56.

40.   "The Translation of Verse," p. 151.

41.   Letter (28 March 1946).

42.   Norton's introduction, p. xi, quoted by DeSua, *Dante into English*, p. 68.

43.   Letter (7 July 1954).

44.   *The Mind of the Maker*, pp. 217–25.

45.   *Ibid.*, p. 183.

46.   Reviews of her translation are listed together, chronologically, in order to avoid a folly of footnotes in the discussion that follows: *New Statesman and Nation*, 38 (10 December 1949), 709; *Times* (London) *Literary Supplement*, 49 (14 April 1950), 224; Angelina LaPiana, *Italica*, 27 (1950), 300–01; Charles Singleton, *Speculum* (July 1950), 394ff. *et seq.;* C[esare] F[oligno]?, *Studi Danteschi*, 30 (1951), 226–32; Peter Russell, *Nine*, No. 6 (Winter 1950/51), 394–95. The *Hell* and *Purgatory* volumes were reviewed together by Dudley Fitts, New York *Times Book Review* (6 November 1955), 58, and by Theodore Holmes, *Comparative Literature*, 9 (Summer 1957), 275–83. In the Translator's Note to his 1961 version of the *Inferno*, Warwick Chapman calls her work "brilliant: I pay it my humble tribute . . ." (London, Oxford University Press), pp. viii–ix. Gilbert Cunningham surveys some of this criticism in *The Divine Comedy in English: A Critical Bibliography, 1901–1966* (New York: Barnes & Noble, 1967), pp. 211–19 and 278–79. An unsigned review in the *Times Literary Supplement* of 27 July 1962 of the Sayers/Reynolds *Paradise* spoke of the "many in whom she first kindled an interest in Dante" and lauded her "first-

class brain," her skill in drama and poetry and her strong religious sense. Scott-Giles's diagrams and maps received general praise.

47.   Charles Singleton, *Speculum*, 25 (July 1950), 394.

48.   Janet Hitchman, *Such A Strange Lady: An Introduction to Dorothy L. Sayers* (London: New English Library, 1974), pp. 185ff.

49.   This comment raises an interesting issue. Are half rhymes, and eccentric rhymes too essentially comic in themselves to be properly used in the *Commedia?* Does Sayers's stress on Dante's humour make her especially receptive to their use —or occasional over use?

50.   It seems to have been this review (although Hitchman does not mention it or any other) that incited Sayers to write the passionate letter to Dr. E. V. Rieu which Hitchman quotes in her book. In that letter, Sayers urged that Penguins play up her academic qualifications in seeking publicity for the book and play down Lord Peter. She stressed that she had previously translated medieval verse in 1930, when Benn published her version of the *Tristan* of Thomas the Anglo-Norman.

51.   "Introduction" to *Hell*, p. 64

52.   In April 1956 *Nine* published the following *anonymous* sonnet:

> *On First Looking into Miss Sayers's 'Dante'*
> Oft have I paused at some cathedral door
> To hear its vaulted canopy prolong
> The murmured adoration of the throng
> Swelled by the pipes to muffle thunder's roar;
> Oft was I told of Dante, skilled to pour
> The medieval miracle of song
> And never dared to deem the verdict wrong
> Till Sayers rearranged the vocal score.
> Then felt I like some nightlong penitent
> Who hears at dawn the minster gates flung wide
> And, hungry for the Blessed Sacrament,
> Scans the dim nave, and shrinks back horrified
> To see the madcaps of the motley season
> Capering round their Abbot of unreason.

The author has the stereotyped vision of what the *Commedia* is like with which Sayers disagreed and tried to combat. Perhaps it *is* a matter of taste.

53.   "Translator's Note," *The Purgatorio* (New York: New American Library [Mentor Books]), pp. xxiv–xxix. This paragraph is based on Ciardi's note and on his article, "Translation: The Art of Failure," *Saturday Review*, 44 (7 October 1961), 17–19.

54.   See Cunningham, *Divine Comedy in English,* pp. 229–33, for some of these.

55.   Joan Ross Acocella, "The Cult of Language: A Study of Two Modern Translations of Dante," *Modern Language Quarterly,* 35 (June 1974), 140–56. It was Ciardi's rendering of the last line of Ulysses's speech, "ma per seguir virtute e conoscenza" as "but to press on toward manhood and recognition" which prompted Theodore Holmes in his review (*Comparative Literature*, 9 [Summer 1957], 278–83), to accuse him of lacking the humility "that lies in the realisation that his author knew best what words he wanted."

56.   *Gaudy Night*, Ch.9.

Artist, Artifact, and Audience:
The Aesthetics and Practice of Dorothy L. Sayers

1.   *The Mind of the Maker*, p. 213.

2.   *Ibid.*, p. 22.

3.   *Ibid.*, p. 21.

4.   "Creative Mind," *Unpopular Opinions*, p. 52.

5. *Ibid.*, p. 57.
6. *The Mind of the Maker*, p. 24.
7. *Ibid.*, p. 37.
8. *Ibid.*, p. 26.
9. "Toward a Christian Aesthetic," *Unpopular Opinions*, pp. 40–41.
10. *The Mind of the Maker*, p. 41.
11. "Toward a Christian Aesthetic," p. 43.
12. *The Mind of the Maker*, p. 29.
13. *Ibid.,* p. 193.
14. *Ibid.*, p. 211.
15. *Ibid.*, p. 66.
16. *Creed or Chaos,* p. 53.
17. *Ibid.*, p. 56.
18. "Toward a Christian Aesthetic," p. 40.
19. *Mind of the Maker*, p. 13.
20. *Creed or Chaos*, p. 59.
21. *Mind of the Maker*, pp. 51–52.
22. *Ibid.*, p. 28.
23. *Creed or Chaos*, p. 59.
24. "Toward a Christian Aesthetic," p. 46.
25. M. H. Abrams, *The Mirror and the Lamp: Romantic Theory and Critical Tradition* (New York: W. W. Norton, 1958).
26. See Vernon Ruland, *Horizons of Criticism: An Assessment of Religious-Literary Options* (Chicago: American Library Association, 1975), pp. 57–8.
27. "The Zeal of Thy House," in *Religious Drama*, I, ed. by Marvin Halverson (New York: Meridian Books, 1957), p. 339.
28. *Unpopular Opinions*, p. 40.

THE MIND OF THE MAKER: THE THEOLOGICAL AESTHETIC OF DOROTHY L. SAYERS AND ITS APPLICATION TO POETRY

1. *The Mind of the Maker* (1941; rpt. Cleveland, Ohio: Meridian, 1956), p. 34.
2. In *The Mind of the Maker*, p. 208.
3. As an epigraph to her chapter "Pentecost," Sayers selects this statement of Christ: "And if any man hear my words and believe not, I judge him not; for I came not to judge the world, but to save the world. He that rejecteth me, and receiveth not my words, hath one that judgeth him: the word that I have spoken, the same shall judge him in the last day."—St. John 12:47, 47, 48 [*The Mind of the Maker*, p. 109].
4. F. Cayré, *Manual of Patrology* (Paris: Desclée, 1927), I, 646.
5. Trans. Stephen McKenna (Washington, D.C.: Catholic University Press, 1967), X, 18.
6. Sayers assumes St. Augustine's discussion of the trinity into her own argument: but with the exception of a quotation or two, she does not relate Augustine specifically to her discussion as I am doing here.
7. The passages from Hesiod are from the *Theogony* as translated by Rhoda A. Henricks in *Classical Gods and Heroes* (New York: Frederick Ungar, 1972), pp. 40–41.
8. Etienne Gilson, *The Christian Philosophy of St. Augustine* (1960; rpt. New York: Vintage-Random House, 1967), p. 222.
9. "Creative Mind," in *Christian Letters to a Post-Christian World*, compiler, Roderick Jellema (Grand Rapids, Mich.: William B. Eerdmans, 1969), p. 89.
10. *Ibid.*, p. 90.
11. This view weakens, for example, Marchette Chute's biography, *Ben Jonson of Westminster*; a number of recent critics have, however, helped make clear the emotion which could be

packed into Jonson's classical modes (Wesley Trimpi's *Ben Jonson's Poems: A Study of the Plain Style* [Stanford: Stanford University Press, 1962] is a good example). None, however, so far as I am aware, discuss the importance of his diction in the manner of this essay.

12.   Sayers writes about "scalene trinities," the emphasizing of one part of the creative trinity at the expense of the other two, in *The Mind of the Maker* [ch. 10].

13.   *Ben Jonson*, ed. C. H. Herford and Percy and Evelyn Simpson (Oxford: Clarendon Press, 1947), VIII, 636.

"THE LAUGHTER OF THE UNIVERSE": DOROTHY L. SAYERS AND THE WHIMSICAL VISION

1.   Quoted by Dorothy L. Sayers in *The Mind of the Maker*, p. 179.

2.   Sayers, in "Selections from the Pantheon Papers," in her *Christian Letters to a Post-Christian World*, pp. 3–10, satirically reverses the perspective and shows how a future generation might look back on our own dead "Modernity" and apparent progess.

3.   *Christian Letters*, pp. 49–65.

4.   *Mind of the Maker*, p. 28.

5.   *Murder Must Advertise*, Ch. 15.

6.   *Mind of the Maker*, p. 203.

7.   *Ibid.*, p. 77.

8.   This point is made by two essayists: H. P. Rickman, "From Detection to Theology (The Work of Dorothy Sayers)," *Hibbert Journal*, 60 (1962), 290–96; and Carolyn Heilbrun, "Sayers, Lord Peter and God," in *Lord Peter: A Collection of All the Lord Peter Wimsey Stories*, compiled by James Sandoe (New York: Harper & Row, 1972), pp. 454–69.

9.   *Gaudy Night*, Ch. 23.

10.   *Begin Here: A Statement of Faith* (New York: Harcourt, Brace and Company, 1941), p. xi.

11.   *Mind of the Maker*, p. 186.

12.   *The Zeal of Thy House* in *Four Sacred Plays*, p. 36.

13.   Cf. *Mind of the Maker*, pp. 25–35.

14.   *Ibid.*, p. 105.

15.   *Introductory Papers on Dante*, p. 180.

16.   *Further Papers on Dante*, p. 48.

17.   *Further Papers*, p. 50.

18.   *The Man Born to Be King*, p. 11.

19.   *Further Papers*, p. 185.

20.   *Mind of the Maker*, p. 102.

21.   *Four Sacred Plays*, p. 108.

22.   Marion B. Fairman, "The Neo-Medieval Plays of Dorothy L. Sayers" (Dissertation, Pittsburgh, 1961), pp. 131, 136–37.

23.   "Towards a Christian Aesthetic," in *The New Orpheus: Essays Toward a Christian Poetic*, ed. Nathan A. Scott, Jr. (New York: Sheed and Ward, 1964), pp. 3–20.

24.   *Lord, I Thank Thee* (1942; rpt. Stamford, Connecticut: Overbrook Press, 1943).

Index

Contributors and Editor

LIONEL BASNEY, Professor of English at Houghton College, is the author of numerous articles on contemporary fiction and eighteenth-century history of ideas, and is currently writing a book-length study of Dorothy L. Sayers.

JOE R. CHRISTOPHER, Associate Professor of English at Tarleton State University, is the author of several articles on detective fiction, and has been involved in two previously published checklists: with Dean W. Dickensheet and Robert E. Briney, *A. Boucher Bibliography* (White Bear Lake, Minnesota: Allen J. Hubin, 1969); and with Joan K. Ostling, *C. S. Lewis: An Annotated Checklist of Writings About Him and His Works* (Kent, Ohio: Kent State University Press, 1974).

TERRIE CURRAN, Assistant Professor of English at Providence College, is a specialist in medieval English literature.

ALZINA STONE DALE, author and editor, has presented several scholarly papers on Sayers, and has recently completed the juvenile biography, *Maker & Craftsman: The Story of Dorothy L. Sayers* (Grand Rapids, Mich.: William B. Eerdmans, 1978).

BARBARA DUNLAP, Associate Professor in the Library Department at the City College of New York, is Chief of the Archives and Special Collections Division. Her notes toward a Sayers bibliography appeared in *Unicorn* in 1970 and 1972; she is currently at work on a study of Sayers's debt to John Ruskin and William Morris.

ROBERT DUNN, Associate Professor and Chairperson of the English Department at Loma Linda University, holds graduate degrees in both English literature and in theology, and has a special interest in religious approaches to literature.

E. R. GREGORY, Professor of English at the University of Toledo, has published a number of essays in both Renaissance and modern literature. He has edited

Dorothy L. Sayers's *Wilkie Collins* (Toledo, Ohio: Friends of the University of Toledo Libraries, 1977) and is currently editing Sayers's previously unpublished essays on detective fiction.

MARGARET P. HANNAY, author of many articles on Sayers and on C. S. Lewis, served as chairperson of the Seminar on Dorothy L. Sayers for the Modern Language Association conventions in 1977 and 1978. She is currently a Lecturer in English Literature at the State University of New York at Albany.

RICHARD L. HARP, Associate Professor of English at the University of Nevada (Las Vegas), has written numerous articles on Renaissance literature, on aesthetics, and on the teaching of writing.

R. RUSSELL MAYLONE, curator of the special collections department, Northwestern University Library, Evanston, Illinois.

R. B. REAVES, Associate Professor of English, University of Rhode Island, has given several conference papers on Sayers and other twentieth-century British and American authors.

BARBARA REYNOLDS, Professor of Italian at the University of Nottingham, England, invited Dorothy L. Sayers to speak at the summer school for Italian Studies she had established in Jesus College, Cambridge; Sayers's lectures were later published in *Introductory Papers on Dante* (London: Methuen, 1954) and *Further Papers on Dante* (London: Methuen, 1957). Prof. Reynolds maintained an extensive correspondence with Sayers as she worked on her Dante translation; after Sayers's death in 1957, Professor Reynolds completed the *Paradiso* translation and commentary for the Penguin edition. She has also translated *Orlando Furioso* (Harmondsworth: Penguin Classics,1975), *La Vita Nuova*(Harmondsworth:Penguin Classics,1969), and edited the Cambridge Italian Dictionary. She has written extensively both on Italian literature and on the work of Dorothy L. Sayers.

WILLIAM REYNOLDS, Associate Professor of English at Hope College, organized and served as chairperson of the Seminar on Dorothy L. Sayers for the Modern Language Association conventions in 1974, 1975, and 1976. He has written several articles on Sayers and other Christian writers.

ROBERT D. STOCK, Professor of English at the University of Nebraska, has written *Samuel Johnson and Neoclassical Dramatic Theory* (Lincoln: University of Nebraska Press, 1973) and several articles on the Neohumanists and C. S. Lewis. BARBARA STOCK is pursuing her M.A. in English at the University of Nebraska.

LEWIS THORPE, Professor of French, University of Nottingham, was the editor of the *Nottingham Medieval Studies* since its inception in 1957, and wrote numerous scholarly articles and books on medieval languages and literature. His books include *Geoffrey of Monmouth: The History of the Kings of Britain* (Harmondsworth: Penguin Classics, 1966), *Le roman de Silence:a Thirteenth century verse-romance* by *Heldris de Cornualle* (Cambridge: W. Heffer, 1972), and *The Bayeux Tapestry and the Norman Invasion* (London: Folio Society, 1973). He helped Sayers with the translation of *La chanson de Roland*, her last published work. Professor Thorpe died suddenly in October 1977.

NANCY TISCHLER, Professor of English and Humanities at the Pennsylvania State University (Capitol Campus), is the author of several books on Southern fiction, including *Tennessee Williams, Rebellious Puritan* (New York: Citadel Press, 1961), and *Black Masks: Negro Characters in Modern Southern Fiction* (University Park: Pennsylvania State University Press, 1969). She has written numerous articles on Southern literature, drama, and Christianity and literature, and is currently working on a book-length study of Dorothy L. Sayers, *A Pilgrim Soul* (John Knox Press).

RICHARD WEBSTER has worked mainly for the British Council in various European universities, especially in Italy, and has specialized in the relations between British and Italian philosophy and literature. His publications include *Equilibrium* (Rome: Officium Libri Catholici, 1966) and *New Dialogue* (Rome: Officium Libri Catholici, 1972) and many articles on Shakespeare and Dante both English and Italian, as well as a chapter on Italian philosophy for Methuen's forthcoming *Companion to Italian Studies*. Now retired, he is actively interested in questions of modern theology.